9-10-94

CONTEMPORARY
Black Biography

ISSN 1058-1316

CONTEMPORARY
Black Biography

Profiles from the International Black Community

Michael L. LaBlanc, Editor
Volume 1

 **Gale Research Inc.** · DETROIT · LONDON

R920.009296
Contemporary
1992
V.1-6

STAFF

Michael L. LaBlanc, *Editor*

Julia M. Rubiner, *Associate Editor*

David Bianco, John Cohassey, David Collins, Christine Ferran, Joan Goldsworthy,
Anne Janette Johnson, Mark Kram, Jeanne M. Lesinski, Louise Mooney,
Michael E. Mueller, Nancy Pear, Bryan Ryan, *Contributing Editors*

Peter M. Gareffa, *Senior Editor*

Jeanne Gough, *Permissions Manager*
Margaret A. Chamberlain, *Permissions Supervisor (Pictures)*
Pamela A. Hayes, *Permissions Associate*
Keith Reed and Nancy Rattenbury, *Permissions Assistants*

Mary Beth Trimper, *Production Manager*
Arthur Chartow, *Art Director*
Cynthia Baldwin, *Graphic Design Supervisor*
C.J. Jonik, *Keyliner*

Cover design by Jeanne M. Moore

Special thanks to the Biography Division Research staff

Special thanks to Filomena Sgambati for her assistance with photos

10 9 8 7 6 5 4 3

The paper used in this publication meets the minimum requirements of American National Standard for Information Sciences—Permanence Paper for Printed Library Materials, ANSI Z39.48-1984.   ∞™

Printed in the United States of America
Published simultaneously in the United Kingdom
by Gale Research International Limited
(An affiliated company of Gale Research Inc.)

ISBN 0-8103-5546-9
ISSN 1058-1316

CILR

Contemporary Black Biography
Advisory Board

Contents

Introduction

Contemporary Black Biography provides informative biographical profiles of the important and influential persons of African heritage who form the international black community: men and women who have changed today's world and are shaping tomorrow's.

Contemporary Black Biography covers persons of various nationalities in a wide variety of fields, including architecture, art, business, dance, education, fashion, film, industry, journalism, law, literature, medicine, music, politics and government, publishing, religion, science and technology, social issues, sports, television, theater, and others.

In addition to in-depth coverage of names found in today's headlines, *Contemporary Black Biography* provides coverage of selected individuals from earlier in this century whose influence continues to impact on contemporary life. *Contemporary Black Biography* also provides coverage of important and influential persons who are not yet household names and are therefore likely to be ignored by other biographical reference series.

Designed for Quick Research *and* Interesting Reading

- **Attractive page design** incorporates textual subheads, making it easy to find the information you're looking for.

- **Easy-to-locate data sections** provide quick access to vital personal statistics, career information, major awards, and mailing addresses, when available.

- **Informative biographical essays** trace the subject's personal and professional life with the kind of in-depth analysis you need.

- **To further enhance your appreciation** of the subject, most entries include photographic portraits.

- **Sources for additional information** direct the user to selected books, magazines, and newspapers where more information on the individuals can be obtained.

Helpful Indexes Make It Easy to Find the Information You Need

Contemporary Black Biography includes cumulative Nationality, Occupation, Subject, and Name indexes that make it easy to locate entries in a variety of useful ways.

We Welcome Your Suggestions

The editors welcome your comments and suggestions for enhancing and improving *Contemporary Black Biography*. If you would like to suggest persons for inclusion in the series, please submit these names to the editors. Mail comments or suggestions to:

The Editor
Contemporary Black Biography
Gale Research, Inc.
835 Penobscot Bldg.
Detroit, MI 48226-4094
Phone: (800) 347-GALE
FAX: (313) 961-6815

Photo Credits

Ralph David Abernathy

1926-1990

Clergyman, civil rights leader

The Reverend Ralph David Abernathy, closest friend and adviser of civil rights leader Martin Luther King, Jr., was also King's hand-picked successor as president of the clergy-led Southern Christian Leadership Conference (SCLC). Abernathy became president of the SCLC after King's assassination in 1968 and continued the organization's nonviolent campaign for civil rights for blacks and other oppressed people in the United States. The alliance between Abernathy and King stretched back to the mid-1950s, when the two were Baptist ministers in Montgomery, Alabama, coordinating a boycott by local blacks to end segregation of the city's buses. The historic Montgomery Bus Boycott, which would come to mark the beginning of the modern-day Civil Rights Movement, thrust King into the national spotlight as the inspirational leader of a nonviolent struggle to desegregate the South, with Abernathy at his side as chief confidant and most trusted official.

"To a lot of people, King and Abernathy seemed an odd pair," wrote Stephen B. Oates in *Let the Trumpet Sound: The Life of Martin Luther King, Jr.* "Largely northern educated and a scion of Atlanta's black middle class, King was learned, fastidious, and urbane. Abernathy, by contrast, came from a bucolic background and was so slow and earthy that some thought him crude." Both men, however, had mutual admiration for their accomplishments as ministers, and their styles complemented each other as leaders in the Civil Rights Movement. In a review of Abernathy's 1989 autobiography, *And the Walls Came Tumbling Down,* Henry Hampton, executive producer of the award-winning civil rights documentary *Eyes on the Prize,* commented in the *New York Times Book Review:* "Mr. Abernathy was known as the 'other-side' of Martin King, and there is much evidence that King could not have succeeded without him. Mr. Abernathy was earthy and outgoing, connecting to the rural masses in a way that King, especially in the early years, could not. His ease with poor and working-class people, joined with King's intellectual appeal to the middle class, made the pair a powerful magnet for a community that needed to overcome class differences."

Abernathy was born the tenth of twelve children on his family's farm in Linden, Alabama, in west-central rural Marengo County. Originally named David, he was nick-

At a Glance. . .

Born March 11, 1926, in Linden, AL; died of cardiac arrest, April 17, 1990, in Atlanta, GA; son of William L. (a farmer) and Louivery Valentine (Bell) Abernathy; married Juanita Odessa Jones, August 31, 1952; children: Juandalynn Ralpheda, Donzaleigh Avis, Ralph David III, Kwame Luthuli. *Education:* Alabama State College (now Alabama State University), B.S., 1950; Atlanta University, M.A. in sociology, 1951. *Politics:* Democrat. *Religion:* Baptist.

Ordained Baptist minister, 1948; radio disc jockey, Montgomery, AL, 1950; Alabama State College, Montgomery, dean of men, 1951; First Baptist Church, Montgomery, pastor, 1951-61; West Hunter Street Baptist Church, Atlanta, GA, pastor, beginning 1961; Southern Christian Leadership Conference (SCLC), Atlanta, president, 1968-77, president emeritus, 1977—. Founder, Montgomery Improvement Association, 1955; co-founder, SCLC, 1957; leader, Poor People's Campaign, Resurrection City, Washington, DC, 1968; organizer and chairman, Operation Breadbasket, Atlanta; founder, Foundation for Economic Enterprises Development (FEED). Advisory committee member of the Congress on Racial Equality (CORE); participant in World Peace Council presidential committee meeting, Santiago, Chile, 1972. *Military service:* Served in U.S. Army, beginning in 1944.

Awards: Numerous honorary degrees, including LL.D.s from Allen University, 1960, Southampton College and Long Island University, both 1969, and Alabama State University, 1974, and D.D.s from Morehouse College, 1971, and Kalamazoo College, 1978; Peace Medal, German Democratic Republic (East Germany), 1971.

Member: National Association for the Advancement of Colored People (NAACP), Atlanta Ministers Union, American Cancer Society, American Red Cross, Young Men's Christian Association (YMCA), Kappa Alpha Psi, Phi Delta Kappa.

farmer and church deacon, owned a 500-acre self-sufficient farm and was respected by both blacks and whites in the community. Deeply committed to education, Abernathy's father served on the board of the local black high school, Linden Academy, and frequently made large financial donations to its operations. Abernathy aspired early on to become a preacher and his mother continually encouraged him in that ambition. As he noted in *And the Walls Came Tumbling Down,* "The preacher, after all, was the finest and most important person around, someone who was accorded respect wherever he went." Abernathy's father often impressed upon him that "Preaching is not a vocation for a boy but for a man" and "David, if you ever see a good fight, get in it—and win it."

After graduating from Linden Academy, Abernathy was drafted into the then-segregated U.S. Army, in which he served during the final months of World War II. He returned to Alabama after the war and enrolled in Montgomery's Alabama State College. A good student and natural leader, Abernathy was elected president of the student council and successfully led protests to obtain better cafeteria conditions and living quarters. Instead of drawing the wrath of school officials, however, Abernathy earned their respect and was later hired as the school's dean of men. Abernathy formally announced his calling as a Baptist minister in 1948; but he was also very interested in learning more about civil rights in his classes at Alabama State, a subject handled with much discretion by the faculty.

After graduation Abernathy worked during the summer of 1950 as a disc jockey at a white Montgomery radio station; he was the first black to do so. In the fall he enrolled at Atlanta University, where he received his masters degree in sociology. While in Atlanta, Abernathy had the opportunity to hear Martin Luther King, Jr., preach for the first time. The location was the Ebenezer Baptist Church, where King's father had been minister for many years. Abernathy introduced himself to the young King, with whom he was very impressed. Abernathy recounted in his autobiography: "He was about my age, but already he had begun to build a reputation in a city the size of Atlanta. So I sat there burning with envy at his learning and confidence. Already he was a scholar; and while he didn't holler as loud as some of the more famous preachers I had heard, he could be loud enough when he wanted to. Even then I could tell he was a man with a special gift from God."

Formed a Bond With King

After obtaining his masters degree Abernathy returned to Alabama and worked part-time as minister for the

named Ralph by one of his sisters after a favorite teacher. Growing up, Abernathy was strongly influenced by both his Christian parents. His father, William, a hardworking

Eastern Star Baptist Church in Demopolis, near his hometown of Linden. Abernathy was very popular with the congregation; under his stewardship Eastern Star became the most active church in Demopolis. About this time Abernathy also began substituting at one of Montgomery's leading black churches, First Baptist. When a permanent vacancy in the pulpit opened there, Abernathy, only 26 years old at the time, was named minister of the congregation. Three years later King accepted a call to another of Montgomery's leading black churches, Dexter Avenue Baptist, and he and Abernathy became close friends. The King and Abernathy families socialized together; the topic of conversation was frequently civil rights. Abernathy recalled in *And the Walls Came Tumbling Down:* "As Martin expounded philosophy, I saw its practical applications on the local level. . . . To use a military analogy, while he was talking about strategy (the broad, overall purpose of a campaign), I was thinking about tactics (how to achieve that strategy through specific actions)."

In 1955 a black seamstress from Montgomery named Rosa Parks refused to relinquish her bus seat to a white passenger, for which she was arrested and later fined. City buses in Montgomery, as was the case throughout the South, were segregated—black sections were in the back and reserved white seats were in the front. In between the two sections was an area in which blacks could sit, but they were required to move if there were white passengers without seats. Parks, tired after a long day at work, refused the order of the white bus driver to move from her seat, and was turned in to the local police and arrested. The incident, though not the first of its kind in Montgomery, stood out in that Parks was a quiet and well-respected woman of the community who had served as secretary of the local branch of the NAACP (National Association for the Advancement of Colored People).

Helped Launch Historic Bus Boycott

A local group called the Women's Political Council

Abernathy (left) with Martin Luther King, Jr., (center), and W.G. Anderson at a 1962 protest march in Albany, Georgia.

suggested a boycott by blacks of the city's buses, while King and Abernathy—both still in their twenties—moved to form what became known as the Montgomery Improvement Association (MIA). Through hurried meetings in their churches, Abernathy and King readily rallied the support of Montgomery blacks to boycott the segregated buses. The MIA, under King's principles of a nonviolent campaign, worked feverishly to coordinate the boycott. Announcements were made in black churches that blacks should stay off the buses. The city's black taxi companies were contacted to transport people; later a carpool was organized after the city ruled that the reduced fares charged by the taxi drivers were illegal. King, as the head of the MIA, and Abernathy, as program chief, became responsible for maintaining the momentum of the boycott within the scope of a nonviolent protest. "Martin's task was to teach them; mine was to move them to act—or rather not to act—in accordance with those principles," Abernathy noted. "So at each meeting I would take the pulpit to whip them into a fervor, exhorting them to remain true to our cause."

Despite numerous threats and other intimidation, the boycott persisted for over a year until the federal courts in June of 1956 upheld an injunction against the bus company's segregation policies. Having successfully led the rally against segregation in Montgomery, King was eager to push for civil rights for blacks in all areas of life. In January of 1957 King and Abernathy met in Atlanta with other Southern clergymen to form the Southern Christian Leadership Conference, an organization of churches and civic groups that would lead nonviolent desegregation protests across the South. King was elected president of the SCLC and Abernathy its secretary-treasurer. While at the Atlanta meeting, Abernathy's home and First Baptist Church were bombed, in addition to other homes and churches in Montgomery. Abernathy's family barely escaped injury; the minister hurriedly returned to Montgomery to tend to his family and oversee the rebuilding of his church.

Later in 1957 King and Abernathy met with then-Vice-President Richard M. Nixon to petition Nixon and President Dwight D. Eisenhower to speak in the South on the importance of governmental compliance with the Supreme Court's landmark *Brown vs. Topeka Board of Education* ruling, which had outlawed segregation in public schools. In 1960 King moved to Atlanta to devote his full time to SCLC activities; a year later, at King's urging, Abernathy also moved and became pastor of the West Hunter Street Baptist Church. In the next few years King, Abernathy, and the SCLC led desegregation protest movements across the South, including marches, rallies, and sit-ins in cities like Birmingham and Selma, Alabama, Albany, Georgia, Greensboro, North Carolina, and St. Augustine, Florida. They were arrested nu-

merous times; violence and threats against their lives became routine occurrences. In 1965 King named Abernathy vice-president at large of the SCLC, perhaps foreseeing the possibility that he might not be around forever to lead the organization.

Assumed Leadership of SCLC

In 1968 King—who was in Memphis, Tennessee, to support a strike by city sanitation workers—was assassinated by a sniper as he stood on the balcony of his motel room. Abernathy was at King's side when he died. Later, SCLC board members unanimously named Abernathy leader of the organization. One of his first moves was to proceed with King's proposed Poor People's Campaign march on Washington, D.C. In 1968 Abernathy led a demonstration on the nation's capitol to protest for economic and civil rights for poor people and oversaw the construction of a shantytown called Resurrection City near the Lincoln Memorial. Resurrection City drew poor and homeless people from around the country. In May of 1968 Abernathy met with members of Congress to petition for help for the nation's unemployed and poor. He was later arrested when the group refused to move from the site after its demonstration permits had expired.

As president of the SCLC Abernathy led several other desegregation protests in the South, including a major one in Charleston, South Carolina. He resigned from the SCLC in 1977 and made an unsuccessful bid for the Georgia fifth district U.S. Congressional seat vacated by prominent black statesman Andrew Young. Undaunted, Abernathy formed an organization called Foundation for Economic Enterprises Development (FEED)—designed to help train blacks for better economic opportunities—and carried on his ministerial duties at West Hunter Street Baptist. In his later years Abernathy lectured across the United States, but was hampered at times by health problems.

In 1989 Abernathy's autobiography, *And The Walls Came Tumbling Down,* was criticized by some black leaders for the minister's inclusion of details regarding King's well-known extramarital affairs. Hampton questioned Abernathy's motives, suggesting jealousy and a smearing of the record. "Does it really add to the record or does it simply provide fodder for blaring headlines?" Hampton asked in his book review. Others rose to Abernathy's defense, however, stating that he had included information about King that was common knowledge, and that a respectable autobiography should not censor facts, especially from Abernathy, who knew King best. Beyond this controversy *And the Walls Came Tumbling Down* is noteworthy, Hampton wrote, for being the story "of a man at the core of a great social movement." Hampton praised Abernathy's recounting of his own involvement in the Civil Rights Movement, noting that "his storytelling is gripping, even moving."

Selected writings

And the Walls Came Tumbling Down: An Autobiography, Harper & Row, 1989.
"The Natural History of a Social Movement: The Montgomery Improvement Association," from *The Walking City: The Montgomery Bus Boycott, 1955-1956,* edited by David J. Garrow, Carlson, 1989.

Selected discography

Birmingham, Alabama, 1963: Mass Meeting, Folkway Records, 1980.
The Sit-in Story, Folkway Records, 1961.

Sources

Books

Abernathy, Ralph David, *And the Walls Came Tumbling Down: An Autobiography,* Harper, 1989.

Branch, Taylor, *Parting the Waters: America in the King Years, 1954-63,* Touchstone, 1988.
Oates, Stephen B., *Let the Trumpet Sound: The Life of Martin Luther King, Jr.,* New American Library, 1982.
Voices of Freedom: An Oral History of the Civil Rights Movement From the 1950s Through the 1980s, edited by Henry Hampton and Steve Fayer, with Sarah Flynn, Bantam, 1990.
The Walking City: The Montgomery Bus Boycott, 1955-1956, edited by David J. Garrow, Carlson, 1989.

Periodicals

New York Post, April 13, 1968.
New York Times, March 24, 1990.
New York Times Book Review, October 29, 1989; November 26, 1989.

—Michael E. Mueller

Maya Angelou

1928—

Author, performing artist

The life experiences of diversely talented Maya Angelou—author, poet, actress, singer, dancer, playwright, director, producer—are the cornerstone of her most acclaimed work, a five-volume autobiography that traces the foundations of her identity as a twentieth-century American black woman. Beginning with the best-selling *I Know Why the Caged Bird Sings,* Angelou's autobiographical books chart her beginnings in rural segregated Arkansas and urban St. Louis, her turbulent adolescence in California, and through her adult triumphs as a performing artist and writer, her work in the Civil Rights Movement, and her travels to Africa. "One of the geniuses of Afro-American serial autobiography," according to Houston A. Baker in the *New York Times Book Review,* Angelou has been praised for the rich and insightful prose of her narratives and for offering what many observers feel is an indispensable record of black experience. Author James Baldwin wrote on the publication of *I Know Why the Caged Bird Sings:* "This testimony from a Black sister marks the beginning of a new era in the minds and hearts and lives of all Black men and women."

Born in St. Louis, Missouri, Angelou was sent at the age of three to live with her paternal grandmother in Stamps, Arkansas, an event that served as the starting point for *I Know Why the Caged Bird Sings.* The book depicts Angelou's early years in Stamps, where her grandmother ran the town's only black-owned general store, and is a revealing portrait of the customs and harsh circumstances of black life in the segregated South. Economic hardship, murderous hate, and ingrained denigration were part of daily life in Stamps, and Angelou translates their impact on the formative and cognizant child. "If growing up is painful for the Southern Black girl, being aware of her displacement is the rust on the razor that threatens the throat," she wrote in the book. "It is an unnecessary insult."

Angelou also spent part of her youth in St. Louis with her mother—a glamorous and dynamic figure who occasionally worked as a nightclub performer. The book concludes with Angelou's early adolescent years in California and the birth of her illegitimate son. Much of *I Know Why the Caged Bird Sings* is grim—particularly Angelou's rape at the age of eight—yet it marks her distinct ability to recollect personal truth through insightful and powerful images, sights, and language. In so doing

At a Glance. . .

Born Marguerite Johnson, April 4, 1928, in St. Louis, MO; daughter of Bailey and Vivian (Baxter) Johnson; married Tosh Angelou (divorced c. 1952); married Paul Du Feu, December 1973 (divorced); children: Guy Johnson. *Education:* Attended public schools in Arkansas and California; studied dance with Martha Graham, Pearl Primus, and Ann Halprin; studied drama with Frank Silvera and Gene Frankel.

Toured with U.S. State Department production of *Porgy and Bess,* 1954-55; worked as a nightclub performer in California, Hawaii, and New York City; performed in, produced, and directed *Cabaret for Freedom,* Village Gate theater, New York City, 1960; northern coordinator of Southern Christian Leadership Conference c. 1960-61; appeared Off-Broadway at St. Mark's Playhouse in *The Blacks,* 1961; associate editor, *Arab Observer* (English-language newsweekly), Cairo, Egypt, 1961-62; assistant administrator, School of Music and Dance, University of Ghana, Accra, 1963-66; feature editor, *African Review,* and writer for *Ghanian Times* and Radio Ghana c. 1964-66; directed film *All Day Long,* 1974; directed own play *And Still I Rise,* 1976; lifetime appointment as Reynolds Professor of American Studies, Wake Forest University, 1981—; producer, *Moon on a Rainbow Shawl,* 1988. Taught modern dance at Rome Opera House and Hambina Theatre, Tel Aviv, Israel.

Awards: National Book Award nomination, 1970, for *I Know Why the Caged Bird Sings;* Golden Eagle Award for documentary, 1977, for *Afro-American in the Arts;* Matrix Award, Women in Communications, Inc., 1983; North Carolina award in literature, 1987.

Addresses: *Home*—Sonoma, CA. *Office*—c/o Dave La Camera Lordly and Dame Inc., 51 Church St., Boston, MA 02116.

Angelou earned high marks from critics who praised her narrative skills and eloquent prose. Christopher Lehmann-Haupt in the *New York Times* called *I Know Why the Caged Bird Sings* "a carefully wrought, simultaneously touching and comic memoir . . . [the] beauty [of which] is not in the story but in the telling." Sidonie Ann Smith wrote in the *Southern Humanities Review* that Angelou's "genius as a writer is her ability to recapture the texture of the way of life in the texture of its idioms, its idiosyncratic vocabulary and especially in its process of image-making. . . . That [Angelou] chooses to recreate the past in its own sounds suggests to the reader that she accepts the past and recognizes its beauty and its ugliness, its assets and its liabilities, its strength and its weakness. . . . Ultimately Maya Angelou's style testifies to her reaffirmation of self-acceptance, [which] she achieves within the pattern of the autobiography."

Angelou's next volume of autobiography, *Gather Together in My Name,* begins with Angelou leaving her mother's home in California at the age of seventeen to forge an independent life with her infant son. The book describes the chaotic years that follow, during which Angelou worked a variety of jobs—cook, waitress, brothel madam—and also suffered a brief drug addiction. Selwyn R. Cudjoe in *Black Women Writers (1950-1980)* noted that the book describes how "rural dignity gives way to the alienation and destruction of urban life. . . . The violation which began in *Caged Bird* takes on a much sharper focus in *Gather Together.* . . . The author is still concerned with the question of what it means to be Black and female in America, but her development is . . . subjected to certain social forces which assault the black woman with unusual intensity." Critics again praised Angelou's skillful prose, but also noted that the book lacked a certain cohesiveness. Lynn Sukenick in the *Village Voice* called the book "sculpted, concise, rich with flavor and surprises, exuding a natural confidence and command." Sukenick added, however, that "in the tone of the book . . . [Angelou's] refusal to let her earlier self get off easy, and the self-mockery which is her means to honesty, finally becomes in itself a glossing over. . . . It eventually becomes a tic and a substitute for a deeper look." Sondra O'Neale similarly commented in *Black Women Writers* that "the writing flows and shimmers with beauty; only the rigorous, coherent and meaningful organization of experience is missing."

Launched Performing Career

In the 1950s Angelou embarked upon a career as a stage performer, working as an actress, singer, and dancer. *Singin' and Swingin' and Gettin' Merry Like Christmas* recounts Angelou's transition from late adolescence to early adulthood, when she began to define herself as a performing artist. She toured Europe with a U.S. State Department production of the black opera *Porgy and Bess* in the mid 1950s, a period that became a turning point in her life. While with the theater company Angelou began to link the turmoil of her past with her identity as a black adult, and, as Cudjoe commented, the book documents the "personal triumph of [a] remarkable black woman." Cudjoe wrote: "The pride which she takes in her company's professionalism, their discipline onstage, and the wellspring of spirituality that the opera emoted, all seem to conduce toward an organic harmony of her personal history as it intertwined with the social history of her people."

In *The Heart of a Woman* Angelou covers the late 1950s and early 1960s, a period in which black artists in the United States were increasingly addressing racial abuse and black liberation. In the book Angelou herself makes a decision to move away from show business in order to, as she describes it, "take on the responsibility of making [people] think. [It] was the time to demonstrate my own seriousness." She joined a group called the Harlem Writers Guild and in 1960 co-wrote the musical revue *Cabaret for Freedom,* which opened in New York City. Later that year she was asked by Martin Luther King, Jr., to become northern coordinator for the then-fledgling civil rights organization he had helped found, the Southern Christian Leadership Conference. *The Heart of a Woman* concludes with Angelou and her son, Guy, moving to Africa, where she first worked for an English-language newsweekly in Cairo, and then at the University of Ghana. *Dictionary of Literary Biography* contributor Lynn Z. Bloom called *The Heart of a Woman* a particularly inspired book. Angelou's "enlarged focus and clear vision transcend the particulars," Bloom wrote, and like *I Know Why the Caged Bird Sings,* the book presents "a fascinating universality of perspective and psychological depth."

Explored African Sojourn

Angelou more fully explored her Africa experience in her fifth book, *All God's Children Need Traveling Shoes,* of which a reviewer in *Time* noted that the author "meditates on the search for historical and spiritual roots." According to Baker in the *New York Times Book Review,* one of the interesting aspects that Angelou explores is her realization that Africa is "a homeland that refuses to become 'home.' Though independence and prosperity make Ghana a festival in black, there is no point of connection between Miss Angelou and what she calls the 'soul' of Africa." Barbara T. Christian likewise observed in the *Chicago Tribune Book World* that Angelou's "sojourn in Africa strengthens her bonds to her ancestral home even as she concretely experiences her distinctiveness as an Afro-American." Wanda Coleman in the *Los Angeles Times Book Review* called *All God's Children Need Traveling Shoes* "an important document drawing more much-needed attention to the hidden history of a people both African and American."

Commenting on Angelou's autobiographical writings, O'Neale wrote that one of the author's overall achievements is the elevation of the black female in literature. "One who has made her life her message and whose message to all aspiring Black women is the reconstruction of her experiential 'self,' is Maya Angelou. With the wide public and critical reception of *I Know Why the Caged Bird Sings* in the early seventies, Angelou bridged the gap between life and art, a step that is essential if Black women are to be deservedly credited with the mammoth and creative feat of noneffacing survival." Cudjoe similarly commented that Angelou's autobiographies rescue not only her personal history, but the

> If we [black women] look out of our eyes at the immediate world around us, we see whites and males in dominant roles. We need to see our mothers, aunts, our sisters, and grandmothers.

collective history of all black women: "It is in response to these specific concerns that Maya Angelou offered her autobiographical statements, presenting a powerful, authentic and profound signification of the condition of Afro-American womanhood in her quest for understanding and love rather than for bitterness and despair. Her work is a triumph in the articulation of truth in simple, forthright terms."

Articulated the Struggle of Black Women

Angelou commented to Claudia Tate in *Black Women Writers at Work* on the special importance of images for black women. "Image making is very important for every human being. It is especially important for black American women in that we are, by being black, a minority in the United States, and by being female, the less powerful of the genders. . . . If we look out of our eyes at the immediate world around us, we see whites and males in dominant roles. We need to see our mothers, aunts, our sisters, and grandmothers." Angelou also described the awareness and responsibility she feels in providing images for black women: "In one way, it means all the work, all the loneliness and discipline my work exacts, demands, is not in vain. It also means, in a more atavistic, absolutely internal way, that I can never die. It's like living through children. So when I approach a piece of work, *that* is in my approach, whether it's a poem that might appear frivolous or is a serious piece. In my approach I take as fact that my work will be carried on.''

In addition to her books of autobiography, Angelou has written several volumes of poetry that further explore the South, racial confrontation, and the triumph of black people against overwhelming odds. According to Tate, Angelou's poems ''are characterised by a spontaneous joyfulness and an indomitable spirit to survive.'' Among her many accomplishments, Angelou wrote the screenplay and score for the 1972 film *Georgia, Georgia,* and in 1979 penned the screen adaptation of *I Know Why the Caged Bird Sings.* She has made numerous television appearances, including her 1977 role in the landmark television movie, *Roots,* and as a guest on many talk shows. Angelou speaks French, Spanish, Italian, Arabic, and Fanti, a language of southern Ghana. She is a popular lecturer throughout the United States.

Selected writings

Autobiography

I Know Why the Caged Bird Sings, Random House, 1970.
Gather Together in My Name, Random House, 1974.
Singin' and Swingin' and Gettin' Merry Like Christmas, Random House, 1976.
The Heart of a Woman, Random House, 1981.
All God's Children Need Traveling Shoes, Random House, 1986.

Poetry

Just Give Me a Cool Drink of Water 'fore I Diiie, Random House, 1971.
Oh Pray My Wings Are Gonna Fit Me Well, Random House, 1975.
And Still I Rise, Random House, 1978.
Shaker, Why Don't You Sing? Random House, 1983.
Poems: Maya Angelou, Bantam, 1986.
Now Sheba Sings the Song, Dial Books, 1987.
I Shall Not Be Moved, Random House, 1990.

Plays

(With Godfrey Cambridge) *Cabaret for Freedom* (musical revue), produced at Village Gate, New York City, 1960.
The Least of These, produced in Los Angeles, 1966.
Ajax (adaptation of Sophocles's *Ajax*), produced at the Mark Taper Forum, Los Angeles, 1974.
And Still I Rise, produced in Oakland, Calif., 1976.

Film and television scripts

Blacks, Blues, Black (ten television programs), National Educational Television, 1968.
Georgia, Georgia (film), Cinerama, 1972.
All Day Long, American Film Institute, 1974.
I Know Why the Caged Bird Sings (film), 1979.
Sister, Sister, NBC-TV, 1982.
Three-Way Choice, CBS-TV.

Also author of the fiction work *Mrs. Flowers: A Moment of Friendship,* Redpath Press, 1986. Contributor of articles, short stories, and poems to periodicals, and of material to books. Composer of songs, including two for the film *For the Love of Ivy.*

Sources

Books

Angelou, Maya, *I Know Why the Caged Bird Sings,* Random House, 1970.
Angelou, Maya, *Gather Together in My Name,* Random House, 1974.
Angelou, Maya, *Singin' and Swingin' and Gettin' Merry Like Christmas,* Random House, 1976.
Angelou, Maya, *The Heart of a Woman,* Random House, 1981.
Angelou, Maya, *All God's Children Need Traveling Shoes,* Random House, 1986.
Black Women Writers (1950-1980): A Critical Evaluation, edited by Mari Evans, Anchor Press/Doubleday, 1983.
Black Women Writers at Work, edited by Claudia Tate, Continuum, 1983.
Black Writers: A Selection of Sketches From Contemporary Authors, Gale, 1989.
Contemporary Literary Criticism, Gale, Volume 12, 1980, Volume 35, 1985.
Dictionary of Literary Biography, Volume 38: *Afro-American Writers After 1955: Dramatists and Prose Writers,* Gale, 1985.

Periodicals

Black Scholar, Summer 1982.
Chicago Tribune Book World, March 23, 1986.
Harper's Bazaar, November 1972.
Los Angeles Times Book Review, April 13, 1986; August 9, 1987.
New York Times, February 25, 1970.
New York Times Book Review, June 16, 1974; May 11, 1986.
Southern Humanities Review, Fall 1973.
Time, March 31, 1986.
Village Voice, July 11, 1974; October 28, 1981.

Washington Post Book World, October 4, 1981; June 26, 1983; May 11, 1986.

—Michael E. Mueller

Arthur Ashe

1943—

Professional tennis player, commentator, writer

The first black man to reach the top ranks of international tennis, Arthur Ashe is the very personification of the educated gentleman-athlete. Ashe's talents on the tennis courts not only secured his personal fame, they also opened the sport to greater black participation—both on a professional and recreational basis. *Wichita Eagle* columnist Fred Mann noted that the dignified Ashe has had "as much to do as anyone with transforming tennis in the 1970s into a sport that was popular with the masses." Mann added that the former winner of the prestigious Wimbledon and U.S. Open matches and Tennis Hall of Famer "conducted himself on the court with grace and composure at all times, unlike some of his Caucasian colleagues."

Arthur Ashe was certainly a phenomenon during his playing career and remains one to this day. In the *Richmond Times-Dispatch* Bob Lipper wrote that Ashe "is wealthy and famous, . . . a certified American hero whose visibility endures a decade after his playing career ended. More, he's a voice of reason in a minefield of rhetorical overkill, a conscience on matters of race and sport. And he's an accomplished man of letters." Lipper

referred to the critically acclaimed role Ashe has assumed as an author, columnist, and lecturer on issues concerning blacks in sports. "As a tennis player, Arthur Ashe was first-rate—not as successful as he might've been minus the self-imposed emotional constraints that governed his existence in an Anglo world of country clubs and garden parties—but a major force nonetheless," Lipper continued. "Still, it's been during the 1980s— as an ex-athlete—that Ashe has truly become world-class, establishing his credentials as businessman, author, commentator and champion of just causes. He's made it look easy, but then grace always was part of his essence."

Arthur Ashe, Jr., was born July 10th, 1943, in Richmond, Virginia. His ancestry is Native American and Mexican as well as black. While Ashe was a youngster growing up in segregated Richmond, his father ran the largest park for blacks in the city. In fact, the Ashe family lived in a caretaker's cottage right in the park, so young Arthur spent many hours engaged in athletic pursuits. Lipper described Arthur Ashe, Sr., as a hardworking man who "subscribed to such fuddy-duddy virtues as diligence and respect and honest labor, and he expected

At a Glance. . .

Full name, Arthur Robert Ashe, Jr.; born July 10, 1943, in Richmond, VA; son of Arthur, Sr. (a park superintendent) and Mattie (Cunningham) Ashe; married Jeanne-Marie Moutoussamy (a photographer), February 20, 1977; children: Camera Elizabeth. *Education:* University of California, Los Angeles, B.A. in business administration, 1966.

Amateur tennis player, 1958-69; professional tennis player, 1969-80; has finished first at least once in the U.S. Open, Wimbledon, and Davis Cup championships and was number-one-ranked player in the world, 1968 and 1975; elected to the United States Tennis Hall of Fame c. 1985. Writer, lecturer, tennis coach, and television commentator, 1980—. *Military service:* United States Army, first lieutenant, 1967-69.

Awards: Honorary doctorates from Virginia Commonwealth University, Princeton University, Dartmouth College, Le Moyne University, and others. Emmy Award for television adaptation of *A Hard Road to Glory*. A tennis club in Manayunk, Pennsylvania, has been named in Ashe's honor.

nothing less from his children." From his father Ashe inherited a sense of pride, dedication, and dignity. His mother's influence led to a measure of introversion that translated to studied calm on the court. Ashe's was not a trouble-free childhood. He told the *Chicago Tribune:* "My mom died when I was six, and books and sports were my way of bandaging the wound. I was too light for football and not quite fast enough for track, which left tennis as a logical choice."

The choice might have been more logical for a white youngster in those last days of nationally legislated racism. Black players—with the outstanding exception of Althea Gibson—were almost nonexistent in the highest amateur and professional ranks. Still Ashe persevered, taking encouragement from the success of baseball player Jackie Robinson. He was also encouraged in his all-black school in Richmond, where he says he received an excellent education. "It was part of a curious phenomenon I call the paradoxical advantage of segregation," Ashe told the *Chicago Tribune.* "Discrimination plus the bias women faced in the job market combined to provide us with some truly remarkable teachers. . . . Every day

we got the same message drummed into us. 'Despite discrimination and lynch mobs,' teachers told us, 'some black folks have always managed to find a way to succeed. Okay, this may not be the best-equipped school; that just means you're going to have to be a little better prepared than white kids and ready to seize any opportunity that comes your way.'" Ashe did seize the opportunity—he was an honors student in high school and was accepted at the University of California, Los Angeles, on a tennis scholarship.

Began Playing Tennis in His Father's Park

Ashe began playing tennis at the age of seven in the playground that his father maintained. Ronald Charity, a part-time instructor at the playground, noticed Ashe's talent and arranged for the boy to meet Dr. Walter Johnson, a black doctor based in Lynchburg, Virginia. In addition to his medical practice, Johnson enjoyed coaching promising black tennis players and provided them with proper equipment and courts. He detected Ashe's potential very early and did everything he could to advance the youngster's career. Unfortunately, Johnson's lessons also necessarily had to stress court etiquette for black players; since the game was so dominated by whites, and Johnson and his charges lived in the South, he taught his players to accept defeat graciously and to celebrate victories with humility.

Ashe was playing as a nationally ranked amateur by the time he turned 14. In both 1960 and 1961 he won the junior indoor singles title, a feat that brought him to the attention of Richard Hudlin, a tennis coach in the St. Louis area. Hudlin invited Ashe to St. Louis to continue his tennis training. Ashe accepted the offer and finished high school there. By 1962 he was the fifth-ranked junior player in the United States.

Such a dry recital of the facts makes Ashe's accomplishments sound easy. In reality he faced a multitude of race-related obstacles, including being barred from competition because his application arrived "too late"—a favorite excuse of segregated country clubs. When he was allowed to play Ashe often found himself surrounded by a sea of white faces, both on and off the court. He was the lone black star in his sport and he remained ever conscious of the example he was setting. Ashe told the *Wichita Eagle* that despite his success, his self-esteem suffered from the treatment he had received from whites while growing up in the South. "You never fully overcome [racism]," he said. "I hate to say it, but you live with it all your life. You get the undeniable impression that the world doesn't like you."

Accepted UCLA Scholarship

After graduating from high school Ashe accepted a scholarship at the University of California, Los Angeles (UCLA). There he perfected his skills with UCLA coach J. D. Morgan and tennis legend Pancho Gonzalez, who lived near the campus. In 1963 Ashe earned a place on the Davis Cup team and earned a victory in his first national contest, the U.S. Men's Hard Court championship. The following year saw him ranked sixth nationally among amateurs, and in 1965—after singles victories in the Davis Cup finals and a tour of Australia—he became the second-ranked amateur in the nation. Ashe closed out his collegiate tennis career by leading UCLA to the NCAA national championship, winning in both singles and doubles competition. Not one to neglect his studies in favor of tennis, however, Ashe earned a bachelor's degree in business administration in June of 1966.

Ashe continued to play tennis during his military service, which he served as a first lieutenant from the Reserve Officers' Training Corps. In the midst of his stint with the army he won the 1967 Men's Clay Court championship and the United States amateur title. The latter victory earned him an invitation to the U.S. Open tournament; it came as little surprise to tennis observers when Ashe won the Open and became the top-ranked player in the nation in 1968. Even in those glory days, however, the tennis star felt isolated by his race. He told *Sports Illustrated:* "It's an abnormal world I live in. I don't belong anywhere. It's like I'm floating down the middle. I'm never quite sure where I am. . . . I do get lonely and it does bother me that I am in this predicament. But I don't dwell on it, because I know it will resolve itself."

Displaying a composure well beyond his years and a vast repertory of power backhands, Ashe remained among the top-five-ranked tennis stars internationally between 1969 and 1975. Observers noted his relaxed demeanor on the court and the calm but grim determination that often unnerved his more volatile opponents. Few in the audience realized that Ashe was far more emotional than he seemed. Before important matches he would sometimes be stricken with nervous stomach cramps; Ashe has since admitted that he wishes he could have been more free with his feelings during those crucial years.

Ashe turned professional in 1969 and played numerous important matches throughout the following decade. His game peaked in 1975 when he won both the prestigious Wimbledon Singles championship and the World Championship Tennis Singles. By that time the changing racial climate had improved sports opportunities for black athletes and Ashe was hailed as a pioneer in his field: He was the first black man to win at Wimbledon and the first to receive a number-one ranking internationally.

Suffered Major Heart Attack

In 1979, at the age of thirty-five, Ashe suffered a major heart attack. He underwent quadruple bypass surgery, vowing to return to tennis as soon as he healed. Upon recovery, however, he still suffered chest pains and was threatened with further surgery. He announced his retirement from tennis in April of 1980. "An athlete retires twice," Ashe told the *Chicago Tribune.* "The first time is when they don't renew your contract. But for a couple of years afterwards you still think you could get in shape again and play another season or two. Then one day you look in the mirror and the reality finally sinks in that it's time to find something else to do with the rest of your life."

So Arthur Ashe the tennis star became Arthur Ashe the author, lecturer, and social critic. Few former athletes of any race have put their college educations to greater use than has Ashe. In 1982 he was invited to give a seminar on the history of blacks in sports at Florida Memorial

> You never fully overcome racism. I hate to say it, but you live with it all your life. You get the undeniable impression that the world doesn't like you.

College. When he went to the library to research the topic, he found very little documentation of black accomplishment in professional sports, especially before the days of Negro League baseball. Investing $250,000 of his own money and several years in the process of research and writing, Ashe produced *A Hard Road to Glory,* a three-volume comprehensive history of America's black athletes. "The project was a natural," Ashe told the *Chicago Tribune,* "since it brought both sides of me, the bookish and the sports-minded, together. Once I made the decision to do it, I had to go at the book the way I've always done things—the way our teachers at Maggie Walker High School insisted upon—all out, with everything I've got." *A Hard Road to Glory* received critical acclaim and went into a second printing. It earned Ashe a number of honorary doctorates from the nation's universities and even an Emmy award when it was produced as a television documentary.

Authority on Minorities in Sports

Today Ashe is recognized as an important spokesman on the issues of minorities in collegiate and professional athletics. He serves as a television commentator at tennis matches, a sports consultant at tennis clinics, and writes columns for the *Washington Post.* Having had two heart attacks and undergone brain surgery, Ashe guards his health with great care. He told the *Seattle Post-Intelligencer* that heart disease "changes your diet, it changes your stress level, it changes the way you work." Ashe has also served as campaign chairman for the American Heart Association.

A dedicated family man, Ashe lives with his wife and daughter near New York City. He also retains close ties to his brother and sister, who live in the South. *Philadelphia Inquirer* columnist Claude Lewis described Arthur Ashe as "a world-class athlete and . . . a world-class man." Reflecting on his career both on the court and since, Ashe told the *Richmond Times-Dispatch:* "I guess I appreciate the fact some people take my views seriously. I'm in a stage of my life in which I have confidence in my opinions. I have the experience and the courage and the background to say some things about some subjects I feel I have expertise in." He continued: "I feel I've made a small contribution to American history. And I've definitely plugged a huge gap in the knowledge of African-American history. It is an incredible history of achievement. African-American athletes outdid themselves." The same can certainly be said of Arthur Ashe.

Selected writings

(With Frank DeFord) *Portrait in Motion,* Houghten, 1975.
Arthur Ashe's Tennis Clinic, illustrations by Jim McQueen, Golf Digest/Tennis Magazine, 1981.
(With Neil Amdur) *Off the Court,* New American Library, 1981.
A Hard Road to Glory, 3 volumes, Warner Books, 1988.

Sources

Chicago Tribune, November 28, 1988.
Life, October 15, 1965.
Newsday, February 12, 1991.
New York Times Magazine, January 2, 1966.
People, March 6, 1989.
Philadelphia Inquirer, April 25, 1990.
Richmond Times-Dispatch, May 21, 1989.
Seattle Post-Intelligencer, May 26, 1988.
Sports Illustrated, September 20, 1965; August 29, 1966.
Wichita Eagle, February 21, 1990.

—Mark Kram

James Baldwin

1924-1987

Writer

The American Civil Rights Movement had many eloquent spokesmen, but few were better known than James Baldwin. A novelist and essayist of considerable renown, Baldwin found readers of every race and nationality, though his message reflected bitter disappointment in his native land and its white majority. Throughout his distinguished career Baldwin called himself a "disturber of the peace"—one who revealed uncomfortable truths to a society mired in complacency. As early as 1960 he was recognized as an articulate speaker and passionate writer on racial matters, and at his death in 1987 he was lauded as one of the most respected voices—of any race—in modern American letters.

Baldwin's greatest achievement as a writer was his ability to address American race relations from a psychological perspective. In his essays and fiction the author explored the implications of racism for both the oppressed and the oppressor, suggesting repeatedly that whites as well as blacks suffer in a racist climate. In *The Black American Writer: Poetry and Drama,* Walter Meserve noted: "People are important to Baldwin, and their problems, generally embedded in their agonizing souls, stimulate him to

write. . . . A humanitarian, sensitive to the needs and struggles of man, he writes of inner turmoil, spiritual disruption, the consequence upon people of the burdens of the world, both White and Black."

James Arthur Baldwin was born and raised in Harlem under extremely trying circumstances. The oldest of nine children, he grew up in an environment of rigorous religious observance and dire poverty. His stepfather, an evangelical preacher, was a strict disciplinarian who showed James little love. As John W. Roberts put it in the *Dictionary of Literary Biography,* the relationship between the youngster and his stepfather "served as a constant source of tension during [Baldwin's] formative years and informs some of his best mature writings. . . . The demands of caring for younger siblings and his stepfather's religious convictions in large part shielded the boy from the harsh realities of Harlem street life during the 1930s." During his youth Baldwin read constantly and slipped away as often as he dared to the movies and even to plays. Although perhaps somewhat sheltered from the perils of the streets, Baldwin knew he wanted to be a writer and thus observed his environment very closely. He was an excellent student who earned

At a Glance...

Born August 2, 1924, in New York, NY; died of stomach cancer December 1, 1987, in St. Paul de Vence, France; son of David (a clergyman and factory worker) and Berdis (Jones) Baldwin. *Education:* Graduate of De Witt Clinton High School, New York, NY.

Writer, 1944-87. Youth minister at Fireside Pentecostal Assembly, New York City, 1938-42; variously employed as a handyman, dishwasher, waiter, and office boy in New York City, and in defense work in Belle Meade, NJ, 1942-46. Lecturer on racial issues in the United States and Europe, 1955-87. Director of play *Fortune and Men's Eyes,* Istanbul, Turkey, 1970, and film *The Inheritance,* 1973.

Awards: Eugene F. Saxton fellowship, 1945; Rosenwald fellowship, 1948; Guggenheim fellowship, 1954; National Institute of Arts and Letters grant for literature, 1956; Ford Foundation grant, 1959; George Polk Memorial Award, 1963; American Book Award nomination, 1980, for *Just above My Head;* named Commander of the Legion of Honor (France), 1986.

Member: Congress of Racial Equality (member of national advisory board), American Academy and Institute of Arts and Letters, International PEN.

special attention from many of his teachers.

In the summer of his fourteenth birthday Baldwin underwent a dramatic religious conversion during a service at his father's church. The experience tied him to the Pentecostal faith even more closely; he became a popular junior minister, preaching full sermons while still in his teens. Students of Baldwin's writings see this period as an essential one in his development. The structure of an evangelical sermon, with its fiery language and dire warnings, would translate well onto the page when the young man began to write. As he grew older, however, Baldwin began to question his involvement in Christianity. His outside readings led him to the conclusion that blacks should have little to do with a faith that had been used to enslave them.

Shortly after he graduated from high school in 1942, Baldwin was compelled to find work in order to help support his brothers and sisters. College was out of the

question—mental instability had crippled his stepfather and the family was desperate. Eventually Baldwin secured a wartime job with the defense industry, working in a factory in Belle Meade, New Jersey. There he was confronted daily by the humiliating regulations of segregation and hostile white workers who taunted him. When his stepfather died Baldwin rebelled against family responsibilities and moved to Greenwich Village, absolutely determined to be a writer. He supported himself doing odd jobs and began writing both a novel and shorter pieces of journalism.

Literary Prowess Blossomed in Europe

In 1944 Baldwin met one of his heroes, Richard Wright. A respected novelist and lecturer, Wright helped Baldwin win a fellowship that would allow him the financial freedom to work on his writing. The years immediately following World War II saw Baldwin's first minor successes in his chosen field. His pieces appeared in such prestigious publications as the *Nation,* the *New Leader,* and *Commentary,* and he became acquainted with other young would-be writers in New York. Still, Baldwin struggled with his fiction. By 1948 he concluded that the social tenor of the United States was stifling his creativity. Using the funds from yet another fellowship, he embarked for Paris and commenced the most important phase of his career.

"Once I found myself on the other side of the ocean," Baldwin told the *New York Times,* "I could see where I came from very clearly, and I could see that I carried myself, which is my home, with me. You can never escape that. I am the grandson of a slave, and I am a writer. I must deal with both." Through some difficult financial and emotional periods, Baldwin undertook a process of self-discovery that included both an acceptance of his heritage and an admittance of his bisexuality. In *Tri-Quarterly* Robert A. Bone concluded that Europe gave the young author many things: "It gave him a world perspective from which to approach the question of his own identity. It gave him a tender love affair which would dominate the pages of his later fiction. But above all, Europe gave him back himself. The immediate fruit of self-recovery was a great creative outburst."

In short order Baldwin completed his first novel, *Go Tell It on the Mountain,* and a play, *The Amen Corner.* In addition to these projects he contributed thoughtful essays to America's most important periodicals and worked occasionally as a journalist. Most critics view Baldwin's essays as his best contribution to American literature. Works like *Notes of a Native Son* and *Nobody Knows My Name* served to illuminate the condition of the black man in American society on the eve of the civil rights era. Baldwin probed the issues of race with emphasis on self-determination, identity, and reality. In *The Fifties: Fiction, Poetry, Drama,* C. W. E. Bigsby wrote that Baldwin's central theme in his essays was "the need to accept reality as a necessary foundation for individual identity and thus a logical prerequisite for the kind of saving love in which he places his whole faith. . . . Baldwin sees this simple progression as an urgent formula not only for the redemption of individual men but for the survival of mankind. In this at least black and white are as one and the Negro's much-vaunted search for identity can be seen as part and parcel of the American's long-standing need for self-definition."

The Fire Next Time Predicts 1960s' Racial Unrest

Baldwin's essays tackled complex psychological issues but remained understandable. His achievements enhanced his reputation both among America's intellectuals and with the general public. In the mid-1950s he returned to America and became a popular speaker on the lecture circuit. The author quickly discovered, however, that social conditions for American blacks had become even more bleak. As the 1960s began—and violence in the South escalated—he became increasingly outraged. Baldwin realized that his essays were reaching a white audience and as the Civil Rights Movement gained momentum he sought to warn whites about the potential destruction their behavior patterns might wreak. In 1963 he published a long essay, *The Fire Next Time,* in which he all but predicted the outbursts of black anger to come. *The Fire Next Time* made bestseller lists, but Baldwin took little comfort in that fact. The assassination of three of his friends—civil rights marcher Medgar Evers, the Reverend Martin Luther King, Jr., and black Muslim leader Malcolm X—shattered any hopes the author might have had for racial reconciliation. Completely disillusioned with the United States, he returned to France in the early 1970s and made his home there until his death in 1987.

Baldwin's fiction and plays also explored the burdens a callous society can impose on a sensitive individual. Two of his best-known works, the novel *Go Tell It on the Mountain* and the play *The Amen Corner* were inspired by his years with the Pentecostal church in Harlem. In *Go Tell It on the Mountain,* for instance, a teenaged boy struggles with a repressive stepfather and experiences a charismatic spiritual awakening. Later Baldwin novels dealt frankly with homosexuality and interracial love affairs—love in both its sexual and spiritual forms became an essential component of the quest for self-realization for both the author and his characters. Fred L.

Standley noted in the *Dictionary of Literary Biography* that Baldwin's concerns as a fiction writer and a dramatist included "the historical significance and the potential explosiveness in black-white relations; the necessity for developing a sexual and psychological consciousness and identity; the intertwining of love and power in the universal scheme of existence as well as in the structures of society; the misplaced priorities in the value systems in America; and the responsibility of the artist to promote the evolution of the individual and the society."

Inspired a Generation of Artists

Baldwin spent much of the last fifteen years of his life in France, but he never gave up his American citizenship. He once commented that he preferred to think of himself as a "commuter" between countries. That view notwithstanding, the citizens of France embraced Baldwin as one

> I could see where I came from very clearly, and I could see that I carried myself, which is my home, with me. You can never escape that. I am the grandson of a slave, and I am a writer. I must deal with both.

of their own. In 1986 he was accorded one of the country's highest accolades when he was named Commander of the Legion of Honor. Baldwin died of stomach cancer in 1987, leaving several projects unfinished. Those who paid tribute to him on both sides of the Atlantic noted that he had experienced success in theater, fiction, and nonfiction alike—a staggering achievement. One of his last works to see print during his lifetime was a well-regarded anthology of essays, *The Price of the Ticket: Collected Nonfiction 1948-1985.* In her book *James Baldwin,* Carolyn Wedin Sylvander concluded that what emerges from the whole of Baldwin's output is "a kind of absolute conviction and passion and honesty that is nothing less than courageous. . . . Baldwin has shared his struggle with his readers for a purpose—to demonstrate that our suffering is our bridge to one another."

Baldwin was laid to rest in a Harlem cemetery. A funeral service in his honor drew scores of black writers, politicians, entertainers, and other celebrities, many of whom offered fond eulogies for the pioneering author. The *New York Times* quoted writer Orde Coombs, for one, who said: "Because [Baldwin] existed we felt that the racial miasma that swirled around us would not consume us, and it is not too much to say that this man saved our lives, or at least, gave us the necessary ammunition to face what we knew would continue to be a hostile and condescending world." Poet and playwright Amiri Baraka likewise commented: "This man traveled the earth like its history and its biographer. He reported, criticized, made beautiful, analyzed, cajoled, lyricized, attacked, sang, made us think, made us better, made us consciously human. . . . He made us feel . . . that we could defend ourselves or define ourselves, that we were in the world not merely as animate slaves, but as terrifyingly sensitive measurers of what is good or evil, beautiful or ugly. This is the power of his spirit. This is the bond which created our love for him."

Perhaps the most touching tribute to Baldwin came from the pen of *Washington Post* columnist Juan Williams. Williams concluded: "The success of Baldwin's effort as the witness is evidenced time and again by the people, black and white, gay and straight, famous and anonymous, whose humanity he unveiled in his writings. America and the literary world are far richer for his witness. The proof of a shared humanity across the divides of race, class and more is the testament that the preacher's son, James Arthur Baldwin, has left us."

Selected writings

Fiction

Go Tell It on the Mountain, Knopf, 1953.
Giovanni's Room, Dial, 1956.
Another Country, Dial, 1962.
Going to Meet the Man, Dial, 1965.
Tell Me How Long the Train's Been Gone, Dial, 1968.
If Beale Street Could Talk, Dial, 1974.
Just Above My Head, Dial, 1979.

Nonfiction

Autobiographical Notes, Knopf, 1953.
Notes of a Native Son, Beacon Press, 1955.
Nobody Knows My Name: More Notes of a Native Son, Dial, 1961.
The Fire Next Time, Dial, 1963.
No Name in the Street, Dial, 1972.
The Devil Finds Work, Dial, 1976.
The Evidence of Things Not Seen, Holt, 1985.
The Price of the Ticket: Collected Nonfiction 1948-1985, St. Martin's, 1985.

Plays

The Amen Corner (first produced in Washington, D.C. at Howard University, 1955; produced on Broadway at Ethel Barrymore Theatre, April 15, 1965), Dial, 1968.
Blues for Mister Charlie (first produced on Broadway at ANTA Theatre, April 23, 1964), Dial, 1964.

Other

Contributor of book reviews and essays to numerous periodicals, including *Harper's, Nation, Esquire, Playboy, Partisan Review, Mademoiselle,* and *New Yorker.*

Sources

Books

The Black American Writer, Volume 2: *Poetry and Drama,* edited by C. W. E. Bigsby, Everett/Edwards, 1969.
Concise Dictionary of American Literary Biography: The New Consciousness 1941-1968, Gale, 1987.
Critical Essays on James Baldwin, edited by Fred Standley and Nancy Standley, G. K. Hall, 1981.
Dictionary of Literary Biography, Gale, Volume 2: *American Novelists Since World War II,* 1978, Volume 8: *Twentieth-Century American Dramatists,* 1981, Volume 33: *Afro-American Fiction Writers after 1955,* 1984.
The Fifties: Fiction, Poetry, Drama, edited by Warren French, Everett/Edwards, 1970.
James Baldwin: A Collection of Critical Essays, edited by Kenneth Kinnamon, Prentice-Hall, 1974.
Pratt, Louis Hill, *James Baldwin,* Twayne, 1978.
Sylvander, Carolyn Wedin, *James Baldwin,* Frederick Ungar, 1980.

Periodicals

New York Times, May 3, 1964; April 16, 1965; May 31, 1968; February 2, 1969; May 21, 1971; May 17, 1974; June 4, 1976; September 4, 1977; September 21, 1979; September 23, 1979; November 11, 1983; January 10, 1985; January 14, 1985; December 2, 1987; December 9, 1987.
Tri-Quarterly, Winter, 1965.
Washington Post, December 2, 1987; December 9, 1987.

—*Anne Janette Johnson*

Amiri Baraka

1934—

Writer, educator

Amiri Baraka is one of the most controversial writers in recent history, one whose influence on Afro-American literature has been profound. Plays, poems, novels, essays, short stories, and music criticism are all included in his body of work, and all have served as vehicles for his outspoken social and political commentary. According to *Dictionary of Literary Biography* contributor James A. Miller, Baraka is "a protean personality, fond of manifestos and vehement repudiations, [who] has shifted guises and discarded identities with such astonishing rapidity that critics have often been frustrated, suspended in the act of defining a man who is no longer there, while his admirers have been left abandoned or challenged to readjust themselves to his new position."

Born LeRoi Jones in Newark, New Jersey, Baraka grew up in a family of distinctly middle-class aspirations. He was one of a handful of blacks in his high school. While his parents apparently took pride in this fact, Baraka's unique status caused him tremendous feelings of alienation and isolation. Later in life he would mercilessly lampoon the values of assimilation his parents held dear. Baraka won a scholarship to Rutgers University in 1951, but a continuing sense of cultural dislocation prompted him to transfer in 1952 to Howard University, a black college. He would eventually attack the school as the citadel of the black bourgeoisie he disdained, writing in an essay: "Howard University shocked me into realizing how desperately sick the Negro could be, how he could be led into self-destruction and how he would not realize that it was the society that had forced him into a great sickness." Despite his later criticism, however, Baraka benefitted greatly from his years at Howard. He studied philosophy, religion, and literature, and was exposed to the ideas of prominent black poets, music critics, and scholars. After earning a bachelor's degree there, he enlisted in the U.S. Air Force, serving in Puerto Rico and Germany as a weatherman and gunner.

Three years later Baraka returned to civilian life. At the time, the social and artistic phenomenon known as the Beat Generation was just beginning to touch the consciousness of a complacent America. The Beats were challenging the stagnant literary establishment and the rigid moral code of the country; Baraka quickly aligned himself with them, seeing them as fellow outsiders. The

At a Glance...

Name originally Everett LeRoi Jones, changed to Imamu Ameer Baraka in 1968, later modified to Amiri Baraka; born October 7, 1934, in Newark, New Jersey; son of Coyette LeRoy (a postman and elevator operator) and Anna Lois (maiden name, Russ) Jones; married Hettie Cohen, October 13, 1958 (divorced, August 1965); married Sylvia Robinson (Bibi Amina Baraka), August 1966; children: (first marriage) Kellie Elisabeth, Lisa Victoria Chapman; (second marriage) Dbalaji Malik Ali, Ras Jua Al Aziz, Shani Isis, Amiri Seku, Ahi Mwenge. *Education:* B.A., Howard University.

Writer. Founded *Yugen* magazine and Totem Press, 1958; New School for Social Research, New York City, instructor, 1961-64; State University of New York at Stony Brook, associate professor, 1983-85, professor of Afro-American studies, 1985—. Founded Black Arts Repertory Theatre School, 1964, director, 1964-66. *Military service:* U.S. Air Force, 1954-57.

Awards: John Hay Whitney fellowship, 1960-61; Longview Award for best essay of the year, 1961, for "Cuba Libre"; Obie Award, 1964, for *Dutchman;* Guggenheim fellowship, 1965-66; Yoruba Academy fellow, 1965; second prize at the First World Festival of Negro Arts, Dakar, Senegal, 1966, for *The Slave;* Doctorate of Humane Letters, Malcolm X College, 1972; Rockefeller Foundation fellow, 1981; National Endowment for the Arts poetry award, 1981; New Jersey Council for the Arts award, 1982; American Book Award, 1984, for *Confirmation: An Anthology of African-American Women;* Drama Award, 1985.

Addresses: *Office*—Department of African Studies, State University of New York, Long Island, NY 11794. *Agent*—William Morrow & Co., 105 Madison Ave., New York, NY 10016.

ideal shared by the Beats and Baraka was to look beyond, or rise above, racial barriers. Baraka explained to David Ossman in *The Sullen Art: Interviews with Modern American Poets:* "I'm fully conscious all the time that I'm an American Negro, because it's part of my life. But I also know that if I want to say, 'I see a bus full of people,' I don't have to say, 'I am a Negro seeing a bus

full of people.' I would deal with it when it has to do directly with the poem, and not as a kind of broad generalization that doesn't have much to do with a lot of young writers today who are Negroes."

Baraka took up residence in Greenwich Village, a center of the budding cultural revolution. He soon met and married Hettie Cohen, a young Jewish woman who shared his tastes in music and literature. Cohen worked for the *Partisan Review,* where Baraka's first published piece appeared in 1958. It was a defense of the innovations of Beat writing declaring that young writers "must resort to violence in literature, . . . to shake us out of the woeful literary sterility which characterized the '40s." Baraka and Cohen organized *Yugen,* a literary magazine showcasing the new poets. Baraka wrote a letter—on toilet paper stationery—to Beat poet Allen Ginsberg soliciting works and was rewarded with contributions from Ginsberg, Philip Whalen, Gregory Corso, Gary Snyder, Jack Kerouac, and other notables.

A vital relationship with Ginsberg developed. Baraka recalled in the *Village Voice:* "We talked endlessly about poetry, about prosody, about literature and it is clear to me that my poetry would not have evolved as it has without A. G.'s ideas. He let me in on poetry as a living phenomenon, a world of human concern, and literature as a breathing force in one's life, the task of a lifetime. I absorbed and grew because of these ideas, and even in resisting some of Ginsberg's other ideas, I still grew and developed because of contact with them." Baraka's association with Ginsberg, his editorship of *Yugen,* and establishment of Totem Press quickly made him one of the leading figures of the Greenwich Village scene. He began to write prolifically, contributing poetry and reviews of books and music to the important smaller magazines of the day.

Visit to Cuba Encouraged Social Activism

But even as he was becoming a key member of the Beat Generation, Baraka was drifting away from the movement. His fellow poets were, for the most part, apolitical. They criticized the system, but had no agenda for changing it. Baraka felt a growing sense of dissatisfaction with this kind of passivity. In 1960 he reached a turning point in his life when he visited Fidel Castro's Cuba. There he encountered many forceful, politically committed young artists and intellectuals who challenged him to abandon the Beat preoccupation with the soul and to tackle society's problems in a more aggressive fashion. Baraka did not change overnight; he did, however, return from Cuba with a new sense of political mission and a stronger identification with artists of the Third World than with those of the white vanguard. Though he remained a resident of Greenwich Village, he became increasingly involved in the social life of Harlem.

During the early 1960s Baraka seemed to regard himself as a bridge between the black and white worlds. He wrote two of his most serious works of fiction at this time, *The System of Dante's Hell* and *Tales*. Both reflect his struggle to pull away from Greenwich Village. He told Kimberly Benston in *Boundary 2:* "I was really writing defensively. I was trying to get away from the influence of people like [Robert] Creeley and [Charles] Olson. I was living in New York then and the whole Creeley-Olson influence was beginning to beat me up. I was in a very closed circle . . . and I felt the need to break out." Still, he continued to work closely with Beat writers; in 1961 he and poet Diane Di Prima founded another important underground magazine, *Floating Bear*. The two were also instrumental in organizing the American Theatre for Poets. Baraka ridiculed the notion of a separate black society in his essay "Black Is a Country," insisting that "America is as much a black country as a white one. The lives and destinies of the white American are bound up inextricably with those of the black American." He clung to his belief in a world free of color lines even as he sought to establish for himself a stronger ethnic identity.

Dutchman Exposes Disillusionment

Eventually Baraka's writing revealed the slow disintegration of his faith in racial harmony. In the poem "Black Dada Nihilismus" he ponders the many nonwhite cultures destroyed by Western civilization and concludes by calling on the African god Damballah for help in the destruction of the West. In his most well-known and highly praised play, *Dutchman,* he depicts a subway encounter between Lula, a white, Bohemian woman, and Clay, a young, middle-class, black man. At first Clay seems to represent the aspects of black life Baraka harshly criticized in his earlier works, while Lula appears to embody the values the author prized. Lula taunts Clay about his repressed identity, urging him to release his true black self. When he finally does, it pours forth as a violent tirade against Lula and the larger white world. At the drama's conclusion Lula calmly stabs Clay to death and sits back to await her next victim. *Dutchman* "merges private themes, mythical allusion, surrealistic techniques, and social statement into a play of astonishing power and resonance," stated Miller. It won the 1964 Obie Award for best American play, was performed internationally, and propelled its author into a whirlwind of lectures, panel discussions, readings, and teaching assignments at liberal universities. Years after the play's debut Darryl Pinckley wrote in the *New York Times Book Review:* "[Baraka] is a highly gifted dramatist. Much of the black protest literature of the 60s now seems diminished in

power, even sentimental. But 'Dutchman' immediately seizes the imagination. It is radically economical in structure, striking in the vivacity of its language and rapid shifts of mood."

By mid-1964 Baraka had completely rejected the cultural and political values of the Beats and had begun verbally attacking his Greenwich Village friends, white liberals, and the white community in general. His anti-bourgeois stance had been transformed into a militant black nationalism inspired by Malcolm X. An integrated society was not only impossible, he now believed, but undesirable. Ironically, Baraka's diatribes against the white world boosted his popularity even further—at least temporarily. For a time he was swamped by invitations to hip, white, New York City high-society parties. But he meant what he said about turning his back on that world. "Now there could be absolutely no ties with whites, and certainly not any intimate ones," he later wrote. "These in themselves, we reasoned, would make us traitors." By

> It is a narrow nationalism that says the white man is the enemy. . . . Nationalism, so-called, when it says 'all non-blacks are our enemies,' is sickness or criminality, in fact, a form of fascism.

the end of 1965 he had ended his marriage to Hettie Cohen, broken his ties with the white literary establishment, and moved to Harlem.

Embraced Black Nationalism

In Harlem he founded the Black Arts Repertory Theatre School. It was a short-lived but highly influential project that revolutionized black theater in the United States. Contemporary dramas shaped by black nationalist philosophy were performed there and institutions modeled after it sprang up all over the country. The theater—which was funded with federal money—was shut down by police in 1966, allegedly because an arms cache had been discovered there. Returning to his birthplace, Newark, Baraka dropped the name LeRoi Jones in favor of the Bantu Muslim appellation Imamu (meaning "spiritual leader," later dropped) Ameer (later changed to Amiri, meaning "blessed") Baraka ("prince"). In the essay "state/meant" he summarized his new sense of purpose: "The Black Artist's role in America is to aid in the destruction of America as he knows it. His role is to report and reflect so precisely the nature of the society, and of himself in that society, that other men will be moved by the exactness of his rendering and, if they are black men, grow strong through this moving, having seen their own strength, and weakness; and if they are white men, tremble, curse, and go mad, because they will be drenched with the filth of their evil."

As the dominant black theorist and artist of the late 1960s, Baraka was responsible for shifting the focus of black literature from an integrationist art that conveyed a raceless and classless vision to a literature rooted in the black experience. The era over which he presided is considered the most important in black arts since the Harlem Renaissance of the 1920s. And despite Baraka's rejection of the ideal of an integrated world, his work affected all races. As Native American author Maurice Kenny wrote in *Amiri Baraka: The Kaleidoscopic Torch,* "He opened tightly guarded doors for not only Blacks but poor whites as well and, of course, Native Americans, Latinos and Asian-Americans. We'd all still be waiting for the invitation from the *New Yorker* without him. He taught us all how to claim it and take it."

Turned to Marxism

As a black nationalist political leader Baraka was a key figure in the organization of the Congress of African Peoples in 1970 and the National Black Political Assembly in 1972. But by 1974 he had undergone yet another reassessment of his cultural and political orientation. In a dramatic turnabout he rejected black nationalism and proclaimed himself a Marxist-Leninist-Maoist. He stated in the *New York Times:* "It is a narrow nationalism that says the white man is the enemy. . . . Nationalism, so-called, when it says 'all non-blacks are our enemies,' is sickness or criminality, in fact, a form of fascism." Since 1974 Baraka has produced a great deal of socialist poetry and essays and names the destruction of the capitalist state and the creation of a socialist community as his goal. William J. Harris quoted him in *The Poetry and Poetics of Amiri Baraka* as saying: "I think fundamentally my intentions are similar to those I had when I was a Nationalist. That might seem contradictory, but they were similar in the sense that I see art as a weapon, and a weapon of revolution. It's just now that I define revolution in Marxist terms. . . . I came to my Marxist view as a result of having struggled as a Nationalist and found certain dead ends theoretically and ideologically, as far as Nationalism was concerned and had to reach out for a communist ideology." Nonetheless, Baraka's many philosophical shifts are far from capricious, attested Arnold Rampersad, who

wrote in *Amiri Baraka: The Kaleidoscopic Torch:* "His change of heart and head is testimony to his honesty, energy, and relentless search for meaning."

Writings

Under name LeRoi Jones until 1967

Plays

Dutchman [and] *The Slave,* Morrow, 1964.
The Toilet, Sterling Lord, 1964.
The Baptism: A Comedy in One Act, Sterling Lord, 1966.
Slave Ship, Jihad, 1967.
Arm Yourself or Harm Yourself! A One-Act Play, Jihad, 1967.
Four Black Revolutionary Plays: All Praises to the Black Man, Bobbs-Merrill, 1969.
(Contributor) *New Plays from the Black Theatre,* edited by Ed Bullins, Bantam, 1969.
J-E-L-L-O, Third World Press, 1970.
(Contributor) *Black Drama Anthology,* edited by Woodie King and Ron Milner, New American Library, 1971.
(Contributor) *Spontaneous Combustion: Eight New American Plays,* edited by Rochelle Owens, Winter House, 1972.
What Was the Relationship of the Lone Ranger to the Means of Production?: A Play in One Act, Anti-Imperialist Cultural Union, 1978.
The Motion of History and Other Plays, Morrow, 1978.
The Sidnee Poet Heroical, in Twenty-Nine Scenes, Reed & Cannon, 1979.
Selected Plays and Prose of LeRoi Jones/Amiri Baraka, Morrow, 1979.

Also author of the plays *Home on the Range* and *Police,* published in *Drama Review,* Summer 1968, *Rockgroup,* published in *Cricket,* December 1969, and *Black Power Chant,* published in *Drama Review,* December 1972.

Screenplays

Dutchman, Gene Persson Enterprises, Ltd., 1967.
Black Spring, Black Arts Alliance (San Francisco), 1968.
A Fable (based on *The Slave*), MFR Productions, 1971.
Supercoon, Gene Persson Enterprises, Ltd., 1971.

Poetry

April 13 (broadside), Number 133, Penny Poems (New Haven), 1959.
Spring & So Forth (broadside), Number 111, Penny Poems, 1960.
Preface to a Twenty Volume Suicide Note, Toteni/Corinth, 1961.
The Dead Lecturer, Grove, 1964.

Black Art (also see below), Jihad, 1966.

Black Magic (also see below), Morrow, 1967

A Poem For Black Hearts, Broadside Press, 1967.

Black Magic: Sabotage; Target Study; Black Art; Collected Poetry, 1961-1967, Bobbs-Merrill, 1969.

It's Nation Time, Third World Press, 1970.

Spirit Reach, Jihad, 1972.

Afrikan Revolution: A Poem, Jihad, 1973.

Hard Facts: Excerpts, People's War, 1975.

Spring Song, Baraka, 1979.

AM/TRAK, Phoenix Bookship, 1979.

Selected Poetry of Amiri Baraka/LeRoi Jones, Morrow, 1979.

In the Tradition: For Black Arthur Blythe, Jihad, 1980.

Reggae or Not! Poems, Contact Two, 1982.

Essays

Blues People: Negro Music in White America, Morrow, 1963.

Home: Social Essays (contains "state/meant"), Morrow, 1966.

Black Music, Morrow, 1968.

Raise, Race, Rays, Raze: Essays Since 1965, Random House, 1971.

Strategy and Tactics of a Pan-African Nationalist Party, Jihad, 1971.

Kawaida Studies: The New Nationalism, Third World Press, 1972.

Crisis in Boston!, Vita Wa Watu—People's War, 1974.

Daggers and Javelins: Essays, 1974-1979, Morrow, 1984.

(With wife, Amina Baraka) *The Music: Reflections on Jazz and Blues,* Morrow, 1987.

Other

The Disguise (broadside), [New Haven], 1961.

Cuba Libre, Fair Play for Cuba Committee (New York City), 1961.

(Contributor) *Soon, One Morning,* edited by Herbert Hill, Knopf, 1963.

The System of Dante's Hell (novel), Grove, 1965.

Striptease, Parallax, 1967.

Tales (short stories), Grove, 1967.

Focus on Amiri Baraka: Playwright LeRoi Jones Analyzes the 1st National Black Political Convention (recording), Center for Cassette Studies, 1973.

The Autobiography of LeRoi Jones/Amiri Baraka, Freundlich, 1984.

Works represented in more than 75 anthologies, including *A Broadside Treasury, For Malcolm, The New Black Poetry, Nommo,* and *The Trembling Lamb.* Editor with Diane Di Prima, *The Floating Bear,* 1961-1963. Contributor to periodicals, including the *Evergreen Review, Poetry, Down Beat, Metronome,* the *Nation, Negro Digest,* and the *Saturday Review.*

Sources

Books

Amiri Baraka: The Kaleidoscopic Torch, edited by James B. Gwynne, Steppingstones Press, 1985.

Baraka, Amiri, *The Autobiography of Leroi Jones/Amiri Baraka,* Freundlich, 1984.

Baraka: The Renegade and the Mask, edited by Kimberly A. Benston, Yale University Press, 1976.

Benston, Kimberly A., *Imamu Amiri Baraka (LeRoi Jones): A Collection of Critical Essays,* Prentice-Hall, 1978.

Black Theatre, U.S.A., edited by James V. Hatch, Free Press, 1974.

Brown, Lloyd W., *Amiri Baraka,* Twayne, 1980.

Contemporary Literary Criticism, Gale, Volume 1, 1973, Volume 2, 1974, Volume 3, 1975, Volume 5, 1976, Volume 10, 1979, Volume 14, 1980, Volume 33, 1985.

Cook, Bruce, *The Beat Generation,* Scribner, 1971.

Dace, Letitia, *LeRoi Jones (Imamu Amiri Baraka): A Checklist of Works By and About Him,* Nether Press, 1971.

Dictionary of Literary Biography, Gale, Volume 5: American Poets Since World War II, 1980, Volume 7: Twentieth-Century American Dramatists, 1981, Volume 16: The Beats: Literary Bohemians in Postwar America, 1983, Volume 38: Afro-American Writers After 1955: Dramatists and Prose Writers, 1985.

Fox, Robert Elliot, *Conscientious Sorcerers: The Black Post-Modernist Fiction of LeRoi Jones/Baraka, Ishmael Reed and Samuel R. Delany,* Greenwood Press, 1987.

Harris, William J., *The Poetry and Poetics of Amiri Baraka: The Jazz Aesthetic,* University of Missouri Press, 1985.

Hudson, Theodore, *From LeRoi Jones to Amiri Baraka: The Literary Works,* Duke University Press, 1973.

Lacey, Henry C., *To Raise, Destroy, and Create: The Poetry, Drama, and Fiction of Imamu Amiri Baraka (LeRoi Jones),* Whitson, 1981.

Ossman, David, *The Sullen Art: Interviews with Modern American Poets,* Corinth, 1963.

Sollors, Werner, *Amiri Baraka/LeRoi Jones: The Quest for a "Populist Modernism,"* Columbia University Press, 1978.

Periodicals

Black American Literature Forum, Spring 1980; Spring 1981; Fall 1982; Spring 1983; Winter 1985.

Boundary, Volume 2, Number 6, 1978.

Chicago Defender, January 11, 1965.

Chicago Tribune, October 4, 1968.

Detroit Free Press, January 31, 1965.

Detroit News, January 15, 1984; August 12, 1984.

Down Beat, January 2, 1964; August 1987.

Ebony, August 1967; August 1969; February 1971.

Esquire, June 1966.

Essence, September 1970; May 1984; September 1984; May 1985.

Jet, January 16, 1975; July 23, 1984.

Modern Drama, February 1971; Summer 1972; September 1972; June 1974.

Ms., September 1983.

Nation, October 14, 1961; November 14, 1961; March 13, 1964; April 13, 1964; January 4, 1965; March 15, 1965; January 22, 1968; February 2, 1970.

Negro Digest, December 1963; February 1964; August 1964; March 1965; April 1965; March 1966; April 1966; June 1966; April 1967; April 1968; January 1969; April 1969.

Newsweek, March 13, 1964; April 13, 1964; November 22, 1965; May 2, 1966; March 6, 1967; December 4, 1967; December 1, 1969; February 19, 1973.

New Yorker, April 4, 1964; December 26, 1964; March 4, 1967; December 30, 1972.

New York Review of Books, January 20, 1966; May 22, 1964; July 2, 1970; October 17, 1974; June 11, 1984; June 14, 1984.

New York Times, April 28, 1966; May 8, 1966; August 10, 1966; September 14, 1966; October 5, 1966; January 20, 1967; February 28, 1967; July 15, 1967; January 5, 1968; January 6, 1968; January 9, 1968; January 10, 1968; February 7, 1968; April 14, 1968; August 16, 1968; November 27, 1968; December 24, 1968; August 26, 1969; November 23, 1969; February 6, 1970; May 11, 1972; June 11, 1972; November 11, 1972; November 14, 1972; November 23, 1972; December 5, 1972; December 27, 1974; December 29, 1974; November 19, 1979; October 15, 1981; January 23, 1984.

New York Times Book Review, January 31, 1965; November 28, 1965; May 8, 1966; February 4, 1968; March 17, 1968; February 14, 1971; June 6, 1971; June 27, 1971; December 5, 1971; March 12, 1972; December 16, 1979; March 11, 1984; July 5, 1987; December 20, 1987.

Saturday Review, April 20, 1963; January 11, 1964; January 9, 1965; December 11, 1965; December 9, 1967; October 2, 1971; July 12, 1975.

Studies in Black Literature, Spring, 1970; Volume 1, Number 2, 1970; Volume 3, Number 2, 1972; Volume 3, Number 3, 1972; Volume 4, Number 1, 1973.

Time, December 25, 1964; November 19, 1965; May 6, 1966; January 12, 1968; April 26, 1968; June 28, 1968; June 28, 1971.

Village Voice, December 17, 1964; May 6, 1965; May 19, 1965; August 30, 1976; August 1, 1977; December 17-23, 1980, October 2, 1984.

Washington Post, August 15, 1968; September 12, 1968; November 27, 1968; December 5, 1980; January 23, 1981; June 29, 1987.

Washington Post Book World, December 24, 1967; May 22, 1983.

—Joan Goldsworthy

Regina Belle

1963—

Singer

Singer Regina Belle has dazzled critics and fans alike since her debut album, *All By Myself,* was released in 1987. Acclaimed as one of the most exciting new singers to emerge on the rhythm and blues scene, the New Jersey songstress boasts a style that recalls some of the most successful black pop female singers in the industry, yet is nonetheless distinctive. Jim Miller in *Newsweek* heralded Belle's entry onto the music scene in 1987: "Move over, Anita Baker—and make way for Regina Belle, who may be the most electrifying new soul singer since Baker herself. . . . Imagine a singer who simultaneously recalls Aretha Franklin, Sade and Anita Baker, and you'll get a fair idea of Belle's singular style."

Belle's wide vocal range has particularly impressed reviewers. "She has a strong, expressive voice and she's versatile, dealing well with sultry ballads ('Baby Come to Me') or sassy jump-ups ('When Will You Be Mine')," wrote David Hiltbrand in *People* of *Stay With Me,* Belle's follow-up to *All By Myself.* Steve Bloom commented in *Rolling Stone* that Belle's "full-throated, pop-gospel vocal style brings to mind Anita Baker, Patti LaBelle, and Stephanie Mills." A number of critics have similarly

compared Belle's vocals to those of soul-jazz phenomenon Baker. Hiltbrand noted that, like Baker, Belle "displays a voice of tantalizing quality. . . . She can sound both promisingly intimate and world-weary without sacrificing vibrancy."

Belle has remarked, however, that comparisons to Baker are off-target. She told Bloom: "Because Anita Baker is prominent right now, Regina Belle sounds like Anita Baker. . . . I've been singing since I was three years old. By the time [Baker's 1986 album] *Rapture* came out, my style was already developed. People say I got certain inflections from Anita, but I got them from Phyllis Hyman. *That* was my girl." In addition to Hyman, Belle lists other musical influences as Billie Holiday, Donny Hathaway, and Nancy Wilson; she refers to the latter as her "show business mother." Belle met famous song stylist Wilson at a music convention in Los Angeles. "When I met her she told me that Billie Holiday did it for Dinah [Washington], Dinah did it for her and she has to do it for me," Belle was quoted as saying in *Jet.*

Belle's musical roots are in gospel, which she grew up singing in church with her family. She told an *Ebony*

At a Glance...

Born in 1963; native of Englewood, NJ; daughter of Eugene and Lois Belle; formerly married to Horace A. Young III; children: Tiy Chreigna (daughter). *Education:* Attended Rutgers State University.

Singer and recording artist, 1987—.

Awards: Nomination for best rhythm and blues female singer, American Music Awards, 1991.

Addresses: *Record company*—Columbia Records, 51 West 52nd St., New York, NY 10019.

---

contributor that she was raised in a house where music was "something . . . involuntary." Her mother's specialty was gospel, and she learned rhythm and blues from her father. "The music was the same, just the message was different," she told Bloom. Belle sang during high school and on weekends attended classes at New York City's Manhattan School of Music, where she studied opera and classical music. Belle did not study jazz until college, when she enrolled in the Jazz Ensemble at Rutgers University. Belle told Bloom that with jazz she learned "to listen for colors, as opposed to trying to sing just notes. For the longest time, I couldn't figure out what that meant."

Not sure that music would be her career, Belle majored in accounting and history at Rutgers. Her big break as a singer came when disc jockey Vaughn Harper heard her open a concert on the Rutgers campus. Impressed, Harper introduced Belle to the manager of the singing group The Manhattans, who were looking for a female backup singer. Shortly thereafter Belle was touring with the group; a recording contract from the group's label, Columbia, soon followed.

Belle's 1987 debut, *All By Myself,* was an instant success; *Stay With Me,* her 1989 effort, established Belle as a major singer on the rhythm and blues scene. Both albums generated a string of solo hits, including "Show

Me the Way," "Make It Like It Was," and "When Will You Be Mine." Belle has been primarily popular on the black charts, something she would like to see eventually change. "It's insulting to me when somebody says, 'You're Number One on the *black* charts.' It suggests that nobody appreciates my music but black people," she told Bloom. "I'd love to have a Number One pop single, but I'm not at the point where I *have* to. It doesn't plague me."

In addition to receiving acclaim as a recording artist, Belle is also considered an outstanding live performer who is not afraid to take chances musically. "Her gifted voice and stage presence make her a tough 'opening' act," noted *Ebony.* "She is said to hold her own on any given night, and on others make the 'headliner' acts sweat for their star-status." Peter Watrous of the *New York Times* reviewed a show-stealing opener by Belle in 1989, noting that "Ms. Belle, who has an extraordinary voice, dug deep into gospel and blues melodies, letting the grit of her voice show, often tearing apart the original impulse of a song." The following year Watrous reviewed Belle as a headliner at New York's Avery Fisher Hall, commenting that "though she's not working as a jazz singer, she is an exceptional improviser." Belle's shows, Watrous continued, are "expansive and improvisatory, old-fashioned qualities that make her one of the most exciting pop singers working."

Selected discography

All By Myself, Columbia, 1987.
Stay With Me, Columbia, 1989.

Sources

Ebony, June 1990.
Essence, May 1990.
Jet, May 14, 1990.
Newsweek, June 22, 1987.
New York Times, September 16, 1989; June 30, 1990.
People, June 22, 1987; October 2, 1989.
Rolling Stone, April 5, 1990.

—Michael E. Mueller

Manute Bol

1963—

Professional basketball player

Manute Bol is the tallest player in the history of the National Basketball Association. He is also the only player in the NBA to have killed a lion with a spear and to have paid 80 cows for his wife. Bol, a native of the Sudan and member of the Dinka tribe, left his troubled homeland to play basketball in the United States. At just under 7' 7", he towers over almost everyone, drawing stares wherever he goes. The stately Bol has learned to handle the attention, though—just as he learned to speak English and block his opponents' shots on the basketball court.

Washington Post correspondent Blaine Harden noted that Bol "has traveled farther and faster than almost any African. The particulars of his cultural dislocation are as exaggerated as his height. The life he knew in Dinka land was among the most arduous, violent and isolated in Africa. The life he knows now is among the highest paid, most transient, least secure in America. Lions, spears and malaria end the careers of Dinka cowherds. Cocaine, coaching changes and stress fractures bring down NBA players. As they grow older, Dinka men become respected elders who give advice on cows and marriage. NBA players can expect an average career of less than four years before they are cut."

Perhaps this is why Bol has never severed the ties with his homeland, even though a civil war there makes it impossible for him to visit. He is supporting a number of family members who are stranded in Khartoum, the Sudanese capital, and is married to a Dinka woman. Bol is proud of his heritage and deeply concerned about his native country, but he is also proud of the success he has achieved in the United States. Bol told the *San Jose Mercury News:* "God gave me [this] height. He gave me a chance to play in the NBA. I have a good life. I'm going to raise my kids to have the good life. I'm really happy with it."

In the Dinka language the name Manute means "special blessing." Bol was given that name because his mother had miscarried twins before he was born. Although no birth certificate exists to document the fact, Bol says he was born on October 16, 1963, near the Dinka village of Turalei. He is a descendent of Dinka nobility—his great-great grandfather, Bol Nyuol, was a chief of the Tuic Dinka of the northwest Sudd, and his grandfather was also a wealthy chief who had some 40 wives and 80 children. Although Bol's father did not inherit the family

At a Glance. . .

Born October 16, 1963, in Turalei, Sudan; son of Madut (a cowherd) and Okwok Bol; married, wife's name, Atong; children: Abuk (girl), Madut (boy). *Education:* Attended University of Bridgeport, 1984.

Professional basketball player, 1985—. Drafted in second round by Washington Bullets; traded to Golden State Warriors, 1988; traded to Philadelphia 76ers, 1990.

wealth, he was nonetheless quite comfortable, with a herd of 150 cows and a position as tribal elder.

Young Manute enjoyed a number of privileges as the descendent of a chief, but he also rebelled against some of the Dinka customs, especially the manhood rites that all teenage boys must undergo. Several times he ran away rather than face the ritual scarring of his face and—worse—the removal of six of his teeth. His education was entirely practical, concerning only the care and sale of cows; Bol never learned to read or write his native tongue. But he did learn every aspect of animal husbandry necessary to insure the health of his cows, including how to kill a sleeping lion with a spear before it could harm his herd.

Bol was also forced to attend "milk camp" as a teenager. The purpose of the camp was to see which young man could gain the most weight over four months. "From May to August, or September, you're not doing nothing, you're just sitting there drinking milk," Bol told the *Philadelphia Inquirer.* "You just sit there and sleep and drink milk. You take 10 cows. One gallon of milk is not enough. I can drink three gallons of milk a day. Some people in the camps weigh almost 400 pounds." What weight Bol gained at milk camp was just as quickly lost again; he grew taller and taller, but remained slender as a reed.

A Cousin Suggested Basketball

The Dinkas are among Africa's tallest people, but even so, Manute Bol was a phenomenon. In 1978, during a lull in the almost constant civil war that has engulfed the Sudan, a national politician visited Bol's village. Bol posed for a picture with the official, and that photograph came to the attention of Nyuol Makwag Bol, a cousin in Khartoum. The cousin suggested that Bol take up basketball. The nearest town with a team was Wau, a city of

some 80,000 residents. Manute journeyed to Wau and began to play for the police team. Not surprisingly his father objected, saying that basketball was "not good work for a Dinka," but Bol persisted. "I started playing basketball more and more," he told the *Washington Post.* "I went on the court to shoot, dribble, and then lay-ups, whatever. And then my cousin . . . told me, 'Why don't you try dunk?' And then I tried. I took one dribble and then I went up to dunk the ball. When I came down I hurt my teeth in the net."

Even his fear of dental distress did not deter Bol however. In 1979 he joined his cousin in Khartoum and won a position on the city's Catholic Club team. Khartoum, however, was not an ideal place for Bol; its largely Arab population—much like that of the northern Sudan—harbors an intense hatred of blacks. "I did fight a lot in Khartoum," Bol said. "I was bad. I don't take anything. Sometimes I can say we Dinkas are crazy. That is what I can say. We don't give up. In the United States they call black people nigger, you know, that thing. In my country, the Moslem people call us the abid (Arabic for slave). Really, I don't like. If they say it to somebody, not even me, I fight them." Bol's cousin had to counsel him to save his aggression for the basketball court, where he was still clumsy and slow-footed.

Bol played basketball in Khartoum for three years, both for the Catholic Club and for the military team. While living in the capital he fell in love with a Dinka girl. His father disapproved of the match, however, and the girl's father demanded a large payment for her. Eventually the marriage negotiations broke down and the girl married another man. "I was hurt really. It bust me up," Bol told the *Washington Post.* That breakup—and hostile conditions in Khartoum—made Bol willing to leave the Sudan behind. Since his departure he has returned only once, for a brief visit.

Don Feeley, a coach from Fairleigh Dickinson University, met Bol in Khartoum and convinced him to come to the United States. Bol was drafted sight unseen by the San Diego Clippers, but when Clipper scouts saw the gangly, 180-pound Bol they decided he needed some time with a college team. This proved to be a problem, of course—Bol could not even speak English, let alone read it. Kevin Mackey of Cleveland State University invited Bol to Cleveland, where the young African took English classes at Case Western Reserve. Although Bol never played for Cleveland State—never even practiced with the team—his presence in the city was viewed as a violation of NCAA rules. Even after he had left Cleveland for the University of Bridgeport in Connecticut, CSU and its coach were placed on probation.

The Washington Bullets Took a Chance

Bol was enrolled as a student at Bridgeport and for the first time played with an American team. There he averaged 22.5 points, 13.5 rebounds and 7.5 blocked shots per game. After one season with Bridgeport he was signed by the United States Basketball League's Rhode Island Gulls. Bol quickly became a presence there as well, with an average of 12.3 blocks in eight games. NBA scouts attended Bol's games in droves, but opinion was mixed on the tall, skinny player; some found him clumsy and hesitant on the court, while others were awed by his height and blocking ability. In 1985 the Washington Bullets decided to take a chance on Bol and he was drafted in the second round.

The Bullets were reluctant to use Bol at first, but when center Jeff Ruland was sidelined by injuries in 1986, Bol got the job. He quickly became a factor on defense, just missing the record for most blocked shots in the history of the NBA—he had 397 for the season—and was runner-up for defensive player of the year. Almost overnight Bol found himself a star in his new country. He was recruited for product endorsement of fried chicken and athletic gear and was credited with increasing attendance at Bullets away games in every American city. In the *Boston Globe* Charles Kenney observed that Bol was "portrayed by the media as a man who grabbed hold of a jungle vine, let out a Tarzan whoop, and swung out of primitive times, forsaking loincloth, spear, and grass hut in favor of the jet age, America, and basketball."

Those who know Bol best—other players and NBA coaches—offer a more realistic picture. Bol is from a culture that in fact champions many so-called "American" values: courage, pride in one's heritage, and the accumulation of wealth. With his custom-built car and suburban townhouse, Bol has assimilated quickly and is still somewhat reluctant to speak about the political troubles in his homeland. On the basketball court he has never quite equalled the statistics of his starting season. Although he has gained in strength and poise over the years, he is still working at a disadvantage; Bol began playing basketball late and has never developed instinctive reactions to the game's flow. He is also hampered by three clawed fingers on his right hand, a birth defect. Nevertheless, the athlete's fantastic height and grim determination have made him a potent force in the NBA—first for the Bullets, then the Golden State Warriors, and most recently the Philadelphia 76ers.

Ties to the Sudan Remain Strong

Conditions in the Sudan have become desperate since Bol left in 1983. Rebels from the country's south—

including many Dinkas—have taken arms against the repressive tactics of the Arab-run government. Many of Bol's family members have lost crops and cattle in government raids; he supports some forty relatives who live in cramped quarters in Khartoum. Bol himself cannot travel to the Sudan because he fears the government there might harm him. "There are rumors I was helping the rebels," Bol told the *Philadelphia Inquirer.* "They think I am sending food to the rebels. If I have anything to send, I send it to the hungry people, to help those people live."

Bol has indeed become more outspoken on the plight of his Sudanese countrymen. A sizeable portion of his $1.3 million annual salary goes to family in Khartoum, Red Cross relief efforts, and to the Sudan Relief and Rehabilitation Association in Silver Spring, Maryland. Still, he says, all he can send is not nearly enough. "I love to help," he said, "but . . . food is very expensive. Sometimes, even if you have money for food you cannot buy

> Manute Bol is the tallest player in the history of the National Basketball Association. He is also the only player in the NBA to have killed a lion with a spear and to have paid 80 cows for his wife.

it. . . . My people just sit there. There are no jobs." Bol hopes that by speaking about the Sudan he can educate the American people—and the American government—about the needs of his homeland's black citizens.

Before the situation in the Sudan became so dire, Bol married a Dinka woman for whom he paid eighty cows. Manute and Atong Bol have two children whom they plan to raise in America. Bol has often been the butt of jokes—comedian Woody Allen once quipped that Bol's team "doesn't bother taking him on the road. It just FAXes him from town to town"—but he has met the laughter with a quiet dignity and intelligence that inevitably win people over. He is very glad to be living in America, far from the war that has claimed the lives of so many of his kin. Asked what he might be doing now had he never left Africa, Bol speculated: "I might be in trouble. I might be dead. Nobody knows. I just thank God I'm not there anymore."

Sources

Akron Beacon Journal, December 11, 1987.

Boston Globe, September 16, 1984; June 16, 1985; August 18, 1985; November 16, 1988.

Chicago Tribune, July 1, 1985.

Orlando Sentinel, October 16, 1985.

Philadelphia Daily News, January 11, 1985.

Philadelphia Inquirer, October 27, 1985; November 6, 1990.

San Jose Mercury News, December 18, 1988.

Washington Post, March 22, 1987.

—Mark Kram

Omar Bongo

1935—

President of Gabon

Gabon's relative prosperity among African nations and its stable political regime have kept it from appearing often in the media. Ruled by President (El Hadj) Omar Bongo since 1967, Gabon is a former French colony in West Africa that enjoys a per capita income of approximately $3,000—high by African standards—due largely to its oil-driven economy. However, depressed oil prices in the world market have resulted in a continued shortfall in oil earnings, which forced the government to adopt austerity budgets in the late 1980s. Like many other African nations with single-party political systems, Gabon has also felt the effects of the democratic reforms that swept through Eastern Europe in 1989-90. Economic and political unrest made 1990 the most turbulent year in President Bongo's 23-year rule.

Gabon saw rapid economic growth in the 1970s through a liberal economic system that encouraged and protected foreign capital investment. When President Bongo visited the United States in 1987, President Reagan noted that the U.S. had $700 million invested in Gabon. Reagan called Bongo "a champion of African development," and agreed to reschedule Gabon's $8-million debt to the U.S. Bongo's visit came during a year of economic crisis for Gabon that was brought on by declining world oil prices. While Gabon maintains friendly relations with the U.S., France remains the country's primary trading partner and source of foreign aid.

Since the early 1970s Bongo has imposed a policy of "Gabonization," in which the government demands state participation in foreign-based companies operating in Gabon, enforces the employment of indigenous Gabonese in managerial positions, and negotiates advantageous terms for the exploitation of Gabon's natural resources. Although Gabon is sub-Saharan Africa's most prosperous nation, there has always been concern and disquiet over the dominant role of foreign companies and the excessive and conspicuous wealth of some Gabonese and Europeans living in the country.

To counter worsening economic circumstances in the 1980s, Bongo frequently resorted to imposing strict controls on immigration. In 1985 he criticized the activities of foreign residents in Gabon, notably the 600-member Lebanese community. When his remarks touched

At a Glance. . .

Born Albert-Bernard Bongo, December 30, 1935, in Lewai, Franceville, Gabon; given name changed to El Hadj Omar in 1973. Divorced first wife, 1988; married Edith Lucie Sassou-Nguesso, 1990; children: Ali (son). *Religion:* Muslim.

President of Gabon. Served in Ministry of Foreign Affairs c. 1960; served as vice-president; became president, 1967; served as minister of the interior, 1967-1970, prime minister, 1967-75, minister of planning, 1967-77, minister of information, 1967-80, and minister of defense, 1967-81. *Military service:* Gabonese Air Force, 1958-60.

off looting and vandalism in Libreville, the nation's capital, Bongo appealed for calm and condemned the looters. During this crisis foreigners without proper papers were arrested. That same year Bongo ordered a census of aliens during which Gabon's borders were closed and illegal immigrants expelled. Employers were told to give priority to employing Gabonese.

In 1986 worsening economic circumstances led to even stricter controls on immigration. Resident permits were introduced and financial restrictions were imposed on immigrants wishing to leave and reenter the country. In June of 1988, 3,500 foreign nationals described as illegal immigrants were arrested. This was followed by the announcement of new nationality regulations. The measures to restrict immigration were designed to insure the employment and prosperity of native Gabonese; they were economically rather than politically motivated.

Became President at the Age of 31

Bongo began his political career in the Ministry of Foreign Affairs in 1960 after serving two years in Gabon's Air Force. He held several administrative posts and was vice-president under Leon M'ba, the first president of the Gabonese Republic. With M'ba's death in 1967, Bongo became president; he was 31. In January of 1968 a government reshuffle resulted in several close associates of President Bongo becoming ministers. In March he announced the formal institution of a one-party government and created the Parti democratique gabonais (PDG). The party's motto was "Dialogue-Tolerance-Peace," and it stood for national unity, the abolition of ethnic and tribal discrimination, and the principles of the RDA

(Rassemblement democratique africain). The RDA, based in the neighboring Ivory Coast, stood for independence rather than federation with other former French colonies in West and Central Africa.

In the 1973 elections for the national assembly and the presidency, Bongo was the sole candidate for president. He and all PDG candidates were elected by 99.56% of the votes cast. In addition to the presidency, Bongo held several ministerial portfolios from 1967 onward, including Minister of Defense (1967-1981), Information (1967-1980), Planning (1967-1977), Prime Minister (1967-1975), the Interior (1967-1970), and many others.

In April 1975 Bongo abolished the post of vice-president and appointed his former number-two man, Leon Mebiame, as prime minister, a position Bongo held concurrently with his presidency from 1967. Mebiame would remain as prime minister until his resignation in 1990. Following an extraordinary congress of the PDG in January 1979 and the December 1979 elections, Bongo gave up some of his ministerial portfolios and surrendered his functions as head of government to Prime Minister Mebiame. The PDG congress had criticized Bongo's administration for inefficiency and called for an end to the holding of multiple offices. A measure of democracy was introduced into PDG party politics at the congress; elections were held for the central committee, and several senior party members lost their seats.

During the 1979 election campaign Bongo toured the country, appealing for national unity and an end to tribal differences. Gabon is home to at least 40 distinct tribal groups, the Fang group accounting for roughly 40% of the population. Bongo is a member of the Bateke tribe, which along with the Eshira and Bapounou are other dominant tribal groups in Gabon. Throughout his tenure as president, Bongo has sought to maintain a delicate ethnic balance in his administration. Bongo was again reelected for a seven-year term in 1979, receiving 99.96% of the popular vote.

Economic Woes Sparked Opposition

Opposition to President Bongo's regime first appeared in the late 1970s, as economic difficulties became more acute for the Gabonese. The first organized, but illegal, opposition party was MORENA, the Movement for National Restoration (Mouvement de redressement national). This moderate opposition group sponsored demonstrations by students and academic staff at the Universite Omar Bongo in Libreville in December of 1981, when the university was temporarily closed. MORENA accused Bongo of corruption and personal extravagance and of favoring his own Bateke tribe; the group demanded that a multi-party system be restored.

Further arrests were made in February of 1982, when the opposition distributed leaflets criticizing the Bongo regime during a visit by Pope John Paul II. In November of 1982, 37 MORENA members were tried and convicted of offenses against state security. Severe sentences were handed out, including 20 years of hard labor for 13 of the defendants; all were pardoned, however, and released by mid-1986. Despite the pressure, Bongo remained committed to one-party rule. Pledged to non-violence, MORENA continued to play a role in Gabonese politics, often from exile.

The 1985 legislative elections followed past procedures; all nominations were approved by PDG, which then presented a single list of candidates. The candidates were ratified by popular vote on March 3, 1985. During that year Bongo repeated an earlier invitation to opposition members in exile to return to Gabon. His mid-year tour of the country was conducted with extremely tight security following an attempted assassination in May of 1985.

In November of 1986 Bongo was reelected by 99.97% of the popular vote. The third congress of the PDG, held in September of 1986, displayed an orientation toward liberalization. The central committee was increased to 297 members, with many new entrants from the young, the armed forces, and even one former MORENA member. Five women were appointed to the central committee's political bureau. Following his reelection Bongo restated his opposition to a multi-party system, contending that the introduction of choice into local government elections had led to unacceptable conflict within Gabonese communities. Economic circumstances forced the government to impose compulsory reductions in salaries in late 1988, which resulted in strikes by the staff of Air Gabon and other public-sector employees. The situation was resolved following negotiations. Labor unrest continued, however, as the government was forced to introduce austerity budgets for 1989 and 1990.

Plot to Overthrow Government Discovered

In September of 1989 a conspiracy to overthrow the government was discovered. The plot involved senior members of the security forces and prominent public officials acting on behalf of Pierre Mamboundou, leader of a little-known opposition group based in Paris, the Union des peuples gabonais (UPG). Although Amnesty International and other international humanitarian organizations were invited to "witness further developments," two of the principals in the plot died, reportedly from disease. In February of 1990 Mamboundou was

expelled from France and relocated to Senegal under the auspices of the French Minister of the Interior.

In January of 1990 legal proceedings continued against 21 Gabonese for their alleged roles in plots against Bongo; these stemmed from the Mamboundou affair and an internal conspiracy led by Lt.-Col. Georges Moubandjo, a former aide-de-camp to Bongo. At an extraordinary session of the central committee of the PDG, Bongo called for urgent action to stamp out corruption. He stressed the need for greater democratization of the country's institutions in the face of political unrest. However, he continued to reaffirm the PDG's leading role and dismissed the possibility of a multi-party system.

Immediately following the close of the session, students boycotted classes at Universite Omar Bongo, protesting inadequate facilities and a shortage of academic staff. The unrest escalated and Lebanese shops were looted, resulting in 250 arrests. In February doctors and teachers

> Although Amnesty International and other international humanitarian organizations were invited to "witness further developments," two of the principals in the plot against Bongo's government died, reportedly from disease.

went on strike demanding better pay and conditions; they were joined by telecommunications workers and airport staff. President Bongo blamed the wave of strikes on reduced purchasing power, the result of austerity measures imposed at the insistence of the International Monetary Fund.

As labor unrest continued a "special commission for democracy" established in January by the PDG condemned Gabon's single-party system. Bongo announced that immediate reforms would be introduced and that a national conference would be held later in March to discuss democracy and political reform. Before the national conference began, though, over 1,000 demonstrators, many of them unemployed, looted supermarkets and shops owned by Lebanese traders in Port Gentil, where oil workers had gone on strike on March 21st. Strikes by civil servants and bank employees continued in Libreville.

When the national conference began on March 27th, the government imposed a curfew and banned strikes. In his opening address President Bongo said that anarchy would impede economic development and drive away foreign investors. The conference was attended by some 2,000 delegates representing over 70 political organizations, professional bodies, and other special interest groups. Rejecting Bongo's earlier proposal for a five-year transitional period, the conference voted for the immediate creation of a multi-party system and the formation of a new government to hold office until legislative elections were held in October of 1990.

Concessions Made to Opposition

Bongo agreed to abide by the decisions of the conference and appointed a new prime minister, Casimir Oye Mba, a prominent banker. Making several concessions, Bongo granted legal status to all opposition groups participating in the conference; some 13 groups immediately formed a United Opposition Front. On May 3rd Oye Mba was formally installed as prime minister, replacing Mebiame and heading a 29-member transitional administration. Several members of opposition movements received ministerial posts. Father Paul Mba Abessole, former leader of MORENA, was nominated for a post but declined to accept. President Bongo resigned as secretary-general of PDG, claiming that such a partisan role was incompatible with his position as head of state. On May 22nd the PDG central committee and the national assembly approved constitutional amendments to facilitate the transition to a multi-party system. The existing presidential mandate, effective through 1994, was to be respected. Subsequent elections to the presidency would be contested by more than one candidate, and the presidential term of office was changed to five years with a limit of one re-election to the office.

The very next day, May 23rd, a vocal critic of Bongo was found dead in a hotel, reportedly murdered by poison. The death of Joseph Rendjambe, a prominent business executive and secretary-general of the opposition group Parti gabonais du progres (PGP), touched off the worst rioting in Bongo's 23-year rule. Presidential buildings in Libreville were set on fire and the French consul-general and ten oil company employees were taken hostage. A state of emergency was declared in Port Gentil, Rendjambe's hometown and a strategic oil production site. During this emergency Gabon's two main oil producers, Elf and Shell, cut output from 270,000 barrels per day to 20,000. Bongo threatened to withdraw their exploration licenses unless they restored normal output, which they soon did. France sent in 500 troops to reinforce the 500-man battalion of Marines permanently stationed in Gabon to protect the interests of 20,000 resident French nationals.

The first multi-party elections under President Bongo's rule were held on September 16th. Only the 13 legalized opposition parties that had participated in the national conference earlier in the year were allowed to put up candidates. The most serious challenge to the PDG was mounted by MORENA-Bucherons, a splinter group led by Mba Abessolo. Mba Abessolo had been dismissed as leader of MORENA in January of 1990, when he decided to return to Gabon from exile and participate in national politics.

Elections Initially Marred by Corruption

In the first round of elections on September 16th voters attacked election officials and smashed ballot boxes, claiming the election was rigged in favor of Bongo. The largest polling station, in the city hall in Libreville, was forced to close when angry voters ransacked the building, reportedly having discovered ballot boxes already stuffed as voting began at 6 a.m. There were also disturbances at Port Gentil. The government annulled results of 32 out of 120 constituencies. A second round of voting scheduled for September 23rd was suspended after the government acknowledged irregularities at a number of voting centers. Opposition groups claimed the government had halted voting in areas where the PDG appeared close to defeat. Fresh elections were set for October.

Legislative elections were completed in November, with the PDG winning 63 seats out of 120. The largest opposition party, MORENA-Bucherons, won 20 seats. A total of eight parties were to be represented in the new parliament. On November 19th Prime Minister Oye Mba tendered the resignation of his transitional government, but was re-appointed two days later by President Bongo. On November 26th a government of national union was announced, with the PDG holding one-third of the ministerial portfolios and the five largest opposition parties represented. After considerable unrest, difficulty, and debate, democratic pluralism had come to Gabon.

Sources

Books

Africa South of the Sahara 1991, Europa, 1990.
International Who's Who 1990-91, Europa, 1990.
Keesing's Record of World Events, Longman, 1990.

Periodicals

Business America, April 11, 1988; April 25, 1988; November 20, 1989.
Department of State Bulletin, October 1987.

Economist, June 2, 1990.
Jet, October 8, 1990.
Time, May 21, 1990.

—*David Bianco*

Gwendolyn Brooks

1917—

Poet, novelist

A leading contemporary American poet and the first black writer to be honored with a Pulitzer Prize, Gwendolyn Brooks is acclaimed for her technically accomplished and powerful portraits of black urban life. Throughout a career that has spanned six decades and includes both poetry and fiction, the prolific Brooks is noted for her carefully wrought and insightful portraits of everyday black life, in which she illuminates racism, poverty, intraracial prejudice, and personal alienation. Brooks is also known as one of the most wide-ranging of contemporary black poets; while her earlier work is marked by social realism contained in masterful poetic form, technique, and language, her later efforts display a more open, free-verse style and are increasingly direct in exploring themes like social protest, revolution, and black nationalism. Brooks has been praised throughout her career for the complexity and technical skill of her work, which she combines with a compassion for the ordinary that speaks universally to many readers. She commented to Claudia Tate in *Black Women Writers at Work* that she would prefer not to be known as an "intellectual," explaining: "I do write from the heart, from personal experience and from the experiences of other people whom I have observed.

Very early in life I became fascinated with the wonders language can achieve. And I began playing with words. That word-play is what I have been known for chiefly."

Much of Brooks's work is set in her native Chicago, where she has lived since she was an infant. Her path to becoming a writer started with her parents, who early on encouraged her in reading and writing. Her father, David, regularly told her stories and read aloud from his set of Harvard Classics, while her mother, Keziah, a schoolteacher, composed songs for her children and commissioned Brooks to write plays for the children of a church group she led. When Brooks's parents discovered she had promising writing abilities, they relieved her of many household duties and her father set up a working desk for her. As a young girl Brooks read widely and especially admired L. M. Montgomery's "Anne of Green Gables" books, in addition to the poems of black writer Paul Laurence Dunbar. Fascinated with words, she would spend many hours composing rhymes and poems and record them in a notebook. Confident of her talent, her mother, as Brooks related in her 1972 autobiography, *Report From Part One,* assured her that one

At a Glance. . .

Full name, Gwendolyn Elizabeth Brooks; born June 7, 1917, in Topeka, KS; daughter of David Anderson (a janitor) and Keziah Corrine (a schoolteacher; maiden name, Wims) Brooks; married Henry Lowington Blakely, Jr., September 17, 1939; children: Henry Lowington III, Nora. *Education:* Graduated from Wilson Junior College, 1936.

Poet and novelist. Publicity director, NAACP Youth Council, Chicago, IL, 1937-38; poetry instructor at numerous colleges and universities c. 1963-69, including Elmhurst College, Northeastern Illinois State College, Columbia University, and the University of Wisconsin—Madison; poet laureate of Illinois, beginning 1968; distinguished professor of the arts, City College of the City University of New York, 1971; poetry consultant to Library of Congress, 1985-86.

Awards: Midwestern Writers Conference poetry award, 1943; Patron Saints Award, Society of Midland Authors, 1945; named one of ten "Women of the Year," *Mademoiselle,* 1945; National Institute of Arts and Letters grant, 1946; American Academy of Arts and Letters creative writing award, 1946; Guggenheim fellowship, 1946 and 1947; Eunice Tietjens Memorial Prize, *Poetry,* 1949, and Pulitzer Prize in Poetry, 1950, both for *Annie Allen;* Robert F. Ferguson Memorial Award, Friends of Literature, 1964, for *Selected Poems;* Thormod Monsen Literature Award, 1964; Anisfield-Wolf Award, 1968, for *In the Mecca;* Black Academy of Arts and Letters Award, 1971; Shelley Memorial Award, 1976; *Essence* Award, 1988; inductee, National Women's Hall of Fame, 1988; Frost Medal, Poetry Society of America, 1989; lifetime achievement award, National Endowment for the Humanities, 1989.

Addresses: *Home*—7428 South Evans Ave., Chicago, IL 60619.

day she would become the "*lady* Paul Laurence Dunbar."

Brooks published her first poem when she was 13 in a popular children's magazine called *American Childhood.* When she was 16 she had the opportunity to meet James Weldon Johnson and Langston Hughes, two of the most famous poets of the 1920s literary movement known as the Harlem Renaissance. Brooks's mother had prompted her to send samples of her work to Johnson and Hughes; they both assured her that she indeed possessed talent and urged her to continue writing and studying poetry. Johnson encouraged Brooks to study the Modernist poets T. S. Eliot, Ezra Pound, and e. e. cummings, to, in his words, "cultivate the highest possible standards of self-criticism." Johnson served, as Gary Smith noted in *MELUS,* as Brooks's "literary mentor," yet Hughes, with whom Brooks would later become great friends, was an even more profound influence. As Brooks described in *Report From Part One,* "The words and deeds of Langston Hughes were rooted in kindness, and in pride. His point of departure was always a clear pride in his race. . . . Mightily did he use the street. He found its multiple heart, its tastes, smells, alarms, formulas, flowers, garbage and convulsions. He brought them all to his table-top. He crushed them to a writing-paste. He himself became the pen." Smith commented that "Hughes underscored the value of cultivating the ground upon which [Brooks] stood," and convinced her "that a black poet need not travel outside the realm of his own experiences to create a poetic vision and write successful poetry."

While in high school Brooks focused heavily on her writing and study of poetry, and was a regular contributor of poems to the *Defender,* a black daily newspaper in Chicago. Brooks graduated from Wilson Junior College in 1936 with a degree in English and went on to work for Chicago's NAACP Youth Council, where she met her future husband, himself an aspiring writer. In 1941 her writing received a boost when she enrolled in a workshop led by Inez Cunningham Stark, a wealthy writer and scholar who traveled to Chicago's predominantly black south side to instruct aspiring poets. Brooks drew much from the comments and criticism of her peers in the workshop and was introduced by Stark to a wealth of contemporary poetry. The poet wrote in *Report From Part One* that while Stark guided the group in the principles of poetry, their own voices were allowed to develop: "If, in spite of everything that she could tell us, we stubbornly clung to our own ways and words, and we often so clung, she bowed gracefully and let us alone, trusting to time to further instruct us, or trusting to the possibility that she herself might be wrong." Throughout the early 1940s Brooks developed a substantial local reputation for her poetry, and, in 1943, received a poetry award from the Midwestern Writers Conference. Soon thereafter her work would gain national attention.

Around 1943 Brooks submitted a manuscript of "Negro poems" to Harper & Row, who published them in 1945 as *A Street in Bronzeville.* The poems received wide critical acclaim and Brooks was hailed as a major new voice in contemporary poetry. Drawn from scenes and characters in Brooks's Chicago neighborhood, *A Street in Bronzeville* offers insight into the aspirations and struggles of ordinary black people. The first section of the book depicts life in the Bronzeville neighborhood, while the second section—a sequence of twelve sonnets entitled "Gay Chaps at the Bar"—explores prejudice against blacks serving in the Armed Forces during World War II. Demonstrating a mastery of the sonnet, quatrain, and ballad, Brooks was praised for her high level of craft, innovative and distinctive use of idiom and imagery, and fresh glimpse into the lives of blacks. George E. Kent noted in *Black World* that Brooks's first book revealed obsessions which would characterize all of her poetry. "Brooks revealed in her first book considerable technical resources, a manipulation of folk forms, a growing sense of how traditional forms must be dealt with if the power of the Black voice is to come through with integrity. *A Street in Bronzeville* . . . committed its author to a restless experimentation with an elaborate range of artistic approaches." William H. Hansell similarly noted in *CLA Journal* that *A Street in Bronzeville* demonstrated "Brooks' commitment to a concept of art which she has never surrendered: the artist must work with the materials most familiar to him, with his own milieu."

First Black to Win a Pulitzer Prize

Following the success of *A Street in Bronzeville,* Brooks received a Guggenheim fellowship and was named by *Mademoiselle* magazine as one of their "Ten Women of the Year." Brooks received even greater honors with her next book of poetry, *Annie Allen,* which won the 1950 Pulitzer Prize, marking the first time the award had been bestowed upon a black writer. A complex sequence of poems that trace the coming-of-age of a black woman, *Annie Allen* is, according to Claudia Tate in *A Life Distilled: Gwendolyn Brooks, Her Poetry and Fiction,* a "collection of rigorously technical poems, replete with lofty diction, intricate word play, and complicated concatenations of phrases." George Kent in *Black Women Writers (1950-1980): A Critical Evaluation* described the highly crafted poems as "an attempt to give artistic structure to tensions arising from the artist's experience in moving from the Edenic environment of her parents' home into the fallen world of Chicago tenement life in the roles of young wife, mother, and artist." Regarding the centerpiece poem of the collection, "The Anniad," Brooks said in an interview reprinted in *Report From Part One* that she was "very interested in the mysteries and magic of technique" and that she "wanted every phrase to be beautiful, and yet to contribute sanely to the whole . . . effect."

Established as a poet, Brooks next ventured to write her first and only novel, *Maud Martha,* which was published in 1953. Like *Annie Allen* the novel focuses on the life of a young black woman and, as with all of Brooks's poetry, scrutinizes the ordinary and everyday to illuminate larger issues and themes. Patricia H. and Vernon E. Lattin in *Critique: Studies in Modern Fiction* noted that "Maud's stage is the home in which she grew up, the schools she attended, the kitchenette where she lives after marriage, and most often her own mind and heart as she struggles to be creative and to be an individual in a gray, oppressive world." On a different scale than sweepingly dramatic black novels like Richard Wright's *Native Son, Maud Martha* has been largely overlooked, according to the Lattins: "With a very loose organization consisting of a series of short vignettes, and with lyrical language never far from poetry, this short novel has a deceptively light and simple exterior which belies the complexity of the interior." David Littlejohn in *Black on White: A Critical*

> [These black authors] seemed proud and so committed to their own people. . . . The poets among them felt that black poets should write as blacks, about blacks, and address themselves *to* blacks.

Survey of Writing by American Negroes, similarly called *Maud Martha* accomplished, "a striking human experiment, as exquisitely written and as effective as any of Gwendolyn Brooks's poetry."

In her 1960 book of poems, *The Bean Eaters,* Brooks continued "to portray the immediate environment and ordinary people and events," noted Hansell. The book also, however, showed Brooks becoming more direct in her concern about black social issues. In *The Bean Eaters* Brooks writes about the integration of the Little Rock, Arkansas, school system, the lynching of blacks in the South, and the misguided efforts of cultured whites to help blacks. Due to its timing—*The Bean Eaters* appeared just as the Civil Rights Movement was gaining momentum—and political overtones, the book received mixed reviews. Maria K. Mootry reported in *A Life Distilled* that "some reviewers found *The Bean Eaters* sufficient in content and form, while others found it too tame in its protest mission; still others were upset and put off by what they deemed an unseemly social emphasis."

Brooks's thematic transition in *The Bean Eaters* was also reflected in a further evolution in her poetic style, which Kent described as a "bolder movement into a free verse appropriate to the situation."

Black Consciousness Influenced Poetry

In 1967 Brooks attended a writers' conference at Fisk University and became acquainted with a group of young writers, including John Killens, Ron Milner, and LeRoi Jones, who were advocating a new perspective for black authors. She commented to Tate on this new breed of black writers: "They seemed proud and so committed to their own people. . . . The poets among them felt that black poets should write as blacks, about blacks, and address themselves *to* blacks." Their message took hold of Brooks and profoundly influenced the direction of her poetry. Beginning with her 1968 book of poetry, *In the Mecca*, Brooks displayed what Toni Cade Bambara called in the *New York Times Book Review* "a new movement and energy, intensity, richness, power of statement and a new stripped lean, compressed style." The title poem of *In the Mecca*, set in an inner-city apartment building, traces a mother's search for her missing daughter among the tenants, only to discover in the end that the little girl has been murdered. The *Virginia Quarterly Review* called the poem "both an impressionistic and naturalistic journey through a huge ghetto apartment house, through the black precincts of despair." R. Baxter Miller in *Black American Poets Between Worlds, 1940-1960* deemed *In the Mecca* "a most complex and intriguing book; it seeks to balance the sordid realities of urban life with an imaginative process of reconciliation and redemption." Other poems in the book treated contemporary black heroes Medgar Evans and Malcolm X; another was dedicated to the Rangers, a Chicago street gang. Frederick C. Stern in *MidAmerica* called the latter "quite powerful, an appreciation for those outside the system, which comes quite close to being revolutionary."

In a move to support black publishers, Brooks left her longtime publisher Harper & Row after *In the Mecca* and chose to have her next several books published by Broadside Press, run by Detroit poet Dudley Randall. *Riot* (1969), *Family Pictures* (1970), and *Beckonings* (1975) further displayed Brooks's evolution in theme and style. Most noticeably, Brooks began to discuss revolution, black power, and black nationalism and her style became almost totally free verse. Norris B. Clark in *A Life Distilled* noted a difference from her earlier work in that Brooks's "emphasis shifted from a private, internal, and exclusive assessment of the identity crises of twentieth-century persons to a communal, external, and inclusive assessment of the black communal experi-

ence." Brooks described her change in focus to Tate: "What I'm fighting for now in my work, [is] for an *expression* relevant to all manner of blacks, poems I could take into a tavern, into the street, into the halls of a housing project. I don't want to say these poems have to be simple, but I want to *clarify* my language. I want these poems to be free. I want them to be direct without sacrificing the kinds of music, the picturemaking I've always been interested in." Critics noted that Brooks was no less masterful in her craft in these later poems, and, as in her earlier work, still focused on the situations of individuals with compassion and understanding.

Kent in *Black World* summarized Brooks's overall stature as a poet: "Brooks shares with Langston Hughes the achievement of being most responsive to turbulent changes in the Black Community's vision of itself and to the changing forms of its vibrations during decades of rapid change. The depth of her responsiveness and her range of poetic resources make her one of the most distinguished poets to appear in America during the 20th Century." Throughout her writing career Brooks has been noted for maintaining a level of objectivity which, however specific and direct her subject matter, gives her poetry a universal appeal. According to Blyden Jackson in *Black Poetry in America: Two Essays in Historical Interpretation,* Brooks offers "the close inspection of a limited domain, . . . a view of life in which one may see a microscopic portion of the universe intensely and yet, through that microscopic portion see all truth for the human condition wherever it is."

In addition to her own writing, Brooks is active in promoting and encouraging the work of other poets. In her native Illinois, where she was named poet laureate in 1968, Brooks has organized numerous poetry competitions, often offering prize money from her own funds. She has visited elementary schools, colleges, prisons, and drug rehabilitation centers, bringing people the art of poetry. In 1985, at the age of 68, she was appointed poetry consultant to the Library of Congress, the first black woman to be named to the post. Among the many other honors she has received in her distinguished career, The Gwendolyn Brooks Center for African-American Literature was established at Western Illinois University, and a junior high school in Harvey, Illinois, was named for her.

Selected writings

Poetry

A Street in Bronzeville, Harper, 1945.
Annie Allen, Harper, 1949.
Bronzeville Boys and Girls (juvenile), Harper, 1956.
The Bean Eaters, Harper, 1960.

Selected Poems, Harper, 1963.

In the Mecca, Harper, 1968.

Riot, Broadside Press, 1969.

Family Pictures, Broadside Press, 1970.

Aloneness, Broadside Press, 1971.

(Editor) *A Broadside Treasury,* Broadside Press, 1971.

(Editor) *Jump Bad: A New Chicago Anthology,* Broadside Press, 1971.

Aurora, Broadside Press, 1972.

The Tiger Who Wore White Gloves (juvenile), Third World Press, 1974.

Beckonings, Broadside Press, 1975.

Primer for Blacks, Black Position Press, 1980.

To Disembark, Third World Press, 1981.

Black Love, Brooks Press, 1982.

Mayor Harold Washington [and] *Chicago: The I Will City,* Brooks Press, 1983.

The Near Johannesburg Boy, and Other Poems, The David Co., 1987.

Other

Maud Martha (novel), Harper, 1953.

The World of Gwendolyn Brooks (contains *A Street in Bronzeville, Annie Allen, Maud Martha, The Bean Eaters,* and *In the Mecca*), Harper, 1971.

Report From Part One: An Autobiography, Broadside Press, 1972.

Young Poet's Primer (writing manual), Brooks Press, 1981.

Very Young Poets (writing manual), Brooks Press, 1983.

Also author of short stories. Contributor to numerous anthologies. Contributor of poems, articles, and reviews to periodicals.

Sources

Books

Black Women Writers (1950-1980): A Critical Evaluation, edited by Mari Evans, Anchor Press/Doubleday, 1984.

Black Writers: A Selection of Sketches from Contemporary Authors, Gale, 1989.

Brooks, Gwendolyn, *Report From Part One: An Autobiography,* Broadside Press, 1972.

Concise Dictionary of Literary Biography, 1941-1968, Gale, 1985.

Contemporary Literary Criticism, Gale, Volume 1, 1973; Volume 2, 1974; Volume 4, 1975; Volume 5, 1976; Volume 15, 1980; Volume 49, 1989.

Contemporary Poets, edited by Harold Bloom, Chelsea House, 1986.

Dictionary of Literary Biography, Volume 5: *American Poets Since World War II,* Gale, 1980.

Jackson, Blyden, and Louis D. Rubin, Jr., *Black Poetry in America: Two Essays in Historical Interpretation,* Louisiana State University Press, 1974.

Kent, George, *Gwendolyn Brooks: A Life,* University Press of Kentucky, 1988.

A Life Distilled: Gwendolyn Brooks, Her Poetry and Fiction, edited by Maria K. Mootry and Gary Smith, University of Illinois Press, 1987.

Littlejohn, David, *Black on White: A Critical Survey of Writing by American Negroes,* Viking, 1966.

Madhubuti, Haki R., *Say That the River Turns: The Impact of Gwendolyn Brooks,* Third World Press, 1987.

Melhem, D. H., *Gwendolyn Brooks: Poetry and the Heroic Voice,* University Press of Kentucky, 1987.

Miller, R. Baxter, *Black American Poets Between Worlds, 1940-1960,* University of Tennessee Press, 1986.

Shaw, Harry F., *Gwendolyn Brooks,* Twayne, 1980.

Tate, Claudia, *Black Women Writers at Work,* Continuum, 1983.

Periodicals

Black World, September 1971.

CLA Journal, March 1987.

Critique: Studies in Modern Fiction, Summer 1984.

MELUS, Fall 1983.

MidAmerica, Volume 12, 1985.

New York Times Book Review, January 7, 1973.

Virginia Quarterly Review, Winter, 1969.

—Michael E. Mueller

Lee P. Brown

1937—

New York City Police commissioner

In 1990 Lee P. Brown was sworn in as police commissioner of New York City, taking command of the nation's largest police force with more than 26,000 officers. Formerly Houston's chief of police, Brown became the first non-New Yorker in a quarter century to hold the post; he was chosen by Mayor David N. Dinkins for his effective community policing programs. While in Houston in the 1980s Brown transformed what was considered one of the nation's worst police departments into, as Peter Blauner describes it in *New York,* "a model of modern 'community-based' policing studied throughout the world." A nationally renowned criminologist and former police officer, Brown promotes a return to old-fashioned police foot patrols as a way to combat crime. Ralph Blumenthal noted in the *New York Times* that Brown's "Community Patrol Operations Program" (CPOC) advocates "replacing emergency response with beat patrols working with neighborhood figures to head off crime problems before they develop."

Brown plans to usher in a new era in New York City policing with CPOC. As Blumenthal noted, "the new program . . . would bring a new kind of policing to New York City, where officers, over the last 50 years, have been moving inexorably off the sidewalks and into speedy radio cars and talking to dispatchers instead of to citizens." One of the objectives of CPOC is to decentralize the department and encourage individual patrol officers to come up with new solutions for fighting crime. "Community policing is a new way of thinking about policing," Brown told Blumenthal. "It says that police officers are creative intelligent individuals who can do more than just respond to incidents. They should be working with the people who live and work in that area and identify the problems to jointly determine the best strategy to solve the problem and use the combined resources of the police and the community to solve the problem." Brown intends to transform the New York Police Department from one where officers move towards specialized "desk jobs." "Rather than taking the first opportunity to enter the more highly paid specialized units and get out of uniform," noted Blumenthal, Brown wants the "Police Department to be such that people come in to be patrol officers, spend their whole careers as patrol officers."

Brown's plans for New York City are to eventually establish foot patrols in each of New York's 75 precincts.

At a Glance...

Full name, Lee Patrick Brown; born October 4, 1937, in Wewoka, OK; son of Andrew and Zelma (Edwards) Brown; married Yvonne Carolyn Streets (a librarian), July 14, 1958; children: Patrick, Torri, Robyn, Jenna. *Education:* Fresno State University, B.A., 1960; San Jose State University, M.A., 1964; University of California, Berkeley, M.S., 1968, Ph.D., 1970. *Politics:* Democrat.

San Jose Police Department, San Jose, CA, officer, 1960-68; Portland State University, Portland, OR, professor, 1968-72; Howard University Institute for Urban Affairs and Research, Washington, D.C., associate director, 1972-75; Sheriff's Department, Mulnomah County, OR, sheriff, 1975-76; Department of Justice Services, Mulnomah County, director, 1976-78; Department of Public Safety, Atlanta, GA, commissioner, 1978-82; Houston Police Department, Houston, TX, chief of police, 1982-90; New York City Police Commissioner, 1990—. Adjunct professor, University of Houston, University of Texas Health Science Center, and Texas Southern University. Consultant to U.S. Department of Justice and Police Foundation, both Washington, DC, and state and local governments.

Awards: Honorary doctorate in public affairs, Florida International University, 1982, and honorary L.L.D., John Jay College, 1985; Robert J. Lamb Humanitarian Award, 1987.

Member: International Association of Chiefs of Police (president), National Organization of Black Law Enforcement Executives (vice president), National Minority Advisory Council on Criminal Justice (chairman), and many others.

Addresses: *Office*—Office of Police Commissioner, Police Plaza, New York, NY 10038.

By 1994 he hopes to have over 10,000 officers on daily patrol, an increase of over 50 percent of the number in 1991. Brown's plans received a boost in February of 1991 when the New York State legislature approved financing for a major anti-crime plan for New York City, which will allow Brown to hire 3,500 new officers over a

six-year period. Although Brown had planned to hire the new officers over two years, CPOC is proceeding within the legislative specifications. "We're not going to wait," Brown was quoted as saying in the *New York Times.* "We're going to incrementally and in a planned fashion do that which is necessary to change our dominant style of policing. . . . My vision is to have every block, every neighborhood of the city be the responsibility of a police officer or a group of police officers."

Many New York police officers are positive about the change to foot patrols, yet there is also an acknowledgement, as Blumenthal notes, that "they are fighting a public consciousness of police work modeled on 'Lethal Weapon,' 'Hill Street Blues' and 'Miami Vice'—car chases and shootouts." Brown has publicly lauded the efforts of the New York police force in adapting to the new style, yet has also stressed that the cooperation of city residents is essential. One frequent problem is in the area of drug dealing, where Brown sees a need for the public to speak up. "People know who are the drug dealers but all too often we don't get the cooperation that we need to address that as a major concern," he told Blumenthal. "We don't want people to do police work. We want them to be our eyes and ears."

Selected writings

(With Eugene Beard and Lawrence E. Gary) *Attitudes and Perceptions of Black Police Officers of the District of Columbia Metropolitan Police Department,* Howard University Institute for Urban Affairs and Research, 1976.
(With Thomas A. Johnson and Gorden E. Misner) *The Police and Society: An Environment for Collaboration and Confrontation,* Prentice-Hall, 1981.

Author of paper *The Death of Police Community Relations,* 1973, and editor of paper *The Administraition of Criminal Justice: A View From Black America,* 1974, both published by the Howard University Institute for Urban Affairs and Research. Also Editor of *Neighborhood Team Policing,* 1976, and *Violent Crime,* 1981. Contributor to books. Also author of numerous articles.

Sources

Jet, January 8, 1990.
New York, January 22, 1990.
New York Times, December 19, 1989; January 23, 1990; February 2, 1990; May 10, 1990; August 3, 1990; August 8, 1990; September 17, 1990; September 25, 1990; February 9, 1991; February 15, 1991.

—Michael E. Mueller

Dorothy Brunson

1938—

Broadcasting executive

Dorothy Brunson is recognized as one of radio's leading marketing and managerial talents. The owner of three radio stations and developer of the "urban contemporary" radio format, Brunson "is a dynamic entrepreneur whose hard work, persistence, imagination and business acumen have worked to her advantage in the hardball game of broadcasting," wrote Ken Smikle in *Black Enterprise.* In 1979 Brunson began a successful career revitalizing black urban radio stations after having previously establishing herself as the savvy manager of New York City's WBLS-Radio. During her tenure at WBLS Brunson gained renown for transforming it from a failing black-oriented station into the sixth-largest U.S. radio station—black or white. The key to WBLS's turnaround was Brunson's innovation of the urban contemporary format, which offers listeners Top Forty pop music mixed with black rhythm and blues. Due to Brunson's programming brainstorm WBLS's listener base and advertising revenues greatly increased and Brunson, "one of radio's true innovators" as Peggy Simpson called her in *Working Woman,* had initiated a trend that was later emulated by numerous other U.S. stations. According to Dwight Ellis, vice-president of the National Association of Broadcast-

ers, as quoted by Simpson, Brunson's career is unique in that "she has demonstrated not only great business skill but a great deal of vision."

Born in rural Georgia and raised in Harlem, Brunson graduated from college with a business and finance degree and took a job as assistant controller of WWRL-Radio in New York City; after only three months she became controller, and eventually, assistant general manager. Wanting greater challenges, in 1969 she cofounded Howard Sanders Advertising, one of the first black advertising agencies in America. Brunson left with $115,000 in buyout money the following year and, after a dress shop she'd purchased went out of business, was asked by a start-up company, Inner City Broadcasting, to organize investors for its radio stations. After only four months in operation, Inner City—which directed the black community-oriented station, WLIB-AM Radio—was over $1 million in debt and Brunson was hired as general manager. Brunson quickly took steps to turn the station around; in her first year she reduced staff size from 35 to eight, restructured the station's debt arrangement, and secured a loan to purchase WLIB-FM, the music counterpart of WLIB-AM.

At a Glance. . .

Born March 13, 1938, in Glensville, GA; daughter of Wadis and Naomi (Ross) Edwards; married James Brunson (an electrician), 1964 (divorced c. 1976); children: Edward, Daniel. *Education:* Empire State College, B.S.

Worked in print communications, 1960-62; WWRL-Radio, New York City, 1964-70, began as assistant controller, became controller, assistant general manager, and corporate liaison to company board of directors; Howard Sanders Advertising, Inc., New York City, 1971-72, co-founder and vice-president; owned retail dress shop, 1972; Inner City Broadcasting Corporation, New York City, 1973-79, began as general manager, became vice-president; owner and president, WEBB-Radio, Baltimore, MD, 1979—, WIGO-Radio, Atlanta, GA, 1981—, and WBMS-Radio, Wilmington, NC, 1984—. Lecturer and speaker. Contributor of articles to *Vogue, Black Enterprise,* and *Newsweek.*

Addresses: *Home*—Baltimore, MD. *Office*—Brunson Communication, Inc., 6821 Reistertown Rd., Suite 205, Baltimore, MD 21215.

Brunson's strategy was to operate both stations under one staff and broaden the playlist of the FM station—renamed WBLS—to include not only its established rhythm and blues catalog, but also recordings by white artists with a black audience. Over the next five years this "urban contemporary" format resulted in a tremendous increase in both listeners and advertising revenues. By 1978 Inner City Broadcasting had expanded from a company with $500,000 in annual sales to one that owned seven major-market radio stations, the billing of which exceeded $23 million. Brunson's urban contemporary sound tapped into a huge and lucrative interracial audience, according to Simpson, "of the very 12- to 39-year-olds advertisers sought." Brunson commented to Simpson on her objective: "We didn't design it to pioneer anything. We designed urban contemporary to be competitive. Advertisers were only buying black radio for products specifically geared to blacks. We tried to defy the myth and came up with the concept that people at the same economic levels generally purchase goods in a similar fashion. For example, for a woman to purchase boutique clothing, eat yogurt, be on a diet crossed all ethnic groups."

After her success at Inner City Broadcasting Brunson was ready to establish her own radio empire. In 1979 she purchased WEBB-Radio in Baltimore, where seven years later she would elevate ratings from the cellar of a thirty-five-station market to Number Ten. The rise of WEBB did not come about, however, without Brunson having to overcome tremendous difficulties: Shortly after she purchased the station Brunson learned of the large back taxes owed and 600 FCC violations amassed by WEBB. "I was naive," she told Simpson. Complicating her position further, local stations fiercely opposed Brunson's efforts to establish what they claimed was an unnecessary additional station serving the black community. Neighborhood groups meanwhile protested Brunson's construction of radio towers in a section of the city where it was believed they would interfere with radio and television reception. WEBB operated in the red its first four years; the first year Brunson took no salary. Confident in her ability and proven track record in revitalizing radio stations, however, investors supplied Brunson with the capital she needed to transform the station. Greg Forest, vice-president of the firm investing in Brunson, told Simpson: "We didn't invest in Dorothy because she was a woman or because she was black but because we thought she knew what she was doing and could make a profit for her and for us. . . . She's one of the hardest-working people I've ever met."

By 1986 Brunson had succeeded in transforming WEBB into a profitable black community-oriented station. She went on to purchase two more stations, WIGO-AM in Atlanta and WBMS-AM in Wilmington, North Carolina, which became part of her burgeoning company, Brunson Communications. She commented to Lloyd Gite in *Essence* of her intent to use the stations "as a propaganda tool, if you will, to enlighten and inform the Black community." She told Simpson that WEBB is known in Baltimore as "the community voice. We do a lot of very positive things like have basketball teams for little kids, a concert, Father's Day awards to highlight the importance of the father." Positive sales figures helped Brunson fulfill these community roles; after six years of operation WEBB increased its advertising billing from $100,000 to over $800,000, while WIGO more than doubled revenues in its first few years of operation.

Brunson described herself to Gite as someone who considers "power . . . part of my motivation." Revealing her entrepreneurial spirit, she told Smikle that "there's a subliminal comfort in knowing the buck stops with you. You've got to make it or break it." She disclosed to Smikle another motivation: "I want to leave my children and grandchildren with a mentality that says, 'I can fight to get a piece of the American pie.'"

Sources

Black Enterprise, April 1987.
Ebony, December 1985.
Essence, June 1984.
Working Woman, August 1986; November 1986.

—Michael E. Mueller

Naomi Campbell

1970—

Model

Deemed "the reigning mega-model of them all" in *Interview* magazine, London-born Naomi Campbell is one of the world's most in-demand and highly paid models. Campbell earns over $1 million annually; for a single day's work she can bring in upwards of $10,000. With looks that some have described as ex-·otic—her grandmother was a Chinese native of Jamaica—Campbell is a familiar figure on the covers of leading American and European fashion publications. She has appeared in *Cosmopolitan, Vogue,* and *Elle,* and holds the distinction of being the first ethnic woman ever to appear on the cover of the French edition of *Vogue.*

One reason Campbell is so highly sought after is what many in the fashion industry have praised as her natural modeling ability. "She's one of the most delightful girls I've ever worked with, one of my favorite models," exalted renown fashion photographer Francesco Scavullo in *Harper's Bazaar.* "No one else has such an amazing body. She makes clothes come alive." Fashion coordinator Audrey Smaltz also commented in *Harper's Bazaar* on Campbell's magnetism on style show runways: "She's doesn't realize how wonderful she is. . . . She has terrific

body language—most models don't—and can translate this into whatever she's wearing." Designer Azzedine Alaia, one of Campbell's personal favorites, calls her "a little marvel."

The daughter of a modern ballet dancer, the brown-eyed brunette Campbell entered modeling when she was fifteen and a student at London's Academy of Performing Arts. An agent discovered her in a shopping arcade of Covent Gardens, which Campbell frequented after school. Campbell described the encounter to George Wayne in *Interview:* "I was just hanging out, and this woman comes up to me and says, 'I'm a modeling agent.' I didn't believe her, but I took her card home and gave it to my mother. And then I saw an interview of her in *Tatler,* so I knew she was legitimate. After that I started pleading with my mother to let me go see her. At the end of the school year, I did. She took a picture of me in my school uniform . . . then she sent me to a photographer who was working on an assignment for British *Elle* in New Orleans, and he booked me." Superstar model Christy Turlington, a close friend of Campbell's, first met the teenage hopeful at the agency where Turlington was working. "She was wearing her school uniform," Turlington related to Eliza-

At a Glance...

Born May 22, 1970, in London, England; mother was a ballet dancer. *Education:* Attended London Academy of Performing Arts c. 1985.

Model, 1986—. Appeared on London stage in *The King and I,* in films *Quest for Fire* and *The Wall,* both 1982, and on television series *The Cosby Show.*

beth Sporkin in *People.* "The next time I saw her, a few months later, she was on her own in Paris, dancing until 4 a.m."

Campbell has worked with some of the biggest names in the fashion industry. She described in *Interview* some of her favorite fashion photographers: "I like working with Herb Ritts, and I do very much like working with [Francesco] Scavullo. He makes me feel like a woman. Herb makes you feel very innocent. Steven [Meisel] makes you feel like a character. When you work with him he'll give you postcards and books to look at and study.

He makes me look different in every picture." Campbell's assignments have taken her to many locations around the world. For one of her most exciting—and harrowing—photo shoots, she found herself, standing atop a volcano in Lanzarote, Spain—in heels.

Campbell's future may hold more than modeling. She has an ambition to act; prior to her modeling career, Campbell appeared on the London stage in a production of *The King and I* and in two 1982 movies, *Quest for Fire* and Pink Floyd's *The Wall.* More recently she played the character of Julia on NBC-TV's *The Cosby Show.* Campbell hopes to expand her acting career and appears confident that the jet-set life of an international model is ample preparation. She remarked to Wayne: "You can't learn it all. As they tell you, acting is reacting. So it's all about going through life, having experiences."

Sources

Harper's Bazaar, March 1990.
Interview, May 1990.
People, June 11, 1990.

—*Michael E. Mueller*

Benjamin Carson

1951—

Neurosurgeon

The director of pediatric neurosurgery at Johns Hopkins Hospital in Baltimore, Dr. Benjamin Carson is "one of the acknowledged miracle workers of modern medicine," wrote Christopher Phillips in *Reader's Digest.* Carson has received recognition throughout the medical community for his prowess in performing complex and delicate neurosurgical procedures, primarily on children. Among his accomplishments are a number of faultless hemispherectomies, a complicated surgical process in which a portion of the brain of a critically ill seizure victim or other neurologically diseased patient is removed to restore normal functioning. Carson's most famous operation—one that gained him international acclaim—came in 1987 when he separated a pair of West German Siamese twins, who had been joined at the backs of their heads. In the landmark operation, which lasted 22 hours, Carson led a surgical team comprised of 70 doctors, nurses, and technicians.

Carson's rise to the top of his field began in the rough inner-city neighborhoods of Detroit. Raised by his divorced mother, Carson—who always dreamed of becoming a doctor—was a failing student with a penchant for fighting, until the age of ten, when his mother imposed a reading program—two books weekly—on him and strictly limited his television viewing. Carson soon became an avid reader and his grades improved, putting him near the top of his class. In high school he continued to excel and received offers from several Ivy League universities. Carson eventually attended Yale University on a scholarship and went on to study medicine at the University of Michigan, where his initial plan was to become a psychotherapist. In his first year of medical school, however, he discovered neurosurgery. "I loved dissecting things," Carson told *Ebony.* "And I always felt that I was very good with my hands. Neurosurgery was a natural for me."

Carson did both his internship in general surgery and residency in neurosurgery at Baltimore's Johns Hopkins Hospital, considered one of the nation's elite medical centers. He became the hospital's first-ever black neurosurgical resident. In 1983 he moved with his wife to Perth, in Western Australia, to became senior neurosurgical resident at the Sir Charles Gairdner Hospital, one of Australia's leading centers for brain surgery. Due to the lack of neurosurgeons in Australia and Carson's advanc-

At a Glance...

Full name, Benjamin Solomon Carson; born September 18, 1951, in Detroit, MI; son of Robert Solomon and Sonya (Copeland) Carson; married Lacena Rustin, July 6, 1975; children: Murray Nedlands, Benjamin Solomon, Jr., Rhoeyce Harrington. *Religion:* Seventh Day Adventist. *Education:* Yale University, B.A., 1973; University of Michigan, M.D., 1977.

Diplomate, American Board of Neurological Surgery. Johns Hopkins Hospital, Baltimore, MD, surgical intern, 1977-78, neurosurgical resident, 1978-82, chief resident, 1982-83, director of pediatric neurosurgery, 1985—; Sir Charles Gairdner Hospital, Perth, Western Australia, senior registrar in neurosurgery, 1983-84. Member of medical advisory board, Children's Cancer Foundation, Baltimore, 1987—; Maryland Red Cross honorary medical chairman, Baltimore, 1987—.

Member: American Association of Neurological Surgeons, Congress of Neurological Surgeons, AAAS, Pediatric Oncology Group, National Medical Association.

Awards: Cum laude award, American Radiological Society, 1982; Paul Harris fellow, Rotary International, 1988; American Black Achievement Award, *Ebony*, 1988; Candle Award, Morehouse University, 1989. Honorary doctorates of science from Gettysburg College, 1988, North Carolina Agricultural and Technical State University, Andrews University, and Sojourner-Douglas College, all 1989, and Shippensburg University, 1990.

Addresses: *Home*—Columbia, MD. *Office*—Johns Hopkins Hospital, 600 North Wolfe St., Baltimore, MD 21205.

Carson rapidly gained a reputation within the medical community as an exceptionally skilled surgeon—especially adept at safely performing operations that typically carried high mortality rates. Such is the case with hemispherectomies and the separation of Siamese twins, which usually results in the loss of one twin. The West German twins that Carson operated on in 1987 were joined through a common blood vessel in the back of their heads. The surgeon devised a plan to separate the twins by completely shutting down their blood flow, severing their common vessel, and then restoring their individual vessel systems. Although the entire procedure lasted 22 hours, Carson and another surgeon had only one hour to conduct the actual surgery and restoration. Carson commented to *Ebony* on the success of the operation. "Not only was it exciting to be part of a history-making event, but the significant fact is that we put together an incredibly complex scene with a team of incredibly competent people who submerged their egos and pulled off what was perhaps the most complex surgical feat in the history of mankind."

Carson remains modest about his individual achievements. A devout Seventh Day Adventist, he views his medical accomplishments in terms of his religious faith. "God created the body," he told *Ebony*. "He knows more about it than anybody else and can heal virtually every problem. It's only a matter of whether we're willing to let Him work through us." In an article Carson wrote for *Ebony* he cited his mother's influence as crucial to his success. He singled out her philosophy of "no excuses for anything" and "if anybody can do something, you can do it better."

Selected writings

Published by Zondervan Books

Pediatric Neuroncology, 1987.
Achondroplasia, 1988.
(With Cecil Murphey), *Gifted Hands*, 1990.

Contributor of numerous articles to journals, including the *Journal of the American Medical Association*.

Sources

Black Enterprise, October 1988.
Ebony, January 1988; May 1990.
Jet, September 28, 1987.
Reader's Digest, April 1990.

ing medical skills, he obtained much valuable work experience in his year at the hospital. "I was operating so much," he told *Ebony*, "I was able to concentrate several years of experience into one year." He returned to Johns Hopkins in 1985 and quickly became one of the hospital's leading surgeons. Within a year he was promoted to director of pediatric neurosurgery and, at the age of thirty-four, was one of the youngest directors of a surgical division in the United States.

—Michael E. Mueller

Joe Clark

1939—

Public school administrator

Principal Joe Clark came into the national spotlight in the late 1980s for his controversial methods of management at Eastside High, an inner-city school in Paterson, New Jersey. Symbolized by his familiar bullhorn and Louisville Slugger baseball bat, which he toted as he patrolled the halls of Eastside, Clark maintained an environment of staunch authoritarian discipline at the school, regularly expelling what he called "parasites": students who were disruptive, truant, or "hoodlums, thugs and pathological deviants."

Clark's drastic methods have won him the support and admiration of many students and teachers and the public praise of President Ronald Reagan, who said Clark represented the tough leadership necessary to manage inner-city schools in crisis. Numerous critics and educators, however, have denounced Clark's autocratic hardline methods of dealing with students and have questioned the real benefits of his law-and-order approach to education. Clark's struggle to restore order at Eastside became "a kind of allegory for all the tribulations, dangers and scattered triumphs of cities large and small, where public education is undergoing its most severe challenge," wrote Ezra Brown in a *Time* cover story on the celebrated principal. Clark emerged as "the touchstone of a rekindled national debate about how to put things right in a city schoolhouse gone wrong."

Clark was appointed principal of Eastside in 1982. A twenty-year veteran of the Paterson school district, Clark had previously been principal at PS 6, a troubled inner-city grammar school, which he transformed into what people referred to as the "Miracle on Carroll Street." Eastside, a predominantly black and Hispanic high school with a student body numbering 3,200, had a reputation for violence and incompetence in a district that state officials once listed as on the verge of "educational bankruptcy." According to Clark in his 1989 book *Laying Down the Law: Joe Clark's Strategy for Saving Our Schools,* "bedlam reigned" at Eastside prior to his arrival. Fighting in school halls and in classrooms was common and weapons had been used against both students and teachers. Drug dealers worked the school daily, both outside and inside the building, and marijuana smoke could often be smelled throughout corridors and in restrooms. Walls and hallways were sprayed throughout with graffiti and broken fencing, windows,

At a Glance. . .

Born May 7, 1939, in Newark, NJ; wife's name, Hazel; children: Joetta, Joe, Jr., Hazel. *Education:* Graduate degree from Seton Hall University.

Worked as grade school teacher in Paterson, NJ, and director of camps and playgrounds, Essex County, NJ, c. 1962-late 1970s; principal of PS 6 (elementary school), Paterson, late 1970s-1982; principal of Eastside High School, Paterson, 1982-89; lecturer, 1989—. Has appeared on numerous television programs, including *Donahue, Nightline, 60 Minutes,* and *A Current Affair.* Addressed U.S. Senate subcommittee on state of education in the United States. *Military service:* U.S. Army Reserve sergeant.

Addresses: *Home*—South Orange, NJ.

doors, and furniture frequently went unrepaired. The educational process at Eastside was equally run-down. Students and teachers worked in a state of perpetual fear, truancy and dropout rates were high, and student academic test scores were among the lowest in the state.

Took Troubled High School by Storm

Clark moved quickly to devise a new order for Eastside. He reorganized the administrative structure at the school, replaced officials whom he considered "loafers," and set up a chain-of-command that clearly defined responsibilities and problem-solving channels. He drew up new student policies, including a rigorous suspension system, student photo identification tags, dress code guidelines, and corridor traffic-flow management. The summer before his first term as principal he coordinated a major renovation of the building itself in order to, as he stated in *Laying Down the Law,* "have it as a powerful and constant ally to my disciplined program for creating and maintaining an atmosphere conducive to learning." Broken fences, windows, and door locks were repaired, while security patrols were beefed up to monitor school grounds and keep out drug pushers. Throughout, Clark kept the extent of his plans for transforming Eastside quiet; as he recounted in *Laying Down the Law,* "too often, an administrator kills or weakens a good plan by telegraphing in advance what he is going to do—instead of just doing it."

On opening day of his Eastside tenure Clark greeted students with his bullhorn: "I am your new principal, Joe Clark. Mr. Clark to you. This is the new Eastside High School. What was, exists no more. Go to your classrooms. Please walk to the right." In his first week Clark suspended 300 students for violations of his new suspension code, which encompassed, among other things, verbal and physical assault, vandalism, graffiti, defiance of authority, threatening staff members, the wearing of hats, and tardiness. Over the next few years Clark established a strict and disciplined feeling at Eastside. Suspensions and expulsions were consistently and regularly enforced and became Clark's way of ridding the school of what he called "leeches, miscreants and hoodlums." In accordance with his belief that "discipline establishes the format, the environment for academic achievement to occur," Clark demanded from both students and faculty a uniform adherence to rules and regulations. Students who failed to comply to Clark's code were suspended; teachers who disagreed with his policies were either dismissed or asked to leave. Clark was a high-profile presence at Eastside, giving daily messages over the public address system, tirelessly patrolling the halls, chatting with students and visiting classrooms, berating teachers he felt weren't doing their job, and praising those who were. "In this building, everything emanates and ultimates from me," he was often quoted as saying. "Nothing happens without me."

Expulsions Drew National Attention

Clark's policies came to national attention in December of 1987 when he expelled over 60 "parasite" students from Eastside. The group included students past the age of 18 who were severely short of credits for graduation and whom Clark felt were an obstacle to the education of others. The Paterson school board voted to draw up insubordination proceedings against Clark, charging that he had suspended students without their right to due process. Clark was also charged with violating fire codes for keeping school exit doors chained, a move he claimed was necessary in order to keep out drug dealers. While many among the Paterson school board wanted to see Clark dismissed as principal, his hard-line efforts at Eastside had won him widespread support throughout the larger community. At a crowded school board meeting in January of 1988 hundreds of parents and students turned up to voice their support for Clark, shouting "Without No Joe, Where Will We Go?" Further support came when a representative of the Reagan administration called to offer Clark a position in the Office of Policy Development, pending the outcome of the school board's ruling. Clark turned down the offer, saying his job would remain at Eastside. He told the board that by "making allowances for inner-city kids," they were "making a bunch of parasites out of black and Hispanic kids." Insubordination proceedings were eventually dropped against Clark and he reinstated some of the expelled students; nonetheless, a formal inquiry was eventually launched into the expulsions.

The expulsions investigation gained national media attention and Clark found himself at the center of a national debate on educational reform of inner-city schools. In addition to his *Time* cover stint in February of 1988, he made numerous appearances on television talk shows and news programs. U.S. secretary of education William J. Bennett praised Clark's tough stance, stating, "Sometimes you need Mr. Chips, sometimes you need Dirty Harry." Philadelphia principal Odetta Dunn Harris in *Time* commended Clark as "a principal with principles," adding, "He is trying to develop strong, independent, law-abiding citizens and is trying to provide the students with a safe, secure place to learn, and for this he is going to be nailed to the wall." Others, however, questioned the concrete benefits of Clark's reforms and

denounced his autocratic approach to education. Los Angeles principal George McKenna stated in *Time:* "We want to fix the schools, but you don't do that by seeing the kids as the enemy. Our role is to rescue and be responsible. . . . If the students were not poor black children, Joe Clark would not be tolerated."

Stirred Debate Among Educators

Professor Irwin A. Hyman in an *Education Week* article reprinted in *Education Digest* said that Clark typified "the charismatic authoritarian who offers himself as an answer to social crises. . . . Most people, he knows, will not complain about the suspension of a few civil liberties of obviously undeserving groups. . . . For Clark and his followers, the 'enemy' is teenagers—minority adolescents, in particular." Ernest Boyer, president of the Carnegie Foundation for the Advancement of Teaching, told Michael Norman in the *New York Times* that Clark deserved commendation for restoring order to Eastside, but that his policies could result in serious problems:

Clark, sporting his customary baseball bat and bullhorn, addresses a rally at East Side High School.

"You've removed the problem from the school system, but you haven't removed it from society and the whirlwind of that will be catastrophic." Other critics condemning Clark's actions pointed out that the expulsions illuminated the urgent need to provide alternative means of education for students who do not fit into the mainstream.

In *Laying Down the Law* Clark describes his career at Eastside, gives insight into the motivations and objectives behind his policies, and outlines a management plan for other educators. Clark describes how Eastside, like many inner-city schools in the United States, suffered from widespread "ignorance." Administrators and teachers stood by and tolerated sub-standard academic performance and disruptive behavior, while the futures of students with potential were put in peril. As a result, many black and Hispanic students, who already encounter greater obstacles in society, faced the prospect of losing a crucial opportunity to acquire the skills they need to succeed as adults. The majority of school administrators and bureaucrats are, according to Clark, unable to "see the main issues clearly enough or long enough," and "take the wrong action, or settle for wrong-headed inaction." The crux of Clark's philosophy is his belief in the "fruitlessness of egalitarianism," embodied in his statement, "You can't save everybody." His critics point to this attitude as illustration of Clark's disregard for problem students; in his defense, Clark maintains that his focus is to ensure that education can actually occur in schools. Commenting in the *New York Times Book Review* Elizabeth Lyttleton Sturz called *Laying Down the Law* "a fascinating picture of a man obsessed with the nuts and bolts that make or break programs in education and elsewhere."

Clark underwent open-heart surgery in May of 1989; two months later he resigned from Eastside. Prior to his departure newspaper editorials had increasingly called for his resignation; the *New York Times* referred to him as an "unguided missile" who had been "abusive of students, parents and teachers, insubordinate to authority and contemptuous even of constructive criticism." Frank Corrado, a vice-principal under Clark, commented positively, however, in *Laying Down the Law* on the "tyranny" of Clark and his battle against the status quo: "Joe Clark understands the value, and the real necessity, of a principal being the sole person in charge, and constantly promotes that. He knows better than most that, in the changeable and potentially explosive atmos-

phere of an inner-city high school, authority must not be demeaned, or all order may break down. . . . He took me aside once . . . and said, 'To be an effective principal in an inner-city school one must be controversial.' He did not mean that he planned to provoke controversy *per se.* He meant that erroneous thought and processes had become so endemic to the system that any principal properly doing the job would inevitably meet resistance."

Since leaving Eastside Clark has lectured on school management, education reform, and drug control measures for inner cities. His larger-than-life story at Eastside was the basis of the 1989 Warner Bros. film *Lean on Me.*

Selected writings

(With Joe Picard) *Laying Down the Law: Joe Clark's Strategy for Saving Our Schools,* Regenery Gateway, 1989.

Sources

Books

Clark, Joe, and Joe Picard, *Laying Down the Law: Joe Clark's Strategy for Saving Our Schools,* Regnery Gateway, 1989.

Periodicals

American Spectator, August 1989.
Black Enterprise, May 1988.
Education Digest, November 1989.
Education Week, April 26, 1989.
Jet, July 31, 1989; March 12, 1990.
Nation, January 30, 1988.
National Review, May 5, 1989.
New York Times, January 5, 1988; January 11, 1988; January 14, 1988; January 15, 1988; January 16, 1988; January 23, 1988; January 27, 1988; January 29, 1988; March 6, 1988; April 5, 1988; June 6, 1988; February 11, 1989; March 11, 1989; March 14, 1989; July 15, 1989.
New York Times Book Review, July 9, 1989.
People, March 27, 1989.
Time, February 1, 1988; March 13, 1989.

—*Michael E. Mueller*

Constance Clayton

1937(?)—

Superintendent of the Philadelphia Public School System

The tasks confronting Constance Clayton are enormous. As superintendent of Philadelphia's public schools, Clayton presides over the sixth-largest school system in the nation—a massive enterprise employing some 24,526 teachers, administrators, and support staff at more than 250 locations citywide. The energetic Clayton faces many challenges in her far-flung district, from budget setbacks to a poverty-stricken student body; but since her tenure began in 1983 she has set out to improve Philadelphia's educational system with the zeal of a crusader.

Philadelphia Inquirer columnist Claude Lewis attested: "It's no secret that Philadelphia public schools have problems trying to upgrade the level of education offered by a system that must cater to a large population of students who are among the poorest of the poor. School Superintendent Constance E. Clayton has done a highly respectable job under circumstances that might cause a lesser educational leader to throw up her hands in frustration." Lewis added: "Has Clayton solved most of the system's ills? Not by a long shot. But she has made meaningful improvement and provided a measure of hope for students and teachers alike who live with despair."

Under Clayton's leadership, student math and reading scores in Philadelphia's elementary schools have improved substantially. Parents express more confidence in the city's public education, and, through special efforts on Clayton's part, private businesses have pumped millions of dollars in grant money into the beleaguered urban schools. Under Clayton's management huge budget deficits have been erased and most of her tenure in office has seen balanced school budgets with some surplus. Clayton is best known, however, as an administrator, with her priorities fixed firmly on the most important link in the school system's chain—the students themselves. "Somebody had better step forward and be the advocate for kids," she told the *New York Times*. "We have a moral responsibility to these youngsters."

Constance Elaine Clayton was born and raised in the city she now serves. Her father was a plumber and her mother a counselor for the Opportunities Industrialization Center. Clayton's parents divorced when she was two and she grew up with her mother and grandmother in a middle-class black neighborhood. To this day she

At a Glance. . .

Full name, Constance Elaine Clayton; born c. 1937 in Philadelphia, PA; daughter of Levi (a plumber) and Willabell (a social worker; maiden name Harris) Clayton. *Education:* Temple University, B.A. and M.A., 1955; Pennsylvania State University, Ph.D., c. 1974.

Philadelphia Public School System, Philadelphia, PA, fourth grade teacher at William H. Harrison School, 1955-64, social studies curricula designer, 1964-69, head of African and Afro-American studies program, 1969-71, director of Early Childhood Program, 1973-83, superintendent, 1983—. United States Department of Labor, Washington, D.C., director of Women's Bureau for Middle Atlantic States, 1971-c. 1972

Awards: Rockefeller Foundation fellowship, c. 1974.

Member: NAACP, Delta Sigma Theta.

Addresses: *Home*—Mount Airy, Philadelphia, PA.

still lives with her mother, now in the Mount Airy section of Philadelphia.

Those who knew her as a child describe Clayton as an obedient, highly motivated youngster who would have rather read books than do just about anything else. "It was as though she was on a straight line just headed from the classroom to where she is now," her fourth grade teacher told the *Philadelphia Inquirer.* "I'm not gilding the lily," the teacher added. "She was a wonderful little girl. . . . Every teacher should have one Constance Clayton in their classroom." In addition to her studies Clayton was active at the St. Paul's Baptist Church, took piano lessons, and regularly attended concerts and museums in the city. Clayton told the *Philadelphia Inquirer:* "I think, as a kid, I had everything I needed and most of the things I wanted. I really was very fortunate in that regard. People might interpret that as being materialistic, but I had a lot of love, and [my family] did a lot of things together."

Clayton attended the Philadelphia High School for Girls, where she played the cello and earned top grades. After high school she entered Temple University. She had planned originally to become a physician, but after spending summers as a camp counselor discovered that she loved working with children. "I had plenty of friends who were interested in teaching," she told the *Philadelphia Inquirer.* "And then also at that time—which was more than 30 years ago—there weren't a lot of avenues open for women and minorities. And generally, success could come if you went into that particular endeavor. I think there were multiple factors in the decision. I have no regrets whatsoever."

Launched Afro-American Studies Program

Clayton earned both her bachelor's and master's degrees at Temple, specializing in elementary school administration. She began her career as a fourth grade teacher in 1955 at the William H. Harrison School in North Philadelphia. Clayton taught at Harrison until 1964, when she was given the task of designing social studies curricula for the city school system's elementary grades. She quickly earned a reputation as a hard-working and dedicated administrator and in 1969 was put in charge of the fledgling African and Afro-American Studies program. In that position she designed curricula on black issues for students of all ages.

For the only time in her career, Clayton left Philadelphia in 1971 to serve in the United States Department of Labor. She directed the Women's Bureau for the region covering Pennsylvania, Delaware, Maryland, Virginia, and West Virginia, organizing seminars on women's employment status and pay equity. Clayton only held the position for a year, however, as she found herself at odds with the Nixon administration over its educational policies. To this day she is an advocate of federal aid to schools and has called President Bush's stand on national education "empty rhetoric." She told the *New York Times:* "The President has come forward with a lot of lofty goals, but where are the fiscal and human resources to back that up and make those goals a reality?"

Clayton returned to The City of Brotherly Love in 1972 as director of the Philadelphia school system's Early Childhood Program. Eventually she became associate superintendent for Early Childhood Education in the city, while at the same time earning her Ph.D. from the University of Pennsylvania. *Philadelphia Inquirer* contributor Martha Woodall noted that Clayton turned Philadelphia's Early Childhood Education program "into a national model and cemented her professional reputation. . . . Within the school district, Clayton became known for her organizational skills and her professionalism. She submitted balanced budgets and operated her programs within them. She kept meticulous records and produced studies demonstrating that children who participated in the district's preschool programs performed better in school. She also was seen as a talented, outspoken, independent official who was never identified with any single superintendent.''

Selected for the Top Job From a Field of 84

Her independence may have helped Clayton survive the administration of Michael P. Marcase, superintendent from 1975 until 1982. Woodall wrote of the Marcase years: ''The district was in turmoil. Test scores were low, and absenteeism among pupils and staff was high. Year after year, students were promoted to the next grade, not because they had learned the material but because they were a year older. The district was bloated with patronage positions, and jobs were parceled out according to an informal ethnic quota system. . . . The school district faced perennial budget deficits.'' In 1983 the Philadelphia Board of Education ousted Marcase and interviewed eighty-four applicants for the superintendent position. Clayton got the job. Woodall concluded that, as Philadelphia's first black woman superintendent, Clayton ''emerged as the closest thing to a miracle worker the board was likely to find.''

Three days after she was hired Clayton submitted a ten-page, 58-point statement of her administration's goals for the city's schools. She planned to balance the budget without cutting student services, standardize curriculum, and attract help of every sort from the private sector. To Clayton's credit, these goals have been largely accomplished. More than 170 businesses have ''adopted'' a local school and helped equip it with better resources. ''Even Clayton's detractors concede that she has been masterful in improving public confidence by fostering a belief that educational change in Philadelphia is possible,'' Woodall wrote. ''As Clayton sees it, her mission is nothing less than transforming the city's school system into the best in the country. She approaches the task with a messianic zeal. Many say her fervor is her greatest strength. They also say it could turn out to be her most troubling weakness: She expects everyone to share her devotion to The Cause and has little tolerance for those she believes are not advancing it.''

Philadelphia Inquirer columnist Acel Moore noted that Clayton has not advanced her cause without alienating people along the way. ''The rap on Clayton throughout her . . . tenure has been that she is autocratic and abrasive and that she can't take criticism—no matter how constructive—from anyone, particularly subordinates,'' Moore reported. The columnist conceded, however, that the tough decisions Clayton has had to make have called for a forceful personality and a no-nonsense approach. Moore ventured: ''I doubt that a male superintendent whose . . . style matched Clayton's would have been faced with the same criticism. And I would bet that

he would have been paid as much as Clayton—or more—by now.'' Clayton herself told the *Philadelphia Inquirer* that she has always encouraged candor and creativity on the part of her subordinates, but she does become impatient with shoddy preparation and illogical or poorly-presented arguments. ''This administration is asking people to do what they should have been doing all along,'' she said. ''This administration is asking people to do what is right and fair for kids.''

City's Fiscal State Provided Challenges

In 1991 Clayton's contract was extended for four years. Her salary was raised from $100,000 to $115,000 in the first year and to $140,000 by the end of the third year of the contract. Clayton drew some criticism for accepting such a generous increase in light of Philadelphia's precarious fiscal outlook, but her supporters have pointed out that the raises only keep her on par with superintendents of other major city school districts.

> ''The President has come forward with a lot of lofty goals, but where are the fiscal and human resources to back that up and make those goals a reality?''

A conscientious worker who often puts in fourteen-hour days, Clayton feels that her work in Philadelphia is far from finished. While test scores have improved, the city still ranks low in statewide measures of student achievement. Clayton's biggest problem is the nature of her student body—some 42 percent of Philadelphia's 197,000 public school students are below the poverty level. Their ''schooling'' must also include nutritious meals, counseling, and even child care for teenage parents. These extra services must be provided at a time when federal and state aid are being decreased, and when Philadelphia itself stands on the brink of bankruptcy.

Superintendent Clayton has faced these challenges with a credo she inherited from her mother: ''There's no such word as can't.'' She told the *Philadelphia Inquirer:* ''There are many people who have come from economically poor circumstances who have succeeded. We have to search out those models. We have always to give the children hope in the expectation that they will break out of the cycle and the chains of poverty. . . . We really can't play catchup. . . . We have to do the job right the first time." Clayton remains optimistic about the school district's future because she has seen how many of its students are striving for an education. "We have splendid children in our system," she concluded. "We have enormously talented kids who have a great deal of potential, children who are aspiring."

Sources

New York Times, February 20, 1991.
Philadelphia Inquirer, September 30, 1984; September 13, 1987; March 8, 1991; May 1, 1991.

—Anne Janette Johnson

Sharon Pratt Dixon

1944—

Mayor of the District of Columbia

In November of 1990 Sharon Pratt Dixon of Washington, D.C., a lawyer and public utility executive, became the first black woman to be elected mayor of a major American city. Dixon's mayoral victory was virtually assured two months earlier in the Democratic primary, in which she not only upset four better-known candidates, but overcame the race's smallest campaign staff and budget and lowest standing in the polls. Dixon pulled off her stunning win on a campaign theme of promising to "clean house—with a shovel, not a broom," referring to the troubled administration of former Washington mayor Marion S. Barry. In a city beset by spiraling crime and deficit problems, Washington voters turned out in record numbers to voice the message that they wanted a major turn-around in city government. B. Drummond Ayres, Jr., commenting in the *New York Times,* wrote that Dixon's victory "provided the strongest reading yet on how deeply troubled Washington residents are by the city's fiscal, administrative, racial, ethical and law-and-order problems, many of which emerged in the latter years of Mr. Barry's 12-year tenure." Barry himself was quoted as saying in *Time* after the election: "Sharon Pratt Dixon represented drastic change."

Although all the candidates in the primary stressed new leadership to restore Washington's tarnished image, Dixon was the only one to openly attack Barry as responsible for many of the city's problems. She was also the only candidate to directly call for his resignation in light of his 1990 arrest for cocaine possession. "I am not prejudging the innocence or guilt of the mayor," Dixon was quoted as saying in a March, 1990, article in the *Washington Post.* "However, if he is to responsibly defend himself against criminal charges and at the same time responsibly come to grips with his admitted chemical substance abuse problem, he cannot give time, energy and attention to the serious problems plaguing our city." Columnist Judy Mann wrote in the *Washington Post* that "Dixon, who was the first candidate to announce for mayor, showed extraordinary courage from the outset. She was willing to go up against an incumbent who had a political machine and would be a formidable fund-raiser. When Barry, shortly before his trial, announced he would not seek reelection . . . she was in an open race."

Dixon's stance as a reform-minded outsider—in a city famous for its powerful political circles—distinguished

At a Glance. . .

Born January 30, 1944, in Washington, DC; daughter of Carlisle Edward (a District of Columbia Superior Court judge) and Mildred (Petticord) Pratt; married Arrington Dixon (former District of Columbia Council chairman), divorced; children: Aimee, Drew (daughters). *Education:* Howard University, B.A., 1965, J.D., 1968. *Politics:* Democrat. *Religion:* Episcopalian.

Joint Center for Political Studies, house counsel, 1970-71; Pratt and Queen, associate, beginning 1971; Antioch School of Law, attorney and professor, 1972-76; Potomac Electric Power Co., associate general counsel, 1976-79, director of office of consumer affairs, 1979-83, vice president, 1983-86, vice president of public policy, 1986-89; mayor of Washington, DC, 1991—. Democratic National Committeewoman, beginning 1971; Democratic committee, Washington DC, acting general counsel, 1976-77; Democratic National Convention, co-chair of Rules Committee, member of Ad Hoc Credentials Committee, and member of Judicial Council, all 1980; Eastern Regional Caucus, chair, 1981; Democratic National Committee, treasurer, 1985-89.

Awards: Falk Fellowship, Howard University, 1962-65; Harvard University Cooperative Scholarship, 1964.

Member: American Bar Association, National Women's Political Caucus, Unified Bar of the District of Columbia, District of Columbia Women's Bar Association, District of Columbia Democratic State Committee (national committeewoman), District of Columbia Law Revision Committee (vice-chair, 1977-83), Democratic National Committee (former treasurer), National Political Science Honor Society, Pi Sigma Alpha.

Addresses: *Office*—District Building, Washington, DC 20004.

date who created a perception that she was different and that the other candidates were part of the problem and she was the one to solve it." In response to the city's financial crisis she promised to cut 2,000 city workers in an effort "to get the city's bureaucracy under control," as reported by the *Washington Post.* Dixon also emphasized throughout her campaign the priority of better assisting working women, students, and families as a way to prevent the social ills of homelessness and drugs. The day after her election she began initiating her primary campaign pledge to "clean house" when she called for the immediate resignation of 177 of Barry's top city appointees. "We said it in the campaign and I meant it," she said in the *Washington Post.* "We're going to have a new team all the way around."

Although she ran as an outsider, Dixon brings valuable "inside" experience to being mayor. In addition to her work as a lawyer and in business, she has been a prominent leader in the Democratic National Committee for years and previously served as its national treasurer. A number of political observers praised Dixon's qualifications for mayor. Ronald H. Brown, chairman of the Democratic National Committee, told Ayres that Dixon was "one of the most persistent, tenacious, focused people I have ever known." Plotkin similarly commented to Ayres: "She's been around a good long time—I think of her as the insider running as an outsider—and you don't ever want to forget how persistent she can be." District of Columbia Council member H. R. Crawford in the *Washington Post* called Dixon "an articulate, outstanding role model [with] professionally impeccable character." Looking back to Dixon's experience as a corporate executive, Crawford stated that the District of Columbia was "fortunate to have a businesswoman with proven ability."

Sources

New York Times, September 12, 1990; September 16, 1990.
Time, September 24, 1990; November 19, 1990.
U.S. News & World Report, September 24, 1990.
Washingtonian, June 1990.
Washington Post, March 6, 1990; March 30, 1990; April 20, 1990; June 28, 1990; August 7, 1990; September 13, 1990; September 14, 1990; September 16, 1990; September 17, 1990.

her from the field of candidates. Political analyst Mark Plotkin noted in *Time* that Dixon "was the only candi-

—*Michael E. Mueller*

Forest J. Farmer

1941—

Automotive executive

In 1988, Forest J. Farmer was named president of Acustar, Inc., the electronic components subsidiary of the Chrysler Corporation. A spin-off of Chrysler's consolidated parts-making division, Acustar was established in 1987 as an independent company in order to encourage innovation and be more competitive with other electronic parts manufacturers. When Farmer took over as president of the growing company, Acustar's sales exceeded $3 billion dollars and the company employed approximately 28,000 personnel in 30 manufacturing facilities. Farmer, a 20-year Chrysler employee with a reputation as an outstanding manager, became responsible for overseeing all operation activities of Acustar's three main units: Diversified Products, Electronic Products, and Engineered Products.

Farmer's road to Chrysler began in the early 1960s at Purdue University, where he was an All-American linebacker and captain of the football team. He left college just before graduating to play professional football with the Denver Broncos, yet was forced to quit during his first year due to an injury. In 1962 Farmer returned to Purdue and received a degree in physical education and biology,

and went on to teach school in Indianapolis for four years. Wanting new opportunities and challenges not provided by teaching, he joined a foreman training program in 1968 for Chrysler, which was actively seeking minority candidates with leadership potential.

Over the next 20 years, Farmer rapidly advanced through a number of manufacturing managerial positions at Chrysler. From 1968 to 1978, he progressed from industrial engineer to foreman, and then to labor supervisor. He briefly left Chrysler for nine months in 1979, when the corporation was on the brink of bankruptcy, and rejoined after the federal government bailed out the struggling auto giant through the Loan Guarantee Act. During the 1980s, Farmer successfully managed a number of Chrysler manufacturing plants throughout the United States and developed, as Charles Whitaker wrote in *Ebony,* "a reputation as something of a miracle worker . . . [by] gaining the cooperation of recalcitrant workers."

One reason that Farmer is successful as a manager is his "hands-on" approach to working with employees. Thomas Stallkamp, who was named chairman of Acustar at

At a Glance. . .

Full name, Forest Jackson Farmer; born January 15, 1941, in Zanesville, OH; father worked in a steel mill; married wife Rosalyn, c. 1967; children: Forest, Jr., Christopher. *Education:* Purdue University, B.S., 1962.

Played linebacker with Denver Broncos of National Football League, 1962; teacher in schools in Indianapolis, IN, 1965-68; Chrysler Corporation, 1968-79, began in foreman training program at Indianapolis Electrical Plant, became industrial engineer, foreman, and labor supervisor; worked for Volkswagen of America, 1979; Chrysler Corporation, 1979-88, worked as plant manager of Jefferson Avenue Assembly Plant, Detroit, MI, beginning 1981, assembly plant manager, Newark, DE, beginning 1983, plant manager, Sterling Heights, MI, beginning 1984, director of advance manufacturing planning, Sterling Heights, 1986-87, and general plant manager, Highland Park, MI, 1987-88; Acustar, Inc., Troy, MI, president, 1988—.

Addresses: *Home*—Rochester Hills, MI. *Office*—Acustar, Inc., 1850 Research Dr., Troy, MI 48083.

the same time Farmer came on board, commented to Whitaker on Farmer's managerial skills: "There are peo-

ple who manage by momentum—sort of let events carry them through. And there are people who manage by getting in there and doing something. . . . Forest has the reputation of being the latter kind of manager. He assesses a situation and then tries to do something about it." Farmer will be expected to use these skills to the fullest at Acustar, since one of the company's financial goals is to not be solely reliant on the business of Chrysler. In order to do that, Acustar will have to be a competitive company, and Farmer commented to Whitaker that his football background will provide a helpful contribution. "I think the automobile industry lends itself to a background in competitive sports. It's a competitive industry, especially with the challenge we've been getting by offshore competitors. You need managers who can respond to that challenge, who are used to pulling people together to work as a team." Farmer voiced enthusiasm about his responsibilities at Acustar: "What I have liked about Chrysler is that they have always challenged me, and this is one of the greatest challenges yet. . . . To be in charge of a whole operation like this—to put in products, bid on contracts, develop my own profitability—it's a chance of a life time."

Sources

Ebony, March 1989.
Jet, September 26, 1988.
New York Times, August 31, 1988.
Wall Street Journal, August 31, 1988.

—*Michael E. Mueller*

Fela

1938—

Musician, singer, political activist

One of Africa's most acclaimed musicians, Nigerian Fela Anikulapo Kuti is "a peculiar late-twentieth-century mix of shaman, politician, ombudsman, activist and musical genius," according to Gene Santoro in the *Nation*. Fela, as he is popularly known, writes and performs political protest songs that have won him a large following both at home and abroad, to the frequent chagrin of government authorities. His music—dubbed "Afro-Beat,"—is an amalgam of American blues and jazz blended with African rhythms, while his pointed lyrics—in pidgin English and African—confront government corruption, multi-national corporations, and police brutality. In a career that has spanned four decades Fela has recorded over 50 albums and performs frequently in concert.

Fela is a flamboyant singer and musician and his concerts—many held at his Lagos nightclub, The Shrine—are lengthy and infectious. Fela belts out his driving songs, gyrating as he performs on saxophone or keyboards, directing his thunderous 27-member band, Egypt 80. Fela's "songs, which usually ride sloganlike lyrics over a densely woven web of cross-rhythms, have titles like 'Beasts of No Nation' (which deals with the way

various governments abet South African repression) and 'Just Like That' (a sneeringly witty list of Nigeria's current shortcomings)," noted Santoro. John Darnton wrote in the *New York Times* that one of Fela's most popular songs, "Upside Down," describes a traveler who finds an organized, well-planned world everywhere except in Africa, where there are villages, but no roads, land, but no food or housing. "These things are the daily lot of all Lagosians," Darnton noted. "When Fela sings this song, . . . listeners nod their heads solemnly and look into their beers."

Fela's musical upbringing spanned three continents. Born and raised in Nigeria, he initially studied piano and percussion and, as a youth, led a school choir. In the late 1950s Fela moved to London, where he studied classical music and was exposed to American jazz artists Charlie Parker, John Coltrane, and Miles Davis. His music did not become political, however, until the late 1960s, when he visited the United States and was exposed to the black power movement. Influenced by the teachings of Malcolm X, Fela began to realize the implications for Africa of white oppression, colonialism, Pan-Africanism—the unity of African nations—and revolution. The young

At a Glance. . .

Full name, Fela Anikulapo Kuti; surname originally Ransome-Kuti; born in 1938, in Abeokuta, Nigeria; son of Reverend Ransome-Kuti (father; a minister and educator) and Funmilayo (mother; a political activist); married, 29 wives, including musical collaborator Sandra; children: six. *Education:* Attended Trinity College of Music, London, late 1950s-early 1960s.

Musician, singer, and political activist. Formed band "Koola Lobitos" c. 1963; band name changed to "Afrika 70," and later to "Egypt 80." Recording artist for Celluloid, Shanachie, Capitol, and Mercury labels. Toured the U.S., 1986.

Addresses: *Home*—Lagos, Nigeria.

musician's work would never be the same; as quoted by Jon Pareles in the *New York Times,* Fela said, "The whole concept of my life changed in a political direction."

Fela returned to Nigeria and began to write politically charged songs that rocked his country. Inspired by Pan-Africanism, he incorporated African instruments into his band, including Konga drums, klips sticks, and the sekere, a percussion instrument. "I'm playing deep African music," he said at the time, as Pareles noted. "The rhythm, the sounds, the tonality, the chord sequences, the individual effect of each instrument and each section of the band—I'm talking about a whole continent in my music." Fela's protest music became very popular among the ranks of Nigeria's unemployed, oppressed, and politically dissident. These groups remain a large part of his audience.

Fela's music and politics have made him a cult figure in Nigeria; he has run for the presidency twice. His openly confrontive messages have, however, repeatedly irked government authorities, who have found reason to jail Fela for a variety of offenses throughout his career. In 1977 official rancor turned violent when the Nigerian military leveled Fela's Lagos residence after he had declared it an independent republic. Before burning the house down, soldiers went on a rampage in which Fela's mother, a prominent women's rights activist, was hurled from a second-story window. She later died from her injuries and Fela, in protest, dumped her coffin at the house of then-president General Olusegun Obasanjo.

Although such incidents have rallied support for Fela, he is notorious for a lifestyle that has alienated many Nigerians;

he unabashedly preaches the virtues of sex, polygamy, and drugs, in particular the use of marijuana as a creative stimulant. In 1978 Fela shocked his countrymen when he married his harem of 27 women, in protest he said, against the Westernization of African culture. His commune, the KalaKuta Republic—which was established to protest the military rule of Nigerian society—was reportedly itself run like a dictatorship. According to Darnton: "[Fela] ruled over the KalaKuta Republic with an iron hand, settling disputes by holding court and meting out sentences—cane lashings for men and a tin shed 'jail' for women in the backyard. . . . To some degree, these trappings of power account for his popularity among authority-conscious Nigerians."

While Fela's politics and lifestyle are controversial, few quibble over the power of his music. In 1986 he and Egypt 80 made their first tour of the United States, where Fela's audience is limited but growing. He has influenced the work of singer Jimmy Cliff and the Talking Heads' David Byrne. As Fela becomes better known outside of Nigeria he feels that his music will increasingly hold an international message. Fela told Nolan: "America needs to hear some good sounds from Africa, man. The sanity of the world is going to be generated from Africa through art. Art itself is knowledge of the spiritual world. Art is information from higher forces, by those who are talented. I'm not jiving. I've been living with my art for 23 years. My music has never been a failure."

Selected discography

Army Arrangement, Celluloid.
Beasts of No Nation, Shanachie.
Black President, Capitol.
Coffin for the Head of State.
Fela, Celluloid.
Fela and Ginger Baker, Live, Celluloid.
Mr. Follow Follow, Celluloid.
(With Roy Ayers) *Music of Many Colours,* Celluloid.
(With Lester Bowie) *No Agreement,* Celluloid.
Original Sufferhead, Capitol.
Overtake Done Overtake Overtake, Shanachie.
Shuffering and Shmiling, Celluloid.
Teacher Don't Teach Me Nonsense, Mercury, 1987.
(With wife, Sandra) *Upside Down,* Celluloid.
Zombie, Celluloid.

Sources

Books

Moore, Carlos, *Fela Fela,* Schocken, 1987.

Periodicals

Maclean's, October 13, 1986.
Nation, August 13, 1990.
New York Times, July 24, 1977; November 7, 1986.
People, December 1, 1986.

—Michael E. Mueller

George Foreman

1949—

Professional boxer

George Foreman is an unlikely hero in a savage sport. A former heavyweight champion of the world, Foreman has returned to professional boxing after a ten-year retirement with the idea of regaining his lost crown. Even though he is well over 40—an unheard-of age for a boxing comeback—he has earned a respectable record and a chance to meet top-ranked Evander Holyfield in a title match. "On the seniors boxing tour," wrote William Gildea in the *Washington Post,* "Foreman is undisputed champion. And among the over-40 set he'll remain king. Nobody his age would pick on him."

Foreman's checkered career includes juvenile delinquency, an Olympic gold medal, dramatic victories and defeats in boxing's professional ranks, and years spent as a preacher and youth leader. Even in his years away from boxing he has been the subject of media attention—not all of it flattering—and his return to the ring has sparked heated debate about his talents and potential. The boxer, a fundamentalist Christian, declares that he has returned to his sport in order to raise money for the youth center he is developing in the suburbs of Houston, Texas. He refuses to concede that his advancing age could weigh against him in a field where stamina and agility factor heavily into most victories. "Forty is no death sentence," he told *Time* magazine. "Age is only a problem if you make it one."

If he seems assured at mid-life, Foreman was certainly adrift as a youth. He was born and raised in the Fifth Ward, a poor neighborhood on the north side of Houston. There he made a name for himself as a brawler, drinker, petty thief, and gang leader, quitting school before he got to the ninth grade. Lester Hayes, a member of the Los Angeles Raiders football team, grew up in the same neighborhood and described the George Foreman he remembered in *Sports Illustrated.* Foreman, Hayes said, "was a very, very big kid and had a reputation for savage butt kickings. That was his forte. So by the early age of 12, I had met George Foreman twice and I found both occasions extremely taxing." Hayes added: "I will say this of George. He was a smart gangster in that he would tax you first and then kick your butt. But he wasn't a very nice thing."

Foreman told *Sports Illustrated* that he thought a hero was someone with "a big, long scar down his face, a guy who'd come back from prison, a guy [who] maybe killed a man once." He even went so far as to wear bandages on his own face so it would seem like he had a scar. Without any proper role models Foreman just drifted, with no clear idea how to make a life for himself. He was growing up in a single-parent family and spending most of his time in the streets. "I remember once," he said in *Sports Illustrated,* "two boys and myself, we robbed a guy. Threw him down. I could hold the guy because I was strong, and the sneaky fella would grab the money. And then we'd run until we couldn't hear the guy screaming anymore. And then we'd walk home as if we'd just earned some money on a job, counting it. We didn't even know we were criminals."

One day Foreman was watching television at his Houston home. A commercial came on featuring athlete Jim Brown, one of the few men Foreman actually admired. In the commercial, Brown urged young people to join the Job Corps in order to "be somebody." Foreman took the challenge. All alone, the teenager traveled from Texas to Oregon, where he joined a Job Corps camp. All was not rosy right away though—*Sports Illustrated* contributor Richard Hoffer described the youth as "principally a thug in a new outfit." Shortly after joining the Job Corps, Foreman was involved in a savage fistfight in the town of Pleasanton, California. When a group of counselors could not pull Foreman off his victim, they called upon the supervisor, Doc Broadus, for help. Broadus stepped in and stopped the fight, noticing in the process that Foreman seemed to be crying out for understanding,

that he was indeed a confused boy wasting his strength in fits of frustration.

Broadus's special interest was developing boxers. He took Foreman to the gym and began to teach him how to channel his energy for productive purposes. In a short two years, Foreman developed into a powerful amateur heavyweight. He not only qualified for the 1968 Olympic Games, he won the gold medal in his division. His many victories notwithstanding, Foreman still remembers his moment in the 1968 games as the highlight of his life. He told *Sports Illustrated:* "None of it felt as good as when I was poor and had just won that gold medal, when I wore it so long I had to have the ribbon restitched."

Won championship bout with Frazier

Foreman turned pro in 1969 and began to move through the ranks toward the championship. He made his mark quickly, going undefeated through forty fights and winning more than half of those within *two* rounds. "My opponents didn't worry about losing to me," Foreman told *Sports Illustrated.* "They worried about getting hurt." Despite this track record, Foreman was an underdog when he entered the ring against world champion Joe Frazier in 1973. Frazier had stunned the world by beating Muhammad Ali and was thought to be invincible. Not only did Foreman beat Frazier, he knocked the champion down six times in a brutal TKO victory. Foreman went on to defend his championship belt against Ken Norton, another highly-ranked contender, and knocked him out in less than two rounds.

This set the stage for one of the most dramatic fights in modern history, the October 30, 1974 meeting between Foreman and Ali in Zaire. The crowd of 60,000 was squarely in Ali's corner, booing Foreman loudly as he attacked the former champion with flurry after flurry of punches. In Muhammad Ali, Foreman had finally met his match. The wily Ali absorbed six rounds of punishment from Foreman, taunting him all the while, and then Foreman was spent. Ali knocked Foreman down in the eighth round, and Foreman was unable to rise before the count of ten. It was his first loss, and it came in spectacular fashion.

The impact of that loss rocked Foreman for years to come. *Sports Illustrated* correspondent Gary Smith wrote: "Out of nowhere, [Foreman] had won adulation by mauling people in a boxing ring; now that he had lost for the first time, he lived with a quiet terror. He couldn't stop spending money or conquering women. . . . He was flailing at love and acceptance the same way he did at Ali, thinking he could win them by exertion of muscle and might." Foreman does not like to dwell on those years now. He admits his life was completely out of control. "After I'd lost to Ali," he said, "I'd decided I needed more hate. I'd hit you in the kidneys or on the back of the head. I'd beat women as hard as I beat men. You psyche yourself to become an animal to box, and that's what you become. A lion sleeps 75 percent of the day, the rest he eats and breeds—just like a boxer."

An unexpected loss marked a milestone

Surrounded by false friends and the useless trappings of a lavish lifestyle (including a lion, a tiger, a $21,000 German shepherd, and a half dozen luxury cars), Foreman more or less made a spectacle of himself. On March 17, 1977, he climbed into the ring in San Juan, Puerto Rico, for a match with lightly-regarded Jimmy Young. For Foreman the fight was no more than a tune-up match for a return against Ali, but he lost a twelve-round decision to Young. That fight marked a true milestone in Foreman's career. After returning to the dressing room, Foreman became ill and began to be obsessed with

death. He told *Sports Illustrated* that he found himself plunged "into a deep, dark nothing, like out in a sea, with nothing over your head or under your feet. Nothing but nothing. A big dark lump of it. And a horrible smell came with it. A smell I haven't forgotten. A smell of sorrow. . . . And then I looked around and I was dead. That was it. I thought of everything I worked for. I hadn't said goodbye to my mother, my children. All the money I hid in safe-deposit boxes! You know how paper burns and when you touch it, it just crumbles. That was my life. I looked back and saw it crumble, like I'd fallen for a big joke."

Foreman began babbling in his terror and was taken to the hospital. On the way, he said, he felt the saving grace of God restoring him to life. "I said, I don't think this is death," he remembered. "I still believe in God. And I said that and I was back alive. . . . I could feel the blood flowing through my veins. For a moment, I felt I was somebody."

Foreman became a zealous Christian. He quit the ring and began a new career, preaching on Houston street

Foreman (right) en route to a second-round knockout of Gerry Cooney in 1990.

corners and in fundamentalist churches. Eventually he opened his own church, the Church of the Lord Jesus Christ, in a mobile home. There he ministered to a small flock, trying to avoid the limelight as much as possible.

Even though he had found Jesus Christ, Foreman still had not taken a firm grasp of his life. Within a space of two years—1981 to 1983—he was married and divorced three times. One of his wives fled to Barbados with the couple's two children, and he flew there and literally stole them back. That experience forced him to face yet more unsavory facts about his life. Foreman told *Sports Illustrated:* "We're all like blind men on a corner—we got to learn to trust people, or we'll never cross the street. I've come to find out love is allowing yourself to be weak and vulnerable and hurt. I used to think that was weakness, even after I'd become a preacher. All those women that were leaving me were just trying to get me to say 'I love you' like I really meant it, instead of just giving them things."

Between 1983 and 1986 Foreman seemed to have found peace at last. His small church and a gym he had built next to it filled his days. He remarried and fathered the last of three sons—all named George. Gradually, however, the expenditures for the church and gym began to erode what funds he had left from his boxing days. At the same time, some of his eight children were nearing college age. Foreman tried to raise money by serving as a guest minister, but he found that experience humiliating. At the age of forty, he decided to return to the career that has proven so lucrative for him in his twenties—boxing.

Immediately he faced yet another challenge. His love of fast food and home cooking had sustained him through the 1980s, but it had also caused his weight to balloon. He estimates that on his first day back in training he weighed nearly 315 pounds. As reporters scoffed, he announced his intentions to fight and began to work out vigorously, eventually bringing his weight down to 267. Few in the boxing establishment praised Foreman for his comeback, especially when he began to book "easy" fights against no-name opposition. NBC boxing commentator Ferdie Pacheco told *Sports Illustrated:* "This is pathetic. It shouldn't be allowed. He's overage, inept. This whole thing is a fraudulent second career to build a money fight with [Mike] Tyson."

Indeed, Foreman did have his eye on "Iron Mike"

Tyson, then the heavyweight champion. "Tyson was 10 years old the last time I had a match," Foreman said in the *Boston Globe.* "I'm fighting guys he just fought and beating them. It still only takes me one punch. Whump. The power is still there." Foreman proved that power to a certain extent by turning in 20 victories, 19 by knockout, between 1986 and 1990. In January of 1990 he met former contender Gerry Cooney in Atlantic City (a match locally known as "The Geezers at Caesars"), knocking him senseless in the second round. Despite his constant battles with weight and the slower reflexes of age, Foreman finally signed for a title match, not against Tyson but against 28-year-old Evander Holyfield. That bout, which took place in April of 1991, ended in defeat for Foreman, although he was not easily beaten—the fight went twelve rounds.

With the strikes of age and weight against him, it is unlikely that Foreman will ever win another championship belt. By boxing standards, he is absolutely ancient—the best talent can easily dance circles around him. On the other hand, he has accomplished the task he set for himself. The money he has earned since making his comeback has enabled him to build a spacious new athletic center for underprivileged youngsters in Houston. He plans to spend the rest of an active life there, training others in the sport that had provided him with so many ups and downs. "I think it's a crime for a man who's made as much as me to ask for donations," he told *Sports Illustrated.* "I want kids with murder on their faces. I'll trick 'em with boxing and sports to get them straightened out and going to school." Reflecting on his unlikely return to boxing prominence, Foreman told the *Boston Globe:* "The second time around is for fun. We've already been through the serious stuff. After you've been the heavyweight champion, you got nothing to prove."

Sources

Boston Globe, March 11, 1987.
Philadelphia Inquirer, September 17, 1989, September 23, 1990.
Sports Illustrated, October 8, 1984, July 17, 1989, January 29, 1990.
Time, July 24, 1989.
Washington Post, January 12, 1990, January 17, 1990.

—Mark Kram

Grant Fuhr

1962—

Professional hockey player

The Edmonton Oilers dominated the National Hockey League throughout the 1980s in no small part due to the goaltending talents of Grant Fuhr. Fuhr was an indispensable component of a team that won five Stanley Cups in seven years, a sometimes brilliant defender who was particularly effective in playoff games. In 1988 Ralph Wiley called Fuhr—who was then 25—"the best goalie in the NHL. The best on earth."

playing professional football. Grant Fuhr was no exception to this rule. At the age of seven he announced that he was going to become a goaltender in the NHL, and he made good on his promise. Fuhr was born in Edmonton in the autumn of 1962 to teenage parents who gave him up for adoption. Even though he considers himself black—or at least of mixed race—he was placed with a white family. Initially his adoptive parents were reluctant to accept him, fearing that they would not be able to instill in him a sense of racial pride. They found that most people accepted their unorthodox family, however, and they were able to deal honestly with their son and his concerns. "We were always honest with Grant," Betty Fuhr told *Sports Illustrated.* "We asked him to be fair in his judgments, to not judge a person—or himself—on social or economic standing, but on their honesty and integrity."

Fuhr is now almost 30, and his once stellar reputation has been tarnished by injuries and the admission of substance abuse. Suspended from the Oilers in 1990 for drug use that occurred during the team's glory years, Fuhr is struggling to regain his place in the league and to remain drug-free (he has not tested positive for cocaine or other drugs for several years). Reflecting on the negative headlines he earned after so much success, Fuhr told *Sports Illustrated:* "I was living life to have some fun. I wasn't worrying about the responsibilities that go along with life. I was just young."

Hockey is nothing less than an obsession for many Canadians. Children learn to skate at an early age and dream of the NHL the way American boys dream of

Fuhr's father was an insurance salesman who was fond of both golf and hockey. He allowed his son to turn the family basement into a makeshift rink and bought the boy a pair of skates when he was four. Grant skated constantly, developing coordination far beyond the norm for one of his tender age. In school he excelled at other sports as well, but hockey remained his favorite. In 1979, when he was 16, he turned down a chance to play catcher with the Pittsburgh Pirates' baseball farm team because "hockey was in." Needless to say, this fascination with sports left little time for formal studies. Fuhr dropped out of high school at 16 and joined the Victoria Cougars of Canada's Western Hockey League. Wiley described the young athlete as "5 ft. 9 in., with strong legs, good eyes, and hands that defied description. He was . . . different."

Fuhr was also black, and he was attempting to make the majors in a sport that is still almost exclusively white. Bob White, a coach in Montreal, told *Sports Illustrated* that Fuhr might have been steered away from hockey had he grown up in eastern Canada. "If Fuhr had been born in Quebec, he might not have made it to the NHL," White said. "You can be recruited with a mask on, like Grant Fuhr. He was lucky he was out west. . . . And it's good he wears the mask." If this harsh judgment speaks to inherent racism in hockey's ranks, it also speaks to Fuhr's outstanding ability, mask or no mask. As a teenager, Fuhr showed such obvious potential that he was made a member of the Edmonton Oilers as a number one draft choice before his eighteenth birthday.

Ron Low, a former Oiler, remembered Fuhr's early years in a *Sports Illustrated* feature. "Grant never played in the minors," Low said. "We all knew he was great from the first day of camp. A natural. Yet he had no style. Or, rather, his style was all styles. He would come out 15 feet to challenge the shot on one offensive rush. The next time he would be back in his crease. He could read the game so well. He anticipated the game. Grant was just . . . different. Different from anyone I'd ever seen." Fuhr honed his skills by practicing against his high-scoring teammates such as Wayne Gretzky and Mark Messier, as formidable a pair of offensive players as can be found

anywhere. Quickly Fuhr improved his reflexes and grasped every nuance of the game, becoming expert at both instinctive plays and strategic moves.

Fuhr helped the Oilers to advance to the playoffs in his rookie season as well as his sophomore year. By 1984 the seeds of the dominant Oilers team had been sown. In that Stanley Cup season, Fuhr turned in ten playoff wins. The following season he stunned the league by earning 15 playoff victories as the Oilers won another Cup. In the 1985-86 season the team once again advanced to the playoffs, and Fuhr stood in the goal even though he had spent several sleepless nights by his adoptive father's deathbed. When Edmonton contended for the Stanley Cup again in the spring of 1987, Fuhr had an astounding goals-against average of 2.46 through nineteen games. He was universally feared as a cool hand in the game's most stressful position and was considered nearly unbeatable in the clutch. Barry Pederson of the Vancouver Canucks summed up the exceptional talents of Grant Fuhr in *Sports Illustrated*. "Bar none, Grant Fuhr is the best goalie in the league," Pederson said. "He has the fastest reflexes. Sometimes his concentration might drift during inconsequential games. But in the big-money games Fuhr is the best. He's the Cup goalie. It's sure not by luck."

A five-time All-Star, Fuhr was chosen to be the starting goalie in the 1987 Canada Cup games against the Soviet Union's national team. Although Team Canada's roster also featured star goalies Kelly Hrudey of the New York Islanders and Ron Hextall of the Philadelphia Flyers, Fuhr started all three games and helped the Canadians to beat the Soviets for the Cup. Wiley called Fuhr's performance in that series "breathtakingly effective." Fuhr then turned in yet another stellar season with Edmonton in 1988, earning the Vezina Trophy as the league's best goaltender.

With such success to his credit, Fuhr was allowed to go his own way off the ice with little supervision. Perhaps not surprisingly, he ran into trouble, financial and otherwise. In the early years of his contract, Fuhr's salary was extremely modest by the standards of professional sports. He paid little attention as his extravagant ways led him into debt. In retrospect, Fuhr told *Sports Illustrated* that he was "a kid who did some dumb things." He added, for instance: "When my clothes were dirty, I just threw them in the closet and went out and bought something else." Fuhr now admits that overspending was only one of his problems. He fell in with a fast crowd and began to use cocaine—not to the point of addiction, but certainly to the point that it added to his financial woes.

In 1990 Fuhr came forward about his drug use after spending two weeks in a counseling center in Florida. He admitted that he used "a substance"—he did not say cocaine—for some seven years, or most of the period that the Oilers rested at the top of the NHL. Details of Fuhr's drug use were supplied by the player's ex-wife, Corrine, who told the press in Edmonton that she often found cocaine hidden in Fuhr's clothing and that she fielded numerous threatening telephone calls from drug dealers who had not been paid. These embarrassing details no doubt added to the severity of Fuhr's one-year suspension from the National Hockey League. The suspension was handed down in September of 1990 by NHL president John Ziegler, who called Fuhr's conduct "dishonorable and against the welfare of the league."

Many observers felt that the year-long suspension was too harsh. Fuhr had, after all, acknowledged the problem and had sought treatment for it. He had also tested free of drugs for a year before the suspension even began. Taking these factors into consideration, the NHL reinstated Fuhr in Februrary of 1991. However, age will inevitably become a factor in Fuhr's play as he tops thirty, but his worst enemy is injury. After years of recurring tendonitis in his left shoulder, he has undergone surgery and has had the joint pinned. He will also rejoin a team that has lost Wayne Gretzky and must therefore work twice as hard to retain its luster.

These difficulties do not seem insurmountable to Grant Fuhr. Now remarried, he is taking each day in stride and is even planning for his future beyond professional hockey. "Life is going to happen," he told *Sports Illustrated.* "That's a goalie's philosophy." The former Vezina Trophy winner said that nothing—not bad publicity, not race, and especially not public opinion—will shake his confidence in himself and his game. "You're an individual," he said, "and you should be accepted as such. Some people don't like to do that, so they might have a problem. Well, it doesn't bother me. If it doesn't bother me, then it shouldn't bother anybody else. See, I know that I'm not dumb, or anything else anybody says I am. And as long as I know that, I have no problem."

Sources

Los Angeles Times, September 1, 1990, September 28, 1990.

San Francisco Chronicle, May 21, 1990.

Sports Illustrated, January 11, 1988, September 10, 1990.

—Mark Kram

Harvey Gantt

1943—

Architect, politician

In June of 1990, Harvey Gantt was chosen the North Carolina Democratic Party's candidate for the U.S. Senate, earning the right to challenge the state's Republican incumbent. The Democrat/Republican match-up in this statewide election soon gained nationwide attention. For, not only was Gantt attempting to become the South's first black senator since Reconstruction, he was also attempting to unseat the voice of conservative morality in the Senate, Jesse Helms.

Gantt's liberal campaign, which stressed increased funding for social programs, decreased funding for defense, opposition to the death penalty, support for abortion rights, as well as tolerance of free expression and alternative lifestyles, drew backing from prominent blacks such as Bill Cosby and from groups adversely affected by Helms's legislative record—artists, feminists, homosexuals, and civil libertarians. Political polls found the race close throughout most of the campaign season, but in the end, Gantt received just 47 percent of the vote and Helms returned to office for his third term.

Gantt had hoped to add his name to that of Edward W.

Brooke of Massachusetts, the first African-American since Reconstruction to serve in the U.S. Senate (from 1967 to 1979). He began campaigning in April 1990 against three other Democratic hopefuls and won the right to face Michael F. Easley in a runoff by earning 38 percent of the vote in the May primary. He secured the Democratic candidacy with a strong showing in the June 5 runoff, polling 58 percent of the vote.

Once chosen to represent the Democrats, Gantt offered himself to the people of North Carolina as the candidate for the New South and characterized Helms as the representative of the Old South. He criticized Helms's record on education and the environment; he also took issue with the Republican incumbent's efforts to control the National Endowment for the Arts. He told Joseph Papp of *Interview:* "As for Helms and the NEA, I believe that people ought to be allowed to pursue their dreams in this country—more than any other place—without fear of persecution. I just don't feel that Helms has the moral authority, given his own history, to begin to tell us what is right and wrong."

At first Helms, who was occupied in Washington with

At a Glance. . .

Full name, Harvey Bernard Gantt; born January 14, 1943, In Charleston, SC; son of Christopher Columbus Gantt (a shipyard worker) and Wilhelmenia Gantt; married, wife's name, Cindy; children: Sonja, Erika, Angela, Adam. *Education:* Attended Iowa State University, 1961-62; Clemson University, B.Arch., 1965; Massachusetts Institute of Technology, M.A., 1970. *Politics:* Democrat. *Religion:* Baptist.

Architect with large firms in Charlotte, N.C., 1965-70; planner for Soul City, N.C., experimental community, 1970-71; Gantt-Huberman architectural firm, Charlotte, partner, 1971—; City of Charlotte, member of city council, 1974-79, council member and mayor pro tem, 1981-83, mayor, 1983-87; Democratic candidate for U.S. Senate from North Carolina, 1990. Lecturer at the University of North Carolina at Chapel Hill, 1970-72; visiting critic at Clemson University, 1972-73. Gantt has served on the U.S. Council of Mayors, as an uncommitted delegate to the 1984 Democratic Convention, and on the Democratic National Committee. Speaker to numerous organizations in the United States and abroad.

Awards: Citizen of the year, Charlotte NAACP, 1975 and 1984. Has received honorary degrees from Belmont Abbey College, Johnson C. Smith University, and Clemson University.

Addresses: *Home*—517 North Poplar St., Charlotte, N.C. 28202.

budget hearings, simply criticized Gantt for his stand on the issues, calling him a liberal out of step with the people of North Carolina. But, as election day grew closer and the polls continued to show Gantt even, or in some cases ahead of Helms, the campaign rhetoric heated up. Helms's campaign ads began to accuse Gantt of unfairly profiting from a federal program that sold television stations to minorities and of supporting racial quotas in hiring practices. Gantt was able to respond to these and other attacks, but he was not able to counter the effect they had on some undecided voters.

Complicating the battle between the candidates was a controversy involving the two political parties. The

Democrats claimed that the 150,000 post cards explaining voting regulations sent by the Republican Party to North Carolina voters were targeted at blacks in an attempt to frighten them away from the polls. The Republicans countered that the Democrats were trying to stir up a voter backlash against Helms. In the end, the contest between liberal and conservative issues became a contest about race and negative campaigning. Gantt polled 47 percent of the overall vote, and 54 percent of the under-30 vote, but he received only 35 percent of the white vote.

Harvey Bernard Gantt was born January 14, 1943, in Charleston, South Carolina, the historic Southern port city overlooking Fort Sumter where the Civil War had begun just over 80 years before. By the time Gantt was born, Charleston, like most of the South, had swung from slavery to Reconstruction, then back to segregation. As a teenager, Gantt took part in sit-ins to desegregate Charleston lunch counters and he graduated from all-black Burke High School.

Career as Architect

Wanting to pursue his ambition to become an architect, he chose to leave the segregated South for the Midwest, attending Iowa State University in 1961 and 1962. But, the young Southerner disliked Iowa's harsh winters and he decided to return to South Carolina to complete his degree. To do so, however, he had to break the color barrier in the state's educational institutions. After a lengthy court case, Gantt became Clemson University's first black student in 1963. Two years later he graduated third in his architecture class.

Gantt chose to pursue his new career in Charlotte, North Carolina's largest city, and along with Atlanta one of the New South's emerging centers. During the five years from 1965 to 1970, he worked as an architect for large firms in the city and also completed a master's degree in urban planning at the Massachusetts Institute of Technology. In 1970 and 1971, Gantt worked with civil rights activist Floyd B. McKissick as a planner for Soul City, North Carolina, an experimental community planned for a rural site north of Durham. After leaving the Soul City project, he returned to Charlotte to launch his own architectural firm along with Jeffrey Huberman. Since 1971, the firm has handled numerous building projects in and around the city.

The young architect's political career began in 1974 when he was appointed to the Charlotte City Council to fill the seat vacated by Fred Alexander, the council's only black member. Once on the council, Gantt urged the city leaders to reform the method of electing council members in order to give a greater voice to minority voters. Under the reform, instead of having citywide contests for every seat, some were set aside for election by district. In his term as an appointed member of council, Gantt earned enough support from city voters to be elected to one of the city-wide seats in 1975. In 1979, his service was interrupted when he lost in a bid to become the Democratic candidate for mayor of Charlotte. He regained his city-wide council seat in the 1981 election.

Elected Mayor of Charlotte

Two years later, having been chosen the Democratic candidate for mayor, Gantt was elected Charlotte's mayor. He was the city's first black mayor, having won 52 percent of the overall vote and 36 percent of the white vote. It was a historic event for this Southern metropolis, but Gantt and his white opponent had both avoided raising the issue of race, and Gantt had refused to enlist the support of national black leaders. The city had, in Gantt's view, shown the spirit of the New South. He was quoted by Ron Martz in the *Atlanta Journal:* "It is sensing that spirit that led me to dream and believe that I could run for the city's highest office and expect to be judged by my character, my competence and my understanding of the critical issues and nothing more."

In his two terms, Gantt faced the problems common to the mayor of a city experiencing growing pains. He struggled to raise the revenue necessary to pay for $200 million worth of road projects not funded by the state while at the same time easing property taxes. His tax plans drew criticism from some on the city council. He worked to improve the city's relationship with surrounding Mecklenburg County, to find summer jobs for area youth, to preserve neighborhoods, and to renew the city center. Even so, his black constituents complained that there was not enough attention paid to their issues.

To maintain the city's economic growth, he lobbied at home and abroad to lure industry and investment. He was also involved in securing a National Basketball Association franchise, the Charlotte Hornets, for the city. But he battled the council over the location of the team's coliseum. Gantt's Republican opponent in the 1987

election, Suellen Myrick, focused on two of the city's growing pains—traffic and taxes—and surprised the incumbent, beating him by approximately one thousand votes.

Senate Campaign

Gantt rebounded from this defeat to make a strong showing in his 1990 campaign for the U.S. Senate. Although he lost, in the process he gained attention and respect, both in North Carolina and across the nation. His name has been raised in connection with future campaigns for senator or governor. He is well regarded within the Democratic Party and may again be tapped to serve on the national committee to help plan its presidential bid for 1992.

Although some analysts have characterized Gantt as a public servant who lacks the hard edge of a politician, he maintains that he shares the motivation of all who work in politics. He once told J. A. C. Dunn of the *Winston-Salem Journal,* "I like [politics] for all the things that normal human beings like—the power, the potential . . . to do some good. Politics, it immediately became clear to me, was the one way to do things easier, to be at the table, to stir the soup a little bit yourself."

Sources

Atlanta Journal, January 29, 1984.
Charlotte Observer, July 12, 1984; August 12, 1984; April 3, 1985; November 4, 1987; October 14, 1990.
Columbia State, October 31, 1990.
Interview, October 1990.
Newsweek, November 19, 1990.
New York Times, May 8, 1990; June 7, 1990; October 13, 1990; November 1, 1990; November 2, 1990, November 7, 1990; November 8, 1990.
Raleigh News and Observer, September 2, 1990.
Time, November 19, 1990.
Winston-Salem Journal, July 19, 1987.

—Bryan Ryan

Marcus Garvey

1887-1940

Political leader

Marcus Garvey was one of the twentieth century's most influential leaders of black nationalism. In establishing the United Negro Improvement Association (UNIA), Garvey hoped to build—through enterprise and mass education—a unified nation of people of African blood. A powerful orator, organizer, and writer, Garvey recruited nearly one million UNIA members worldwide. In 1919 he charted the Black Star Shipping Line (B.S.L.), which promoted black crosscontinental trade. Under his red, black, and green banner of Pan-Africanism—a commitment to the solidarity of all black peoples—Garvey encouraged the worship of a black deity and the study of black history. Devoted to the separation of the black and white races, a position that he believed was vital to racial prosperity and cultural development, Garvey warned black workers to avoid the possible manipulation of white trade unions and Communist organizations. Although his success was short-lived, Garvey continues to symbolize racial pride and destiny for blacks around the world.

Born in St. Ann's Bay, Jamaica, in August of 1887, Garvey was the youngest of 11 children. A bright student, he acquired a passion for books at an early age.

Family financial problems led to his apprenticeship in the printing trade, where he developed journalist skills. In 1907, participation in a failed printer's strike influenced Garvey to enter politics. Roughly four years later he joined the mass migration of Jamaicans seeking employment in Central and South America. In Costa Rica he contributed to publications that presented the oppressive conditions of black workers. While abroad, Garvey's futile attempts to gain British colonial protection for West Indians promoted his growing racial awareness.

Returning to Jamaica in 1912, Garvey realized that the island offered little opportunity for a young black politician. Traveling to London that same year, he met with black laborers, intellectuals, and businessmen whose descriptions of the injustices suffered under European colonial rule contributed to his gradual path toward racial militancy. The most influential of these acquaintances was a Sudanese-Egyptian actor, journalist, and nationalist named Duse Mohammed Ali. Working for Ali's publication *African Times and Oriental Review* exposed Garvey to the role of African business and the triumphs of Africa's ancestral past. While in London he read Booker

At a Glance. . .

Born Marcus Moziah Garvey, August 17, 1887; died from complications of a stroke, June, 1940; son of Sarah Jane Richards and Marcus Garvey, Sr.; married Amy Ashwood (playwright and lecturer), December, 1919 (divorced, 1921); married Amy Jaques (editor), July, 1922.

T. Washington's autobiography *Up From Slavery.* The book's vivid account of racial conditions in America inspired the young Jamaican to become a "race leader."

On the voyage back to his homeland in 1914, Garvey conceived of the plan to create the UNIA and its coordinating body, the African Communities League. On August l, with the assistance of a few colleagues, he officially launched his organization. Adopting the motto "One God! One Aim! One Destiny!," the UNIA offered opportunity to all blacks. The organization's plan of African redemption centered upon the establishment of black educational institutions. Following Booker T. Washington's Tuskegee model, Garvey sought to build Jamaican trade schools that would provide missionaries for "Mother Africa." Black middle-class Jamaicans, however, remained indifferent to his vision. In need of funds and support, Garvey wrote to Washington, who in turn invited him to come to America. Tragically, Washington died in 1915, before the two could meet.

Success in New York City Prompted A Move

The following year Garvey arrived—at the age of 28— in New York City. Penniless and unknown, he struggled to raise support for his Jamaican educational program. At first, residents of New York City's Harlem were unresponsive to his speeches. Garvey became aware that to gain black support in the U.S. he would have to alter his Jamaican strategy; while his previous orientation had been strictly reformist, Garvey's outlook in America became increasingly revolutionary. He endorsed a broad economic plan for private business and industry. By the end of World War I in 1918, black migration, racial violence, and continuing segregation had provided a climate that vastly benefitted the expansion of Garveyism. The UNIA's economic strategy and publication, *Negro World,* attracted thousands of new proponents. Rapid success encouraged Garvey to move his base of operations from Jamaica to New York.

On August l, 1920, the first UNIA convention opened with a parade that stretched for miles along Lenox avenue in Harlem. That evening, before a crowd of 25,000 in Madison Square Garden, Garvey boldly announced his plan to build an African nation-state. Sympathizing with the plight of Irish Home Rule and Jewish Zionism advocates, he called upon blacks to seek their own "place in the sun." The highlight of the weeklong convention was the adoption of the Declaration of the Rights of the Negro Peoples of the World. Containing a bill of rights, the document proclaimed the equality of the black race and included resolutions for the creation of independent legal and educational systems.

Around the time of the convention, Garvey organized several business enterprises. These included the Negro Factories Corporation, a restaurant, a millinery, a publishing house, and a chain of cooperative grocery stores. But most importantly, he attempted to create a maritime fleet that he hoped would give blacks political power and bring them to the forefront of worldwide trade. Selling shares of five-dollar stock through the mail enabled him to acquire enough capital to purchase three ships for the Black Star Shipping Line. The shipping company contributed to Garvey's growing prominence as an international champion of Pan-Africanism. Consequently, he introduced a plan to transfer his organization's headquarters to Monrovia, Liberia.

Some Blacks Rejected Separatist Ideals

Despite his emerging popularity, Garvey received widespread opposition among both black and white political, labor, and religious organizations. During the postwar era, a growing fear of Socialist and Communist conspiracies led many to view Garvey's movement as a harbinger of radical black power. In 1919 Garvey was summoned by the U.S. State Department regarding the legality of the B.S.L. operation. Although the investigation failed to produce any evidence against Garvey, the State Department pursued a plan for his eventual deportation.

Harshest resistance arose among black leaders, including Socialist Labor Party spokesman A. Philip Randolph and the African Blood Brotherhood's Cyril V. Briggs. After 1920 Garvey suffered continual attacks from the Negro publications *Chicago Defender* and *Crisis,* the journal of the National Association for the Advancement of Colored People (NAACP). W.E.B. DuBois, cofounder of the NAACP, was one of the leading adherents to the mounting "Garvey Must Go" campaign. Although he was a black nationalist and Pan-Africanist, DuBois rejected Garvey's segregationist and economic policies. As a result, the two became embroiled in bitter dispute over black progress and African liberation.

In the years following the first UNIA convention, the organization began to decline. After a trip to Central America in 1921 Garvey was denied a visa by the State Department, thereby delaying his reentry into the United States for several months. A year later, federal officials convicted Garvey of mail fraud. Released on bail, he tried to rescue the failing B.S.L. from collapse. Due to the poor condition and exorbitant operating costs of the company's vessels, however, the B.S.L. was forced into insolvency. During the same year, Garvey's meeting with the acting Imperial Wizard of the Ku Klux Klan (KKK) greatly contributed to his faltering status. His statements that the UNIA and the KKK shared a similar policy of racial separation spread outrage throughout the black community. Garvey's demand for a unified African Orthodox church left him almost entirely alienated from conventional black religious denominations.

Charges of Mail Fraud Led to Incarceration

In 1923 the murder of former UNIA member Reverend James Eason generated further controversy. Eason's death motivated eight of Garvey's enemies to send an incriminating letter to Attorney General Harry Dougherty. The correspondence hastened the State Department's decision to bring Garvey to trial. With Garvey acting as his own defense, the hearing became a forum for his racial beliefs. Unable to adequately defend against the charge of mail fraud, he was incarcerated; six months later he was released on $25,000 bail. In 1924 he attempted to establish a second commercial fleet—the Black Cross Navigation and Trading Company—but facing a shortage of funds, the business soon folded. UNIA efforts to found an independent Liberian republic also proved unsuccessful. In 1925, despite an appeal to the Supreme Court, Garvey was sent to the Atlanta penitentiary. After serving two years, federal authorities ordered his release and immediate deportation.

Upon his return to Jamaica in 1927 Garvey entered local politics. Struggling to form the People's Political Party, he developed a program of national economic, agricultural, labor, and political reform. Although the UNIA's 1929 convention in Kingston, Jamaica, recaptured some of the splendor and enthusiasm of its earlier Harlem era, the organization never again amassed a substantial membership. Under a new charter, Garvey returned the UNIA headquarters to Jamaica, causing widespread fragmentation and desertion among branches in the United States. In 1935, confronted with ensuing political defeat and financial problems, Garvey took up permanent residence in London. But in England his racial program and political aspirations were met with indifference. From 1936 to 1938 Garvey attended conventions in Toronto, Canada, where he set up the School of African Philoso-

phy. After a long period of failing health, he suffered a stroke in 1940 that led to his death in June of that year.

Regarded as Pioneer of Black Pride

Despite limited success in his lifetime, Garvey has become an international symbol of black freedom. The Reverend Martin Luther King, Jr., called him "the first man, on a mass scale to give millions of Negroes a sense of dignity and destiny." During its heyday the UNIA claimed as members Black Muslim leader Elijah Mohammed and the father of Malcolm X. In 1964 the Jamaican government proclaimed Garvey a national hero. His legacy served as an integral force in the "Black is Beautiful" consciousness of the 1960's. More recently, Garvey has become an inspirational figure within the Jamaican

> At first, residents of New York City's Harlem were unresponsive to his speeches. Garvey became aware that to gain black support in the U.S. he would have to alter his Jamaican strategy; while his previous orientation had been strictly reformist, Garvey's outlook in America became increasingly revolutionary.

Rastafarian religious movement. Indebted to the perseverance and dedication of Garvey's Pan-African struggle, Malcolm X wrote, "Each time you see another independent nation on the African continent you know Marcus Garvey is alive."

Sources

Books

Black Leaders of the Twentieth Century, edited by John Hope Franklin and August Meir, University of Illinois Press, 1982.

Clarke, John Henry, with Amy Jaques Garvey, *Marcus Garvey and the Vision of Africa,* Random House, 1974.

Cronon, Edmund David, *Black Moses: The Story of Marcus Garvey and the Universal Improvement Association,* foreword by John Hope Franklin, University of Wisconsin Press, 1955.

Garvey, Amy Jaques, *Garvey and Garveyism,* United Printers Ltd., 1963.

The Marcus Garvey and Universal Negro Improvement Association Papers, edited by Robert Hill, University of California Press, 1983.

Irvin, Jeannette Smith, *Marcus Garvey's Footsoldiers,* African World Press, Inc., 1988.

Lewis, Rupert, *Marcus Garvey: Anti-Colonial Champion,* African World Press, Inc., 1988.

Philosophy and Opinions of Marcus Garvey; or, Africa for Africans, compiled by Amy Jaques Garvey, second edition, Frank Case and Co., Ltd., 1967.

Stein, Judith, *The World of Marcus Garvey: Race and Class in Modern Society,* Louisiana State University Press, 1986.

Vincent, Theodore G., *Black Power and the Garvey Movement,* Ramparts, 1971.

Periodicals

Crisis, May 1924.
Ebony, November 1926.
Journal of Negro History, January 1951.
Journal of Southern History, May 1988.
New York Times, February 1922.
Time, August 1924.

—John Cohassey

Dizzy Gillespie

1917—

Trumpeter, composer, bandleader

In 1989, the year he became 72 years of age, Dizzy Gillespie received a Lifetime Achievement Award at the National Association of Recording Arts and Sciences' Grammy Award ceremonies. The honor—one of many bestowed on the trumpet virtuoso—recognized nearly 50 years of pioneering jazz performances. That same year he received the National Medal of Arts from President George Bush "for his trail-blazing work as a musician who helped elevate jazz to an art form of the first rank, and for sharing his gift with listeners around the world."

Not letting age slow him down, Gillespie in 1989 gave 300 performances in 27 countries, appeared in 100 U.S. cities in 31 states and the District of Columbia, headlined three television specials, performed with two symphonies, and recorded four albums. He was also crowned a traditional chief in Nigeria, named Commandeur d'Ordre des Artes et Lettres—France's most prestigious cultural award—was named regent professor by the University of California, and received his fourteenth honorary doctoral degree, this one from the Berklee College of Music. The next year, at the Kennedy Center for the Performing Arts ceremonies celebrating the centennial of American jazz, Gillespie received the American Society of Composers, Authors, and Publishers' Duke Award for 50 years of achievement as a composer, performer, and bandleader.

Fifty years after helping found a new style of progressive jazz that came to be known as bebop, Dizzy Gillespie is still contributing all he can to the development of modern jazz. His band is a virtual training ground for younger musicians. In 1990 he led and wrote the arrangements for a group that included bassist John Lee, guitarist Ed Cherry, drummer Ignacio Berroa, conga drummer Paul Hawkins, and saxophonist Ron Holloway. More than 40 years earlier Gillespie was the first bandleader to use a conga player. Employing Latin rhythms and forging an Afro-Cuban style of polyrhythmic music was one of Gillespie's many contributions to the development of modern jazz.

As a trumpet virtuoso Gillespie stands firmly as a major influence in the development of the jazz trumpet. Before Gillespie there was New Orleans musician Buddy Bolden—the earliest known jazz cornetist—who was followed by King Oliver, Louis Armstrong, and Roy Eldridge. In his memoir, *To Be Or Not To Bop,* Gillespie described the

At a Glance. . .

Real name, John Birks Gillespie; born October 21, 1917, to James (a bricklayer and musician) and Lottie Gillespie; youngest of nine children; raised in Cheraw, SC; married Lorraine Willis (a dancer), 1940. *Education:* Attended Laurinburg Institute.

Moved to New York City in 1937 and began playing trumpet in jam sessions with various musicians; played with the Teddy Hill Orchestra, beginning in 1937, and the Cab Calloway Orchestra, 1939-41; made first recording in 1939 with Lionel Hampton; joined Earl "Fatha" Hines band, 1942; with Sarah Vaughan, Charlie Parker, and others, formed new group headed by Billy Eckstein, 1943; also played for other bands, including the Duke Ellington Orchestra, c. 1943; formed quintet, 1944; has played in, led, and composed for numerous big bands, orchestras, and small groups throughout the world.

Awards: New Star Award from *Esquire* magazine, 1944; Lifetime Achievement Award from the National Association of Recording Arts and Sciences, 1989; National Medal of Arts from President George Bush, 1989; Commadre d'Ordre des Artes et Lettres (France), 1989; Duke Award from the American Society of Composers, Authors, and Publishers, 1989; and numerous other awards and honors, including several honorary degrees.

Addresses: *Home*—Camden, NJ.

influence of Armstrong and Eldridge on his trumpet playing: "Roy Eldridge was a French-style trumpet player. Eldridge was in a direct line from Louis Armstrong, and he was the voice of that era, the thirties. I hardly ever listened to Louis, but was always aware of where Roy's inspiration came from. So I was looking at Louis Armstrong, you see, because they are one and the same. My inspiration came through Roy Eldridge, from Louis Armstrong and King Oliver and Buddy Bolden. That's the way it happened."

The Legend Gets His Name

Gillespie played with bands in Philadelphia from 1935 to

1937 before moving to New York. In Philadelphia, where his family had moved from Cheraw, South Carolina, Gillespie learned Eldridge's trumpet solos from fellow trumpeter Charlie Shavers. It was then that Gillespie earned his nickname for his erratic and mischievous behavior. When Gillespie was in the Frankie Fairfax band in Philadelphia he carried his new trumpet in a paper bag; that inspired fellow musicians like Bill Doggett to call him "Dizzy." While Gillespie himself acknowledges the paper bag incident, he says the nickname didn't stick until later.

Gillespie's basic style of solo trumpet playing at that time involved "running them changes"—improvising on chord changes in a song and introducing new chord changes based on the song's melody. He had taught himself piano and used the instrument to experiment with new melodies and chord changes. When he went to New York in 1937 he did not have a specific job but was introduced to other musicians by Shavers. Gillespie joined in jam sessions, sometimes after hours at clubs in Harlem like Monroe's Uptown House and Dicky Wells's. He would also sit in with bands; while jamming one night with Chick Webb's band at the Savoy Ballroom, Gillespie met Mario Bauza, a Cuban trumpeter who introduced him to Latin rhythms.

Already a Musical Force at 19

Within a year Gillespie was hired by the Teddy Hill Orchestra for a European tour when the regular trumpet player didn't want to go. Hill probably liked Gillespie's style, which was similar at that time to Roy Eldridge's; Eldridge had left Hill's band to join Fletcher Henderson. By 1937—when he was only 19—Gillespie had already made a name for himself among New York musicians, who couldn't help but notice his radically fresh take on solo trumpet playing: he utilized the upper register of notes above high C, played with great speed, and used new rhythms and chord changes. Gillespie made his first recordings with the Teddy Hill Orchestra just prior to leaving for Europe on "The Cotton Club Show."

Gillespie joined the Cab Calloway Orchestra in 1939 and stayed until 1941. He wrote in his memoir, "It was the best job that you could possibly have, high class." Calloway played the Cotton Club and toured extensively. During this period Gillespie continued to play all-night jam sessions at Minton's and Monroe's Uptown House to develop his musical knowledge and style. In 1939 the most in-demand trumpet players for recording dates in New York were Eldridge, Shavers, and Buck Clayton. Gillespie was fourth on the list, but somehow managed to land a recording date with Lionel Hampton, which resulted in the famed "Hot Mallets" session. In this session

Gillespie became the first musician to record in the modern jazz style with a small group. Lionel Hampton said of the session, as quoted in Gillespie's book, "[Gillespie] came out with a new style, came out with a bebop style. He came out with a different style than we'd ever heard before. A lot of people don't know that was the creation of bebop, the beginning of bebop." Of course, it wasn't called bebop just yet.

Gillespie left Calloway in 1941 following a misunderstanding. During a performance someone from the vicinity of the trumpet section was having fun aiming spitballs at the bandleader, who was singing in front of the band at the time. Naturally Calloway assumed Gillespie was responsible. By most accounts, however, Gillespie was completely innocent and had been set up. Words led to action; Gillespie pulled a knife on Calloway and actually cut him a few times. While the two later reconciled and remained friends, Gillespie was forced to leave the band. This well-known incident illustrates the flip side of Gillespie's jovial personality; he often found himself in situations where he might need to defend himself and was fully prepared to do so.

Inspired by Charlie Parker

Gillespie joined the Earl "Fatha" Hines band in 1942, about the same time Charlie Parker did. Although Parker became famous as an alto saxophonist, he was playing tenor sax at that time. Gillespie first met Parker in Kansas City in 1940 when he was on tour with Cab Calloway. The two of them jammed together at the Booker T. Washington Hotel for several hours. Gillespie ventured in *To Be or Not to Bebop,* "I guess Charlie Parker and I had a meeting of the minds, because both of us inspired each other." They spent a lot of time together during their stint with the Hines band.

By the time he joined Hines, Gillespie had composed "A Night in Tunisia," one of his most famous songs. He was also writing arrangements for other bandleaders, including Hill, Calloway, Jimmy Dorsey, and Woody Herman.

Gillespie transcribes a phrase of his musical creation, Bebop, in 1947.

He wrote bebop arrangements, as most bandleaders at that time were interested in having one or two bebop numbers in their repertoires. Several musicians have commented that even if Gillespie had not been able to play the trumpet, he could have made a name for himself on the basis of his original compositions and arrangements. Other jazz standards credited in whole or in part to Gillespie include "Groovin' High," "Manteca," "Woody 'n You," "Con Alma," and "Salt Peanuts."

Bebop Born on 52nd Street

A large part of the Earl Hines band departed in 1943 to form a new group headed by Billy Eckstine. Former Hines members who joined Eckstine included Sarah Vaughan, Gillespie, Parker, and others. The band also featured saxophonists Gene Ammons and Dexter Gordon. Gillespie became musical director for Eckstine, whose backers got him a job on 52nd Street. Gillespie stayed with Eckstine for about seven months, touring and playing on 52nd Street. "The Street," as it was described by critic Pete Migdol in Gillespie's memoir, "was the hippest block with regard to its short distance and that amount of music. . . . This was the top talent street, and it was, of course, discoverer of a lot of the new people for that era."

After leaving Eckstine, Gillespie substituted in the Duke Ellington Orchestra for about four weeks, then formed his own group to play at the newly opened Onyx Club on 52nd Street. Gillespie had been playing bebop whenever he could since 1940, the year he married Lorraine Willis. Now he was able to play it full time. 52nd Street became the proving ground for a new jazz style that had previously been played primarily at late night jam sessions.

"The opening of the Onyx Club represented the birth of the bebop era," Gillespie recalled in his book. "In our long sojourn on 52nd Street we spread our message to a much wider audience." His first quintet at the Onyx Club in 1944 included Oscar Pettiford on bass, Max Roach on drums, George Wallington on piano, and Don Byas on tenor sax. Gillespie had tried to get Parker to join, but he had temporarily returned to Kansas City.

Quintet Revolutionized Jazz

That year Gillespie received the New Star Award from *Esquire* magazine, the first of many awards he would receive in his career. Describing the new style his quintet played, Gillespie wrote, "We'd take the chord structures of various standard and pop tunes and create new chords, melodies, and songs from them." For example,

Tadd Dameron's composition "Hothouse" was based on "What Is This Thing Called Love," and Parker's "Ornithology" came out of "How High The Moon." Gillespie also noted, "Our music had developed more into a type of music for listeners." There would be little dancing to bebop. Rhythm and phrasing, however, were also important to the new jazz style. "The most important thing about our music was, of course, the style, how you got from one note to another, how it was played. . . . We had a special way of phrasing. Not only did we change harmonic structure, but we also changed rhythmic structure."

Gillespie's quintet also played other clubs, including the Downbeat and the Three Deuces, where the group included Charlie Parker—by then on alto sax—and Bud Powell on piano. Gillespie also played for two months in Hollywood with Parker, vibraphonist Milt Jackson, bassist Ray Brown, pianist Al Haig, and drummer Stan Levy. This was the West Coast debut of bebop and it was very well received. In fact, it was around this time that the term "bebop" came into use. Gillespie recalled, "People, when they'd wanna ask for one of those numbers and didn't know the name, would ask for bebop. And the press picked it up and started calling it bebop. The first time the term bebop appeared in print was while we played at the Onyx Club."

1953 Triumph in Toronto

Gillespie's quintet and the presentation of modern jazz in that format reached its apex in 1953—with a concert at Massey Hall in Toronto that featured Gillespie, Parker, Powell, Roach, and legendary jazz bassist Charles Mingus. As Roach recalled in Gillespie's memoir, "The five people that Dizzy had originally thought about in the group at the Onyx didn't really materialize until we did Jazz at Massey Hall, that album, in 1953." Billed by jazz critics as "the greatest jazz concert ever," it was recorded by Mingus—a last-minute substitute for Pettiford—and later released on Debut Records.

From the big bands and orchestras that he first organized in the late 1940s, to the small combos of the early 1950s that served as incubators for young musicians like saxophone giant John Coltrane, Gillespie's influence consistently defined modern jazz. Though the enterprise was short-lived, Gillespie had his own record label, Dee Gee Records, from 1951-53. He appeared at the historic first Newport Jazz Festival in 1954. And he later played the role of unofficial ambassador of jazz, beginning with a 1956 world tour sponsored by the U.S. State Department. These are just a few of the many accomplishments highlighting the career of this remarkably accomplished titan of contemporary American music.

Selected writings

(With Al Fraser) *To Be or Not To Bop: Memoirs of Dizzy Gillespie,* Doubleday, 1979.

Selected discography

(With the Quintet) *Jazz at Massey Hall,* Fantasy/Debut, 1953.
Dizzier and Dizzier, RCA, 1954.
Groovin' High, Savoy, 1955.
The Champ, Savoy, 1956.
The Dizzy Gillespie Story, Savoy, 1957.
Concert in Paris, Roost, 1957.
Jazz From Paris, Verve, 1957.
Dizzy in Greece, Verve, 1957.
The Trumpet Kings, Verve, 1957.
For Musicians Only, Verve, 1958.
Manteca, Verve, 1958.
Birk's Works, Verve, 1958.
Dizzy Gillespie at Newport, Verve, 1958.
Dizzy Gillespie Duets, Verve, 1958.
Have Trumpet Will Excite, Verve, 1959.
The Ebullient Dizzy Gillespie, Verve, 1959.
The Greatest Trumpet of Them All, Verve, 1960.
Gillespiana, Verve, 1961.
An Electrifying Evening, Verve, 1962.
Carnegie Hall Concert, Verve, 1962.
Dizzy on the French Riviera, Philips, 1962.
New Wave, Philips, 1963.
Something Old, Something New, Philips, 1963.
Cool World, Philips, 1964.
The Essential Dizzy Gillespie, Verve, 1964.
Jambo Caribe, Limelight, 1964.
The New Continent, Limelight, 1965.
Montreux '77, Pablo, 1977.

Dee Gee Days, Savoy, 1985.
New Faces, GRP, 1985.
Oo Pop A Da, Affinity, 1985.
Dizzy Gillespie and His Sextets, Musicraft, 1986.
Dizzy Gillespie and His Orchestra, Musicraft, 1986.
Dizziest, RCA Bluebird, 1987.
Enduring Magic, Black Hawk, 1987.
Dizzy Gillespie and His Orchestra, Giants of Jazz, 1988.
Small Combos, Giants of Jazz, 1988.
(With Max Roach) *Max and Dizzy: Paris 1989,* A&M, 1990.

Sources

Books

Feather, Leonard, *The Encyclopedia of Jazz in the Sixties,* Horizon, 1966.
Feather, *The Encyclopedia of Jazz in the Seventies,* Horizon, 1976.
Horricks, Raymond, *Dizzy Gillespie and the Bebop Revolution,* Hippocrene, 1984.
Koster, Piet, and Chris Sellers, *Dizzy Gillespie, Volume 1: 1937-1953,* Micrography, 1986.
McRae, Barry, *Dizzy Gillespie,* Universe Books, 1988.
The New Grove Dictionary of Jazz, Macmillan, 1988.

Periodicals

Down Beat, December 1985; January 1986; September 1989; August 1990.
IAJRC Journal, Winter 1991.
Maclean's, March 20, 1989.

—*David Bianco*

Carole Gist

1970(?)—

Miss USA 1990

Carole Gist of Detroit, Michigan, made history in 1990 when she became the first black woman ever to capture the title of Miss USA, an honor which brought her over $200,000 in cash and prizes, and the opportunity to represent the United States in the Miss Universe pageant. The former Miss Michigan and student of marketing and management—who stated a life ambition of establishing a performing arts foundation for disadvantaged children—beat out 50 other contestants for the prestigious honor. Two months later, the six-foot beauty came very close to yet another milestone, when she finished as first runner-up in the Miss Universe pageant.

Gist's Miss USA pageant victory marked a life achievement of rising above obstacles. As she described herself in *Jet,* Gist was not a "stereotypical all-American winner." Raised in a single-parent home, Gist often relocated with her mother and siblings, and lived in some of the roughest neighborhoods of inner-city Detroit. "My home was broken into a lot," she said. Money was scarce in her family, and Gist's early ambitions towards the arts were affected: "I wanted to dance and I wanted to learn to play the piano and violin. But . . . my mother couldn't afford

all those things," she told Ardis Carthane in *Jet.* Despite such difficulties, however, Gist—who was an honors student in high school—maintained a confident outlook, and today looks at her past as important in building strength. "I do believe that some of the negative things in my childhood are positive for me now. They made me what I am today," she told *Jet,* adding, "I had not the happiest of upbringings, but you don't have to become a statistic just because you grew up in a broken home."

After becoming the first black Miss USA, Gist had these words of advice for other ground-breakers: "It's nice to be the first at something. . . . You know you don't have to wait around and wait for someone else to do it. Go for it. Just because someone else hasn't done it before you . . . you never know, you might have what it takes to be the first." Gist sees her winning the title as another important step in black achievement. As quoted by Carthane, Gist said: "It's all a part of taking pride in our [people's] heritage and culture. . . . We are people destined for greatness. We have it in our blood, we have the knowledge and the knack." Gist is a reminder, according to Carthane, that "though a person doesn't grow up with

At a Glance...

Full name, Carole Anne-Marie Gist; born c. 1970; mother, Joan Gist; father, David Turner; raised in Detroit, MI. Part-time club singer in Midland, MI; crowned Miss Michigan, 1989; crowned Miss USA, 1990; first runner-up, Miss Universe, April, 1990. *Education:* Graduated from Cass Technical High School, Detroit, 1987; attended Northwood Institute, Midland, Mich.

a silver spoon in her mouth, she can still taste the good things in life."

Sources

Jet, March 19, 1990; March 26, 1990.
Los Angeles Times, March 3, 1990.
TV Guide, April 14, 1990.

—*Michael E. Mueller*

Danny Glover

1948—

Actor

In an industry that offers limited screen opportunities for blacks, Danny Glover managed to be one of the busiest actors at work in the 1980s and into the 1990s. He began on the stage in the late 1970s and within ten years had made a successful transformation to the screen, starring in some of the biggest films of the 1980s, including *Places in the Heart, Witness, The Color Purple, Lethal Weapon,* and its sequel, *Lethal Weapon 2*. His stage career had also been quite successful and was highlighted by his acclaimed role in the 1982 award-winning Broadway play *"Master Harold" . . . and the Boys;* throughout, Glover has made frequent appearances on television. The talented actor has displayed great diversity in the roles he has tackled and is regularly noted for his empathetic treatment of the characters he has portrayed, which have ranged from the kind-hearted farmer Mose of *Places in the Heart* to the villainous and abusive husband Mister in *The Color Purple*.

Born in rural Georgia and raised in California, Glover had early ambitions to become an economist, but was exposed to acting while a politically active student at San Francisco State University in the late 1960s. "My [acting] interest began simultaneously with my political involvement," Glover explained to Aldore Collier in *Ebony*. "My acting is also an extension of my involvement in community politics, working with groups like the African Liberation Support Committee, tutorial programs. . . . All of these things, at some point drew me into acting." While in college he obtained roles in several plays by Amiri Baraka, who had traveled to San Francisco to stage new theater productions aiming for a fresh perspective as part of the Black arts movement. "I did activist roles in many of the plays," Glover told Collier. "I felt I was making a statement in the plays."

In addition to his stage experience Glover studied acting formally while in college, yet did not pursue it as a career until years later. After graduation he continued his political activism by working within city government and was employed for five years as an evaluator of community programs for the Mayor's Office in San Francisco. He continued to dabble in local theater, however, and eventually decided that his calling was to be an actor, not a bureaucrat. Glover studied at the American Conservatory of Theatre and the Black Box Theatre Company, moonlighted as a taxi driver, and quickly amassed a great

At a Glance...

Born in 1948 in Georgia; raised in San Francisco, CA; married wife Asake (a jazz singer) c. 1972; children: Mandisa. *Education:* Graduated from San Francisco State University, late 1960s; also studied at the American Conservatory of Theatre and with the Black Box Theatre Company.

Actor, 1977—. Researcher for Mayor's Office, San Francisco, late 1960s-early 1970s. Stage credits include *The Island, Sizwe Bansi Is Dead, "Master Harold"... and the Boys, The Blood Knot,* and *A Lesson From Alloes,* all by Athol Fugard, and *Suicide in B Flat,* by Sam Shepard. Film credits include *Escape from Alcatraz,* Paramount, 1979; *Chu Chu and the Philly Flash,* Twentieth-Century Fox, 1981; *Iceman,* Universal, 1984; *Birdy,* Tri-Star, 1984; *Places in the Heart,* Tri-Star, 1984; *Witness,* Paramount, 1985; *Silverado,* Techniscope, 1985; *The Color Purple,* Warner Bros., 1985; *Lethal Weapon,* Warner Brothers, 1987; *Mandela,* Home Box Office (HBO), 1987; *Bat 21,* 1988; *Dead Man Out,* HBO, 1989; *Lethal Weapon 2,* Warner Bros., 1989; *To Sleep With Anger,* 1990; *Predator 2,* 1990; and *Flight of the Intruder,* 1991. Television performances include *Many Mansions,* PBS-TV; *A Raisin in the Sun,* American Playhouse, PBS-TV, 1989; and *Lonesome Dove,* CBS-TV, 1990. Guest appearances on television series include *Hill Street Blues,* NBC-TV; *Lou Grant,* CBS-TV; *Paris,* CBS-TV; and *B. J. and the Bear,* NBC-TV.

Awards: Theatre World Award, 1982, for performance in *"Master Harold"... and the Boys;* honorary D.H.L., Paine College, 1990.

Addresses: *Home*—San Francisco, CA.

amount of stage experience. He appeared in South African anti-apartheid playwright Athol Fugard's *The Island* and *Sizwe Bansi Is Dead* at the Eureka Theatre in San Francisco and the Los Angeles Actors Theatre, and later at New York City's Roundabout Theatre in Fugard's *The Blood Knot.* He also performed in Sam Shepard's *Suicide in B Flat* at the Magic Theatre in San Francisco and played Shakespeare's Macbeth at the Los Angeles Actors Theatre.

In 1982 Glover received recognition for his performance in Fugard's three-person *"Master Harold"... and the Boys,* which premiered at the Yale Repertory Theatre in New Haven, Connecticut, and eventually moved to Broadway. Glover's performance as Willie, a good-hearted waiter whose white friend turns on him and a fellow black waiter in a vicious barrage spurred by self-hatred, won him a Theatre World Award as one of the most promising new talents of 1982. *Master Harold* was heralded by the *New York Times's* Frank Rich as one of the best and most well-written plays of recent times, which, he speculated, "may even outlast the society that spawned it—the racially divided South Africa of apartheid." Rich noted that "as the easygoing Willie, Mr. Glover is a paragon of sweet kindliness—until events leave him whipped and sobbing in a chair, his low moans serving as forlorn counterpoint to the play's main confrontation."

Places in the Heart Earned Film Respect

Glover's performance in *Master Harold* was seen by film director Robert Benton, who cast Glover in the role of Mose in his 1984 film, *Places in the Heart.* Although the role originally called for an older man, Benton was so impressed with Glover's reading for the part that he had the script rewritten. Glover portrays a black hobo-farmer who helps to save the farm of a Southern white widow played by Sally Field; for character reference Glover drew upon the many years of his youth spent on his grandparents' farm in Georgia. He told Lisa Belkin in the *New York Times* that in playing Mose he continually looked to the image of his ninety-year-old grandfather "picking cotton and trusting in God." Glover was more profoundly influenced, however, by the tragedy of his mother's death in an automobile accident days before he went to work on the film. "She was with me in so many ways," he told Charlene Krista in *Films in Review,* especially in the film's poignant farewell scene. "I mean, she was there when I gave the handkerchief to Sally.... I think as actors, we probably would have found ways to get what we wanted, but what happened with my mother gave us the thrust. At a time I was mourning, it gave me strength."

Places in the Heart was nominated for best picture, as was the next film Glover appeared in, 1985's *Witness,* a romance-thriller set amid the Amish communities of Pennsylvania. *Witness* provided Glover the opportunity to create a completely different type of character—a dapper ex-police officer turned murderer. Also in 1985 Glover appeared in Lawrence Kasden's acclaimed western, *Silverado,* playing the role of Malachi, a black cowboy-hero. Glover told Belkin that feedback from the role, especially from children, reinforced for him the importance of his image as a black screen actor. "I've run into black kids who flash their two fingers at me like guns and who say, 'This ought to do' or 'I don't want to kill you and you don't want to be dead,'" he remarked, citing two of his lines from the film. "They're watching me. That's a responsibility."

The Color Purple Stirred Controversy

The following year Glover appeared in *The Color Purple,* which provided one of his most complex roles and certainly his most controversial. In the Steven Spielberg-directed film based on Alice Walker's Pulitzer Prize-winning novel, Glover plays Mister, a southern black widower who marries a young woman, Celie (Whoopi Goldberg). Not only does he cruelly separate Celie from her beloved sister, but he intercepts and hides her sister's letters over a number of years. Mister is an abusive husband who exploits Celie ruthlessly, openly carrying on a love affair with a sultry blues singer named Shug. *The Color Purple* was protested by the NAACP, which felt the film typecast black characters in stereotypical roles—in particular, Glover's Mister, which allegedly projected a negative image of black men as violent and insensitive. Glover, who'd been criticized by some friends and relatives in the South, held, however, that the character accurately depicted life in the early 1900s. "I hear the criticism," he told Belkin, "... [and] prefer to remember the reaction of older black women who say, 'That's the way it was.'" Glover nonetheless understood the disapproval and explained his character in a broader context. "Mister was an adequate representation of one particular story," he told *People.* "He's a product of his past and his present and I think we showed that he has some capabilities for changing." Glover's empathy with the reprehensible Mister translated onto the screen in a manner that was noted by many critics. Donald Bogle in *Blacks in American Films and Television* wrote that Glover "gave a tightly drawn, highly charged performance of a man who's both brute and simp," while Janet Maslin of the *New York Times* said that Glover "somehow makes a very sympathetic villain."

In 1987 Glover teamed up with screen idol Mel Gibson for the biggest movie hit of the year, the comic-action film *Lethal Weapon.* In it Glover portrays Roger Murtaugh, a homicide detective and dedicated family man, whose partner is a reckless—to the point of suicidal—officer named Martin Riggs (Gibson). Glover's stable character serves as a successful counterpoint to Gibson's crazed persona; their rapport made the movie a blockbuster at both the box office and with critics. Roger Ebert in *Roger Ebert's Movie Home Companion 1988 Edition* claimed that although Glover had important film roles in the past, his performance in *Lethal Weapon* "makes him a star.

His job is to supply the movie's center of gravity, while all the nuts and weirdos and victims whirl around him." Two years later Glover and Gibson teamed up again for the equally successful *Lethal Weapon 2.* "Like its predecessor, *Lethal Weapon 2* is well-written and competently acted," noted Paul Baumann in *Commonweal.* "It's blood-drenched fluff, but there is real chemistry between these two accomplished actors."

Glover's performance in the little-noticed 1990 Charles Burnett film, *To Sleep with Anger,* has been judged by some critics to be among his best. Glover plays a superstitious and manipulative man from the Deep South who pays a visit to old friends who have become a middle-class black family in Los Angeles. Slowly but surely, Harry works to stir up simmering disputes within the family, which eventually come to a head. David Ansen wrote in *Newsweek* that "Glover, in what may be the best role of his film career, makes [Harry] an unforgetta-

> I've always felt my experience as an artist is inseparable from what happens with the overall body of Black people. . . . My sitting here now is the result of people, . . . fighting a struggle in the real world, changing the real attitudes and the real social situation.

ble trickster, both frightening and a little pathetic." Terrence Rafferty in the *New Yorker* noted that Glover turns in "an elegantly suggestive performance."

Sense of Responsibility as Black Role Model

Throughout the diverse roles of his career Glover has been aware of his responsibility as a role model for blacks. Echoing the political activism of his earlier days, Glover was quoted as saying in *Jet:* "I've always felt my experience as an artist is inseparable from what happens with the overall body of Black people. . . . My sitting here now is the result of people, Black people and people of good conscience in particular, fighting a struggle in the real world, changing the real attitudes and the real social situation." This awareness results in a special discretion regarding the roles he plays. "I have to be careful about the parts I take," he told Belkin. "Given how this industry has dealt with people like me, the parts I take have to be political choices.''

Although Glover is a leading screen star whose talents have been praised by many critics, he is modest about his success. ''I was in the right place at the right time,'' he told Collier. ''I was coming along at a time when the roads were available. . . . It's a very simple correlation.'' Glover still lives in his hometown of San Francisco in a house in the Haight-Ashbury district that he purchased years ago. He commented to Ebert in an interview: ''I remember, when I was driving a cab and acting at night, I was in seventh heaven. I'm no happier today than I was in those days when I was living in a house in San Francisco and fixing it up, and I got a paycheck and spent it on sheet rock and worked with a guy putting it into the house, and went out and acted, and I was getting paid for it. How could I be happier than that?''

Sources

Books

Bogle, Donald, *Blacks in American Films and Television: An Illustrated Encyclopedia,* Simon & Schuster, 1988.

Ebert, Roger, *Roger Ebert's Movie Home Companion 1988 Edition,* Andrews, McMeel & Parker, 1987.
People Weekly Magazine Guide to Movies on Video, edited by Ralph Novak and Peter Travers, Macmillan, 1987.

Periodicals

Commonweal, October 6, 1989.
Ebony, March 1986.
Films in Review, April 1985.
Gentleman's Quarterly, July 1989.
Jet, March 17, 1986; April 6, 1987; October 31, 1988; September 18, 1989; March 5, 1990.
Maclean's, November 19, 1990.
Newsweek, October 22, 1990.
New Yorker, November 5, 1990.
New York Times, May 5, 1982; May 6, 1982; May 16, 1982; December 18, 1985; January 26, 1986.
People, March 10, 1986.

—Michael E. Mueller

Berry Gordy, Jr.

1929—

Recording industry executive, entrepreneur

On the night of January 20, 1988, Berry Gordy, Jr., was inducted into the Rock 'n' Roll Hall of Fame. His peers that evening were the Supremes, Bob Dylan, the Beatles, the Beach Boys, the Drifters, folk singer Woody Guthrie, blues and folk singer Leadbelly, and jazz guitarist Les Paul. Gordy was honored in the non-performing category for founding and developing Motown Industries. He originally formed the company in 1959 as the Motown Record Corporation. During the 1960s and early 1970s it grew from a Detroit-based record label specializing in rhythm and blues hits to a full-fledged entertainment corporation based in Los Angeles, active in television and motion pictures as well as records. In 1973 the magazine *Black Enterprise* recognized Motown Industries as the number one black-owned or managed business. In 1988 Gordy sold Motown Records to entertainment giant MCA Inc. for $61 million. The sale did not include Motown's publishing division (Jobete Music Co. and Stone Mountain Music), nor its film and television divisions. Gordy would continue to run these operations as the Gordy Company.

Although Berry Gordy, Jr., the seventh of eight children

of Berry, Sr., and Bertha Gordy, began the Motown Record Corporation in 1959, the entire Gordy family was called on to make their own special contributions. Indeed, Gordy did his best to foster a family feeling at Motown in the early days. Many of the performers were in their teens or early twenties; Gordy himself was barely 30. As performers were signed to the company they became new members of the "Motown family," and as in most families, there were incidents of conflict along the way. Gordy was forced to make some unpopular decisions, but throughout the years he kept the enterprise together and firmly on course, soon coming to be known as "Mr. Chairman."

Despite the fact that none of the Gordys made their names as entertainers, the family was very much a musical one. Its musicality made itself known not in performance, but in the continuing enterprise that has provided the world with numerous performers and countless popular songs. The following excerpt from a speech by the Honorable John Conyers, Jr., of Michigan, to the U.S. House of Representatives on April 19,

At a Glance...

Born November 28, 1929, in Detroit, MI; son of Berry, Sr. (owner of a plastering and carpentry service, a general store, and a printing business), and Bertha Gordy; married Thelma Coleman, 1953 (divorced, 1959); married Raynoma Liles (divorced, 1962); children: (first marriage) Hazel Joy, Berry IV, Terry; (second marriage) Kerry (son); Kennedy (son; with Margaret Norton).

Worked on an automobile assembly line and as a prizefighter c. early 1950s. Owned record store c. 1955. Co-wrote songs, 1957—, including "Reet Petite," 1957, "To Be Loved," and "Lonely Teardrops," both 1958, "That's Why," and "I'll Be Satisfied," both 1959, "Money (That's What I Want)," 1960, "I Want You Back," "ABC," and "The Love You Save"; independent producer, 1958, and music publisher, 1958—. Founded Motown Record Corporation (later Motown Industries) in 1959; resigned as president of Motown Record Corporation, founded and assumed leadership of Motown Industries, 1973; sold Motown Records to MCA Inc. for $61 million, 1988; director of the Gordy Company (comprised of the Motown Industries publishing division—Jobete Music Co. and Stone Mountain Music—and film and television divisions), 1988—. Producer and co-editor of feature films, including *Lady Sings the Blues*, 1972. Director of feature films, including *Mahogany*, 1975, and *The Last Dragon*, 1985. *Military service:* U.S. Army c. 1951-1953.

Awards: Inducted into the Rock and Roll Hall of Fame, 1988.

Addresses: *Office*—The Gordy Company, 6255 Sunset Blvd., 18th Floor, Los Angeles, CA 90028.

1971, ably reflects the familial nature of the Motown enterprise, as well as Gordy's sense of social responsibility.

"Mr. Speaker, ten years ago a Detroit assemblyline worker, who had formerly been a prizefighter, saved $800 and started his own business. Like so many before him, he had ideas of what he could do and wanted to try them in a business of his own. His name was Berry Gordy, Jr., and the company he created was the Motown Record Corp. Starting from their own home, the Gordy family has built Motown into the largest independent record firm in the world, and the only major black company in the entertainment business. Berry Gordy realizes that even in America factory workers cannot all become successful businessmen. Therefore, he believes that it is essential that each and every young person receive the maximum education possible. He knows that education is the passport to the future and that tomorrow belongs to the people who prepare for it today. One of the many ways Gordy puts his belief to work is through the Sterling Ball, a benefit which directly provides assistance in the form of scholarships to inner city high school graduates who wish to continue their education but are financially unable to do so. This annual charitable event has, to date, helped scores of young men and women, black and white, reach an otherwise impossible goal—a college education. The benefit was originally conceived by Mr. Gordy and his sister, Mrs. Esther Edwards, vice president in the corporation, as a continuing and meaningful memorial to their late sister, Mrs. Loucye Gordy Wakefield, who had been the first vice president of Motown and a personal inspiration to all who knew her."

Women in High Places

Gordy's family supported his efforts to establish his own business from the start, with a 1959 loan of $800. Once the company was launched various family members played key roles in its continuing operations. While Gordy's brothers—Fuller, Robert, and George—participated in the Motown enterprise, it was his sisters who provided most of the help in the company's operations. Gordy believed in women as executives. His second wife, Raynoma, was an early vice-president, as was Janie Bradford, with whom Gordy co-wrote the 1960 hit "Money (That's What I Want)." Later, Motown Productions—the film, television, and video arms of the corporation—would be skillfully guided by Suzanne De Passe. As Smokey Robinson wrote in his autobiography, "Berry was big on letting people prove themselves, based on skill, not sex or color."

In 1951 Gordy was drafted into the army, where he received his high school equivalency diploma. In 1953, no longer in the service, he married Thelma Coleman; a daughter, Hazel Joy, was born the following year. The couple would have two more children, Berry IV and Terry, before divorcing in 1959. While working on an auto assembly line, Gordy started a jazz-oriented record store—the 3-D Record Mart—around 1955, but it soon folded. Like Motown, it was financed largely by his family. At the time, Gordy was writing songs constantly, submitting them to magazines and contests. His big break came in 1957, when future soul star Jackie Wilson recorded "Reet Petite," which was written by Gordy, his sister Gwen, and Tyran Carlo. Jackie Wilson had just signed with the Brunswick label in 1956 and "Reet Petite" turned out to be his first hit. Gordy's team wrote four more hits for Wilson over the next two years: "To Be Loved" and "Lonely Teardrops" in 1958, and "That's Why" and "I'll Be Satisfied" in 1959.

Smokey Robinson a Key "Discovery"

In 1957 Gordy "discovered" Smokey Robinson, who would later become a rhythm and blues superstar. Gordy had just written "Lonely Teardrops" when Robinson and his group—then the Matadors—auditioned for Jackie Wilson's representatives. Present at the audition were Nat Tarnapol, owner of Brunswick Records and Wilson's manager, and Alonzo Tucker, generally described as "Jackie's music man." Gordy was also present, though he made it clear to Smokey that he did not work for Jackie Wilson. According to Robinson's oft-repeated account, Tucker rejected the Matadors for being too much like the Platters, another popular group of the time. Gordy, however, appeared very interested in the group, apparently because of their original material. He introduced himself as a songwriter, and Robinson noted in his book *Smokey: Inside My Life* that Gordy looked young for his age: "This boyish face hid the fact that he was eleven years older than me." Robinson also credited Gordy with having more songwriting savvy at that time than he did. He went on to report that Gordy expressed his views on songwriting after complimenting him on his rhymes, saying, "Songs are more than rhymes. Songs need a beginning, middle, and end. Like a story." It was the beginning of a long and beautiful friendship. Gordy is often credited with a discerning eye for talent, of which his "discovery" of Smokey Robinson is a prime example.

By 1958 Gordy was active as an independent producer, forming the nucleus of what would become Motown Records. He recorded and leased recordings of the Miracles, Marv Johnson, and Eddie Holland to the nationally distributed labels Chess, United Artists, and End. The same year he established Jobete to publish his songs. Jobete was named for Gordy's first three children, Hazel Joy, Berry IV, and Terry.

Moving toward becoming a full-fledged entrepreneur, Gordy was motivated by a number of factors. Certainly, his family background contributed to and supported his ambition. By then his friend, Robinson urged him to take control of his operations, especially in light of the pitifully small royalty checks he was receiving from the national labels. As a songwriter Gordy had to split his royalties

with the music publisher; his way around this was to form his own publishing company, which was valued at nearly $100 million 30 years later. Finally, it was widely known that Gordy did not particularly like the way his songs were being produced at Brunswick. To move forward, he needed to take control and form his own corporation.

Company's Beginnings Were Modest

According to Robinson, Motown began with six employees who had been operating in 1958 out of an apartment on Gladstone in Detroit. In addition to Gordy and Robinson, they included Raynoma Liles—not yet Gordy's wife at the time—Bradford, Robert Bateman, and Brian Holland. Holland and Bateman were a songwriting-production duo that evolved a few years later into the famed Holland-Dozier-Holland team, when Brian's brother Eddie returned to Motown after his contract with United Artists expired.

In 1959 Motown released its first single on the newly formed Tamla label. The name "Tamla" is a variation on

> One obstacle that Berry Gordy faced and overcame was the fact that there had never been a big-time record company owner who was black.

"Tammy," a popular song of the period sung by Debbie Reynolds. The Motown label was activated in 1960, and the company's third major label, Gordy, debuted in April of 1962. While the Motown sound had its roots in urban rhythm and blues, it was Gordy's plan to appeal to young people of all races with a kind of music that would retain some of its origins while adding other ingredients. Motown's early advertising slogan, "The Sound of Young America," reflected Gordy's desire for Motown's music to achieve widespread popularity. The company landed its first number-one pop hit in 1961 with the Marvelettes' "Please Mr. Postman."

Crossover Dreams Realized

As late as 1962 Motown's releases were still appealing primarily to black audiences, as evidenced by their success on the rhythm and blues charts. That year the company placed 11 singles on the R & B Top 10. The company's strategy, as mapped out by Gordy, was to "cross over" to the white record-buying public. In fact, four singles managed to reach the Top 10 on the pop charts in 1962. The next year Motown placed six more singles on the pop Top 10, with Stevie Wonder's "Fingertips, Part 2" becoming its second number-one pop hit.

Nineteen sixty-four proved a watershed year for Motown. Four of the company's five Top 10 pop hits went to Number One: "My Guy," "Where Did Our Love Go," "Baby Love," and "Come See About Me." The other song, "Dancing in the Street," went to Number Two. Most importantly, Motown had hit on a winning combination with the Supremes singing songs written and produced by Holland-Dozier-Holland. The next year, five Motown releases reached Number One. Reflecting the company's success, Gordy purchased the Gordy Manor in Detroit.

Gordy's strategy for producing hits was paying off. While Gordy himself was a talented songwriter and hands-on producer, these strengths alone were not enough to make Motown a success. Rather, it was Gordy's ability to surround himself with talented people that made Motown a force in the music business. Motown's greatest songwriters and producers—Smokey Robinson, Eddie Holland, Lamont Dozier, Brian Holland—were complemented by a group of other gifted writers and producers, all competing within the Motown system to produce hits. Often likened to an assembly line, Motown was indeed a music factory that was able to churn out hit after hit.

Gordy Looked Beyond Records

As Motown's popularity in the mid-1960s ensured the company's success, Gordy began to move the company forward by pursuing other entertainment opportunities. As early as 1966 Motown established a West Coast office for expansion into movie production, to secure film roles for Motown stars, and to encourage the use of Motown songs in film soundtracks. Motown also announced its interest in becoming a "Broadway angel," a financial backer for Broadway plays. By 1968 Gordy had purchased a home in Los Angeles and moved there. During the next few years Motown established additional offices on the West Coast; the move from Detroit was finalized in 1972. For some within the company the move was an unpopular decision; for others, it opened up new opportunities. By that time Gordy had purchased comic Red Skelton's Bel Air estate and was living there.

The end of the 1960s brought a talented new group to Motown—the Jackson 5. "Discovered" by Bobby Tay-

lor of Bobby Taylor and the Vancouvers and introduced to the public by former Supreme Diana Ross, the Jackson 5 hailed from Gary, Indiana. The group, and especially youngest member Michael, enjoyed close ties to Gordy, who often let the entire family stay at his home in California. Gordy headed a songwriting and production team within Motown—called the Corporation—that wrote and produced several chart-topping hits for the Jackson 5, including "I Want You Back," "ABC," and "The Love You Save." Michael Jackson was quoted in *The Motown Album* as saying, "Berry was my teacher and a great one. He told me exactly what he wanted and how he wanted me to help him get it. Berry insisted on perfection and attention to detail. I'll never forget his persistence. This was his genius."

Ross Helped Launch Motown Industries

In 1973 Gordy resigned as president of Motown Records to assume leadership of the new Motown entertainment conglomerate, Motown Industries, which included record, motion picture, television, and publishing divisions. His primary star was Diana Ross, whom Gordy began grooming for television and motion pictures as early as 1968, when she was featured with the Supremes and the Temptations on Motown's first television special, "T.C.B.: Taking Care of Business." A second special with the Supremes and Temptations followed in 1969. Ross starred in her first solo television special, "Diana," in 1971. It was widely rumored that Gordy and Ross enjoyed a special personal relationship prior to Ross's 1971 marriage to Robert Silberstein.

Gordy was involved as more than producer in Ross's first film role: singer Billie Holiday in the 1972 Paramount release, *Lady Sings the Blues*. Motown invested heavily in the film and by most accounts Gordy spent a great deal of time personally editing it. It was a promising start for Motown's film ventures; Ross received an Academy Award nomination for her performance. Her second film, 1975's *Mahogany*, marked Gordy's debut as a film director. It was followed by *The Wiz*, a 1978 Universal/Motown musical version of *The Wizard of Oz* that garnered largely negative reviews and did poorly at the box office. Motown would not enter the motion picture business again until Gordy's 1985 effort, *The Last Dragon*, an entertaining kung-fu musical that fared respectably well at the box office.

"Motown 25" Broke New Ground

Motown scored well in television with the NBC-TV special "Motown 25—Yesterday, Today, and Forever," which aired in 1983. Edited to a two-hour television special from a four-hour live performance, the show was a tribute to the genius of Berry Gordy. Among the highlights were reunions of the Jackson 5, the Miracles, and the Supremes, and solo performances by Michael Jackson and Marvin Gaye. The show garnered nine Emmy nominations for Motown; but perhaps more significantly, it was the most-watched variety special in the history of television.

Motown followed its anniversary special with the 1985 broadcast "Motown Returns to the Apollo." The show coincided with the reopening of the newly restored Apollo Theater in Harlem, marking its fiftieth anniversary. The special won an Emmy for best variety, music, or comedy program. Following the formula for success that Gordy implemented as far back as 1960—to reach as wide an audience as possible—Motown has made a number of its productions available for the home video market, including specials featuring Marvin Gaye and the Temptations.

Many books have been written by and about Motown's stars—Marvin Gaye, Smokey Robinson, the Temptations, the Supremes, Diana Ross, Mary Wilson—telling the story of Motown from several perspectives. Perhaps the final word will come from Mr. Chairman himself as Berry Gordy prepares his own autobiography for imminent publication. Through records, movies, videos, and now books, the heritage of Motown—and of the visionary behind it—will be preserved for and appreciated by future generations intrigued by the house that Gordy built.

Sources

Books

Benjaminson, Peter, *The Story of Motown,* Grove, 1979.
Bianco, David, *Heat Wave: The Motown Fact Book,* Pierian, 1988.
Fong-Torres, Ben, *The Motown Album,* St. Martin's, 1990.
Hirshey, Gerri, *Nowhere to Run,* Times Books, 1984.
Robinson, Smokey, with David Ritz, *Smokey: Inside My Life,* McGraw, 1989.
Singleton, Raynoma Gordy, with Bryan Brown and Mim Eichler, *Berry, Me, and Motown: The Untold Story,* Contemporary Books, 1990.
Taraborrelli, J. Randy, *Motown: Hot Wax, City Cool & Solid Gold,* Doubleday, 1986.
Waller, Don, *The Motown Story,* Scribner, 1985.

Periodicals

Detroit Free Press, May 15, 1983.
Rolling Stone, August 23, 1990.

—David Bianco

Earl G. Graves

1935—

Publisher, corporate executive officer

A highly respected and nationally known authority on black business development, Earl G. Graves is the founder and publisher of *Black Enterprise,* a magazine that focuses on issues and news relating to black-owned businesses in the United States. Celebrating its 20th anniversary in 1990, *Black Enterprise*—to which Graves contributes a monthly publisher's column—boasts a circulation of over 230,000 and annual revenues of more than $15 million. A key communicator and spokesman within his field, Graves was once described by the Reverend Jesse Jackson in the *Washington Post* as the "primary educator in the country on black business—on trends and opportunities and the like."

Graves himself is a prosperous businessman; as Margaret K. Webb noted in the *Washington Post,* "Graves's success extends beyond the pages of his magazine." *Black Enterprise* is published by the Earl G. Graves Publishing Company, the parent corporation of which, Earl G. Graves, Ltd., is directed by Graves in his capacities as president and chief executive officer. In addition to these responsibilities Graves serves on the board of directors of several corporations, including the Chrysler

Corporation, and is chairman of the Black Business Council. In 1990 Graves made national business headlines when he purchased the rights for Pepsi-Cola's Washington, D.C., distribution operations. Graves's partner in the venture is Los Angeles Lakers basketball star Earvin "Magic" Johnson, who serves as the partnership's executive vice-president and spokesperson, while Graves acts as chief executive officer. The franchise, which distributes over four million cases of Pepsi annually in the District of Columbia and parts of Maryland, has been estimated to be worth about $60 million and makes Graves and Johnson Pepsi's largest minority franchisees.

Although the Pepsi deal has consumed much of Graves's energy, he remains committed to the concerns of *Black Enterprise.* In his monthly publisher's column Graves often comments on matters important to greater economic power for blacks. In a 1990 essay for the magazine he expressed a stern warning that the publication's annual survey of the top 100 black-owned businesses in the United States showed virtually no growth occurring in the year 1989. As Webb quoted, Graves wrote that black business was threatened not only by a slow econo-

At a Glance. . .

Full name, Earl Gilbert Graves; born in 1935 in Brooklyn, NY; son of Earl Godwin (a shipping clerk) and Winifred (Sealy) Graves; married Barbara Kydd, July 2, 1960; children: Earl Gilbert, John, Michael. *Education:* Morgan State College, B.A. (economics), 1958. *Religion:* Episcopalian. *Politics:* Democrat.

Worked in real estate and as national commissioner of scouting for Boy Scouts of America, New York City, early 1960s; administrative assistant to Senator Robert F. Kennedy, 1965-68; owned management consulting firm, 1968-70; publisher of *Black Enterprise,* New York City, 1970—; co-owner of Pepsi-Cola distributorship, Washington, D.C., 1990—; president and chief executive officer, Earl G. Graves., Ltd.,; president, Earl G. Graves Publishing Co., Inc., Earl G. Graves Marketing and Research Co., Earl G. Graves Development Co., and EGG Dallas Broadcasting Co. Member of board of directors, Rohm & Haas Corp., New York State Urban Development Corp., Chrysler Corp., National Supplier Development Council, and Magazine Publishers Association. Chairman, Black Business Council. *Military service:* U.S. Army, 1958-60; became captain.

Awards: National Award of Excellence, U.S. Department of Commerce, 1972; Black Achiever Award, *Talk* (magazine), 1972; presidential citation, "One of [the] Ten Most Outstanding Minority Businessmen in the United States," 1973; "Outstanding Citizen of the Year," Omega Psi Phi, 1974; one of 200 "Future Leaders of the Country," *Time;* "Outstanding Black Businessman," National Business League; one of 100 "Influential Blacks," *Ebony;* Poynter fellow, Yale University, 1978; numerous awards from the Boy Scouts of America.

Addresses: *Home*—Scarsdale, NY. *Office*—*Black Enterprise,* 130 Fifth Ave., New York, NY 10011.

my but "the Reagan administration's legacy of exclusion . . . realized with the subsequent retrenchment of affirmative action plans and minority business set-aside programs." Graves noted that black businesses will survive if they get "leaner, stronger, better," and urged his readers to "be selective where we spend our money and do business with companies that do business with us."

Graves has always been vocal on the subject of racial discrimination in business. In 1990 he praised the United Way of his hometown, Scarsdale, New York, for moving their kick-off dinner from a club that traditionally excluded blacks from membership. In a speech quoted by James Ferron in the *New York Times* Graves stated that the United Way's action sent "an important signal of equal opportunity," and that a primary cause of human suffering was the "lack of equal economic opportunity in our minority communities." He later commented to Ferron on racial bias: "It is a national problem . . . and the point I was making in this speech is that if there were jobs, people would not have some of the problems they have. If they had equal opportunity, quality schools, all of the above, then people would not have time to get sidetracked by those things that are detrimental to their well-being."

Sources

Business Week, August 13, 1990.
Fortune, August 27, 1990.
Jet, April 2, 1990.
Los Angeles Times, July 1, 1990.
New York Times, September 30, 1989.
Washington Post, July 25, 1990.

—*Michael E. Mueller*

Dick Gregory

1932—

Comedian, social activist, nutrition advocate

Dick Gregory has made a name for himself in many areas: as an athlete, comedian, civil rights activist, author, nutritionist, and, most recently, as a speaker on peaceful solutions to conflict in the Middle East. Perhaps his greatest success, however, was in overcoming the extreme poverty into which he was born in St. Louis, Missouri. Raised by a single mother who often worked late into the evening, Gregory started hustling early in life, shining shoes and doing odd jobs to help support himself and his many siblings. He was a bright child who wished to excel in school, but circumstances at home—often no electricity or food—made it difficult to study. In *Nigger: An Autobiography,* Gregory recalled: "I got picked on a lot around the neighborhood; skinniest kid on the block, the poorest, the one without a Daddy. I guess that's when I began to learn about humor, the power of a joke. . . . They were going to laugh anyway, but if I made the jokes they'd laugh *with* me instead of *at* me. I'd get the kids off my back, on my side."

Gregory decided to go out for track in high school because he knew team members had the luxury of hot showers every day after practice. At first the coach wouldn't let him try out, but Gregory refused to accept that decision. "Every day while the team ran around inside the field, around the track, I ran outside, around a city block," he remembered. The coach began to let Gregory have the hot showers he craved; by the next year Gregory's personal training regimen earned him a spot on the team. Soon he was setting records and winning championships. Success on the team and the celebrity that went with it provided a welcome relief from the pains of being the poorest kid on a poor block. By senior year Gregory was captain of the track and cross-country teams and his self-esteem had developed enough for him to run for president of his class—and win. Gregory's speed and endurance were his ticket into Southern Illinois University, where he continued to set records and win championships. His wins began to seem hollow, however, as he became more and more conscious of the many little injustices he faced daily in the predominantly white university. "Track became something different for me in college," he stated. "In high school I was fighting being broke and on relief. . . . But in college I was fighting being Negro."

At a Glance...

Born October 12, 1932, in St. Louis, MO; son of Presley and Lucille Gregory; married Lillian Smith, February 2, 1959; children: Michele, Lynne, Paula, Pamela, Stephanie, Gregory, Christian, Ayanna, Missy, Youhance. *Education:* Attended Southern Illinois University, 1951-53, 1955-56.

Roberts Show Club, Chicago, IL, master of ceremonies, 1959-60; entertainer and commentator, 1961—; Dick Gregory Health Enterprises, Chicago, chairman, 1984. Lecturer at numerous universities. Candidate for mayor of Chicago, 1966; presidential candidate of Freedom and Peace Party, 1968. *Military service:* U.S. Army, 1953-56.

Awards: Winner of Missouri Mile championship, 1951 and 1952; Outstanding Athlete award, Southern Illinois University, 1953; Ebony-Topaz Heritage and Freedom award, 1978; honorary doctorate of humane letters, Southern Illinois University at Carbondale, 1989; has received more than one hundred civil rights awards; presented with the key to the city of St. Louis.

Addresses: *Home*—Long Pond Rd., Plymouth, MA 02360. *Office*—Dick Gregory Health Enterprises, 39 South LaSalle, Chicago, IL 60603.

He did some satirical comedy work at a few of the school's variety shows and found performing both exhilarating and frightening. "For a while, standing on that stage and watching those people laugh with me, I thought it was even better than winning a track meet," he wrote in *Nigger*. "But running track was safer: You can be saying the funniest thing in the world but if Whitey is mad at you and has hate, he might not laugh. If you're in good condition and you can run faster than Whitey, he can hate all he wants and you'll still come out the better man." Gregory began to develop what he called "an attitude," which accompanied him into the army when he was drafted in 1954. His wisecracks to superiors led to a confrontation with a colonel who challenged him to win the comedy competition at that night's talent show—or face court-martial. Gregory won and was transferred to the army's Special Services entertainment division.

After his discharge from the service Gregory drifted for a while, then headed to Chicago, where he began trying to

carve out a name for himself as a comedian. It was a long struggle. He got some low-paying, short-term jobs as host at various black nightclubs, but between these he was forced to work as everything from a postal clerk to a car washer. In 1958 Gregory borrowed some money and opened his own nightclub, the Apex, on the outskirts of the city. The first weekend seemed to forecast a rosy future for the club, but several successive weekends of fierce winter weather kept the crowds away and nearly wiped Gregory out financially; the Apex closed before a full year had passed. Things began to look up in late 1959, however, when he rented the Roberts Show Club in Chicago and organized a party for the Pan American Games. The success of the event and of Gregory's role as its master of ceremonies convinced the owner of the Roberts to hire the young performer as his regular master of ceremonies. The best black acts in the country played the club, which gave Gregory a chance to study and learn from the likes of funnyman Nipsey Russell and song-and-dance legend Sammy Davis, Jr. Unfortunately, the job lasted only a year and for a short time Gregory was back to scrabbling for one-night stands in small clubs. Then, early in 1961, he got the job that changed his life.

Perseverance Wore Down a Racist Audience

Gregory's agent called to say that a replacement was needed for a comic scheduled to work Chicago's Playboy Club. The comedian raced downtown for this prestigious gig, only to be turned away by the club's booking agent. The explanation was that the room had been booked to a convention of executives from the South who seemed likely to be hostile to a black comedian. Gregory recalled: "I was cold and mad and I had run twenty blocks and I didn't even have another quarter to go back home. I told him I was going to do the show they had called me for. . . . I didn't care if he had a lynch mob in that room." Gregory remembered facing the unreceptive crowd: "I went all the way back to childhood that night in the Playboy Club, to the smile Momma always had on her face, to the clever way a black boy learns never to let the bitterness inside him show. The audience fought me with dirty, little, insulting statements, but I was faster, and I was funny, and when that room broke it was like the storm was over. They stopped heckling and they listened. What was supposed to be a fifty-minute show lasted for about an hour and forty minutes."

The original one-night contract at the Playboy was extended to a two-month engagement, and Gregory's career took off. *Time* ran a feature on him, Jack Paar invited him to appear on his television program, and Gregory was soon one of the hottest acts on the nightclub circuit. He became the first black comedian to break the "color barrier" and perform for white audiences. The key to his comedy success was his satirical approach to race relations and his development of jokes that were about race, but not derogatory. In his autobiography he described his attitude on stage at that time: "I've got to go up there as an individual first, a Negro second. I've got to be a colored funny man, not a funny colored man." After starting off with several jokes poking fun at himself, he would switch to a topical joke. For instance: "They asked me to buy a lifetime membership in the NAACP, but I told them I'd pay a week at a time. Hell of a thing to buy a lifetime membership, wake up one morning and find out the country's been integrated." Having introduced the race issue in a nonthreatening way, Gregory would then confront the audience more pointedly, with a line like: "Wouldn't it be a hell of a thing if all this was burnt cork and all you folks were being tolerant for nothing?"

Elected "President-in-Exile"

Deep-rooted concern about political and social issues

was evident from the beginning of Gregory's career—in his choice of poverty, segregation, and social injustice as satirical targets. As his fame increased he was able to direct the energy he'd previously poured into searching for gigs toward putting his personal convictions into practice. During much of the 1960s Gregory spent his evenings in nightclubs satirizing racism and his days in the street demanding black voting rights. He made appearances at civil rights marches and rallies throughout the United States and performed benefits for SNCC (the Student Nonviolent Coordinating Committee), CORE (the Congress on Racial Equality), and other agents of social change. At one point he commuted daily from San Francisco to Chicago in order to fulfill a nightclub engagement while participating in a series of demonstrations. He was arrested and jailed several times and was beaten severely by police in a Chicago jail. "I wouldn't mind paying my income tax if I knew it was going to a friendly country," he joked during this period.

Concern over America's social problems finally spurred Gregory to enter electoral politics. He was a candidate in

Gregory marches in front of the White House in support of the 1991 Civil Rights Bill.

Chicago's 1966 mayoral race and in 1968 ran for president as a member of the Freedom and Peace Party. His platform, closely linked to the New Left and Black Power movements, called for civil rights, racial and social justice, and peace in Vietnam. Neither of his campaigns were successful, but they did draw attention to issues that Gregory considered too often overlooked. He earned some two hundred thousand votes for president, mostly write-ins, and was sworn in as "President-in-Exile" by some of his supporters. At his "inauguration" in Washington, D.C., Gregory swore to continue fighting "the insane, stinking, rotten racist system in the United States." He presented his political and social beliefs in *The Shadow That Scares Me, No More Lies,* and *Dick Gregory's Political Primer.* Reviewer Charles Dollen found that Gregory "preaches freedom; he teaches it; he satirizes over it, and no one is safe from his keen wit or common sense."

Nutrition and Health Issues Provided Another Passion

Also in the late 1960s Gregory began changing his personal life to bring it into greater harmony with his political and social convictions. He became a vegetarian because of his dedication to nonviolence, but discovered that the dietary change also put an end to lifelong ulcers and sinus trouble. This discovery led him to carefully research diet and health and eventually adopt outspoken positions on the benefits of vegetarianism and the ill effects of the average American diet. Before long Gregory had quit the nightclub circuit in favor of speaking engagements at churches, schools, and universities. Asked by Lawrence Levy of the *Detroit News* what prompted the move from nightclubs, Gregory replied, "They take time away from serving humanity." More importantly, the clubs promoted a lifestyle Gregory no longer supported. He has said: "How can I get up there and tell those students that drugs and alcohol and even meat is bad for them, then afterwards say 'come on down and catch my act at the club and have a drink.'"

In the 1970s Gregory began to explore other areas of health care and nutrition; he became interested in fasting and marathon running, activities he has been occasionally able to translate into a call for scrutiny of social issues. He has fasted many times to publicize world hunger, to draw attention to the nation's drug epidemic, and to emphasize the plight of Native Americans. He has run marathons for similar reasons, from Chicago to Washington, D.C., for example, to urge that action be taken by the government to ease world famine. Gregory's unique career has won him substantial attention and admiration. "Gregory's name," wrote Peter Barry Chowka of *East West Journal,* "is synonymous with progressive social

and political causes. . . . He is that rare combination (like Gandhi) of activist and healer, one whose own life illustrates how real change first must come from within oneself."

Selected writings

From the Back of the Bus, edited by Bob Orben, with an introduction by Hugh M. Hefner, Dutton, 1962.
(With Robert Lipsyte) *Nigger: An Autobiography,* Dutton, 1964.
What's Happening?, Dutton, 1965.
The Shadow That Scares Me, edited by James R. McGraw, Doubleday, 1968.
Write Me In!, edited by McGraw, Bantam, 1968.
(Under name Richard Claxton Gregory) *No More Lies: The Myth and Reality of American History,* edited by McGraw, Harper, 1972.
Dick Gregory's Political Primer, edited by McGraw, Harper, 1972.
Dick Gregory's Natural Diet for Folks Who Eat: Cookin' with Mother Nature, Harper, 1973.
Dick Gregory's Bible Tales, edited by McGraw, Stein & Day, 1974.
(With McGraw) *Up from Nigger* (autobiography), Stein & Day, 1976.
(With Mark Lane) *Code Name "Zorro": The Murder of Martin Luther King, Jr.,* Prentice-Hall, 1977.

Also creator of comedy routines featured on a number of recordings, including *In Living Black and White,* Colpix, 1961, *The Light Side, the Dark Side,* Poppy, 1969, *Caught in the Act,* Poppy, 1973, *Dick Gregory East and West,* and *Dick Gregory at Kent State.*

Sources

Books

Gemme, Leila B., *New Breed of Performer,* Washington Square Press, 1976.
Gregory, Dick, and Robert Lipsyte, *Nigger: An Autobiography,* Dutton, 1965, new edition with Bronson Dudley, McGraw, 1970.
Gregory, Dick, and James R. McGraw, *Up from Nigger,* Stein & Day, 1976.

Periodicals

Best Sellers, February 1, 1968; May 15, 1972.
Booklist, November 15, 1976.
Book Week, November 1, 1964.
Book World, July 21, 1968; September 23, 1973; February 19, 1978.
Christian Century, November 27, 1974.

Christian Science Monitor, January 14, 1977.
Detroit News, April 7, 1974.
East West Journal, July 1981.
Ebony, November 1974.
Esquire, November 1961.
Essence, August 1979.
Library Journal, January 15, 1968.
National Observer, March 17, 1969.
New York Times, September 14, 1961.
New York Times Book Review, February 6, 1972; May 13, 1973; December 26, 1976; January 15, 1978.
New York Times Magazine, April 30, 1961.
Progressive, June 1973.
Time, May 17, 1961.

—Joan Goldsworthy

Gregory Hines

1946—

Dancer, actor

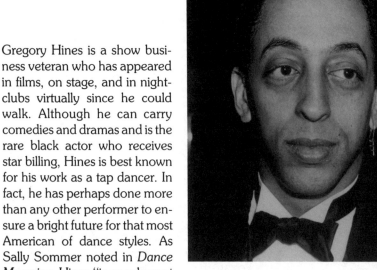

Gregory Hines is a show business veteran who has appeared in films, on stage, and in night-clubs virtually since he could walk. Although he can carry comedies and dramas and is the rare black actor who receives star billing, Hines is best known for his work as a tap dancer. In fact, he has perhaps done more than any other performer to ensure a bright future for that most American of dance styles. As Sally Sommer noted in *Dance Magazine,* Hines "is an adamant advocate for the contemporaneity of tap who wants to push tap beyond the expected conventions and cliched images. . . . Certainly he is in the right position to initiate such changes, because he is both an enormously popular performer in mainstream entertainment and a radical tap artist who keeps experimenting with the form."

Hines told *Dance:* "I can't ever remember *not* tapping." He was born in New York City in 1946 and raised in the middle-class, integrated Washington Heights neighborhood. His father, who sold soda and worked as a night-club bouncer, was the son of dancer Ora Hines, a showgirl at the famous Cotton Club. On his mother's side his ancestors include Portuguese, Jewish, and Irish immigrants. Hines told *People* that he has never felt ambivalent about his ethnicity. "When I was a kid," he said, "blacks would say, 'Oh, we have some Irish in us and some Portuguese. We have better quality hair. We're better than other blacks.' I thought it was a load of bull. I always have considered myself a black man. What my mother has on her side is irrelevant. When I go for a role that was written for a white, it means nothing."

Hines's mother had great ambitions for her sons and thus steered both Gregory and his older brother Maurice toward tap dancing. Gregory literally learned his first tap steps as a toddler and was enrolled in dance school at the age of three. Shortly thereafter he and Maurice became professionals with a song-and-dance act known as the Hines Kids. They toured extensively in America and abroad and also played the prestigious Apollo Theatre in New York. In 1952 they came under the tutelage of Broadway choreographer Henry LeTang; he helped them earn roles in their first musical comedy, *The Girl in Pink Tights.* Gregory in particular rounded out his tap training by watching older tap professionals "Sandman" Sims and Teddy Hale. During breaks in shows these improvisational masters would tutor the youngster, passing on to him a style that might otherwise have been lost in tap's lean years.

In 1963 Maurice Hines, Sr., joined the act as a percussionist and the trio billed themselves as Hines, Hines and Dad. Gregory told *People:* "We weren't ever *really* successful. We were a very strong opening act, but we never got over the hump." Many would-be entertainers would have been more than satisfied with their level of success, however. Throughout the 1960s Hines, Hines and Dad appeared on the *Tonight Show, the Ed Sullivan Show,* and numerous other television programs. They also toured Europe, playing at London's famed Palladium and the Olympia Theatre in Paris. Unfortunately for the Hines family, tap dancing had gone out of vogue by the late 1960s. The trio was reduced to a musical-comedic lounge act, with Maurice as straight man and Gregory as comedian. Slowly the act began to stagnate, and Gregory accordingly revised his ambitions.

In 1973 the Hines brothers disbanded. Almost simultaneously, Gregory's first marriage dissolved. Left to his own resources, he moved to Venice, California, and became "a long-haired hippie," experimenting with the sex, drugs, and rock 'n' roll lifestyle of the West Coast. "Venice Beach was a real charged atmosphere then," Hines told *Ebony.* "It was music, women and drugs, and I had my share of all three." He worked as a waiter, busboy, and karate instructor during the day and played with a jazz-rock group at night. Today Hines remembers those years in Venice as a turning point in his life. "For the first time in my life, I learned how to take care of myself," he told *Ebony.* "Until that time, I always had somebody—my wife, my manager, my parents—taking care of me. There was always somebody between me and what was really happening. I got out to Venice and it was just me and life, and I had to learn how to take care of myself."

Career Sizzled With Broadway Triumphs

During his sojourn in Venice Hines met his second wife, Pamela Koslow. She returned with him to New York City in 1978 and they were married in 1981. For years Hines thought that he had left tap dancing behind, but upon his return to New York he reconciled with Maurice and auditioned for a Broadway revue. Eventually the Hines brothers teamed again with LeTang, appearing on Broadway in *Eubie!* in 1978. That show featured Gregory Hines as a tapper and singer and earned him the first of three Tony Award nominations as outstanding featured actor in a musical. After *Eubie!* closed Gregory starred in two more successful Broadway shows, *Comin' Uptown* and *Sophisticated Ladies.* Both gave Hines the opportunity to shine as a singer, comedian, and dancer, and he again earned Tony nominations for his work.

A national tour of *Sophisticated Ladies* took Hines back to the West Coast; while there he embarked on a film career. In 1981 he earned his first movie roles, appearing in *History of the World, Part I* as a Roman slave and in *Wolfen* as a medical examiner investigating a series of mysterious deaths. Hines absolutely relished film work and aggressively sought further roles. When he heard that producer Robert Evans was casting a major film about the Cotton Club, the dancer-actor "instituted a reign of terror" trying to win a principal role. "I started calling [Evans] every day and going over to his house telling him how perfect I was for the part," Hines told *Ebony.* In fact, Hines was indeed perfect for the role of "Sandman" Williams, an upwardly-mobile Cotton Club dancer. When *Cotton Club* was released in 1984 many reviewers singled Hines out as the bright spot in an otherwise muddled movie.

The appearance in *Cotton Club*—and a now-classic performance on the television show *Saturday Night Live*—virtually assured Hines a measure of stardom. Audiences were thrilled with his fast-paced and insinuatingly sexy jazz-tap routines, many of which featured improvisational, arrhythmic flights that pushed far past tap's traditional boundaries. Sommer wrote in *Dance Magazine:* "Like a jazz musician who ornaments a well-known melody with improvisational riffs, Hines improvises within the frame of a dance. Among many tappers, improvisation is the most revered art, because it is about creation, demanding that the imagination be turned into choreography instantaneously. Certainly it is the most difficult aspect of tap to master. The tap dancer has to have the brilliant percussive phrases of a composer, the rhythms of a drummer, and the lines of a dancer."

Held His Own Opposite Baryshnikov

In 1985 Hines faced a daunting challenge when he was cast opposite Mikhail Baryshnikov in the dance drama *White Nights.* Hines rose to the occasion, matching the classically trained Baryshnikov step for step in a film that became an impressive box-office draw despite its somewhat hackneyed plot. Hines also turned in several striking dance numbers in the 1988 film *Tap,* a movie that featured three generations of great black tap artists. "Finally," noted Sommer, "the movies have caught up with the real world of dance. Now the moviegoing public will find out what the tap dance audience discovered at least ten years ago—the vital black heritage that shaped the look and sound of American tap dance." No one has been more pivotal than Gregory Hines in bringing that heritage to a mainstream audience.

Hines is also considered a bankable romantic actor. *People* correspondent Mary Vespa wrote: "With his dancer's grace, relaxed wit and bedroom eyes, Hines could move into a realm where no black actor has been before—the hip, sophisticated, romantic-comedy territory staked out by Cary Grant and Fred Astaire." Hines has earned top billing in a variety of roles, from the comic *Running Scared,* where he teamed with Billy Crystal, to the science-fiction adventure *Eve of Destruction,* to the critically well-received big-budget drama *A Rage in Harlem.* Director Peter Hyams told *People* that Hines is one black actor who need not fear for his future in the business. "In terms of talent," Hyams said, "Gregory is an absolute ticking thermonuclear weapon just waiting to go off."

Such an assessment should undoubtedly reassure Hines, who still sees himself first and foremost as a tap dancer. As he settles into middle age, Hines has realized that his reflexes are slowing down. "I know I can't dance at this level indefinitely," he told *Ebony.* "Skill diminishes with age; it's just mathematics. But to me, dancing is like sex. Like Nipsey Russell said, 'I'm not as good as I once was, but I'm as good once as I ever was.'" Expectations of Hines's decline seem premature, however; he works out regularly and has kept his 5'10" frame in remarkably sound condition.

Having been in show business for forty-odd years, Hines is used to the frantic pace and months away from home and family. On the rare occasions when he is free, the dancer enjoys spending time with his wife and three children. "My family is very important to my existence," he told *People.* "If there was something beyond the marriage ceremony I could do with [my wife], I would. I have responsibilities as a husband and father that I want to fulfill." With his trademark left earring and drooping eyelids, Hines has an offbeat attractiveness that will undoubtedly sustain him past the age when most dancers retire. Already he has left an indelible mark on the movies by bringing his tough and alluring variety of tap to young audiences. *Dance*'s Sommer concluded that the grand old men of tap, the hoofers of yesteryear, see Gregory Hines as their future, "their immortality, the talented baby of them all, who carries the legacy of their rhythms in the soles of his feet."

Sources

Dance Magazine, December 1988.
Ebony, January 1991.
Glamour, December 1985.
People, August 11, 1986.

—Mark Kram

Billie Holiday

1915-1959

Jazz singer

Billie Holiday is considered by many to be the greatest of all jazz singers. In a tragically abbreviated singing career that lasted less than three decades, her evocative phrasing and poignant delivery profoundly influenced vocalists who followed her. Although her warm, feathery voice inhabited a limited range, she used it like an accomplished jazz instrumentalist, stretching and condensing phrases in an ever-shifting dialogue with accompanying musicians. Famous for delivering lyrics a bit behind the beat, she alternately endowed them with sadness, sensuality, languor, and irony. Rarely singing blues, Holiday performed mostly popular material, communicating deep emotion by stripping down rather than dressing up words and lines. "If you find a tune that's got something to do with you, you just feel it, and when you sing it, other people feel it, too," Holiday once explained. According to the *Penguin Encyclopedia of Popular Music*, "She was the first and is perhaps still the greatest of jazz singers, if the essence of jazz singing is to make the familiar sound fresh, and to make any lyric come alive with personal meaning for the listener."

Holiday's life was a study in hardship. Her parents married when she was three, but her musician father was seldom present and the couple soon divorced. Receiving little schooling as a child, Holiday scrubbed floors and ran errands for a nearby brothel so she could listen to idols Louis Armstrong and Bessie Smith on the Victrola in its parlor. Brutally raped at ten, she was sent to a reformatory for "seducing" her adult attacker; at fourteen she was jailed for prostitution. Determined to find work as a dancer or singer in Harlem, Holiday moved to New York City in 1928 and landed her first job at Jerry Preston's Log Cabin, where her vocals moved customers to tears. Discovered in another Harlem club by jazz record producer John Hammond in 1932, she made her first recording a year later with Benny Goodman's orchestra. She began to record regularly for Columbia, usually under the direction of Teddy Wilson, backed by small studio bands comprised of the day's best jazz sidemen. These included saxophonist and soulmate Lester Young, whose style approximated Holiday's own; it was he who gave the pretty, dignified young singer the nickname "Lady Day."

Intended largely for a black jukebox audience, the Wilson discs—mostly silly and second-rate love songs that

At a Glance. . .

Born Eleanora Fagan on April 7, 1915, in Baltimore, MD; died of cardiac arrest July 17, 1959, in New York City; daughter of Clarence Holiday (a jazz guitarist) and Sadie Fagan (a domestic); married James Monroe (marriage ended); married Louis McKay (separated).

Jazz singer. Began career in Harlem clubs, 1930; made recording debut with Benny Goodman ensemble, 1933; performed and recorded with various jazz bands, including those of Teddy Wilson, 1935-39, Count Basie, 1937, and Artie Shaw, 1938; solo recording artist and performer in theaters and nightclubs, 1940s and 1950s. Appeared in short film *Rhapsody in Black,* 1935, and feature film *New Orleans,* 1946, and on television program *Sound of Jazz,* 1957.

Awards: *Esquire* silver award, 1945 and 1946, gold award, 1944 and 1947; *Metronome* poll winner, 1945-46.

white singers had declined to record—were quickly and cheaply made. But Holiday and company transformed them into jazz treasures, immediately appreciated by musicians, critics, and jazz afficionados, if not the public at large. These hundred-odd songs—delivered in a light, buoyant style—are today considered among Holiday's most significant work. Forgoing club engagements in 1937 to tour with Count Basie's orchestra, Holiday went on to become one of the first black vocalists to be featured with a white band when she fronted for Artie Shaw a year later. Life on the road proved bitter for the singer, though; racial segregation made simple things like eating, sleeping, and going to the bathroom logistically difficult. Fed up when she could not enter one hotel through the front door with the rest of the Shaw orchestra, Holiday abandoned touring, returning to New York clubs and cabarets as a solo artist.

With Columbia's permission Holiday recorded "Strange Fruit," a controversial song about southern lynchings, for Commodore in 1939. It became a favorite of the interracial crowd for whom she performed at the Cafe Society, a Greenwich Village haunt of intellectuals and the political left. Holiday began to attract a popular following and indulged her taste for slow, melancholy songs about love gone bad, which communicated the hunger and despair that were starting to pervade her own life. Introduced to

opium and heroin in the early forties by first husband James Monroe, she began her lifelong struggle with narcotics and alcohol addiction—Monroe the first in a succession of men who would feed that addiction, squander her earnings, and physically abuse her. Jailed for a year on drug charges after a sensational trial in 1947, Holiday had her cabaret license revoked and was thus prohibited from performing in the clubs and nightspots that suited her best. Unable to stay drug-free as long as she remained involved with the music scene, she would face other arrests.

Artistry Prevailed Over Inferior Material

Holiday recorded for Decca from 1944 to 1950. Because the company sought to make her over into a popular singer, much of her material for that label was overarranged, dominated by strings, and largely ordinary. Still, Holiday's artistry prevailed in songs like "Ain't Nobody's Business If I Do" and "Lover Man." Recording for Verve from 1952 to 1957, the singer frequently returned to the small group format that best fit her glimmering voice, but by then her instrument had begun to falter from years of abuse. Her desire and range dwindling, her voice scratchy and tired, Holiday still retained her unique timing and phrasing and—when she wanted—her ability to move listeners. Recording many American standards for Verve by Cole Porter, George Gershwin, and Rodgers and Hart, her personal interpretations made them seem new again. While deemed too painful to listen to by some critics, Holiday's later recordings are esteemed by others, who find the singer's ability to communicate at its peak. In *High Fidelity* Steve Putterman, for instance, judged her Verve recordings "devastating," because "tonal beauty and emotional expressiveness worked inversely for Holiday: The more her pipes gave out, the more penetrating and affecting her delivery became."

Although industry insiders in the late 1950s—Frank Sinatra for one—acknowledged her as "unquestionably the most important influence on American popular singing in the last twenty years," when the singer succumbed in 1959 to cirrhosis of the liver, kidney trouble, and cardiac arrest at the age of forty-four, her passing was noted by the general public as much for her lurid personal life as for her musical contributions. Time has since diminished the glare of Holiday's frailties and her musical gifts shine brighter than ever. Describing Holiday in a *Down Beat* review of one Verve collection as "the woman who taught the world that the interaction and feeling of jazz musicians was the ultimate key to interpreting the great American song lyric," Will Friedwald remarked: "I guess you can't inject so much real passion into a song without scaring the pants off some people. . . . *Billie Holiday on Verve, 1946-59* is essential music by the most haunting and hypnotic voice—indeed, sound—in all of recorded music."

Selected writings

(With William Duffy) *Lady Sings the Blues* (autobiography), Doubleday, 1956.

Compostions

Wrote and co-wrote songs, including "Fine and Mellow," "God Bless the Child," and "Don't Explain."

Selected discography

Holiday's recordings can be divided into four segments: From 1933 to 1942 she largely recorded for Columbia (with some discs for Okeh, Vocalion, and Brunswick); from 1944 to 1950 she was on the Decca (now MCA) label; and from 1952 to 1957 she recorded for Verve. She also recorded two important sessions with Commodore in 1939 and 1944.

Singles

"Did I Remember?"/"No Regrets," Vocalion/Okeh, 1936.
"Billie's Blues," Vocalion/Okeh, 1936.
"Strange Fruit"/"Fine and Mellow," Commodore, 1939.
"Loveless Love," Okeh, 1941.
"God Bless the Child," Okeh, 1941.
"Gloomy Sunday," Okeh, 1941.
"Lover Man," Decca, 1944.

Reissues and compilations

Billie Holiday: The Golden Years (includes "Riffin' the Scotch," "These Foolish Things," "Pennies from Heaven," "I Can't Give You Anything But Love," and "When You're Smiling"), Columbia.
Lady Day, Columbia.
Billie's Blues, Columbia.
Billie Holiday's Greatest Hits, Columbia.
Lady in Satin, Columbia.
The Original Recordings, Columbia.
The Quintessential Billie Holiday, five volumes, Columbia.
The Billie Story, volume 1 (includes "Don't Explain," "Ain't Nobody's Business If I Do," "Lover Man," and "Solitude"), MCA, volumes 2 and 3, Columbia.

From the Original Decca Masters, RCA.
Lady's Decca Days, MCA.
The Best of Billie Holiday (includes "Travelin' Light," "I Thought of You," and "Willow Weep for Me"), Verve.
All of Nothing at All, Verve.
The Billie Holiday Songbook, Verve.
Body and Soul, Verve.
The Complete Billie Holiday on Verve, 1946-1959, Verve.
The Essential Billie Holiday, Verve.
The First Verve Sessions, Verve.
Jazz at the Philharmonic, Verve.
Lady Sings the Blues, Verve.
The Last Recordings, Verve.
Songs for Distingue Lovers, Verve.
Stormy Blues, Verve.
Fine and Mellow/I'll Be Seeing You (includes "Lover Come Back to Me," "Embraceable You," and "My Old Flame"), Commodore.

Sources

Books

Chilton, John, *Billie's Blues,* Stein & Day, 1975.
Feather, Leonard, *The New Edition of the Ecyclopedia of Jazz,* Horizon Press, 1960.
The New Grove Dictionary of Jazz, edited by Barry Kernfeld, Macmillan, 1988.
Penguin Encyclopedia of Popular Music, edited by Donald Clarke, Viking, 1989.
Simon, George T., and others, *The Best of the Music Makers,* Doubleday, 1979.
Tudor, Dean, *Popular Music: An Annotated Guide to Recordings,* Libraries Unlimited, 1983.

Periodicals

Down Beat, February 1986; July 1989.
Esquire, October 1989.
High Fidelity, January 1986; May 1987.
New York Herald Tribune Book Review, August 5, 1956.
People, June 1, 1987.
Stereo Review, March 1981.

—*Nancy Pear*

Jesse Jackson

1941—

Civil rights leader, politician

During the last decade Jesse Jackson has firmly established himself as one of the most dynamic forces for social and political action in both the national and international arenas. His campaigns for economic justice, human rights, world peace, and the United States presidency have earned him recognition in polls as America's most important black leader and the third most admired man in the U.S., as well as celebrity status among journalists and statesmen in the Middle East, Africa, Europe, and Central America. An inspirational speaker, committed activist, and tireless and confident campaigner, Jackson began his career as a foot soldier in the Civil Rights Movement of the 1960s and has developed into a leader of millions of Americans—black and white—a "rainbow coalition" of the nation's dispossessed and disenfranchised.

Jackson's 1988 bid for the Democratic presidential nomination attracted over 6.9 million votes—from urban blacks and Hispanics, poor rural whites, farmers and factory workers, feminists and homosexuals, and from white progressives wanting to be part of a historic change. He finished behind Massachusetts Governor Michael Dukakis in the primaries, but exercised the power of his second-place finish to force his consideration as a vice-presidential running mate and to influence the nature of the Democratic Convention and the issues included on its platform. He called for homes for the homeless, comparable worth and day care for working women, a higher minimum wage, a commitment to the family farm, and an all-out war on drugs. "When we form a great quilt of unity and common ground" he told delegates at the party convention on July 19, 1988, "we'll have the power to bring about health care and housing and jobs and education and hope to our nation."

Jackson has drawn upon his own early experience in Greenville, South Carolina, to relate to his constituency. He was born on October 8, 1941, to a seventeen-year-old unwed high school student and her older, comfortably middle-class neighbor, a married man. Jackson's ancestry includes black slaves, a Cherokee, and a white plantation owner. Although the young Jackson was quite aware of poverty and illegitimacy, his mother, grandmother, and stepfather were always able to see to family needs. Even so, his knowledge of social inequities and of his more privileged half brothers affected him. As Barba-

At a Glance...

Full name, Jesse Louis Jackson; original name, Jesse Louis Burns; born October 8, 1941, in Greenville, SC; son of Noah Robinson (a cotton grader) and Helen Burns Jackson (a hairdresser); adopted by stepfather, Charles Henry Jackson (a postal worker), 1957; married Jacqueline Lavinia Davis, 1964; children: Santita, Jesse Louis, Jr., Jonathan Luther, Yusef Du Bois, Jacqueline Lavinia. *Education:* Attended University of Illinois, 1959-60; North Carolina Agricultural and Technical College, B.A., 1964; attended Chicago Theological Seminary, 1964-66. *Politics:* Democrat. *Religion:* Baptist.

Ordained Baptist minister, 1968. Field representative for the Council on Racial Equality (CORE), 1964; demonstrator in SCLC voting rights campaign, Selma, Alabama, 1965; Chicago coordinator of Operation Breadbasket, 1966-67, national director, 1967-71; Operation PUSH founder, 1971, executive director, 1971-86, also founder of PUSH-Excel and PUSH for Economic Justice; candidate for Democratic presidential nomination, 1983-84 and 1987-88; National Rainbow Coalition Inc., Chicago, founder, 1986, national president, 1986—; statehood senator for the District of Columbia, 1991—. Host of the syndicated television program *Voices of America with Jesse Jackson,* 1989—; also hosted radio broadcasts from Chicago and contributed weekly columns to the *Los Angeles Times* Syndicate.

Awards: Rockefeller grant, c. mid-1960s, Presidential Award, National Medical Association, 1969; Humanitarian Father of the Year, National Father's Day Committee, 1971; numerous honorary degrees from colleges and universities, including Pepperdine University, Oberlin College, Oral Roberts University, Howard University, and Georgetown University.

Addresses: *Office*—National Rainbow Coalition Inc., 30 West Washington, Suite 300, Chicago, IL 60602.

ra Reynolds wrote in her biography *Jesse Jackson: America's David:* "Every teacher Jesse came into contact with took note of his insecurities, masked by a stoic sense of superiority. They never perceived him as brilliant, but rather each saw him as a charmer, a spirited, fierce competitor with an almost uncanny drive to prove himself by always winning, always being number one in everything." At Sterling High School Jackson was elected president of his class, the honor society, and the student council, was named state officer of the Future Teachers of America, finished tenth in his class, and lettered in football, basketball, and baseball.

In 1959 Jackson left the South to attend the University of Illinois on an athletic scholarship. During his first year, however, he became dissatisfied with his treatment on campus and on the gridiron and decided to transfer to Greensboro's North Carolina Agricultural and Technical College, a predominantly black institution. There he was quarterback, honor student, fraternity officer, and president of the student body. After receiving his B.A. in sociology he accepted a Rockefeller grant to attend the Chicago Theological Seminary, where he planned to train for the ministry. Jackson was ordained a Baptist minister in 1968, though he had not finished his coursework at CTS, having instead left in 1966 to commit himself full-time to the Civil Rights Movement.

Jackson first became involved in the Civil Rights Movement while a student at North Carolina A & T. There he joined the Greensboro chapter of the Council on Racial Equality (CORE), an organization that had led early sit-ins to protest segregated lunch counters. In 1963 Jackson organized numerous marches, sit-ins, and mass arrests to press for the desegregation of local restaurants and theaters. His leadership in these events earned him recognition within the regional movement; he was chosen president of the North Carolina Intercollegiate Council on Human Rights, field director of CORE's southeastern operations, and in 1964 served as delegate to the Young Democrats National Convention. In Chicago in 1965 Jackson was a volunteer for the Coordinating Committee of Community Organizations and organized regular meetings of local black ministers and the faculty of the Chicago Theological Seminary.

Joined King and the SCLC in 1965

Jackson joined Martin Luther King, Jr., and his Southern Christian Leadership Conference (SCLC) in 1965 during demonstrations in Selma, Alabama, pushing for expanded voting rights for blacks. When the SCLC launched the Chicago Freedom Movement in 1966, Jackson was there to put his knowledge of the city and contacts within the black community to work for King. He organized local ministers to support the movement, marched through all-white neighborhoods to push for open housing, and began work on SCLC's economic program, Operation Breadbasket. Drawing from successful campaigns in other cities, Operation Breadbasket organized the black community to use selective buying and boycotts to support black manufacturers and retailers and to pressure white-owned businesses to stock more of their products and hire more black workers. Jackson served as Operation Breadbasket's Chicago coordinator for one year and was then named its national director. Under Jackson's leadership the Chicago group won concessions from local dairies and supermarkets to hire more blacks and stock more products from black businesses. It encouraged deposits from businesses and the government for black-owned banks and organized a Black Christmas and a Black Expo to promote black-owned manufacturers.

In addition to his SCLC activities, Jackson led a number of other campaigns in his adopted home city and state. In 1969 and 1970 he gathered Illinois's malnourished and led them on a march to the state capital to raise consciousness of hunger. He led a similar event in Chicago. The state responded by increasing funding to school lunch programs, but Mayor Richard Daley's machine in Chicago was less cooperative. The mayor's power and resistance to change, as well as an Illinois law that raised

difficult barriers to independent candidates, prompted Jackson to run for mayor of Chicago in 1971. He was not successful; some believe, however, that his efforts laid the foundation for Harold Washington's successful bid to become Chicago's first black mayor in 1983.

In 1971 Jackson resigned from the SCLC to found his own organization, People United to Save Humanity (PUSH). Because of his aggressive, impatient, and commanding personality, Jackson had long irritated SCLC leadership; and, in the three and a half years after King's assassination, he had offended others with his public antics to secure a role as leader of the Civil Rights Movement and his feuds with Ralph D. Abernathy, King's successor as president of the SCLC, over leadership, policy, and funding. Through PUSH Jackson continued to pursue the economic objectives of Operation Breadbasket and expand into areas of social and political development for blacks in Chicago and across the nation. The 1970s saw direct action campaigns, weekly radio broadcasts, and awards through which Jackson protected black homeowners, workers, and businesses,

Jackson addresses an anti-Apartheid rally on the steps of the U.S. Capitol in 1988.

and honored prominent blacks in the U.S. and abroad. He also promoted education through PUSH-Excel, a spin-off program that focused on keeping inner-city youths in school and providing them with job placement.

A Force in Politics

Since 1979 Jackson has repeatedly asserted himself as a prominent figure in national and international politics. In that year he traveled to South Africa to speak out against apartheid and to the Middle East to try to establish relations between Israel and the Palestinians. In January of 1984 he returned to the Middle East to negotiate the release of Lieutenant Robert Goodman, a black Navy pilot who had been shot down and taken hostage in the region. Later that year he traveled to Cuba to negotiate the release of several political prisoners held there and to Central America, where he spoke out for regional peace. Nineteen eighty-four was also the year of Jackson's first campaign for the Democratic presidential nomination. His appeals for social programs, voting rights, and affirmative action for those neglected by Reaganomics earned him strong showings in Alabama, Florida, Georgia, New York, Louisiana, and Washington, D.C. He received 3.5 million votes, enough to secure a measure of power and respect at the Democratic convention.

Jackson's 1988 campaign for the Democratic nomination was characterized by more organization and funding than his previous attempt. With the experience he gained from 1984 and new resources, Jackson and his Rainbow Coalition surprised the media and the political pundits. Initially written off as unelectable, Jackson emerged in the primary/caucus season as a serious contender for the nomination. After early respectable losses in Iowa and New Hampshire, he won five southern states on Super Tuesday, March 8, 1988. On March 12 he won the caucus in his birth state of South Carolina and three days later finished second in his home state of Illinois. On March 26 Jackson stunned Dukakis and the rest of the nation in the Michigan caucus: Having won that northern industrial state with 55 percent of the vote, Jackson became the Democratic front-runner. Dukakis later recaptured the lead and the eventual nomination with strong showings in the second half of the primary season. Even so, Jackson had succeeded in bringing Americans of all colors to consider a black man for the presidency and vice-presidency.

After the 1988 elections Jackson moved his home from Chicago to Washington, D.C. There he has campaigned against homelessness in the nation's capital. He was considered one of the top contenders to take over as the capital's mayor after Marion Barry was forced out of office by a drug scandal, but Jackson refused to run.

Instead, he announced in July of 1990 that he would seek election as the District of Columbia's "statehood senator," a position recently established by the city government to push Congress to grant statehood to the district. He was elected in November and sworn into office in January of 1991. Even with his new duties, Jackson remains the most visible and vocal contender for the 1992 Democratic presidential nomination.

Never Far From Controversy

From civil rights activist to presidential candidate, Jesse Jackson has stirred both admiration and criticism. His behavior in the hours immediately following the assassination of Martin Luther King, Jr., was a subject of controversy: Jackson claimed that he had held the dying leader, heard his last words, and had his shirt stained by King's blood. Other SCLC officers present at the murder have disputed those claims. As an organizer Jackson often overstepped his authority in SCLC matters and violated organization policy in a number of his Chicago campaigns. His economic boycotts were criticized by some businessmen as extortion and by some reformers for lacking follow-through. The management of PUSH's people and finances were the subject of close scrutiny and the freewheeling nature of the organization was regularly called into question. Jackson offended some Americans by negotiating with the PLO (Palestine Liberation Organization), Fidel Castro, and the Marxist Sandinista government of Nicaragua. Jackson's connection with the Black Muslim leader and outspoken anti-Semite Louis Farrakhan, as well as the candidate's reference to New York City as "Hymietown," outraged Jews.

The same driving ambition to achieve success that is at the root of Jackson's weaknesses is also the source of his strength. He is a tireless worker who is fiercely committed to his causes, even when bedridden—Jackson suffers from sickle-cell trait. He is an intelligent, creative, and charismatic leader, an inspirational speaker capable of archiving numerous details, then using them to encapsulate his agenda along with the aspirations of many Americans. He has a flair for the dramatic that infuses an increasingly tedious political process with life. And finally, Jackson acts while others talk of action. He has become the leading spokesman for Americans forgotten by the power brokers of the political process, especially blacks. In his speeches Jackson often relates his vision of hope for these Americans: "We have come from the slaveship to the championship, from the guttermost to the uttermost, from the outhouse to the courthouse, and from the statehouse to the White House."

Sources

Books

Abernathy, Ralph David, *And the Walls Came Tumbling Down,* Harper, 1989.

Colton, Elizabeth O., *The Jackson Phenomenon: The Man, the Power, the Message,* Doubleday, 1989.

Reynolds, Barbara A., *Jesse Jackson: America's David,* JFJ Associates, 1985.

Periodicals

Christian Science Monitor, August 15, 1989.

Commonweal, November 7, 1986.

Harper's Magazine, March 1969.

Newsweek, April 4, 1988; October 16, 1989; January 29, 1990.

Vanity Fair, January 1988.

—Bryan Ryan

Mae C. Jemison

1957(?)—

Astronaut, physician

In June of 1987 Dr. Mae C. Jemison made history when she became the first black woman selected to be an astronaut by the National Aeronautics and Space Administration (NASA). Jemison came a step closer to being the first black woman in space when she was assigned the role of mission specialist for the June 1991 shuttle Discovery flight, Spacelab-J. A joint venture with Japan, Spacelab-J is charged with conducting life science and materials processing experiments in space to help scientists better understand the environment. As a mission specialist—or "scientist astronaut"—Jemison's responsibilities include, as she explained to Marilyn Marshall in *Ebony,* being "familiar with the shuttle and how it operates, to do the experiments once you get into orbit, to help launch the payloads or satellites, and also do extra-vehicular activities, which are the space walks."

Becoming an astronaut was, as Marshall noted, a "natural progression" for Jemison. As a young girl and teenager she was always interested in science, especially astronomy, and was encouraged by her parents and teachers to pursue not only her science studies, but also dance and art. She earned a double degree at Stanford Univer-

sity—in chemical engineering and Afro-American studies—and then studied medicine at Cornell University. While at Cornell she traveled to Thailand and Kenya to provide primary medical care services. After completing her medical internship Jemison joined the Peace Corps and worked as a staff physician in West Africa. "I took care of Peace Corps volunteers and State Department personnel in Sierra Leone and I oversaw the medical health care program for volunteers in Liberia," Jemison explained to an *Ebony* contributor.

Jemison was working as a general practitioner in Los Angeles when she first applied to the space program, in October of 1985—three months before the space shuttle *Challenger* accident that killed seven astronauts. NASA postponed the application process because of the *Challenger* incident, but Jemison still aspired to become an astronaut and re-applied in 1986. "I didn't think about [the *Challenger*] in terms of keeping me involved," she told Marshall. "I thought about it because it was very sad because of the astronauts who were lost, but not in any way keeping me from being interested in it or changing my views about things." Jemison was one of 15 candi-

Joseph D. Atkinson, Jr., head of NASA's Equal Opportunity Programs Office, described Jemison as a "very stately, intelligent, sincere and stable young woman." Commenting to Marshall, he added that Jemison earns high marks for being not only "highly qualified technically," but also "extremely sensitive to the social needs of the community." Regarding her role as the nation's first black woman astronaut, Jemison commented to *Ebony* on what her achievement might signify to other women. "The thing that I have done throughout my life is to do the best job that I can and to be me. . . . In terms of being a role model, I really feel like if I'm a role model, what I'd like to be is someone who says, 'No, don't try to necessarily be like me or live your life or grow up to be an astronaut or a physician unless that's what you want to do.'"

At a Glance. . .

Born c. 1957, in Decatur, AL; raised in Chicago, IL; daughter of Charlie (a custodian and contractor) and Dorothy (a teacher) Jemison. *Education:* Graduated from Stanford University (degree in chemical engineering and Afro-American Studies), 1977; Cornell University, M.D., 1981. Medical intern, Los Angeles, CA, beginning 1981; staff doctor with Peace Corps in West Africa, 1983-85; CIGNA Health Plans of California, Los Angeles, general practitioner, 1985-87; National Aeronautics and Space Administration (NASA), Houston, TX, astronaut, 1987—.

Awards: Award from *Essence* magazine, 1988.

Addresses: *Home*—Houston, TX. *Office*—National Aeronautics and Space Administration, Johnson Space Center, Houston, TX 77058.

---

dates selected from a field of nearly 2,000 aspiring astronauts. In addition to her assignment as mission specialist, she works as a liaison between the Johnson Space Center in Houston and NASA crew members in Cape Canaveral, Florida.

Sources

Ebony, October 1987; August 1989; February 1990.
Essence, October 1988.
Jet, June 22, 1987; October 30, 1989.
New York Times, October 1, 1989.
Working Woman, April 1989.

—*Michael E. Mueller*

Ben Johnson

1961—

Olympic runner

Canadian sprinter Ben Johnson has entered the 1990s determined to rescue his tarnished reputation. For most of the 1980s Johnson was among the most famous and best-loved athletes in Canada and his long-standing feud with American runner Carl Lewis earned him great attention in the United States as well. Once an Olympic gold medalist and the fastest man on earth, Johnson was stripped of his honors for using anabolic steroids to enhance his performance. His downfall at the 1988 Olympic games—and his subsequent confession to years of steroid use—came as a blow to track fans worldwide. *Maclean's* contributor Bob Levin wrote: "[Johnson] was a rocket, a role model, a national hero. . . . To Canadians, he was never Johnson, just Ben. . . . But when the steroid scandal burst upon the world, . . . Canadians, who had risen as one to applaud Johnson's triumph, doubled over in sickened disbelief, taking Johnson's humiliation as their own. Children wept openly. Many people clutched at faint hopes of some innocent explanation. Others branded Ben a betrayer, a cheat."

Johnson served a two-year suspension imposed by the International Amateur Athletic Federation and was re-instated for competition in September of 1990. Having spent his days of suspension crusading against drug use in Canada's schools and amateur athletic clubs, the young runner was able to regain some of the respect he had lost. The rest of that respect he hopes to earn back on the track. *Washington Post* correspondent Christine Brennan noted that the citizens of Canada "were embarrassed by [Johnson]; now they love him. Johnson is Canada's prodigal son." Brennan quoted Toronto *Sun* columnist Jim O'Leary, who called the runner "a risk taker" and "a high-wire act in a nation of couch potatoes. [Canadians] admire his flair, applaud his success and now seem determined to cushion his fall with a net of public sympathy."

Ben Johnson, Jr., was born in Falmouth, Jamaica, on December 30, 1961. Falmouth, a formerly prosperous seaport that has fallen upon hard times, is about 17 miles east of Montego Bay. The Johnson family was reasonably successful, with a pleasant home and a large yard. Ben, Sr., had a regular job repairing telephones for the Jamaica Telephone Company; he also raised chickens, ducks, cows, pigs, vegetables, and bees. The fifth of six

At a Glance...

Full name, Benjamin Sinclair Johnson, Jr.; born December 30, 1961, in Falmouth, Jamaica; son of Ben (a telephone repairman) and Gloria (a cook and waitress) Johnson. *Education:* Graduated from Yorkdale High, Ontario, Canada; attended Centennial College, Ontario.

Sprinter and relay runner, 1977-88 and 1990—. Appeared in the Summer Olympics in Los Angeles, 1984, earned two bronze medals, for 100 meter race and 400 meter relay; earned four indoor world records, 1987, including a 9.83-second finish in the 100 meter in Rome; appeared in the Summer Olympics in Seoul, South Korea, 1988, earned gold medal, for 100-meter run, stripped of medal and banned from Olympic competition for two years after urine test revealed steroid use. Re-instated to Olympic eligibility, 1990.

children, Ben, Jr., grew up outdoors, running and swimming in the nearby ocean at every opportunity. "We'd take off all our clothes and swim naked all day," Johnson told *Maclean's.* "We couldn't get our clothes all wet up or everyone would know what we'd been doing. Even in dry clothes, my parents could tell if I'd been swimming, because they could see the sea salt drying white against my black skin and I would get a beating."

Johnson's mother told *Maclean's* that her son would never walk when he could run. "I would turn my head for a moment, and he would be far in the distance." Johnson's childhood heroes included famous sprinters Donald Quarrie of Jamaica and Hasely Crawford of Trinidad, but his most immediate inspiration was his older brother, Edward. While Johnson was still quite young his brother earned a spot with the Conquerors track club. Soon the youngster was tagging along to meets and earning small change in informal street races. In school Johnson was an average student who was bothered by a speech impediment; his teachers remembered him as shy and withdrawn.

In 1972 Johnson's mother decided that her children needed a better education than rural Falmouth afforded them. She had a friend who had emigrated to Toronto, so she boarded a plane and went to look for work in Canada. Eventually she got a full-time job as a cook and moved Johnson and three of his siblings into a two-bedroom flat in suburban Toronto. "I went because

Mom went," Johnson told *Sports Illustrated* of his move north. "I didn't really know where I was going." For a short time Ben, Sr., joined the family, but eventually returned to his job with the Jamaican telephone company. Father and son remained on good terms, however, visiting on holidays and communicating by phone.

Academic Trouble Turned Focus to Athletics

The transition to Canada's schools proved difficult for Johnson. His Jamaican accent and stutter led to placement in remedial classes. "I didn't like to go to school," Johnson confessed in *Sports Illustrated.* He did manage to graduate from Yorkdale High, though his reading and mathematics skills were judged to be very basic. Johnson's interests decidedly lay elsewhere. In 1977 he accompanied Edward to the Scarborough (now Mazda) Optimist Track Club, where both brothers began to train with coach Charles Francis. Francis himself had been an Olympic sprinter for Canada in the early 1970s. He was hardly impressed by the lanky young Johnson. The coach told *Maclean's:* "He was small for his age and so skinny that I thought he was 12, not 14."

When he arrived at the Scarborough Optimist Track Club Johnson could hardly run a lap around the track without collapsing from exhaustion. But after six months of Francis's coaching the youth gained 43 pounds and six inches of height—and became a formidable runner as well. In 1978 Johnson placed fourth in the 50 meter dash at the National Indoor Track and Field Championships in Montreal. Only two years later he ran a close second in the one hundred meter event in the Canadian men's championships. By then Coach Francis was truly excited about his young prospect and the two became fast friends.

In 1980 Johnson encountered superstar Carl Lewis for the first time when both competed in the Pan-American junior championships in Sudbury, Ontario. Lewis easily outdistanced Johnson on that occasion, as he often would over the next four years. The defeat—and Lewis's affable, easygoing manner—galled Johnson, who became determined to run faster than his confident rival. Francis counseled patience and Johnson worked methodically to improve his times and build his upper body strength. "Ben never has to learn anything new," Francis told *Sports Illustrated.* "He can perfect every exercise. . . . The core sprint exercises—the hips, the upper legs, the arms—are where he goes high." At 15 Johnson weighed only ninety-three pounds; seven years later he was a 175-pound marvel who could bench press 335 pounds. He was still unable to defeat Lewis, however, who took four gold medals in the 1984 Olympics. The 1984 Games proved quite disappointing for Johnson; he was forced to settle for two bronze medals while the public fawned over Lewis.

Rivalry With Carl Lewis Proved Inspirational

The feud between Johnson and Lewis grew ever more heated as the two runners exchanged barbs through the press, each predicting the other's defeat and disgrace. In 1985 Johnson finally proved that he could beat Lewis when he won the World Championships in Canberra, Australia. During most of the following two years Johnson absolutely dominated world track events. He won the one hundred meter race at Moscow's 1986 Goodwill Games in record-breaking fashion with a 9.95-second time. The following year he was undisputed champion with four indoor world records and an absolutely stunning 9.83-second finish in the outdoor World Championships in Rome. The dazzling victory in Rome, where Johnson finished a full meter ahead of Lewis, left no room for doubt: Ben Johnson was proclaimed the fastest man on earth and was hailed as Canada's finest athlete.

Even then Carl Lewis suggested—in a roundabout way—that Johnson was using performance-enhancing drugs. Johnson and his trainers countered that he had passed any number of urine tests after his meets. Indeed, a test run just after the Rome race yielded negative results, leaving most observers certain that Lewis's charges were merely a matter of sour grapes. Johnson did face other problems as he reached the height of his profession, however. A hamstring injury sidelined him and he quarreled with Francis over treatment methods. His schedule became clogged with product endorsements and time-consuming business deals and the press questioned his amateur status as he spent lavishly on homes, sportscars, and art objects. Reflecting on his year in the limelight, Johnson told *Maclean's:* "I didn't know what it was going to be like. Now I'm successful, and I'm paying for it."

Discovery of Steroid Use Crippled Career

Johnson entered the 1988 Olympics in Seoul as a heavy favorite for victory in the prestigious one hundred meter dash. As predicted, he won the event, shattering his own record in the process. Even the most jaded running enthusiasts expressed amazement at Johnson's time of 9.79 seconds. The reason for his performance soon became evident, when traces of the drug stanozolol—a banned anabolic steroid—were found in his urine during a post-race test. In the worst scandal in Olympic history, Johnson was stripped of his medal—it went to Lewis, who finished second—and suspended from competition. For some time following the discovery Johnson

denied any wrongdoing. Only after Francis testified to Johnson's steroid use in court did the runner finally admit that he had been taking drugs since 1981.

The scandal held wide implications for amateur athletes throughout Canada, but the burden undoubtedly fell hardest on Johnson. Officials debated rescinding his 1987 win in Rome and a veritable fortune of product endorsement contracts were canceled or allowed to expire. Johnson faced tough times financially and personally, but through the long two-year suspension resolved to make a comeback and prove that he could win without the help of drugs. "Whatever I lost doesn't mean a thing," he told the *Philadelphia Inquirer.* "My health is the most important thing. If I had kept taking [steroids], I could have had side effects with my liver."

Johnson's reinstatement to Olympic competition in 1990 was accompanied by a reinstatement from the Canadian government for appearances as a representative of the nation. Johnson hired a new coach, Loren Seagrave,

> "People won't forget, but they're going to say, 'Great. After his downfall, the guy took care of his problems and won again.' That will be the biggest thrill of my life."

and returned to work, visibly smaller and thinner than he had been in 1988. Although he turned 30 in December of 1991, Johnson predicted that he would make his way to the 1992 Olympics as a champion sprinter. Today his races are run in memory of his father, who died of a heart attack in 1989. Johnson still harbors a grudge for Carl Lewis and lists defeating the American as his number one priority. Still, the former star admits that he has a great deal to prove, both to himself and to the people of his adopted country. "People won't forget," he told the *Chicago Tribune,* "but they're going to say, 'Great. After his downfall, the guy took care of his problems and won again.' That will be the biggest thrill of my life."

Sources

Chicago Tribune, November 20, 1990.
Maclean's, August 8, 1988; September 12, 1988; October 10, 1988.
New York Times, November 19, 1990.

Philadelphia Inquirer, January 13, 1991.

Sports Illustrated, November 30, 1987.

Washington Post, June 17, 1989; January 10, 1990; January 13, 1991.

—*Mark Kram*

Charles R. Johnson

1948—

Novelist, essayist, cartoonist

When Charles Johnson won the 1990 National Book Award in fiction for his third novel, *Middle Passage,* he became the first black man to win the award since Ralph Ellison won in 1953 for *Invisible Man.* It is worth noting too that literary critic Elizabeth A. Schultz equated Johnson with Ellison in her 1978 essay "The Heirs of Ralph Ellison," and that Johnson himself has written with admiration of the "magnificent feast of fictional styles" found in *Invisible Man.*

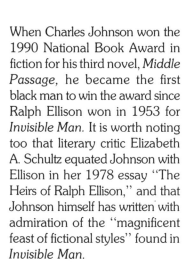

result of his exposure to playwright and social theorist Amiri Baraka and the black arts movement, Johnson came to recognize that "the built-in danger of this cultural nationalism is the very tendency toward provincialism, separatism and essentialist modes of thought that characterize the Anglophilia it opposes."

Before he became a fiction writer, Johnson established himself as a political cartoonist, publishing book-length works and contributing to a variety of newspapers and magazines. In 1970 he produced and co-hosted a how-to-draw television series on the Public Broadcasting Service called *Charlie's Pad.* At the same time, Johnson was heavily involved in cultural nationalism, organizing groups in the newly formed discipline of black studies. Then, he says, "I began to see that the intellectual questions I wanted to pursue, some of them were foreclosed on by some of the principal spokesmen of the black arts movement." In the writings of Toomer, Wright, and Ellison, Johnson found a basis for the type of philosophical fiction he wanted to write. Wright, though recognized as a leading writer of racial protest, also wrote works that Johnson felt were "compatible with the most interesting ideas in continental philosophy during the

Aside from Ellison, Johnson cites Jean Toomer and Richard Wright as writers he admires; moreover, his 11-year association with novelist John Gardner has helped him develop his unique brand of philosophical fiction. In his 1988 article "Where Philosophy and Fiction Meet" Johnson praised Toomer as a writer "whose lovely and language-rich *Cane* ushered in the Harlem Renaissance and advanced the American short story as a form." He noted that Toomer's image of the "blue man" suggested "infinity and the transcendence of dualism," an important concept in Johnson's personal development from a member of the black arts movement of the 1960s to a philosophical novelist. While Johnson's first publication, a cartoon collection titled *Black Humor,* was a direct

thirties and forties." Similarly, Johnson found Ellison's *Invisible Man* "to be, at bottom, about the ambiguities of perception and interpretation in the racial world."

Johnson's development as a first-class novelist and writer began with his association with John Gardner. Feeling out of step with his black arts contemporaries, Johnson wrote in *American Visions,* "I tried to maintain that most insecure of positions demanded by philosophy: namely, a perpetual openness to thoughts and feelings wherever I found them. And a tremendous source of help for this was my 11-year association with John Gardner." Johnson studied under Gardner at

Southern Illinois University as a graduate student, earning a master's degree in philosophy.

Johnson had written six apprentice novels before penning *Faith and the Good Thing,* published in 1974. As described by Arthur P. Davis in his survey *Novels of the New Black Renaissance,* it is "a fascinating melange of classic philosophy, scholasticism, occult writings, folklore (including Southern superstition and Negro tall tales), surrealistic dreams, flashbacks, and down-to-earth realism. . . . Taking Faith from her Deep Southern home to Chicago and back to her native region, the author carries the reader along with a brilliant tour de force of fantasy and realism." Davis found Johnson's refinement and folk knowledge an unusual mixture and called the novel "a strange book, a provocative book, an eminently readable book." It is the "overall mythic design" of *Faith and the Good Thing* that initially led literary critic Schultz to draw her comparison to Ellison's *Invisible Man.*

Eight years passed before Johnson's second novel, *Oxherding Tale,* was published. According to the author, the manuscript "went through 25 publishers before Indiana University Press took the great risk of releasing it." Like his award-winning third novel, *Middle Passage,* his second novel is a slave narrative. Johnson admits that *Oxherding Tale* is more complex than *Middle Passage.* He describes it as "a modern, comic, philosophical slave narrative—a kind of dramatization of the famous 'Ten Oxherding Pictures' of Zen artist Kakuan-Shien." Soon after the publication of *Oxherding Tale* Johnson began research for *Middle Passage.* "I went back and looked at every sea story from Apollonius of Rhodes to Homer—all the way through Melville, Conrad, London, the Sinbad stories, slave narratives that took place on boats—about the middle passage."

Like his previous novels, *Middle Passage* combines the adventures of a roguish main character with philosophical concerns about race, culture, and individual identity. Characteristic of much of Johnson's fiction, humor and satire are also found in abundance. As Linnea Lannon described *Middle Passage* in the *Detroit Free Press,* "It is at once witty and wily, a novel laced with references to great adventures of another age (Moby Dick and "The Rime of the Ancient Mariner") but not weighed down by them, a deeply philosophical book that never leaves the reader mired in symbolism." Johnson himself described *Middle Passage* as "a philosophical sea adventure, a genre-crossing novel, which is itself a kind of genre." In accepting the National Book Award for *Middle Passage,* he predicted that black fiction would become one of "increasing intellectual and artistic generosity, one that enables us as a people, as a culture, to move from narrow complaint to broad celebration."

Selected writings

Black Humor (cartoon collection), Johnson, 1970.
Half-Past Nation Time (cartoon collection), Aware, 1972.
Faith and the Good Thing (novel), Viking, 1974.
Oxherding Tale (novel), Indiana University Press, 1982.
The Sorcerer's Apprentice (short stories), Atheneum, 1986.
Being and Race: Black Writing Since 1970 (essays), Indiana University Press, 1988.
Middle Passage (novel), Atheneum, 1990.

Sources

Books

Contemporary Authors, Volume 116, Gale, 1986.
Contemporary Literary Criticism, Gale, Volume 7, 1977, Volume 51, 1989.

Dictionary of Literary Biography, Volume 33, Gale, 1984.

Periodicals

American Visions, June 1988.
Boston Globe, January 28, 1991.
Callaloo, October 1978.
Chronicle of Higher Education, January 16, 1991.
CLA Journal, June 1978; December 1978.
Contemporary Literature, Autumn 1978.
Detroit Free Press, December 9, 1990.
Detroit News, January 17, 1991.
New York Times Book Review, July 1, 1990.
People, January 14, 1991.
Village Voice, July 19, 1983.

—*David Bianco*

Bill T. Jones

1952(?)—

Dancer, choreographer

Bill T. Jones is an innovative dancer and choreographer whose most famous works have been based on a loving partnership and the pain of loss. Jones and Arnie Zane formed two dance troupes and had established a growing following and earned excellent reviews when Zane fell ill with AIDS. The two continued to dance their characteristically formalist duets until just before Zane's death in 1988. Soon after, Jones created an extraordinary dance called *Absence,* which evoked the memory of his late partner and lover, and addresses the varied feelings associated with bereavement. Zane's death is only one of the many subjects with which the choreographer and his troupe have wrestled; Jones said in *People* that "a dance can come from my fears about aging or about the betrayal of the environment. I just want this funky company to say, 'Yeah, life hurts like hell, but this is how I keep going. I have a sense of humor. I've got my brothers and sisters. I've got this ability to make something out of nothing. I can clap my hands and make magic.'"

Jones's early life was nomadic: His parents and their twelve children worked where they could, mostly in Florida. Jones later became a star high school athlete in New York, where he also gained valuable early stage experience and became an award-winning amateur actor. As a student at the State University of New York in Binghamton Jones began to question his artistic direction and sexual orientation. He told *People:* "A lot of things were changing in my life, one of which was meeting Arnie and starting my first relationship with a man. I didn't feel comfortable being a jock anymore, and the theater department was too conservative for me. So dance reared its beautiful head." Soon after their introduction Jones and Zane traveled together to Amsterdam, where they lived for several years before returning to New York and forming the American Dance Asylum. That troupe performed—completely naked—to great local acclaim. Jones and Zane would manage, nonetheless, to avoid the predictability that early success often creates.

In 1982 Jones and Zane formed another dance troupe; the new group, however, was accused of selling out because they had created what *New York* magazine described as "big, splashy spectacles in which outrageousness or fashion, of social and political attitudes—melded blithely with earlier formalist concerns." Most

At a Glance. . .

Born c. 1952; raised in Florida and Wayland, NY; son of migrant laborers. *Education:* Attended the State University of New York at Binghamton c. 1971.

Dancer and choreographer. Co-founded, with Arnie Zane, the American Dance Asylum c. 1974, and the Bill T. Jones/Arnie Zane dance company, 1982. Principal works include *Absence, D-Man in the Waters,* and *Last Supper at Uncle Tom's Cabin.*

critics, though, agreed that the troupe's progressiveness in both subject and execution demanded serious attention. *Interview* called the Jones/Zane troupe "one of the freshest and most innovative modern dance troupes in the world," relating how at "their breakthrough performance at the Brooklyn Academy of Music's Next Wave Festival in 1982, when they performed with jazz drummer Max Roach, [they] reinvented the language of movement."

The dance company's future hung in the balance when Zane became ill in the mid 1980s. Jones feared that making Zane's illness public might adversely effect their funding, but Zane insisted on going public in hope of educating people about AIDS. By refiguring the crisis as artistic material, the troupe began exploring the emotional and physical impact of AIDS in their dances. "Living and dying is not the big issue," Jones told the *MacNeil/ Lehrer Report* in 1987, as reported in *People.* "The big issue is what you're going to do with your time while you're here. I [am] determined to perform." Zane's death in 1988 was reflected in dances of loss, grieving, anger, and ultimately, acceptance. The company encountered financial problems that year, partly because of Zane's inability to dance. *People* recounted that "the troupe toured less and less often and nearly declared bankruptcy in 1988 but was saved by a group of artist friends who sold their works to raise $100,000."

The company pulled together to support Jones emotionally after Zane's death, again using dance as a catalyst for their grief. The piece *Absence* was composed by Zane to depict the poignancy of a dancer who has lost a partner of many years. Jones called up the memory of Zane by sometimes seeming out of balance on stage, lacking a counterweight, and then pausing forgetfully for his partner's steps. Critic Robert Jones responded in *People* to a 1989 performance of *Absence;* he described "a shimmering, ecstatic quality that was euphoric and almost unbearably moving." Tobi Tobias, dance critic for *New*

York, said that the work took "its shape from Zane's special loves: still images and highly wrought, emotion-saturated vocal music." When another troupe member fell ill with AIDS soon after Zane's death, Jones choreographed *D-Man in the Waters,* which depicted dancers struggling with fateful tides.

Triumphs for the troupe after these painful losses included a premiere at the Houston Grand Opera in the fall of 1989 and a debut at the Munich Opera Festival in 1990. Like *Absence,* Jones's next important piece, *Last Supper at Uncle Tom's Cabin,* was inspired partly by Zane—conflict was still a theme, but not strictly as an effect of death. In the *New York Times* Jones explained the origins of *Last Supper at Uncle Tom's:* "I think of Harriet Beecher Stowe's novel as a wonderful liberal tract. Arnie Zane and I were talking about the Last Supper a couple of months before he died, and the idea of the Last Supper at Uncle Tom's Cabin sort of started as a joke. After Arnie died, I began to look more closely at the idea. There is so much about people being torn from each other and people in pursuit of each other and with the kind of robust athletic partnering that we do, I think we'll produce something quite evocative."

The subjects in conflict are meant to be resolved in the course of *Last Supper at Uncle Tom's Cabin,* which is divided into distinct parts. The opening section of the dance is a fast-paced summation of Stowe's book about slavery, using nontraditional casting, mime, and masks to emphasize the role-playing and absurdity of slavery. The next portion is a series of four solos by women, who in turn present the troubles of a slave, a battered woman, a lesbian, and a prostitute. Jones then dances a solo portrait of Job, the biblical character ravaged by misfortune as a test of his faith in God. Next, the biblical reference to Job becomes a tableau of the Last Supper. The final part of the dance is presented by an enlarged troupe—the core company, joined by others, "stages a sixties love-in," as it was termed in *New York.* "It's amazing how this sort of cheaply sentimental catharsis can still get to you," the magazine ventured.

Tobias took a broad view of Jones's choreography for *Last Supper at Uncle Tom's Cabin.* "Dance is not, primarily, what it's about. In genre, it's a multimedia extravaganza. Although there's plenty of movement—vibrant solos in an eclectic vocabulary, sternly patterned group work—someone's usually talking at the same time. . . . [It is a] work bristling with anger, energy, and provocative questions, but one apparently still 'in progress.'" Commenting to Tobias, Jones said of the work, "This piece must start as a fight and end as a huge song," testimony to his ongoing commitment to take life's jumbled and troubled experiences and make them meaningful and beautiful through his art.

Sources

Interview, March 1989.
New York, January 5, 1987; September 10, 1990; November 26, 1990.
New York Times, December 31, 1989.
People, July 31, 1989.

—Christine Ferran

Ahmed (Mathieu) Kerekou

1933—

President of Benin

Benin, the former French colony of Dahomey, became independent on August 1, 1960. It was renamed the People's Republic of Benin in 1975 as part of an ideological shift to a Marxist-Leninist state following a 1972 military coup led by Mathieu Kerekou. Sandwiched between Nigeria to the east and the even smaller nation of Togo to the west, Benin receives little attention in the United States. The American ambassador left in 1975 and did not return until diplomatic relations were restored in 1983, as the Kerekou regime sought to pursue a policy of liberalization. There is virtually no U.S. investment in this tiny nation, due in large part to its lack of exportable resources and the government's Marxist-Leninist stance for so many years. Only in 1982 did Benin become an oil-producing state.

Kerekou has ruled Benin as its president since he came to power in 1972. He brought to Benin a much-needed political stability, military rather than civilian rule, and a Marxist-Leninist ideology. The twelve years following independence were characterized by extreme political instability, as regional leaders vied for power. Benin's tribal groups fall into three distinct geographical regions, and each region had a powerful political leader. The three-way political competition between Hubert Maga, leader of the northern Bariba ethnic group, Sourou Migan Apithy representing the southeastern Yoruba and Goun tribes, and Justin Ahomadegbe of the southwest and south-central Fon group, created twelve years of continuous ethnic tensions in Dahomey. During this period, military officers intervened six times to quell political bickering and calm ethnic and regional conflicts.

The final military intervention came on October 26, 1972, when Major Mathieu Kerekou established himself as the leader of a new military regime. The coup ended the triumvirate presidential council of Maja, Ahomadegbe, and Apithy, a compromise government that lasted just over two years. Five years earlier, in 1967, then-Captain Kerekou had backed Major Kouandete's seizure of power, which led to the appointment of Emile Zinsou, a conservative politician from the 1940s, as president. In the 1967 coup, the junior officers were content to relinquish power to their seniors; but in the 1972 coup, Kerekou and other junior officers established their own regime and removed the senior officers from command

At a Glance...

Adopted first name, Ahmed, upon conversion to Islam, 1980; born September 2, 1933, in Kourfa, Atakora, Dahomey (now Benin); member of the Somba ethnic group; married with children. *Education:* Attended the Saint-Louis Secondary School, Senegal; attended the Military Training College, Frejus, France; and the Saint-Raphael Military School, France.

Served in the French army 1960-61, joined the Dahomey army, 1961; aide-de-camp to President Hubert Maga, 1961-63; participated in coup that removed President Christophe Soglo, 1967; chairman of Military Revolutionary Council, 1967-68; promoted to rank of major, 1970; deputy chief of staff, 1970-72; Minister of Planning, 1972; led coup, 1972; President of Republic of Benin, 1972—; Minister of National Defense, 1972-90.

Addresses: *Office*—Presidence de la Republique, Cotonou, Benin.

by appointing them to sinecures as heads of state-run companies and other positions. The marginalized senior officers made one attempt to regain power in 1973, but were unsuccessful.

The 1972 coup was instigated by a group of junior officers who asked Kerekou to join them just before the coup took place. At that time, Kerekou had ties to senior as well as junior officers. After the coup, Kerekou took over as chief of staff. In justifying the coup, Kerekou said he had not "seized" power but "collected" it back. His statement reflected a militaristic philosophy of political power as well as the fact that the armed forces had become the vehicle for the political aspirations of certain officers.

Consolidated His Power

Kerekou resolved conflicts with other members of the coup over his authority through a series of administrative changes that strengthened the powers of the presidency and gradually downgraded or removed others from the government. He then brought his own supporters into the government. Following the coup, former heads of state and ministers were placed under arrest, except for Zinsou, who was in France. The ministers were gradually released after they returned some of their corrupt gains

from holding office. Maga, Apithy, and Ahomadegbe were not released from house arrest until 1981.

Kerekou's military regime marked a clear break with all earlier Dahomeyan governments. He introduced revolutionary changes into political and economic life. The state sector was rapidly expanded through nationalization, and the "national revolution" would follow a Marxist-Leninist course that was officially adopted in 1974. The decisive break with the old system was symbolized by changing the name of the country to the People's Republic of Benin in 1975.

In his first major speech in November 1972, Kerekou announced a policy of national independence to represent national interests and an end to foreign influence in education and culture. His core philosophy was one of "militant nationalism," reflecting a common belief among Dahomey's educated citizens that previous governments were too closely aligned with France and French interests. Not allowing the left to replace or control his government, Kerekou would wait for two years before making any official mention of socialization or the nationalization of foreign businesses. Any radical measures in the early years of his regime were modest, including, for example, the opening of diplomatic relations with China, North Korea, and Libya, as Dahomey became part of the non-aligned or "progressive" bloc of nations.

Opposition to the new regime was difficult. As expressed by students, labor, and the Left, the opposition desired the restoration of a civilian, popular-based regime and a reduction in austerity measures and rural exploitation. In January of 1973 Kerekou lifted an existing ban on student organizations that had been imposed on more than 300 student organizations, the largest being the UGEED (Union generale des etudiants et des eleves du Dahomey). After the ban was lifted, the union's leadership helped to radicalize the government by organizing anti-French demonstrations.

The student-dominated FUD (*Front unique democratique*) called for a mass political party and the democratization and civilianization of the regime. Kerekou dismissed their demands but left the organization alone. Following student strikes over conditions and the regime's perceived conservatism in January of 1974, Kerekou dissolved some 180 student organizations, and some students were drafted into the army. Kerekou later denounced the students as "anarchists playing the game of anti-revolutionaries." The UGEED was then banned.

Political Changes

Among the political changes made in the first years of the new regime was the implementation of a plan to reorganize local and regional government. Following high-level deliberations in November of 1973, a "decentralization" of government was implemented to allow "the organized masses to recover control of the state apparatus." In the rural sector, directly elected local revolutionary committees were created at the village, town, and commune levels. Above these were appointed district and provincial councils. By the end of 1974, some 1,500 local committees were said to exist, giving the people a sense of participation that would help the military regime overcome its opponents. Urban changes involved creating CDRs (Committees for the Defense of the Revolution) at places of work and residency. Military officers were appointed as political commissars to be responsible for the organization, instruction, and mobilization of the people.

Kerekou announced the adoption of an official Marxist-Leninist ideology in a speech commemorating the second anniversary of the 1972 coup. His November 1974 speech proposed the same nationalistic goals of 1972, but they now required a socialist strategy. The speech was designed to legitimize his regime and to placate pressures from the left for further radicalization. From the pattern of socialism that evolved in Benin, it was apparent that socialism was not something held as a conviction by Kerekou and the officer corps. It was an *ad hoc* and changing doctrine rather than a cohesive set of premises. As outlined in the anniversary speech of 1974, its main tenets included independence from external economic control through nationalization, the transformation of society through an alliance of farmers and workers, and the realignment of foreign policy toward the "progressive bloc."

Kerekou announced the first nationalizations, of the oil distribution network and private education, on November 30, 1974. In response, France froze all of its subsidies, loans, and grants pending a resolution of the nationalization issue. Since the value of the nationalized assets was worth less than one year of aid from France, Kerekou agreed to compensate the private companies who had suffered nationalization. The deterioration of Benin's economy and balance-of-trade can, in part, be traced to poorly planned extensions of state control over the economy. Declines in productivity and inefficiency associated with the reorganization and centralization of commercial life also led to corruption.

Internal Opposition and Unrest

The Kerekou regime's popularity had diminished by 1975, which became a year of crisis for the government. Austerity measures introduced in 1974 and again in 1975 alienated trade unionists, civil servants, students,

and even many teachers. A January 1975 coup attempt by Captain Assogba on behalf of former President Zinsou was followed by a June murder of one of the coupmakers, Capt. Michel Aikpe, by the presidential guard. The death of Aikpe marked the regime's biggest crisis and was followed by an eruption of internal and external opposition. In protest, trade unions, many urban revolutionary committees and CDRs, and members of the national revolutionary council joined to call for a general strike. The strike was harshly repressed, resulting in several deaths. Many trade unionists were arrested, and the revolutionary council and civil service were purged of suspected opponents. Kerekou withdrew to the army barracks at Cotonou and ruled from there.

Since Aikpe was a southerner and Kerekou was a member of the northern-based Somba ethnic group, Aikpe's murder was seen as part of a pattern of regional favoritism. Following the incident, many southern civil servants and diplomatic staff abroad resigned. In July 1975, many exiled politicians, civil servants, and intellectuals formed a new opposition group, the FLRD (Front for the Libera-

---

Kerekou has ruled Benin as its president since he came to power in 1972

---

tion and Rehabilitation of Dahomey), in Brussels. Kerekou used this as an opportunity to further purge opponents, and a February 1976 trial resulted in many exiles being condemned to death.

By 1975, though, Kerekou's government was strong enough to withstand virtually all opposition, which at the time was weak and unpopular by comparison to the opposition movements of the 1960s. He had created enough popular consent through the impact of his policies and increased participation; and the government had actually begun reforms that promised stability, such as the popular rural literacy campaigns. To further legitimize his regime, Kerekou announced the formation of an official political party toward the end of 1975, in conjunction with changing the name of the country to the People's Republic of Benin. In May 1976, the PRPB (*Parti de la revolution populaire de Benin*) held an extraordinary congress and elected a 27-person central committee with a clear civilian majority. Comprising mainly Kerekou supporters, the central committee of the official party was the first key institution since the coup that was not dominated by the military.

Consolidated Grip on Power

The next five years of Kerekou's regime were devoted to building the state and building socialism. In 1976, several steps were taken to strengthen Kerekou's position and centralize power and authority in the presidency. He expanded the elaborate security apparatus, reorganized ministries, and reorganized the military and paramilitary forces. In 1977, one last surge of opposition appeared in the form of a mercenary invasion that one commentator termed "tragicomic." Gabon and Morocco as well as Emile Zinsou were implicated by a subsequent United Nations inquiry.

The result of the 1977 mercenary invasion was to further legitimize the existing government. Kerekou enjoyed increased popularity, however briefly, and the prospect of former leaders returning to power was eliminated. Kerekou expanded the army from 1,650 to 2,100 members and became the chief of general staff and took charge of the militia. Around this time, complaints of torture of political prisoners began to surface. Benin also responded to the mercenary invasion by becoming more isolated internationally and relying on ties with Libya and other "radical" African states. Benin distanced itself from neighboring states, including Gabon, Ivory Coast, Togo, and other African nations seen as being allied with the exiled opposition.

Political Reform Initiated

In November 1977, a new constitution was drafted and opened to public debate, marking the fifth anniversary of the 1972 coup. Elections were held in November 1979, where a single list of candidates representing different strata and groupings within Benin's society was presented. The final list of candidates was selected from candidates proposed in meetings in villages, towns, and at the district level, giving the general population a greater sense of participation in government.

In late 1979, Kerekou called a meeting of some 400-500 administrators to discuss political matters. Participants freely criticized the regime and some of its reforms. A month later, the PRPB held a congress where these concerns were echoed. As a result, the central committee was nearly doubled from 25 to 45 members, and the political bureau increased from seven to thirteen. These structural changes allowed more civilians and critics to gain access to these hitherto tightly controlled bodies.

In early 1980, a new government was formed amid a sense of political and economic decline. The change also marked a shift toward liberal policies and Western alignments. The early years of the 1980s were a period of broad debate, with the state newspaper *Ehuzu* containing material critical of government policies. Many of the reforms introduced in the 1970s were recognized as ineffective or corrupt. In 1983, a new five-year plan was presented to raise foreign aid, but only one-third of the needed funds were forthcoming. From 1983 onward, Benin's accumulated debts, declining productivity, and failure to control imports drove the economy closer to crisis.

Economic Crisis

In 1987 Kerekou retired from the army to concentrate on the economic crisis. A cabinet reshuffle involving changes in most of the economic ministries left only one military officer in the new government. In March of 1988 a coup attempt involving mainly junior officers, but including two senior military officers who had been involved in the 1972 coup, was preempted. By the time they came to trial in July of 1989 nearly 150 military officials had been arrested. A Libyan official was implicated as the primary instigator and supplier of funds and arms.

One sign of Benin's economic decline was its involvement in the West African toxic waste scandal, in which it was revealed that Benin had agreed to allow dumping of toxic waste at ridiculously low prices. Several ministers were dismissed amid this scandal, which upset Benin's eastern neighbor, Nigeria, whose leader, Gen. Ibrahim Babangida, had declared participation in toxic waste schemes a capital offense.

Opposition to the Kerekou government reflected declining economic conditions in 1989. The year began with student strikes, which were quickly joined by civil servants who paralyzed government offices. Security forces opened fire without warning in response to rioting and the sacking of public buildings. At the end of January, Kerekou ordered civil servants be paid two months salary out of the four months owed to them. In April, teachers in Porto-Novo went on strike to claim three months back salary. They were joined by teachers in Cotonou and in July by state employees. The banks were ordered to pay December's salary to state employees.

In June, direct elections for 200 people's commissioners resulted in an unusually high percentage of "no" votes, which ran as high as 15.8 percent in Mono province and 15.2 percent in Oueme, which includes Porto-Novo, the focus of discontent and student-led disturbances earlier in the year. In August, Kerekou was re-elected as head of state for another five-year term. In October, the government suspended publication of the independent weekly, *La Gazette du Golfe,* one of the few publications critical of the government.

Political Shakeup

As 1989 ended, the mounting crisis included strikes, corruption, and unpopular austerity measures. A special joint session in December of the PRPB, the national assembly, and the executive council agreed to drop Marxism-Leninism as the country's official ideology. Kerekou called for a national conference to be held in the first quarter of 1990 to discuss further political reforms. On February 25, 1990, the National Conference of Active Forces of the Nation proclaimed itself a sovereign body whose decisions were mandatory. It declared the constitution null and void and existing state institutions suspended. The conference, called by Kerekou and held in Cotonou, included 488 delegates representing about 50 opposition groups.

On February 27, Kerekou declared the proceedings of the national conference a "civilian coup d'etat." However, three days later, he endorsed all of its decisions, saying, "This is not a defeat. It is not a capitulation. It is a question of national responsibility." On March 1, the constitution was revoked and the national assembly dissolved. The name of the country was changed from People's Republic of Benin to Republic of Benin, reflecting the disavowal of Marxism-Leninism. During the transition, Kerekou was to remain head of state, but the defense portfolio was removed from his responsibilities.

Nicephore Soglo, a former World Bank administrator, was elected as prime minister by delegates to the national conference. Legislative power was vested in a 50-member High Council of the Republic, with 25 members being elected. This body included the three former civilian presidents who had recently returned from exile: Hubert Maga, Justin Ahomadegbe, and Emile Zinsou. On March 9 Kerekou inaugurated the High Council and formed a 15-member all-civilian government that was accountable to it. Kerekou remained president and head of the armed forces. The new government was headed by Prime Minister Soglo, who also became Minister of Defense.

A press release on the "New Democratic Era in Benin"

set out the political transition program. It involved a new constitution, new electoral laws, and the free formation of political parties. All of this would lead to legislative and presidential elections to be held in February and March 1991. Prime Minister Soglo praised President Kerekou for accepting the political reforms and appealed to all citizens to return to work. Benin thus became the first sub-Saharan African nation to return, by popular coercion, to a multi-party democracy.

Sources

Books

Africa South of the Sahara 1991, Europa, 1990.
Allen, Chris, et al., *Benin, the Congo, Burkina Faso: Economics, Politics and Society,* Pinter Publishers, 1988.
Decalo, Samuel, *Historical Dictionary of Benin,* 2nd edition, Scarecrow, 1987.
Keesing's Record of World Events, Longman, 1990.
The Military in African Politics, edited by John W. Harbeson, Praeger, 1987.
The Performance of Soldiers as Governors: African Politics and the African Military, edited by Isaac James Mowoe, University Press of America, 1980.
Socialism in Sub-Saharan Africa: A New Assessment, edited by Carl G. Rosberg and Thomas M. Callaghy, University of California Institute of International Studies, 1979.

Periodicals

American Spectator, May 1990.
New Republic, March 13, 1989.
Time, May 21, 1990.

—David Bianco

Martin Luther King, Jr.

1929-1968

Civil rights leader

In the years since his assassination on April 4, 1968, as he stood on the balcony of the Lorraine Motel in Memphis, Tennessee, Martin Luther King, Jr., has evolved from a prominent civil rights leader into the symbol for the Civil Rights Movement in the United States. He is studied by schoolchildren of all backgrounds; his words are quoted by the powerless and the powerful, by anyone who has a dream to make her or his life better, to better the nation, or the world. Monuments have been dedicated in his honor and institutions such as the Center for Nonviolent Social Change in Atlanta, which bears his name, have been established to carry on his work. In 1986, the U.S. Congress made King unique among twentieth-century Americans by designating his birthday a federal holiday.

King was born into a family of Baptist ministers. Martin Luther King, Sr., his father and namesake, was the pastor of Ebenezer Baptist Church in Atlanta, a position the elder King had inherited from his wife's father, Adam Daniel Williams. As the son of a pastor growing up among the black middle class, the young King was afforded some opportunities for education and experience not available to children in poorer urban and rural areas. Yet despite his social standing, he was still subjected to the lessons of segregation because of his color. Although his family tradition was intertwined with the church and expectations were high that "M. L." would follow in the footsteps of his father and grandfather, King first resisted the ministry as a vocation, finding it ill-suited to allow him to address the social problems he had experienced in the South. So, after completing high school early, he entered nearby Morehouse College in 1944 with thoughts of becoming a lawyer or doctor. Later, influenced by the teachings of George D. Kelsey, a religion professor, and Dr. Benjamin Mays, the college's president, King came to understand the social and intellectual tradition of the ministry. By graduation in 1948, he had decided to accept it as his vocation.

In 1948 King entered the Crozer Theological Seminary in Chester, Pennsylvania, where for the next three years he studied theology, philosophy, ethics, the Social Gospel of Walter Rauschenbusch, and the religious and social views of Reinhold Niebuhr. It was also during this time that King first learned of the nonviolent activism of Mohandas Gandhi. While at Crozer, King earned the

Original given name, Michael, changed to Martin; born January 15, 1929, in Atlanta, GA; assassinated April 4, 1968, in Memphis, TN; originally buried in South View Cemetery, Atlanta, reinterred at Martin Luther King, Jr., Center for Nonviolent Social Change, Atlanta; son of Martin Luther (a minister) and Alberta Christine (a teacher; maiden name, Williams) King; married Coretta Scott (a concert singer), June 18, 1953; children: Yolanda Denise, Martin Luther III, Dexter Scott, Bernice Albertine. *Education:* Morehouse College, B.A., 1948; Crozer Theological Seminary, S.D., 1951; Boston University, Ph.D., 1955, D.D., 1959; Chicago Theological Seminary, D.D., 1957; attended classes at University of Pennsylvania and Harvard University. *Religion:* Baptist.

Licensed to preach by Ebenezer Baptist Church deacons, 1947; ordained Baptist minister, 1948; Dexter Avenue Baptist Church, Montgomery, AL, pastor, 1954-60; president, Montgomery Improvement Association, 1965-66; Southern Christian Leadership Conference (SCLC), Atlanta, founder, 1957, president and leader of civil rights campaigns, 1957-68; Ebenezer Baptist Church, Atlanta, co-pastor with father, 1960-68. Vice-president, National Sunday School and Baptist Teaching Union Congress of National Baptist Convention.

Awards: Recipient of numerous awards, including Spingarn Medal from the NAACP, 1957; Anisfield-Wolf Award, 1958, for *Stride Toward Freedom;* named Man of the Year, 1963; Nobel Peace Prize, 1964; Judaism and World Peace Award from Synagogue Council of America, 1965; Brotherhood Award, 1967, for *Where Do We Go From Here: Chaos or Community?;* Nehru Award for International Understanding, 1968; Presidential Medal of Freedom, 1977.

respect of his professors as well as his classmates. He was elected student-body president, was valedictorian of his class, won a prize as outstanding student, and earned a fellowship for graduate study. He was accepted for doctoral study at Yale, Boston University, and Edinburgh in Scotland. He chose to attend Boston University, where he studied systematic theology with Edgar Sheffield Brightman and L. Harold DeWolf. Again he impressed his professors with his passion for learning and his intellect. After completing his coursework, King began a dissertation in which he would compare the religious views of Paul Tillich and Henry Nelson Wieman.

Emerging from Boston University, King had a number of avenues available to him—pursuing a career as a professor, returning to Atlanta to join his father at Ebenezer, or becoming the pastor of his own church, in the North or in the South. He decided to accept the pastorship at Dexter Avenue Baptist Church in the Deep South of Montgomery, Alabama. He installed himself as full-time pastor in September of 1954. During his first year at Dexter, King finished his dissertation and worked to organize his new church, to activate the social and political awareness of his congregation, and to blend his academic learning with the emotional oratory of the Southern preacher. He had begun to settle into his role as preacher and new father when the events of December, 1955, thrust upon him the mantle of local civil rights leader.

Montgomery Bus Boycott

On December 1, 1955, Montgomery seamstress Rosa Parks was arrested for refusing to abide by one of Montgomery's laws requiring segregated seating on city buses. In response to this incident, several groups within the city's black community, long dissatisfied with the treatment of blacks on public transportation, came together to take action. The National Association for the Advancement of Colored People (NAACP), the Women's Political Council, the Baptist Ministers Conference, the city's African Methodist Episcopal (AME) Zionist ministers, and the community at large united to organize a boycott of the buses. After a successful first day of boycotting, the groups formed the Montgomery Improvement Association (MIA) to oversee the community action and to work with the city and busline officials to bring about fairer treatment of blacks within the existing laws. King was elected the MIA's first president.

For 382 days, King and the black community maintained the boycott while white officials from the city and the busline resisted their modest demands: courtesy toward black riders, a first-come-first-serve approach to seating, and black drivers for some routes. During this period, the MIA convinced black-owned taxis to reduce their fares to enable boycotters to afford a means of transportation. Then, when the city blocked that measure, the group organized carpools. King was arrested, slandered, received hate mail and phone threats, and his house was bombed; but from the outset he preached nonviolence to the black boycotters. After Montgomery city officials refused to be moved to change by a number of related federal court decisions, the black community finally won more than it had asked for when the U.S. Supreme Court upheld a federal court decision that ruled against segregation in Montgomery. On December 21, 1956, the integration of Montgomery city buses became mandatory.

SCLC Formed

To continue the momentum gained from the victory in Montgomery and to spread the movement across the South, King and other black leaders gathered in early 1957 to form the Southern Christian Leadership Conference (SCLC). As president of the SCLC, King spent the next few years consolidating the organization's position as a social force in the region and establishing himself as its leader. King toured the country giving speeches, appearing at rallies, meeting with elected officials and candidates, and writing a book about the Montgomery experience. In 1958 he traveled to Ghana to join in its independence celebration; in 1959 he traveled to India to meet with Nehru and other associates of Gandhi. With

demands on his time growing, King decided to resign from the Dexter Avenue Baptist Church in Montgomery and to accept his father's offer to become co-pastor of the Ebenezer Baptist Church in Atlanta. This arrangement afforded the younger King the flexibility to devote more time to SCLC activities.

From 1960 to 1962 King and the SCLC renewed their direct action against segregation at the voting booth, at schools, at lunch counters, and at bus stations. King also threw his organization's support behind other groups fighting the same battles. There were black college students, who would later organize as the Student Nonviolent Coordinating Committee (SNCC), staging sit-ins at segregated lunch counters in Nashville, Montgomery, and Atlanta. There were Freedom Rides initiated by the Council on Racial Equality (CORE) to challenge segregation in interstate bus transportation. These efforts contributed to the eventual desegregation of stores, buses and bus stations.

Yet, along with these successes, King and the Civil Rights

Ralph Abernathy (left) and King in 1956 during the Montgomery Bus Boycott.

Movement also encountered failures. In December of 1961 the SCLC joined members of the black community of Albany, Georgia, in their effort to end segregation in that city. In the end, the city government and law enforcement officials refused to make any substantial concessions and avoided resorting to violence. The black organizations involved, on the other hand, were unable to cooperate among themselves and unable to keep Albany's blacks from turning to violence. With the failure in Albany, King's leadership and philosophy of nonviolence as well as the SCLC's planning came under criticism.

Birmingham Protest March

King was able to redeem himself in the spring of 1963 in Birmingham, Alabama, a city considered by many to be the most segregated in the country. King and the SCLC were invited by local black leaders to help organize a protest to end segregation in downtown stores, to achieve equal opportunity in employment, and to establish a biracial commission to promote further desegregation. In order to attract attention to their demands and to put pressure on local businesses, the protesters employed a march. Birmingham police moved against the first march with clubs and attack dogs and the state court issued an injunction barring further protests. When King and close associate Ralph Abernathy defied the court order, they were arrested and placed in solitary confinement. During his incarceration, criticism by local white clergymen of the movement and King's actions prompted him to write his famous "Letter from a Birmingham Jail."

After being tried for contempt and found guilty, King was released on appeal. He rejoined the protesters. When the adult marchers began to lose their enthusiasm, high school students and younger children joined the march. Around 3,000 marchers were arrested, filling up the jails. Later marches were broken up by police using clubs and dogs and firemen with high-pressure hoses. The police brutality directed toward unarmed black men, women, and children outraged the nation and the John F. Kennedy administration. The growing tide of negative publicity soon convinced Birmingham's white businessmen to seek an agreement with the protesters.

In the aftermath of the agreement, white extremists bombed King's hotel and his brother's home, igniting riots by blacks. However, black leaders, white businessmen, and federal troops sent in by the Kennedy administration were successful in their efforts to halt the violence; the agreement was given time to take hold.

"I Have a Dream"

With the success of Birmingham still fresh in the minds of blacks and whites in the South and North, King was poised to assert himself as a national and international leader. On August 28, 1963, approximately 250,000 blacks and whites marched on Washington, D.C., to raise the nation's consciousness of civil rights and to encourage the passage of the Civil Rights Bill before Congress at that time. The march was a cooperative effort of several civil rights organizations—including the Negro American Labor Council, the Urban League, the SCLC, NAACP, SNCC, and CORE—and the movement's largest demonstration. King was the last speaker scheduled to address the crowd gathered in the shadow of the Lincoln Memorial. He began a speech that referred to the lack of progress in securing black rights in the hundred years since Lincoln's Emancipation Proclamation; by the time he finished, he had deviated from his prepared speech to offer one drawn from past sermons and the inspiration of the moment, his famous "I Have a Dream" address.

King's stature as a leader of national and international prominence was confirmed in 1964. In January of that year he became the first black American to be named *Time* magazine's "Man of the Year." And, in December of that year he was awarded the Nobel Peace Prize, the youngest person ever to win the award. The recognition that followed from these and other honors prompted journalists and politicians from around the world to seek King's views on a wide range of world issues. Even so, King remained focused on the "twenty-two million Negroes of the United States of America engaged in a creative battle to end the long night of racial injustice," as he stated in his Nobel acceptance speech. Earlier in 1964 he had attended the signing of the Civil Rights Act of 1964, the law that put the federal government firmly behind ending segregation and discrimination in public institutions. But blacks still faced barriers to voting throughout the South, and more subtle economic barriers in other regions.

Voting and Economic Barriers

In 1965 and 1966 King and the SCLC decided to take on these barriers. Civil rights groups stepped up their voter registration drives in the South and King took his strategy of nonviolent confrontation to Selma, Alabama. Marches in Selma and from Selma to the state capital of Montgomery brought publicity to the movement's voting rights demands and gave momentum to congressional efforts to enact legislation to remedy the situation. In August, the Voting Rights Act of 1965 was passed into law. It gave federal authorities the power to end literacy tests and poll taxes and to monitor all elections.

In 1966 King and the SCLC launched a campaign in Chicago, both to expand their influence into the North and to raise awareness of the issues of urban discrimination and poverty as manifested in housing, schooling, and unemployment. The SCLC influenced some changes and put some long-term operations in place such as Operation Breadbasket. However, the campaign was unable to score the kind of success that it had in Montgomery, Birmingham, and Selma. Discrimination was more subtle in this northern metropolis than in the segregated South; city officials, including Mayor Richard Daley, were less extreme and more politically astute than their southern counterparts in their response to confrontation; furthermore, Chicago's black population was more divided, with some elements very much prone to violence.

Poor People's Campaign

In the last year of his life, King actively expanded the scope of his efforts to include not only civil rights issues but also human rights issues important to people the world over. As the war in Vietnam escalated in the second half of the 1960s, King grew dissatisfied with the situation. In 1967 he began to speak out consistently against the war. In speeches and rallies around the country, he called for a negotiated settlement. King was recruited by anti-war activists to head an independent ticket for the presidential election of 1968, a position he declined in order to keep his social and moral concerns free from political obligations.

Late in 1967 King directed his organization to begin laying the groundwork for what would be known as the Poor People's Campaign. He wanted to recruit the poor from urban and rural areas—men and women of all

King delivers his "I Have a Dream" speech during the 1963 March on Washington.

races and backgrounds—and lead them in a campaign for economic rights. The recruited poor, trained in nonviolent direct action, would descend on Washington, D.C., and begin a three-month campaign of marches, rallies, sit-ins, and boycotts to pressure the Lyndon B. Johnson administration and leading businessmen to put a more human face on American capitalism.

In March of 1968, while touring the U.S. to raise support for this new march on Washington, King accepted an invitation to speak on behalf of sanitation workers in Memphis, Tennessee, who were striking in an attempt to improve their poor working conditions. After a march organized by local leaders was postponed because of a heavy snowstorm, King joined the rescheduled event on March 28. Shortly after the march began, young gang members initiated violence, igniting a riot that ended with one dead, numerous injuries, and widespread property damage. King vowed to return to personally direct another demonstration in order to reestablish nonviolence in this local dispute.

Again in Memphis to plan this march, King was assassinated on April 4, 1968, as he stood on the balcony of the Lorraine Motel. The night before, addressing an audience of 500 at the Mason Temple in downtown Memphis, King had given his last speech, which included these words: "Like anybody, I would like to live a long life. Longevity has its place. But I'm not concerned about that now. I just want to do God's will. And he's allowed me to go up to the mountain, and I've looked over, and I've seen the promised land. I may not get there with you. But I want you to know tonight that we as a people will get to the promised land."

The Man vs. the Myth

Although widely regarded as one of the great social leaders of the twentieth century, King has not been without critics. He was closely scrutinized during his life by his colleagues in the SCLC, by other leaders in the Civil Rights Movement, by those he sought to change, and by state and federal officials affected by his actions; he is still scrutinized today by those trying to get behind the symbol to the man and his place in American history.

In SCLC meetings, King often faced disagreements with his lieutenants and advisers over organization, tactics, and campaigns. He received little initial support for his idea to launch the Poor People's Campaign. Within the Civil Rights Movement of the 1960s, King was not universally accepted as its leader and spokesman. Roy Wilkins, the NAACP, and its strategy of seeking change through legislation and court action were in constant competition with King, the SCLC, and its nonviolent direct confrontation for the support of blacks and white integrationists.

The SNCC criticized King for becoming a symbol and his SCLC adults for interfering with student-initiated grass-roots movements. Later in the movement, the two groups grew farther apart when the SNCC and its leader, Stokely Carmichael, espoused the "black power" ideology of violence and black separatism as the only means to bring about change. Local civil rights organizations were often put off by King's outsiders invading their cities, making headlines, then leaving, never to follow through. Furthermore, numerous civil rights leaders and social commentators severely faulted King for his stand against the war in Vietnam. Some felt he was abusing his prominence to step beyond his expertise; others feared that his linking of the civil rights and anti-war movements would weaken their cause.

King has also received criticism for more personal aspects of his life. During his career as a civil rights leader, his actions and character were repeatedly placed under a microscope through spying and wiretapping ordered by FBI Chief J. Edgar Hoover. Information about King's advisers outside SCLC and their links to communism and homosexuality as well as King's own extramarital relationships was gathered for use to discredit the leader and his organization. Most recently, scholars working on a collection of King's papers confirmed November, 1990, press reports that significant parts of King's Ph.D. dissertation had been lifted from the work of Jack Boozer, a fellow student, and the theologian Paul Tillich.

At a time when new generations of Americans more easily see the symbol of the Civil Rights Movement than the man, the gifted yet human activist, many who were close to King fear that his dream for America runs the risk of fading along with the memories of his life. In his biography of King, *Bearing the Cross,* David J. Garrow quoted one of King's college classmates, educator Charles V. Willie: "By idolizing those whom we honor, we do a disservice both to them and to ourselves. By exalting the accomplishments of Martin Luther King, Jr., into a legendary tale that is annually told, we fail to recognize his humanity—his personal and public struggles that are similar to yours and mine. By idolizing those whom we honor, we fail to realize that we could go and do likewise."

Sources

Abernathy, Ralph David, *And the Walls Came Tumbling Down,* Harper, 1989.
Garrow, David J., *Bearing the Cross: Martin Luther King,*

Jr., and the Southern Christian Leadership Conference, Morrow, 1986.

King, Coretta Scott, *My Life With Martin Luther King, Jr.,* Holt, 1969.

King, Martin Luther, Jr., *A Testament of Hope: The Essential Writings of Martin Luther King, Jr.,* edited by James Melvin Washington, Harper, 1986.

Oates, Stephen B., *Let the Trumpet Sound: The Life of Martin Luther King, Jr.,* Harper, 1982.

Playboy Interviews, Playboy Press, 1967.

—Bryan Ryan

Jennifer Lawson

1946—

Television programming executive

As executive vice president of national programming for the Public Broadcasting System (PBS), Jennifer Lawson is, according to Jeremy Gerard in the *New York Times,* "the most powerful programming executive in public television." Lawson is responsible for overseeing the creation, promotion, and scheduling of national programming for the 330-station public television system. Prior to her tenure at PBS, Lawson was a senior programming executive at the Corporation for Public Broadcasting and also had several years' experience working as a funding liaison with filmmakers. According to PBS president Bruce Christensen in the *New York Times,* Lawson's "strong ties to the independent filmmaking community" made her especially well-qualified to oversee PBS's programming needs.

The naming of Lawson was a landmark appointment for PBS, which, for the first time, centralized national program decision-making in one executive. Among Lawson's primary responsibilities are to expand public television programming and broaden its audience. Lawson's priorities in doing so, as Gerard reported, are "to offer more cultural diversity in public television, to improve and expand programming for children and to increase the audience through better promotion." Already, in her first year, Lawson has recorded two notable achievements for PBS. *The Civil War,* a five-night series, drew over 50 million viewers and became the most-watched show in PBS history. Also under Lawson, PBS began promoting its programming on commercial networks for the first time.

Lawson has stated that her parents were the biggest influence in her life. "From my early childhood, they taught me a whole range of skills, from carpentry to painting," she told Darlene Gavron Stevens in the *Chicago Tribune.* "My father always insisted I learn how to work on cars. His notion was that if I could do a transmission job, I could make my living anywhere in the world." Lawson grew up in the deep South, and in the 1960s the Civil Rights Movement emphasized for her the importance of helping people.

Although Lawson won a scholarship and was in pre-med studies at Tuskegee Institute, she interrupted her career plans and joined black voter registration efforts in the South. She was quoted in *Jet:* "The Civil Rights Movement became the turning point for me because I

At a Glance. . .

Full name, Jennifer Karen Lawson; born in 1946; grew up in Fairfield, AL; daughter of William (owner of a repair shop) and Velma (a schoolteacher) Lawson; married in 1982; children: two sons. *Education:* Attended Tuskegee Institute; received undergraduate and masters degrees from Columbia University.

Student Nonviolent Coordinating Committee (SNCC), staff member, c. 1964-67; worked with National Council of Negro Women, 1968-69; Whitman County, MS, director of adult education program, c. 1969; Drum and Spear (publisher), Washington, DC, art director, c. 1970, lived in Tanzania, 1970-72, and worked on joint government publishing project; William Green Productions (film company), editor; Brooklyn College, Brooklyn, NY, film instructor; The Film Fund, executive director; Corporation for Public Broadcasting, Washington, DC, 1980-89, began as program fund coordinator, became senior programming executive; Public Broadcasting Service, Washington, DC, executive vice president of programming, 1989—.

Awards: Named one of "101 Most Influential People in Entertainment Today," *Entertainment Weekly,* 1990.

Addresses: *Home*—Washington, DC.

began to see that there was a larger ill. To me, it required more courage to try to address that ill than it did to deal with the individual sick person. I felt the time was ripe for us to change this society and eradicate institutionalized racism."

From 1970 to 1972, Lawson worked in Tanzania on an African publishing project, and it was then that she became aware of the power of visual media. She realized, as she told Stevens, "how ironic it was that we were working in print in a society that for the most part did not read. I began to feel that film and TV would be the educational media of the future." Lawson returned to the United States and completed a master's degree in film at Columbia University, after which she worked as a film editor and taught film classes. In 1980, she joined the Corporation for Public Broadcasting as coordinator of their television program fund, and worked as a liaison with independent filmmakers. By the time Lawson left in 1989, she was associate director of drama and arts programming, and was responsible for a $42-million budget.

In her new position at PBS, Lawson is able to further the ideals of the Civil Rights Movement in her work. "In a way," she told Stevens, "I'm still continuing my mission of helping people, but using a different and powerful medium: television." Lawson believes that being the highest-ranking black woman ever to serve in public television sends a positive message to viewers. She told Gerard: "I think it speaks to public television's recognition and tradition of serving the entire country, and in presenting the cultural realities of America in a way not necessarily presented in the rest of television." She added: "When you say public television is an alternative, you should be able to see that clearly."

Sources

Chicago Tribune, June 3, 1990.
Entertainment Weekly, November 2, 1990.
Jet, December 18, 1989.
New York Times, October 20, 1989; June 21, 1990.

—*Michael E. Mueller*

Joie Lee

1962(?)—

Actress

Joie Lee first became familiar to filmgoers in her brother Spike Lee's hit 1986 movie, *She's Gotta Have It,* and has since appeared in three other of his acclaimed films. In Spike's films—which critics have praised as stirring depictions of contemporary black society—Joie regularly portrays characters who represent a voice of conscience. Veronica Webb explained in *Spin:* "Joie's work with her brother, who is fast becoming the pope of polemics in American cinema, seems to take on the role of the benevolent black Madonna that inhabits her brother's imagination. . . . She is the eternal incarnation of the good girl."

Joie's acting style has been described as natural and refreshing; Webb calls her "the Gechee woman in a head-on collision with the fly-girl." Joie has received positive notices for her film performances. She had her most major role in the 1990 film *Mo' Better Blues,* where she played Indigo Downes, the long-suffering girlfriend of an unscrupulous jazz musician played by Denzel Washington. "Lee lights up the screen with her sassy portrayal of the devoted Downes," wrote Victor Dwyer in *Maclean's.* "Hopelessly in love, but pragmatic about the prospects of convincing Gilliam to settle down, she succeeds in bringing a genuine touch of lightness to the overbearing gloom that pervades the movie."

Joie noted to Marjorie Rosen and David Hutchings in *People* the differences between her and Indigo. "I was not raised to be someone's wife. I was raised so that things should be evenly distributed. Indigo is very soft-spoken, and I can get loud." As a youth in Brooklyn, Joie was brought up in an environment that encouraged artistic development and independence. The Lee children—four boys and one girl—were "exposed early to the arts and ideas of black culture—everything from Broadway musical theater to the writings of the abolitionist Harriet Tubman," reported Rosen and Hutchings.

Joie's father, Bill, was a noted jazz trumpeter and composer—(he wrote the score for *Mo' Better Blues*—while her mother, Jackie, was a teacher in an exclusive private school. Jackie, from whom Joie says she got her acting style, taught black pride to the Lee children. "She started experimenting with African hairstyles long before anyone else did," Joie told Rosen and Hutchings. "We'd walk down the street together wearing beads and cornrows.

At a Glance...

First name originally Joy; changed to Joie (pronounced Zhwah); born c. 1962; grew up in Brooklyn, NY; daughter of Bill (a jazz trumpeter and composer) and Jackie (a teacher) Lee; four brothers: Spike, David, Chris, Cinque. *Education:* Attended Sarah Lawrence College.

Actress. Appeared in Spike Lee films, *She's Gotta Have It,* 1986; *School Daze,* 1988; *Do the Right Thing,* 1989; and *Mo' Better Blues,* 1990; appeared in James Dearden film, *A Kiss before Dying.*

Addresses: *Home*—Brooklyn, NY.

She saw it as history, not fashion. She researched everything. People laughed at us, but it didn't matter."

Lee's parents were supportive of her acting. "When I was little my parents always encouraged me to act," she told Webb. "They were never daunted by the fact that there were so few black images on screen." Joie hopes to forge new opportunities for black actresses. She commented to Webb: "I'd like to break all the standards as an actress, and as a black actress. I'd like to bring a different image to the public. I want to see something other than what I've seen. Insightful portraits of black women. I'm only one person, but I'd like to perform in every genre of film: sci-fi, gangster, comedy. There are so many barriers to be broken down."

In 1990, Joie acted in her first non-Spike Lee film, the murder-mystery *A Kiss before Dying,* starring Sean Young and Matt Dillon. "I decided this would be a good time to branch out. People don't know if I can do things on my own," she told Rosen and Hutchings. In addition to more acting, Joie's future plans include developing a children's television pilot with her brother Cinque. Among her other goals in film, she told Webb: "I'd like to find some stability as an actress. I'd like to have my own production company in the next five to ten years, a multimedia ensemble company. I'd like to own the rights to a lot of things. I'd like to be writing my own projects. I'd really like to write something for Spike."

Sources

Jet, August 6, 1990.
Maclean's, August 6, 1990.
Nation, August 13, 1990.
National Review, September 3, 1990.
People, August 27, 1990.
Spin, October 1990.

—*Michael E. Mueller*

Nelson Mandela

1918—

Social and political activist

Nelson Mandela has spent a lifetime fighting for the rights of black South Africans, enduring trial and incarceration for his principles. A political prisoner in his native South Africa for more than twenty-seven years, the eloquent and statesman-like Mandela became the human embodiment of the struggle against government-mandated discrimination. His courage and determination through decades of imprisonment galvanized not only South African blacks, but also concerned citizens on every continent. Since his release from prison on February 11, 1990, Mandela has reclaimed his position in the once-banned African National Congress and has fought tirelessly for democratic reform in his troubled homeland.

With his magnetic personality and calm demeanor, Mandela is widely regarded as the last best hope for conciliating a peaceful transition to a South African government that will enfranchise all of its citizens. "For whites," wrote John F. Burns in the *New York Times,* "a man once presented to them as a threat to everything they prize is now widely viewed as the best hope for a political settlement that will guarantee them a future. For blacks, Mr. Mandela has achieved a legendary stature, towering above most other leaders in the way that Lenin dominated the revolutionary cause in Russia, and Churchill the fight for England's survival in World War II."

Time magazine contributor Richard Lacayo characterized Mandela as a figure who is "unique among heroes because he is a living embodiment of black liberation. . . . His soft-spoken manner and unflappable dignity bespeak his background as a lawyer, a single-minded political organizer and a longtime prisoner still blinking a bit in the spotlight." Lacayo continued: "For the many blacks who have begun to call themselves African Americans, [Mandela] is a flesh-and-blood exemplar of what an African can be. For Americans of all colors, weary of their nation's perennial racial standoffs, [he] offers the opportunity for a full-throated expression of their no less perennial hope for reconciliation."

Nelson Mandela could have lived a relatively comfortable life in obscurity had he wished. He was born in 1918 in rural Umtata in what is now the black homeland of Transkei, the son of a highly placed tribal adviser. As a youth Mandela spent his days farming and herding cattle.

Became Political Activist

Mandela's tribal name, *Rolihlahla*, means "one who brings trouble upon himself." It is therefore quite descriptive of the difficult path the young man chose when he reached adulthood. In his late teens Mandela renounced his hereditary right to the tribal chiefdom and entered college in pursuit of a law degree. He became a political activist in short order and in 1940 was expelled from University College at Fort Hare for leading a student strike. Soon thereafter he moved closer to the commercial capital of Johannesburg, where he worked in the gold mines and studied law by correspondence course. He earned his law degree from the University of South Africa in 1942.

Mandela was twenty-four when he joined the African National Congress, a group that sought to establish social and political rights for blacks in South Africa. In 1944 Mandela and several friends founded a sub-group, the Congress Youth League, and adopted a platform calling for nonviolent protest and black African self-reliance and self-determination. The country Mandela and his Youth League comrades lived in was then, as it is now, populated primarily by blacks but governed completely by whites. Black citizens were legally discriminated against in housing, education, and economic opportunity; they could not vote and were subjected to numerous white-authored laws and restrictions. The Youth League responded to this racist political climate by calling for civil disobedience—nonviolent strikes and "stay-at-home" days in protest of no less than six hundred racist laws.

From his position as a leader of the Youth League, Mandela helped to coordinate labor strikes and campaigns to defy the unjust laws. Unfortunately, ANC protest rallies were often repulsed by police brutality. In 1950 eighteen blacks were killed during a labor walkout, and again in 1952 a great number of protesters—including Mandela—were beaten and jailed for opposing the South African government. On that occasion Mandela received a nine-month suspended jail sentence and was ordered to resign from the ANC leadership. Mandela refused to resign and moved into underground work because he was forbidden to attend public meetings.

By the time Mandela reappeared in public in 1955, *apartheid*—meaning "apartness" in the Afrikaans language—had been taken to extreme ends in South Africa. The government continued to tighten restrictions on its black non-citizens, creating segregated townships and "homelands" where blacks were forced to settle. Late in 1956, Mandela was arrested with 155 other anti-*apartheid* leaders and was charged with treason under a convenient anti-Communist statute. Freed on bail, Mandela mounted his own defense and practiced law on the

After the death of his father in 1930, the twelve-year-old was sent to live with the chief of the Tembu tribe. There he impressed his elders with his quick intelligence and maturity. Many thought he would someday become chief himself.

side as the infamous "Treason Trial" dragged on and on. Although he was again banned from political activity, he persisted in his efforts for the cause of the African National Congress. He also found time to marry his second wife, a social worker named Nomzamo Winnie Madikileza. She too was a dedicated activist who supported her husband's efforts to end *apartheid*.

ANC Banned

Early in 1960, a demonstration in the Johannesburg suburb of Sharpeville turned violent when police killed sixty-nine unarmed protesters. The massacre sparked nationwide outrage, and the government acted quickly to ban the African National Congress and some of its splinter groups. Mandela once again found himself detained by police without being charged with a crime. Sickened by the failure of the nonviolent protests, he quietly decided that more extreme measures needed to be taken against the white supremacist government. In a

1961 speech before the Pan-Africanist Conference in Ethiopia, he said: "Peace in our country must be considered already broken when a minority government maintains its authority over the majority by force and violence."

Meanwhile, the Treason Trial entered its final stages and proved to be an effective forum for Mandela's views. As his own defense attorney, Mandela mounted a spirited justification of the ANC's goals and methods. He insisted that his organization sought the franchise and equal rights for South Africans of all races, and he maintained that nonviolent disruptive tactics were the only means by which South African blacks could air their discontent. Mandela and his co-defendants were acquitted in 1961, but their African National Congress had been declared illegal. Although he was free to go about his business, Mandela realized that he could no longer conduct his "business" without breaking the law.

Forced underground, Mandela founded a new group, *Umkonto we Sizwe* ("Spear of the Nation"), a guerrilla

Mandela (with wife Winnie) triumphantly leaves prison after 27 years.

organization that directed sabotage actions against government installations and other symbols of *apartheid*. Mandela travelled throughout Africa seeking funds for his cause, at every turn eluding capture by South African security police. The hardships he faced affected his family as well, as Winnie Mandela remembered in *People* magazine. "He told me to anticipate a life physically without him, that there would never be a normal situation where he would be head of the family," Mrs. Mandela said. "He told me this in great pain. I was completely shattered."

Sentenced to Life in Prison

Mass protests continued in South Africa, and the Spear of the Nation claimed responsibility for more than seventy acts of sabotage. On August 4, 1962, Mandela was arrested by South African police and charged with organizing illegal demonstrations. Once again he used his courtroom appearance as an opportunity to challenge the legality of South Africa's minority rule. His defense was masterful and eloquent, but he was nevertheless convicted and sentenced to five years in prison. While he was serving this sentence, the police connected him to Spear of the Nation and charged him with the more serious crimes of treason and sabotage. After yet another trial, he was sentenced to life in prison in June of 1964.

Mandela was sent to Robben Island, a prison seven miles off the coast of Cape Town. There he endured years of hard labor quarrying limestone and harvesting seaweed, while his wife faced almost constant police harassment at home. In the eyes of the South African government, Nelson Mandela had effectively ceased to exist. Mere discussions of his views or questions about his health were illegal, and he was allowed no contact with the outside world and few visitors. Mandela never lost faith in his cause, however—and the black people of South Africa never forgot their fearless hero. As his years of imprisonment dragged on, he assumed the mantle of martyrdom and became a symbol of the government's desperate efforts to maintain minority rule.

In 1982 Mandela was moved from Robben Island to the maximum security Pollsmoor Prison outside Cape Town. The authorities offered official administrative reasons for the move, but most observers agree that Mandela was simply exerting a powerful influence over the other inmates of Robben Island. Mandela spent much of the next six years in solitary confinement, bolstered by a weekly thirty-minute visit with his wife. He was offered a conditional freedom in 1984—provided that he would settle in the black "homeland" of Transkei—but absolutely refused this option, affirming his allegiance to the African National Congress.

Inevitably, Mandela's health deteriorated. In 1988 he was hospitalized with tuberculosis. After he recovered he returned to prison, but under somewhat more benign circumstances. By the late 1980s, social conditions in South Africa had become even more desperate, with frequent violent confrontations between young blacks and government forces. The international tide was also turning against South Africa. Many private enterprises and national governments withdrew financial support for the beleaguered nation, and the resulting economic downturn literally forced the South African government to reconsider its dedication to *apartheid*. Finally, after twenty-seven years, the white leadership heeded the calls of citizens of numerous nations to release the most important political prisoner of the late twentieth century, Nelson Mandela.

Freed at Last

The whole world watched on February 11, 1990, as Mandela—thin and gray, but unbowed—walked out of Verster Prison. Cheering crowds met him at every turn. He told *People:* "I was completely overwhelmed by the enthusiasm. It is something I did not expect." Mandela quickly assumed a leadership position in the African National Congress, restored to legal status by the government. Within weeks he and his wife were travelling across their nation, calling for a truce in the armed struggle and open negotiations toward equal rights in South Africa. In July of 1990 Mandela brought his message to the United States when he toured a series of big cities, raising funds for his cause. He also asked the American government to continue imposing economic sanctions against South Africa until *apartheid* is completely dismantled.

Mandela and the ANC continue to face enormous problems in South Africa, some of which involve murderous feuds between black factions and terrorist actions in the townships. *Time* correspondent Michael S. Serrill noted that the violence in his nation has forced Mandela to face a sobering reality: "He may have wielded more moral authority as the world's most famous prisoner than he does as a political leader in his . . . freedom." Serrill continued: "To some South African blacks, . . . Mandela out of prison has become an irrelevant figurehead, a dignified gentleman with utopian socialist ideas that have little to do with their daily lives. . . . Mandela's damaged stature has achieved an important aim of [the] white government: to demystify the A.N.C. and make clear that Mandela is only one of many black players." The role Mandela takes in a more enlightened South Africa may depend on the degree of cooperation he can muster among the country's black majority.

Hopes for South Africa's Future

Now in his mid-seventies with several grown children, Mandela remains ever zealous in his pursuit of rights for all South Africans. He is still a revolutionary who counts as allies anyone who supports his cause—including Cuban dictator Fidel Castro, Libya's Colonel Muammar Kaddafi, and the Palestine Liberation Organization. In *Newsweek,* Tom Masland claimed that Mandela "hasn't renounced the use of violence, he wants to nationalize at least some industries, and he remains willing to take help from anyone and return the favor."

This attitude only illustrates the persistent state of concern Mandela and the ANC feel about social conditions in South Africa. Since 1955, when it published its Freedom Charter, the group's aims have changed little. Its political objectives include a unified South Africa with no artificial homelands, a black representation along with all other races in a central parliament, and a one-man, one-vote democracy in a multi-party system.

In a speech in New York City during the summer of 1990, Mandela thanked the American people for taking such an interest in him and his struggle. "You, the people, never abandoned us," he said. "From behind the granite walls, political prisoners could hear loud and clear your voice of solidarity. . . . We are winning because you made it possible."

Selected writings

No Easy Walk to Freedom, Basic Books, 1965.

The Struggle Is My Life, Pathfinder Press, 1986.

Sources

Books

Benson, Mary, *Nelson Mandela: The Man and the Movement,* Norton, 1986.
Black Writers: A Selection of Sketches From "Contemporary Authors," Gale, 1989.
Mandela, Nelson, *No Easy Walk to Freedom,* Basic Books, 1965.
Mandela, Nelson, *The Struggle Is My Life,* Pathfinder Press, 1986.
Mandela, Winnie, *Part of My Soul Went With Him,* Norton, 1985.

Periodicals

Newsweek, September 9, 1985; July 2, 1990.
New York Times, May 12, 1980; February 2, 1985; August 16, 1985; November 24, 1985; December 1, 1985; February 1, 1986; February 12, 1986; February 4, 1990; February 11, 1990.
Observer, April 22, 1973.
People, February 26, 1990.
Time, January 6, 1986; January 5, 1987; April 9, 1990; July 2, 1990.

—Anne Janette Johnson

Thurgood Marshall

1908—

Former Supreme Court justice

Former United States Supreme Court Justice Thurgood Marshall built a distinguished career fighting for the cause of civil rights and equal opportunity. *Ebony* contributor Juan Williams called Marshall "the most important Black man of this century—a man who rose higher than any Black person before him and who has had more effect on Black lives than any other person, Black or White." Prior to his retirement in June of 1991, Marshall stood alone as the Supreme Court's liberal conscience, the last impassioned spokesman for a left-wing view on such causes as affirmative action, abolishment of the death penalty, and due process.

Duke University professor John Hope Franklin told *Ebony:* "If you study the history of Marshall's career, the history of his rulings on the Supreme Court, even his dissents, you will understand that when he speaks, he is not speaking just for Black Americans but for Americans of all times. He reminds us constantly of the great promise this country has made of equality, and he reminds us that it has not been fulfilled. Through his life he has been a great watchdog, insisting that this nation live up to the Constitution."

Marshall's work on behalf of civil rights spanned five and a half decades and included the history-making *Brown* vs. *Board of Education* ruling that led to integration of the nation's public schools in 1954. As an attorney for the National Association for the Advancement of Colored People, Marshall fought to have blacks admitted to segregated state universities, challenged the armed services to offer equal treatment for black recruits, and even assured that blacks would have the right to serve on a jury. John Hope Franklin put it this way: "For Black people he holds special significance because it was Thurgood . . . and a few others who told us we could get justice through interpretation of the law. . . . Marshall was at the head of these lawyers who told us to hold fast because they were going to get the law on our side. And they did."

Marshall was born in Baltimore, Maryland, in 1908, into modest but prosperous circumstances. His mother worked as a teacher in a segregated public elementary school, and his father was a steward at the staunchly all-white Gibson Island Yacht Club. Marshall's first name derives from a great-grandfather, Thoroughgood Marshall, who was brought to America from the Congo as a slave. Both of Thurgood Marshall's grandfathers owned grocery stores. Marshall told *Ebony* that he rarely felt uncomfortable about his race while growing up in Baltimore. He lived in a nice home on Druid Hill Avenue and played with children of both races. He describes himself as a "mediocre" student and a "cutup," whose punishment was often to read the United States Constitution out loud. By the time he graduated from high school, he knew it by heart.

Planned to Study Medicine

In September of 1925, Marshall became a student at Lincoln University, near Philadelphia. He originally intended to study medicine and dentistry, but he changed to the humanities and began to consider a career in law. Williams noted that in college Marshall still was something of a cutup—"he was thrown out of the college twice for fraternity pranks." During his junior year, how-

ever, he married a student from the University of Pennsylvania, Vivian Burey.

The relationship settled him down, and he graduated *cum laude* from Lincoln in 1930. From there he moved to Howard University in Washington, D.C., where he enrolled in the small, all-black law school. The course supervisor was Charles H. Houston, a demanding but inspiring instructor who instilled in his students a burning desire to change segregated society. Marshall graduated first in his class, earning his LL.B. in 1933. He was admitted to the Maryland Bar the same year.

Joined NAACP Staff

Returning to Baltimore, Marshall began working as a private practice lawyer. Williams noted, however, that the young lawyer "still made time for the fight against segregation. Representing the local NAACP, he negotiated with White store owners who sold to Blacks but would not hire them." Marshall also took the case of a would-be law student who wanted to attend the all-white University of Maryland law school. The case against the university was Marshall's first big one. His former professor came to town to help him argue it, and the judge gave them a favorable ruling. Soon thereafter, Marshall was invited to join the NAACP's national office in New York City as an assistant special counsel. Two years later, in 1938, he became the head special counsel for the powerful organization.

"For the next 20 years," Williams wrote, "[Marshall] traveled the country using the Constitution to force state and federal courts to protect the rights of Black Americans. The work was dangerous, and Marshall frequently wondered if he might not end up dead or in the same jail holding those he was trying to defend." Marshall prepared cases against the University of Missouri and the University of Texas on behalf of black students. He petitioned the governor of Texas when a black was excluded from jury duty. During and after the Second World War, he was an outspoken opponent of the government detention of Japanese Americans, and in 1951 he investigated unfair court-martial practices aimed at blacks in the military in Korea and Japan. William H. Hastie, of the U.S. Third Circuit Court of Appeals, told the *New York Times:* "Certainly no lawyer, and practically no member of the bench has Thurgood Marshall's grasp of the doctrine of law as it affects civil rights."

Helped End School Segregation

The limelight found Marshall in 1954, when he led the legal team that challenged public school segregation in the courts. The case advanced to the U.S. Supreme Court and resulted in a landmark ruling that ended a half-century of segregated schooling. Remembering those days when he worked on *Brown* vs. *Board of Education,* Marshall told *Ebony* that the Court's decision "probably did more than anything else to awaken the Negro from his apathy to demanding his right to equality." At the time, however, Marshall was an opponent of civil disobedience for blacks in the South, feeling that organized opposition might lead to white violence—as indeed it did.

Marshall's first wife died after a long illness in 1955. A year later, he married Cecilia Suyat, a secretary at the NAACP's New York office. The *Brown* vs. *Board of Education* ruling had made Marshall a national figure— he was known for some time as "Mr. Civil Rights"—and when Democrats took control of the White House, the ambitious attorney let it be known that he wanted a judgeship.

Eventually, after much opposition from Southern sena-

tors and even from Robert Kennedy, Marshall was named to the 2nd U.S. Circuit Court of Appeals in 1961. As the Civil Rights Movement gained ground in the 1960s, so did Marshall. In 1965 he was given the post of United States Solicitor General, a position in which he represented the government before the Supreme Court. His most important case during these years was the one leading to the adoption of the Miranda rule, which requires the police to inform suspects of their rights.

Named to Supreme Court

Against stiff opposition even in his own (Democratic) party, President Lyndon Johnson nominated Marshall to the Supreme Court in 1967. Marshall's nomination was opposed most violently by four Southern senators on the Judiciary Committee, but nevertheless he was confirmed by a vote of 69 to 11. He was sworn in and took his seat on October 2, 1967. Williams wrote: "Throughout his time on the court, Marshall has remained a strong advo-

Marshall (center), with George Hayes (left) and James N. Nabrit, successfully argued the unconstitutionality of segregated schools before the Supreme Court in 1954.

cate of individual rights. . . . He has remained a conscience on the bench, never wavering in his devotion to ending discrimination.''

Marshall was known as the most tart-tongued member of the court and was never reticent with his opinions, especially on matters affecting the civil rights agenda. Former justice William Brennan, long Marshall's liberal ally on the court, told *Ebony:* "The only time Thurgood may make people uncomfortable, and perhaps it's when they should be made uncomfortable, is when he'll take off in a given case that he thinks . . . is another expression of racism."

It is therefore no surprise that Marshall was a vocal critic of both Ronald Reagan and George Bush. Few justices have been known to speak out on political matters, and for years Marshall himself refused to grant interviews. In the years just prior to his retirement, however, Marshall was stung by court reversals on minority set-aside programs and affirmative action. In 1987 Marshall dismissed Reagan as "the bottom" in terms of his commitment to black Americans. He later told *Ebony:* "I wouldn't do the job of dogcatcher for Ronald Reagan." In 1990 Marshall heaped equal vitriol on the Bush administration after the president vetoed an important civil rights bill. He told *Newsweek* that the actions of Bush and Reagan reflected a return to the days "when we [blacks] really didn't have a chance."

Last Liberal on Changing Court

More than a decade has passed since a Democrat sat in the White House, and inevitably this has brought changes to the nation's Supreme Court. One by one, retiring justices have been replaced with more conservative

successors. For many years Marshall and Brennan teamed as the high court's true liberals, and Marshall was gravely disappointed when his colleague retired. Marshall was the last outspoken liberal on the nine-member court, and had long voiced his determination to hold his seat despite heart attacks, pneumonia, blood clots, and glaucoma. "I have a lifetime appointment," Marshall told *Ebony* in 1990, "and I intend to serve it. I expect to die at 110, shot by a jealous husband."

One of Marshall's law clerks told *People* magazine that Marshall felt compelled to remain on the Court, perhaps at the expense of his health, because he saw himself as the champion of the underdog. "He's the conscience of the Court," the clerk said, "and he's happy in that role." But on June 27, 1991, Marshall announced his retirement from the high court, citing his advancing age and medical condition as reasons for stepping down.

Marshall and his wife live near Washington, D.C. Their oldest son, Thurgood, Jr. is an attorney on Senator Edward Kennedy's Judiciary Committee staff. The younger son, John, is a Virginia state policeman. The Marshalls also have several grandchildren. In his spare time the Justice enjoys spending a few days gambling in Atlantic City.

Sources

Ebony, May 1990.
Detroit Free Press, June 28, 1991.
Detroit News, June 28, 1991.
Newsweek, September 21, 1987; August 6, 1990.
New York Times, November 23, 1946; April 6, 1951.
People, July 7, 1986.

—*Mark Kram*

Hugh Masekela

1939—

Composer, musician

South African trumpeter, fleugelhornist, composer, and singer Hugh Ramopolo Masekela is an acknowledged master of African jazz. He is also one of his country's most recognizable freedom fighters in the battle against apartheid. Masekela was born on April 4, 1939 in Witbank, a coal-mining town near Johannesburg, South Africa. Although his father was a health inspector and famous sculptor, the home was a modest one, and the young boy was raised by his grandmother. At age six Hugh was singing the songs of the street and from age nine attended missionary schools, where he learned to play the piano.

He first became interested in playing the trumpet after seeing the movie *Young Man with a Horn* (1949), the story of Bix Beiderbecke. Initially his greatest influences were the performers of American swing. Later he became interested in be-bop jazz and the music of Dizzy Gillespie and Charlie Parker, who Masekela credits with the development of his talent.

As a teenager Masekela began playing trumpet with South African dance bands and toured major African cities. In 1958 he joined Alfred Herbert's African Jazz

Revue and the following year he formed his own band—the Jazz Epistles, with Dollar Brand (pianist), Makaya Ntshoko (drummer), Jonas Gwanga (trombonist), and Kippie Moeketsi (alto saxophonist).

Because South African music schools were not open to him, Masekela went abroad to continue his musical training. He studied at London's Guildhall School of Music and received a scholarship from Harry Belafonte to the Manhattan School of Music, in New York City, which he attended from 1960 to 1964. He also worked with Belafonte's Clara Music and arranged several albums for his then-wife, African folk singer Miriam Makeba, from whom he was divorced in 1966.

In 1964 he formed another group and the following year he teamed up with fellow student Stewart Levine to found Chisa Records. The *Emancipation of Hugh Masekela* was the first of the eleven albums the team produced. In 1968 Masekela became one of the first African artists to pierce America's pop music world when his song "Grazing in the Grass" topped *Billboard*'s single's chart for two weeks. Written in *mbaqanga*, a recombination of traditional Zulu music and black Ameri-

Collaborated With Mbongemi Ngema

In 1983 Masekela met South African playwright Mbongemi Ngema, who had written several critically acclaimed plays. One of them was *Woza Albert* in which Ngema used Masekela's song "Coal Train." After seeing a performance of this play, Masekela went backstage to meet Ngema. They became quick friends and decided to collaborate on a play. Winnie Mandela, wife of then-imprisoned South African political activist Nelson Mandela, suggested that they portray the children of South Africa and their resistance to the *bantu* education, a lesson that prepared them to serve the white minority in their country.

Ngema wrote the book and some of the music for what was to become *Sarafina!*, titled for the main character, a woman's name common in the townships around Johannesburg, and asked Masekela to compose additional music. Rather loosely structured, the play is more like a series of choral set pieces than musical theater but the songs and dances are all tied together thematically by the Soweto uprising. The action takes place in schoolyard of the Morris Issacson High School, the site of the 1976 Soweto uprising, during which nearly 600 students were killed and many more shot by police for protesting the teaching of Afrikkans—considered by them the language of oppression—instead of English. In *Sarafina!*, inspired by their student leader, the young Sarafina, the students at the school put on a play that depicts the release of the imprisoned Nelson Mandela.

Ngema auditioned and trained about twenty young South Africans from the townships for roles in *Sarafina!* The members of the ten-piece band that provides the energetic *mbquanga* music are dressed as soldiers in a set that is made up of a chain link fence and a silver tank. At the beginning of the piece, the performers are dressed in the trouser and blouse uniforms of the school, but by the end they are in tribal costumes, dancing and singing their heritage and protesting their oppression.

Musical an International Hit

At its 1987 premier in South Africa, *Sarafina!* was an immediate hit. It went from Johannesburg to the Lincoln Center theater later that year, and in January 1988 it moved to Broadway, where, an instant success, it played for two years to sell-out crowds before beginning a national tour. A second troupe was formed to perform the Tony Award-nominated musical in Europe. "I think it's one of the most rewarding projects I've done," Masekela told *Detroit News and Free Press* writer Cassandra Spratling.

Born April 4, 1931, in Witbank, South Africa; father was a health inspector and a sculptor; divorced Miriam Makeba (a folk singer), 1966. *Education:* Attended missionary schools; studied music at Guildhall School of Music, London, England; attended the Manhattan School of Music, New York City, 1960-64.

Began playing trumpet with South African dance bands while a teenager; member of Alfred Herbert's African Jazz Revue, 1958-59; formed own band, the Jazz Epistles, 1959; studied music in England, and in the United States, 1960-64; co-founder of Chisa Records, 1965; leader of and member of numerous musical groups, 1965—; left United States for Botswana, 1982, joined the Kalahari Band; founded the Botswana International School of Music, 1986; co-wrote (with Mbongemi Ngema) musical play *Sarafina!*; returned to South Africa, 1990.

can pop, "Grazing in the Grass" reflects Masekela's African heritage.

Masekela toured parts of Africa in 1973, performing with African musicians. In Ghana he met Nigerian jazzman Fela Anikulapo-Kuti and the Ghanian group Hedzoleh Soundz. He became the group's leader and made recordings with it, including *Masekela: Introducing Hedzoleh Soundz*. In 1974 the group toured the United States.

Masekela moved back to Africa in 1980, settling in Botswana, where he lived for four and a half years. He had a mobile recording studio shipped from California, and working with Jive Afrika Records, he released an album, *Technobush*. The lead song, "Don't Go Lose It Baby," topped the dance charts in the United States. In 1986 Masekela founded the Botswana International School of Music, a nonprofit institute to train African musicians. The following year he signed on as a guest star for Paul Simon's *Graceland* tour, which was a popular and critical success, though it garnered stiff criticism from those who claimed that Simon had violated a United Nations cultural boycott of South Africa when he recorded parts of the album *Graceland* in Johannesburg. Masekela does not appear on the record.

When Masekela left South Africa to study music, he began what was to become a thirty-year self-imposed exile in protest of apartheid. Despite his physical separation, he never lost his emotional and cultural ties, or the desire to see his homeland freed from racial inequality. "I'm not the kind of musician you hear saying 'my music'," Masekela told Donna Britt of the *Washington Post*. "I don't think I have music. I think everybody gets music from the community they come from. . . . And every note that I play, every song that I've ever worked on is really from the people. And their freedom will usher in a place where I can say, 'Now I'm an artist'."

In late 1990 Masekela returned to South Africa to visit his mother's grave for the first time. He also set up a residence to use during part of the year, thus ending his exile. Masekela told *Boston Herald* writer, "I will go back a lot now I think. There is no doubt in our minds that we will be free one day soon and that South Africa will become a normal society. There's a lot of work to be done with the reconstruction that will be coming up. We'll all have to be a part of it."

Selected discography

Trumpet Africaine, Mercury Records, 1960.
Home Is Where the Music Is, Chisa Records, 1972.
Masekela: Introducing Hedzoleh Soundz, 1973.
I Am Not Afraid, Chisa Records, 1974.
Main Event (with Herb Alpert), A & M, 1978.
Technobush, Jive Afrika Records, 1984.
Waiting for the Rain, Jive Afrika Records, 1985.
Uptownship, Novus/RCA, 1990.

Sources

Africa Report, July-August 1987.
American Visions, April 1990.
Boston Globe, October 26, 1990.
Boston Herald, March 6, 1988; October 26, 1990.
Chicago Sun Times, August 5, 1990.
Detroit News and Free Press, June 3, 1990.
(Hackensack, New Jersey) *Record,* October 26, 1987.
Harford Courant, April 24, 1988; March 21, 1990.
(Madison, Wisconsin) *Times,* April 4, 1989.
Milwaukee Journal, July 29, 1990.
(Newark, New Jersey) *Star-Ledger,* October 3, 1989; January 24, 1988.
New York Post, October 24, 1987; October 26, 1987.
New York Tribune, February 12, 1988.
Philadelphia Inquirer, November 22, 1987.
Pittsburgh Press, June 1, 1989.
Providence Journal, July 20, 1990.
Rolling Stone, June 10, 1982; July 2, 1987.
San Francisco Examiner, June 14, 1990.
(Springfield, Massachusetts) *Sunday Republican,* January 24, 1988.
Washington (D.C.) *Times,* April 27, 1990.

—*Jeanne M. Lesinski*

Erroll McDonald

1954(?)—

Publishing executive

Erroll McDonald, the executive editor of Pantheon Books, is a high-ranking executive in New York's vast and lucrative publishing industry. McDonald—an urbane and outspoken businessman—has cut a controversial swath across the publishing market and has become better known than some of the writers whose books he edits. *Esquire* contributor Vince Passaro calls McDonald "a fast-rising and high-profile editor considered brilliant even by the people who don't like him," adding: "McDonald is something of a loose cannon on the slippery decks of His Majesty's Ship Random House."

Pantheon Books, a subsidiary of Random House, specializes in so-called highbrow works of literature and nonfiction—books with literary value and social awareness by American and foreign authors. McDonald brings to his new position extensive experience editing and publishing important Third World authors, including Wole Soyinka, the first African to win the Nobel Prize for literature. The Yale-educated editor has many admirers in his business, but he also has made enemies across the publishing spectrum, still something of a good-old-boy network. "Many people think I'm an asshole," McDonald

bluntly told *Esquire*. ". . . The reaction to me of many people in this business has been one of condescension and contempt."

McDonald is a self-made man in every respect of the word. He was born in Limon, a village in Costa Rica, and was an illegitimate child who barely knew his father. When he was ten he and his mother moved to New York, to the crowded and rough Bedford-Stuyvesant district of Brooklyn. According to Passaro, McDonald largely missed the debilitating effects of racial antagonism in his youth because he lived first in a country with less racial strife and then in an almost all-black neighborhood. "McDonald didn't perceive himself as a minority until he reached high school," Passaro wrote.

That may be the case, but history caught up with McDonald when he attended the prestigious Bronx High School of Science, commuting across boroughs on the bus for his education. He intended to study elementary particle physics—even in high school—but his experiences of the wider world made him change his mind. "That was when the explosion of the civil rights movement and the black nationalist movement occurred," he told *Publish-*

At a Glance. . .

Born c. 1954 in Limon, Costa Rica; son of a seamstress; married, wife's name, Klara Glowczewska. *Education:* Yale University, B.A., c. 1975, M.A., c. 1977.

Random House Publishing Company, New York, NY, employee, 1978—. Began as sub-rights assistant, became editor, 1979, and senior editor, 1983. Named executive editor and vice-president of Vintage Books (a subsidiary of Random House), 1988, originator of Vintage Books' Aventura line of trade paperbacks; executive editor of Pantheon Books, also a subsidiary of Random House, 1990—.

Addresses: *Office*—c/o Pantheon Books, 201 E. 50th St., New York NY 10022.

ers Weekly. "I became more political than scientific." Whatever his interests, McDonald was an excellent student who attended Yale University on scholarship.

At Yale McDonald pursued a number of options—pre-law, political science, economics, and history—before discovering a passion for literature. "I just started reading fiction," he told *Publishers Weekly.* "I decided to take courses in literature, just to see what they were all about. In fact, even after I decided to become an English major I thought I would go to law school. Literature was just something I thought I should read, not something I wanted to get a job in." Comparative literature intrigued McDonald, and he added a knowledge of French, Russian, and German to his fluency in English and Spanish. Remembering his earliest exposure to books in *Esquire,* McDonald said: "I was amazed at reading this English I didn't understand, this English that didn't have anything to do with the English I knew. It made me feel challenged in an aggressive way."

That challenge extended itself into graduate work. McDonald turned down a place at Yale's law school and continued his studies in literature instead. He earned a Master's Degree in philosophy and comparative literature from Yale and was contemplating his doctoral dissertation when he decided to take a break from the academic world. Author Toni Morrison was teaching at Yale in those years, and she helped McDonald secure summer employment at Random House, where she served as an editor. At summer's end, McDonald decid-

ed to pursue a career in publishing. "The more I stayed in New York, the more arcane comparative literature seemed," he told *Publishers Weekly.*

Made Mark in Publishing

McDonald ascended quickly through the ranks at Random House, beginning as a sub-rights assistant and moving to junior editor in only fourteen months. By 1981 he was editing some of the company's most thought-provoking books, including convicted felon Jack Henry Abbott's *In the Belly of the Beast,* an account of life in a penitentiary. That project dragged McDonald's name into the news for the first time, because just as the book was published, Abbott—on parole—killed another man. Passaro notes of the incident: "McDonald, Norman Mailer (Abbott's chief sponsor), and a number of others were accused of pandering to a homicidal maniac for the sake of literary fashion." McDonald has called the press treatment of the affair "a big distortion," maintaining that neither he nor anyone else in publishing had any influence on Abbott's early parole or on his subsequent manic behavior.

The controversy simmered down shortly thereafter, and McDonald continued to work at Random House, eventually becoming a senior editor. Some of the titles he edited include Manuel Puig's *Kiss of the Spider Woman,* Wallace Terry's *Bloods: An Oral History of the Vietnam War by Black Veterans,* and *Good Morning Blues: The Autobiography of Count Basie.* In 1983 he founded the Aventura series for Random House's Vintage Paperback division. The series brought into English translation works by foreign authors who were well known and respected in their own countries, people such as Timothy Mo, Elsa Morante, Julio Cortazar, and Jamaica Kincaid. *Emerge* magazine contributor Randall Kenan noted that the Aventura series reflected "not only a discriminating sense of high quality but also concern about and commitment to a 'First World' or multicultural vision."

One of the authors published under the Aventura signature was Wole Soyinka, the 1986 Nobel Laureate for literature. McDonald still considers Soyinka's *Ake: The Years of Childhood* one of the best titles he edited. He was invited to the Nobel Prize award ceremony in Stockholm, Sweden, where he celebrated with the author in high style. In *Publishers Weekly,* McDonald called *Ake* a book "by which I can justify to myself my presence in publishing."

Named Executive Editor of Vintage Books

Publishing is a business, and like any other business, the

profit margin is paramount. Soon after Sonny Mehta was named president of Random House's Knopf imprint—which oversees both the Vintage and Pantheon divisions—he discontinued the Aventura line. The end of Aventura did not mean the end of McDonald, however. Within months he had been named executive editor of Vintage Books, and he inaugurated yet another series, Vintage International, that bore great similarities to Aventura. Still, McDonald's experience with Aventura convinced him that his company had a responsibility not only to the stockholders, but to the book authors themselves, to make substantial profits wherever possible.

This philosophy found its way into the public eye in 1990, when Random House ordered severe cost-cutting measures for Pantheon Books, a division long renowned for publishing works of serious literary merit. Rather than face what they considered politically-motivated frugality, the chief of Pantheon and five of his top editors resigned. Shortly thereafter, a group of editors, authors, and assistants staged a protest march outside the Random House offices. McDonald responded to the protests by penning a blistering article for the *New York Times* opinion page, a piece in which he blasted the resignees for their ''support of the welfare mentality.'' McDonald went on to point out that editors must remain accountable for profitability of their merchandise, or else they would face charges of pandering to the notion that ''culture, lofty though it might be, is necessarily unprofitable.''

Takes Over Reins of Pantheon

A few weeks later, McDonald was named the new chief of Pantheon—and two more editors quit. Fred Jordan, Pantheon's president and publisher, defended McDonald's choice in *Publishers Weekly* by stating: ''I maintain that he is an important editor and I would hire him again. It is important to have someone strong, and he has a wonderful reputation among his generation of editors.'' Shrugging off the mass exodus from Pantheon, Jordan added: ''There are thousands who would give their eye teeth to work here, and everybody who comes here will be coming to a new situation.''

''Strong'' is a word that aptly describes McDonald. He is loved by some people and hated by others for his aggressive, forthright stance. One friend, scholar Henry Louis Gates, told *Esquire* that race indeed plays a part in the perception of McDonald as abrasive and arrogant. Gates said that McDonald ''makes for a forbidding and intimidating presence that only adds to his woes. It spells danger, given the stereotypes of black men in American culture, and he has had to develop strategies to counter that.''

McDonald is well aware that some of his associates in the predominantly white publishing industry will react to him in a racially-motivated manner. He intends to press on with his agenda, however, and that agenda does not include any limits set by race. Kenan wrote: ''All eyes are on McDonald, waiting to see how well he will walk the tightrope between art and commerce.''

McDonald and his wife Klara live on the Upper West Side of New York. Lean and handsome, the editor presents a picture of his intellectual background and decade-and-a-half of achievements in a high-risk industry. Fred Jordan offers nothing but praise for his new associate, a man Jordan feels will be able to find and make profitable the best literature in the world. ''It's fun to work with [McDonald],'' Jordan told *Esquire*. ''He has a deep sense of social issues and social consciousness, he's known as an editor with a passion for books. There aren't that many people left who do this kind of publishing.''

Sources

Black Enterprise, February 1991.
Emerge, January 1991.
Esquire, January 1991.
Publishers Weekly, March 6, 1987; May 11, 1990.

—*Mark Kram*

Lori McNeil

1964(?)—

Professional tennis player

Since turning professional in 1983, Lori McNeil is respected as one of the more challenging players on the women's professional tennis tour. Considered one of tennis's best serve-and-volley players, McNeil likes to storm the net, where her lightning-fast responses make it difficult to return shots against her. Retired superstar Chris Evert, in an overview of her own tennis career, cited McNeil as one of the most difficult players she ever faced. "McNeil's reflexes are among the quickest on the tour," Evert wrote in an article for *World Tennis*. "It's also tough to play Lori because you never know what she's thinking. Lori is one of those hot-and-cold players. She can play erratically, then string together five or six brilliant points and make you wonder what you have to do to win a rally."

Many felt that McNeil came into her own in 1987 with her upset of the highly-seeded Evert at the U.S. Open, becoming the first black female since Althea Gibson in 1958 to reach the tournament's semi-finals. McNeil's stunning defeat of Evert, followed by a narrow three-set loss to top-rated Stefi Graf, brought the then 23-year-old player into the national sports headlines as one of tennis's newest stars and made her a tournament crowd favorite. Prior to her achievement at the Open, however, McNeil was an established, if relatively unfamiliar, figure on the professional circuit, with over $400,000 in career earnings.

Primarily a doubles player, McNeil made her first serious mark as a singles player when she reached the 1986 quarterfinals at Wimbledon. While her performance at the 1987 U.S. Open may have surprised some, it did not seem to surprise McNeil. "I feel I'm capable of playing with the best," she was quoted as saying in *Jet* at the time. "I always felt I had the ability, but now I'm a little closer." After her performance at the Open, McNeil vaulted to number 11 in the world tennis rankings.

In a profile for the *New York Times,* Roy S. Johnson described McNeil as a "self-made" success who flourished under the encouragement and understanding of her family. She spent her early years in San Diego, California, where her father, Charlie, played defensive back for the San Diego Chargers football team. At that time, her mother Dorothy used to take breaks from family duties by playing tennis in the courts near their home, and often brought young Lori along with her.

At a Glance...

Born c. 1964; daughter of Charlie (a professional football player) and Dorothy (an office manager) McNeil. *Education:* Attended Oklahoma State University.

Professional tennis player, 1986—; reached quarterfinals at Wimbledon, 1986; reached semi-finals at U.S. Open, 1987.

Awards: Big Eight Conference tennis singles champion; named most improved player, *World Tennis,* 1987; named to the U.S. Wightman Cup Team, 1987.

"Lori was my backboard," Dorothy McNeil told Johnson. "She could almost always get the ball back to me from the baseline. It was a real help because I could practice and keep an eye on her at the same time." Lori, Mrs. McNeil continued, was someone who simply "fell in love with the game" and "spent most of her teen-age years on a tennis court. She missed her prom because of it, but she did make it to graduation. When she went out on her first date in college, I said, 'Finally, it's about time.'"

The McNeil family eventually moved to Houston, Texas, and it was there that Lori was introduced by her mother to tennis coach John Wilkerson. Like fellow black professional player and close friend Zina Garrison, McNeil developed under the tutelage of Wilkerson, and practiced on the public tennis courts of MacGregor Park in Houston. At the age of 14, she was inspired by the performance of Pam Shriver, a 16-year-old, who made it all the way to the finals of the U.S. Open. "That was the first time I really focused on it," she told Johnson. "It gave me the feeling that maybe I could be out there at 16, too." After high school, McNeil went on to a successful college career at Oklahoma State University, where she was the Big Eight Conference singles champion, and shortly afterwards turned professional.

According to Wilkerson, McNeil's primary attributes as a professional are her constancy and determination. She possesses a "laid-back" attitude, he told Johnson, "that . . . will usually come out on top." After reaching the U.S. Open semi-finals in 1987, McNeil was collected when responding to questions about her achievement. "It's great to still be undefeated at this point of any tournament," she was quoted by Johnson. "But I haven't arrived or anything. Arrived at what? I've only arrived at the semifinals."

Sources

Jet, July 20, 1987; September 28, 1987; November 2, 1987.
New York Times, September 11, 1987.
World Tennis, May 1987; July 1988; April 1990.

—*Michael E. Mueller*

Mobutu Sese Seko

1930—

President of Zaire

Mobutu Sese Seko has ruled Zaire, the former Belgian Congo that he renamed in 1971, since he assumed power with a military coup in 1965 and established the Second Republic. His regime has been characterized as repressive, and his critics describe him in terms of his drive for power, his compulsion for personalization, and his hunger for adulation. As an effective statesman, he is considered ambitious, charming, keenly intelligent, and diversely educated. According to J. B. Wright in *Zaire Since Independence,* "[The Mobutu regime's] most striking feature is a certain genius for survival against all the odds," including record indebtedness, opposition from the Catholic church, and two invasions. Zaire's rich mineral resources combined with Mobutu's moderate policies have assured Zaire of powerful foreign support, both military and economic.

When Mobutu seized power on November 24, 1965, the Belgian Congo had endured five years of virtual anarchy during which an estimated one million Congolese were killed. Independence came suddenly and abruptly to the Belgian Congo, with devastating consequences, on June 30, 1960. Fifteen political parties sprang up, primarily centered around tribal differences. While the Belgians

had developed a small African elite, known as evolues, there were few college graduates or experienced administrators to rule the country. The Belgians seemed to think their advisers would effectively rule the country.

When independence was formally declared on June 30, 1960, Joseph Kasavubu was president and Patrice Lumumba his prime minister. They represented two opposite factions, with Kasavubu's ABAKO (Alliance des Ba-Kongo) party favoring a federation of the Congo's provinces, and Lumumba's MNC (Mouvement national congolais) seeking a unified state. The tensions between the two leaders were never resolved.

Within days, the Congo was plunged into crisis when the army mutinied. Lumumba satisfied the army's demands by appointing a new chief of staff, Colonel Joseph-Desire Mobutu; and several noncommissioned officers were appointed to officer ranks from lieutenant to colonel. Mobutu had demonstrated an influence over the army during the mutiny, on several occasions confronting the mutineers and calming them. During the ensuing months of crisis, Mobutu's chief competitor for control

At a Glance. . .

Name originally Joseph-Desire Mobutu; adopted name/title Mobutu Sese Seko Nkuku wa za Banga, 1972; born at Lisala, Equateur province, Belgian Congo (now Zaire), October 14, 1930; son of Alberic Bemany (a cook and domestic servant) and Marie-Madeleine Yemo. *Education:* Attended Catholic missionary schools.

Conscripted into the colonial army for seven years for disciplinary reasons as a result of being expelled from the Catholic missionary schools, 1950; attained the highest rank open to Africans in the colonial army, that of sergeant-major; following independence in 1960, he progressively made higher ranks, eventually promoting himself to the rank of field marshal; seized control of Zaire in military coup, 1960; returned power to civilian rule, 1961; another military coup returned Mobutu to power, 1965—. Also wrote newspaper articles under pseudonym "de Banzy," beginning in 1956.

over the army was its commander-in-chief, Victor Lundula. By August, when there was a rupture between Mobutu and Lumumba, Mobutu had virtual control over centrally located army garrisons.

In the meantime, Europeans in the Congo panicked, and Belgian civil servants fled the country. Belgian troops intervened to protect their nationals. The province of Katanga (later renamed Shaba) decided to secede under the leadership of Moise Tshombe, and South Kasai followed. Lumumba requested assistance from the United Nations and also obtained aid and advice from the Soviet Union. He also named Mobutu secretary of state for defense.

Staged First Coup

By August 1960, tensions had risen dramatically between Mobutu and Lumumba. When a political crisis erupted between President Kasavubu and Prime Minister Lumumba, Kasavubu used his constitutional powers to remove Lumumba from office. Refusing to accept his own dismissal, Lumumba then asked parliament to remove Kasavubu from the presidency. This political deadlock was resolved by the prompt intervention of the military under Colonel Mobutu, who staged his first coup on September 14, 1960. Mobutu immediately announced

his intention to suspend all political institutions until December 31, 1960. Upon taking over, he expelled all Soviet and communist-bloc diplomats and technicians who had been invited to the Congo by Lumumba. He declared both Kasavubu and Lumumba were "neutralized," and on his own authority established an interim regime.

Following the coup, Lumumba was living in the capital under United Nations protection. Held incommunicado, he eventually tried escaping to Kisangani to join his supporters, but he was captured and delivered to his enemies in Katanga province. Lumumba was murdered on his first day there. While no one has been convicted of Lumumba's assassination, allegations have been made regarding possible CIA involvement and Mobutu's complicity, since he was in charge of the forces that arrested Lumumba and delivered him to his enemies.

Of this episode, Mobutu has said, "Kasavubu ordered Lumumba's arrest and his subsequent transfer to Lumubashi in Shaba [then Katanga] province, where he died. When Lumumba was assassinated, I was in Kinshasa [then Leopoldville, the capital], carrying out my duties as chief of staff of the army. I was as surprised as anyone when the news of his death was reported." As president of the Second Republic, Mobutu would later declare Patrice Lumumba a national hero.

Returned Power to Civilian Rule

Mobutu ruled briefly during the First Republic with the assistance of commissioners organized as the College of Commissioners, who were primarily young university graduates. Both a soldier and a political figure, Mobutu was not interested in becoming a military dictator. The army was his prime base, but he sustained his complex political network and was a major participant in government policymaking. He ruled until a new parliament was convened in August 1961, and a new government was formed with Cyrille Adoula as prime minister. Kasavubu remained as president.

During this period, four groups were vying for power: civilians under Kasavubu, northern provinces under Antoine Gizenga, Tshombe in Katanga, and a separatist group in Kasai led by Albert Kalonji. All except Tshombe joined to form the new government under Adoula, who ruled for two turbulent years. In July 1964, President Kasavubu invited Tshombe to assume the post of prime minister and form a new national government, the "government of national reconciliation." A new constitution of August 1, 1964, established a presidential system that incorporated a federalist structure.

Returned to Power

The Congo had been divided into 21 provinces under a new constitutional amendment that allowed the creation of new provinces, and the new constitution formalized the federalists' position. Elections were held in March and April 1965, but by mid-year a deadlock between Tshombe and Kasavubu occurred. Once again, the army, led by Lieutenant-General Mobutu, intervened and neutralized the two executives. On November 24, 1965, all executive powers were transferred to Mobutu.

The diversity of Mobutu's background helped bring him to power. Christened Joseph-Desire, he was born at Lisala, Equateur province, on October 14, 1930. His father, a cook and domestic servant, died in 1938, and his mother placed her family under the protection of the paternal clan of Ubangi. The "Sese Seko" of the title Mobutu adopted in 1972 are the given names of his paternal uncle, a well-known warrior-diviner from the village of Gbadolite. It is Gbadolite, rather than Lisala, that Mobutu considers his ancestral village, and he has transformed it into a model community with a well-appointed presidential palace that is often used as a rural retreat.

In his later life, Mobutu frequently referred to his humble background as the son of a cook and the victim of a difficult childhood. He finished fourth grade when his father died, then spent ten years in and out of school as his mother took the family to different villages. At Gbadolite, there was a conflict with his paternal uncles, one of whom expected a compulsory marriage to Mama Yemo, Mobutu's mother. In 1948, Mobutu was able to advance to junior high school at Mbandaka. He was subject to frequent disciplinary problems at the various Catholic missionary schools he attended, including the Capuchins, Scheutists, and Freres des Ecoles Chretiennes.

Conscripted Into Colonial Army

In 1950, Mobutu was definitively expelled and given a seven-year disciplinary conscription into the colonial army. His excellent command of French won him a desk job there, and he was soon sent to the Kananga military school where noncommissioned cadres were trained. At the Kananga school, he met the military generation that would seize control of the country in 1960 when the Belgian officers fled the country. In 1953, he was transferred to army headquarters in Kinshasa. At the time of his discharge in 1956, he had risen to sergeant-major in the accounting section, the highest rank open to Zairians. There were no African officers in the Belgian colonial army.

In 1956, Mobutu began to write newspaper articles under the pseudonym "de Banzy." Through his military and journalistic careers, he found powerful European patrons, such as Pierre Davisher, a liberal Belgian editor, and Colonel Marliere, a senior Belgian officer. He also acquired visibility among the new African elite in Kinshasa. His only problem was with the Catholic church, which considered him an intelligent but dissolute young man, lacking the proper moral qualities. Mobutu remained antagonistic to the church throughout his life. He refused to perform a Catholic marriage with his wife, and he typically aligned with anti-clerical factions as president.

In 1958, Mobutu went to Brussels with a large contingent of Zairians who were exhibited at the Brussels World Exposition as examples of Belgian colonial achievement. In 1959, he revisited Brussels and secured an apprenticeship in the colonial propaganda agency Inforcongo. This post also gave him opportunities for advanced study in Brussels. In 1959-60, politically ambitious Zairians were busy constructing political networks.

Mobutu continued to live in Brussels and was sought out by diplomatic, intelligence, and financial interests who

> Both a soldier and a political figure, Mobutu was not interested in becoming a military dictator

were making contact with Zairian nationals in Belgium as the prospect for early independence loomed. Mobutu made contacts among financiers, the CIA, Zairian students, and Belgian security forces during this period. Mobutu attended the Round Table Conferences in Brussels that considered the coming independence for the Congo. He had developed a friendship with Lumumba that began in 1957 and was named head of the MNC/L office in Brussels. He returned to Zaire only three weeks before independence.

After the five-year debacle that was the First Republic, Mobutu assumed power, declaring, "The political leaders have settled for a sterile power struggle without any regard for the well-being of the citizens of this country." Following his 1965 coup, Mobutu kept the institutional framework of the government intact and filled posts with new officials. He became head of state and his right-hand man, Colonel (later General) Leonard Mulamba, was named prime minister. Behind a constitutional facade, the army staff became the sole effective authority.

Ended Anarchy in Zaire

The first five years of Mobutu's presidency saw a consolidation of power into his hands and his office. After six years of virtual anarchy, Mobutu succeeded in bringing some law and order to Zaire. When he became head of state, he declared "no party politics were to be practiced in the country for five years." He became the founding president of MPR, the Mouvement populaire de la revolution, in April 1966. The MPR was the country's sole legal political party, and by law every citizen was a member. By 1970 the Congo had regular political institutions for the first time since 1965.

Mobutu said, "After independence, I set out to restore popular sovereignty and national unity, which was in grave jeopardy. In addition, I sought to promote economic development and to forge a national political movement." His ideological objective became known as "authenticity." By ending Zaire's multiparty system, which spawned nearly fifty political parties, Mobutu believed, "I was able to create a new sense of national unity and political stability."

After assuming power, Mobutu sought to make authenticity a political reality. The ideology derives its inspiration from the African experience. And Mobutu felt ideology plays a salient role in the survival and progress of a nation and that without it, a society loses its sense of direction. In line with the doctrine of authenticity, the Democratic Republic of Congo became the Republic of Zaire on October 27, 1971. Zaire is French for the Portuguese name given to the Congo River, from an approximate rendering of the Kikongo word *nzadi* (river). Colonial place names were Africanized, and a new flag and national anthem were adopted. Individuals were required to adopt African names in place of their Christian or other foreign names. Mobutu adopted his ancestral name—Mobutu Sese Seko Nkuku wa za Banga—which translates as "all-conquering warrior who goes from triumph to triumph."

Inspired a Personality Cult

The official ideology became known as Mobutism, and by 1974 it was taught in schools in place of religious instruction. Mobutu's more devoted followers referred to him as the Messiah, and the MPR was equated with the church. Following certain Maoist tendencies, Mobutu's praise was reiterated in the official media with titles like Guide of the Zairian revolution, the Helmsman, Father of

the Nation, and Founding President. Mobutu also designated towns and villages associated with his career as "places of meditation." Mobutu's mother, Mama Yemo, died in 1971. Some commentators believe she exercised a restraining effect over her son. It was in the years immediately following her death that Mobutu's personality cult reached its peak. Mobutu had a new medical facility in Kinshasa named after her.

When the Mobutu personality cult was at its peak in 1974-75, the press carried a front-page photograph of him nearly every day, and other officials could only be mentioned by title, not by name. From 1969 to 1975, Mobutu enjoyed direct communion with the people of Zaire. His brand of personalism is justified on the grounds that the public could not understand power in abstract terms. To achieve full legitimacy, the state needed to be personalized, not unlike a village chief who embodies the people of that village.

The unchecked concentration of power in Mobutu's hands has led to corruption and an intolerance of dissent. He effectively dealt with opposition from political figures, students, labor, and the Catholic church in the early years of his presidency. Mobutu admits the media and flow of information in Zaire is controlled. He considers the media "an excellent vehicle for educating the masses," but "this information must reflect the genuine concerns and major aspirations of the people. . . . The people must not be left to the mercy of the media, which over time and without their knowledge may sow the seeds of strife and discord."

A 1985 article in *Forbes* estimated Mobutu's personal fortune at $5 billion, the equivalent of Zaire's national debt. Mobutu denied the charge and claimed to have about $50 million in assets. With 17-20 percent of Zaire's national budget devoted to "Presidency Services," Mobutu is able to make legal expenditures at his own discretion. He is the largest shareholder in the Banque du Kinshasa, has indirect interest in several Zairian operations of foreign-owned companies, and partially owns an agricultural conglomerate (CELZA) that is one of the country's largest employers.

After 25 years of Mobutu's regime, tensions in Zaire mounted in 1990 as democratic reforms sweeping Eastern Europe took effect in many African nations. In February, an illegal opposition party (UDPS) staged demonstrations to commemorate the death of Lumumba. Further unrest occurred in April, as students staged protests in Kinshasa. Later that month, Mobutu announced that a multiparty system allowing three parties (including the MPR) would be introduced after a transition period of one year.

At that time, he also announced the inauguration of the

"Third Republic" and resigned as chairman of MPR and state commissioner for national defense. He retained the office of president and set up a special commission to draft a new constitution. Presidential elections were scheduled to take place before December 1991, with legislative elections to follow in 1992. Regardless of the election's outcome, Mobutu will have taken care of one of the most difficult aspects of politics in Africa by setting up a constitutional structure for a peaceful and orderly transition of power.

Sources

Books

Africa South of the Sahara, 1991, Europa, 1990.
Elliot, Jeffrey M., and Mervyn M. Dymally, editors, *Voices of Zaire: Rhetoric or Reality,* Washington Institute Press, 1990.

Wright, J. B., *Zaire Since Independence,* Institute for the Study of Conflict, 1983.
Young, Crawford, and Thomas Turner, *The Rise and Decline of the Zairian State,* University of Wisconsin Press, 1985.

Periodicals

Business Week, July 10, 1989.
Current History, April 1985.
Forbes, November 18, 1985.
Harper's, June 1990.
Time, May 21, 1990.

—*David Bianco*

Daniel Moi

1924—

President of Kenya

After more than a decade of ruling Kenya as its elected president, Daniel Moi faces serious problems in political, economic, and social areas. Politically a one-party state since a 1982 constitutional amendment legitimized the Kenya African National Union (KANU) as the country's single party, Kenya now faces increasing pressure from at home and abroad to move toward a multiparty system. The sweeping deomocratic reforms taking place in Eastern Europe and elsewhere have not gone unnoticed in Africa.

Moi has long been a strong advocate of the single-party system as practiced in Kenya. He was responsible for the 1982 constitutional amendment that outlawed opposition parties, and he recently received support on this issue from Nelson Mandela. During his July 1990 visit to Nairobi, the capital of Kenya, Mandela defended Kenya's single-party system by asking the rhetorical question, "What right have the whites anywhere to teach us about democracy, when they executed those who asked for democracy during the time of colonial rule?"

There are at least three strong arguments that Moi puts forth in defense of his one-party rule. Historically, Kenya

has shown an unprecedented political stability for an African nation, and the country is blessed with a high level of economic, intellectual, and political development. A proliferation of political parties, Moi argues, would only encourage tribalism over nationalism. Kenya is an ethnically diverse nation of more than 40 tribes, and Kenyan politics have been intertwined with tribal interests even before independence was achieved in December 1963. Throughout Africa, tribalism has been a major deterrent to economic and political development. Wars in Africa nearly always take place between tribes rather than nations.

As a term, "tribes" is used to refer to specific ethnic groups. Tribalism in Kenya amounts to a fear of the Kikuyu, the country's largest tribe. Historically, the Kikuyu have been prominent in Kenyan politics; it was the tribe of Jomo Kenyatta, Kenya's first president and the man who is considered the father of independent Kenya. While Kenyatta proclaimed a doctrine of nationalism, many of his policies favored his own tribe. When Kenyatta died in 1978, the law required an election within 90 days. The Kikuyu were split between two powerful rivals from their own tribe, Attorney General Charles Njonjo and

At a Glance...

Full name, Daniel Arap Moi; took the name Daniel when baptized by Christian missionaries; born in 1924 to a farming family of the Kalenjin tribe in the Baringo district of the Rift Valley Province of western Kenya; married; children: several. *Education:* Attended missionary and government schools and received teacher training at the Kapsabet Teacher Training College, becoming a teacher at the Government African School in 1945.

Began career as teacher, quickly advanced to head teacher, and following a series of promotions, became the headmaster of the Government African School, 1954-57. Entered politics in 1955 as a black representative from the Rift Valley; Moi became one of the first eight blacks elected to the Legislative Council, 1957; reelected, 1958; went to London in 1960 as one of the African delegates who helped draft a new Kenyan constitution; elected assistant treasurer of the newly formed KANU (political party), 1961; established, with the leaders of other minority tribes, political party KADU, served as chairman for about a year; served in various ministerial capacities, including Minister of Education, 1961-62, Minister of Local Government 1962-64, and Minister for Home Affairs 1964-67; became Jomo Kenyatta's vice-president, 1967, and succeeded as president upon Kenyatta's death in 1978, re-elected in 1983 and 1988.

Mwai Kibaki. With the support of Njonjo, the Kikuyu backed Moi, Kenyatta's vice-president and a member of a smaller tribe, the Kalenjin.

Elected President

Moi ran unopposed and selected Kibaki for his vice-president, letting the Kikuyu think they would soon return to power. However, another powerful tribe, the Luo, gave Moi their backing, not wanting the Kikuyu to return to power. Moi consolidated his power when, in 1982, he persuaded parliament to pass a constitutional amendment that made KANU the country's only legal party.

Fear of Kikuyu dominance in the nation's politics stems from the colonial period, when the Kikuyu both benefitted and suffered from the British presence. The British settled where the Kikuyu lived, in Nairobi and the surrounding highlands, where they established tea estates on some of the most fertile acreage in Kenya. From the British, the Kikuyu were exposed to trade and commerce and other modern ways; they also received some educational benefits. Tribes further from Nairobi enjoyed few, if any, benefits from colonial rule, and they resented the Kikuyu.

The British also exposed the Kikuyu to concepts of freedom and independence, and the Kikuyu-led "Mau Mau rebellion" of the early 1950s was an early attempt to achieve independence. To put down the uprising, the British employed other tribes, thus increasing the animosity between tribes. The Luo, a tribe originally from western Kenya, had their first contact with the Kikuyu in Nairobi, where they came to compete for jobs. In anticipation of independence for Kenya, the British in 1960 allowed the formation of political parties; the Kikuyu and Luo joined together to form KANU. Other tribes formed KADU, the Kenya African Democratic Union, whose largest tribes were the Luhya, Kenya's second largest tribe, and the Kalenjin, Moi's tribe and the nation's fifth largest. Moi was one of the KADU leaders.

One-party rule in Kenya actually began less than a year after independence, when the KADU voluntarily dissolved itself, its members joining KANU. Except for a three-year period in the late 1960s, one-party rule has continued uninterrupted in Kenya to the present time. That three-year exception is notable for the formation in 1966 of the KPU, Kenya People's Union, by Oginga Odinga, Kenyatta's vice-president at the time. "Mr. Double O," as he is known informally, split with Kenyatta's capitalist-oriented policy and formed the KPU as a left wing, ideologically based party. He was a Luo, and most of the party members were Luo, so the party represented a break between the Luo and Kikuyu tribes. The final Luo-Kikuyu break came in 1969 with the assassination of Tom Mboya, a Luo and one of the country's strongest nationalists. The assassin was identified as a Kikuyu, and following incidents of violence against Kenyatta, the KPU was banned and its leaders put in jail. Oginga Odinga, KPU's founder, would later emerge as a voice of socialist opposition against Moi's regime in the 1980s.

In addition to concerns over tribalism, Kenya's one-party system is defended as appropriate for an African nation. It is argued that multiparty systems are being forced on African nations by colonial powers, and they are not consistent with African traditions and cultures. It is also argued that most African countries are not sufficiently developed for a pluralist democracy to take hold.

Resisted U.S. Pressure

While Moi has tolerated debate on multiparty democracy, he has resisted pressures from the United States to practice pluralist politics. As Moi faced the end of 1990, a year that saw considerable unrest in his nation, he was presented with the prospect that future U.S. aid may be tied to the formation of a Western-style democracy and other conditions. Kenya has enjoyed good relations with the West because of its free market and avoidance of communism. With the end of the Cold War, though, he is facing increasing pressure to democratize the country.

The year began with riots in February that resulted when the unsolved murder of Foreign Minister Robert Ouko was linked with possible government involvement and food prices were decontrolled. In June, Kenya's Catholic bishops expressed alarm about the "unlimited authority" of KANU. It was becoming disturbing to the bishops that Moi and KANU were not being held accountable by the country's citizens. It was KANU's policy at the time to purge members with differing views.

Moi's tolerance of debate on the multiparty issue ended in July 1990, when the government began rounding up the leaders of the multiparty movement. Those identified as leaders included former cabinet ministers Kenneth Matiba and Charles Rubia, noted human rights attorney Gibson Kamau Kuria, and Raila Odinga, son of former Kenyatta Vice-President Oginga Odinga. Kuria received asylum in the U.S. Embassy and was later allowed to leave the country for the United States, where he would teach at the Harvard Law School as a visiting scholar. The other three were held without charges, and Moi rebuked the U.S. for interfering in Kenya's internal affairs. The U.S. countered with a statement that it was "distressed" at Kenya's repression and arrest of dissidents. As other dissidents fled the country, four days of riots and street violence engulfed Nairobi and surrounding areas. Following these riots, President Moi appointed a KANU committee to begin hearings around the country to determine what political changes the people of Kenya wanted.

While Moi's adherence to one-party rule may be justifi-

Moi ignites $3 million in illegally poached ivory to show Kenya's commitment to save elephants from extinction.

able, his rule as president has been marked by a steady erosion of the country's democratic institutions, including the press, the judiciary, and the voting system. When Moi was elected to his first term as president in November 1979, five million people, or 80 percent of the electorate, turned out to vote. Over 740 candidates ran for the 158 seats in parliament. At that time, it was typical for only half of the incumbents to retain their seats. In that election, Moi ran unopposed in his own district, and many from the old Kenyatta regime were ousted.

As a result of voting reforms introduced in 1986 that partially eliminated the secret ballot, the turnout in the 1988 election was quite low, and more than three quarters of the incumbent members of parliament retained their seats. In 1986, the secret ballot was replaced in primary elections by a system of queuing, whereby voters stand in front of the picture of the candidate of their choice. While the secret ballot was retained for general elections, a 70 percent rule was also introduced, which gave the primary candidates automatic election if they received more than 70 percent of the primary vote. These reforms served to reduce the possibility of change in the elected government, lessening the accountability of elected officials and consolidating Moi's political support.

Attacked Judicial System and Press

Moi's attack on Kenya's independent judiciary began in 1986, when the constitution was amended to take away life tenure from the attorney general. Two years later, life tenure was taken away from senior judges. These officials now serve at the will of the president, thus effectively eliminating the independent judiciary system. Moi also sought greater control over Kenya's press, long considered one of the country's strong points. In recent years, three magazines have been banned. Government officials often block stories from the newspapers, and the press is reluctant to investigate corruption among cabinet ministers and senior KANU politicians. Moi's actions have fostered a personality cult and left him unwilling or unable to solve the problem of "rampant corruption and maddening excesses of bureaucracy," according to *Time* magazine. Britain's liberal paper, the *Guardian,* has called Moi's regime "one of the world's most corrupt leaderships."

When he first became president, Moi promised to attack the corruption that had grown under Jomo Kenyatta's rule. Kenyatta's estate was valued at $200 million at the time of his death. Moi publicly denounced five members of parliament for illegal practices and began investigating contracts awarded by the Ministry of Works. In an attempt to reduce Kenyatta's estate, he authorized the repossession of property by unpaid creditors and enforced the collection of back taxes. However, it soon became clear that Moi was only pursuing incidents of corruption at the lowest levels of government. In his own government, high-level cabinet ministers reportedly made personal fortunes by importing sugar at a time when Kenya's sugar supply was low.

The first years of Moi's presidency were filled with the promise of positive developments for Kenya. He virtually eliminated the legal killing of game and the smuggling of ivory and coffee, practices that had been tolerated by Kenyatta. He reaffirmed Kenyatta's policy of development along capitalist rather than socialist lines. In a December 1978 speech, he announced the release of 26 political prisoners who had opposed Kenyatta and introduced several social programs to combat illiteracy, increase universal free primary education, strengthen employment, and provide free milk daily to all primary school children.

Weathered Coup Attempt

The first sign of an erosion in Moi's popular support came in mid-1982, when rebels from the Embakasi air force base near Nairobi seized the Voice of Kenya radio station, announced the formation of a provisional National Redemption Council, and promised the release of all political prisoners. The coup attempt was launched by junior or enlisted members of Kenya's air force who were quickly joined by students from the University of Nairobi. Their quick defeat led some commentators to speculate that the coup had been betrayed by another contingent that was to have joined the rebel forces.

Although the coup attempt was quickly stamped out, the rebels were joined by slum dwellers in a looting spree aimed primarily at the Asian shopkeeper of Nairobi's tourist district and causing millions of dollars of damage. The rebels were defeated by loyalists from the Kenyan army and the General Service Unit, a paramilitary police force. Moi, not in Nairobi at the time, returned to the city and quickly launched a crackdown resulting in 3,000 arrests, including four fifths of the 2,500-person air force.

The 1982 coup attempt revealed dangerous tensions in Kenyan politics. Moi had begun showing his authoritarian bent earlier in the year, when he order the detention without charges of seven people, including four lecturers from the University of Nairobi and their lawyer. In June, the constitutional amendment legitimizing KANU as the country's sole political party was passed. Following the coup attempt, Moi in May 1983 called for parliamentary elections that September, fourteen months before they would have been constitutionally mandated. New party rules enabled Moi to handpick the entire slate of election candidates, since they all had to receive the approval of KANU's executive. During the year, Moi succeeded in purging Charles Njonjo, a former supporter and powerful Kikuyu, and his followers from the government. In the 1983 election, only 48 percent of the electorate turned out.

In 1984, Moi demonstrated a willingness to open a dialogue with student dissenters, even as he introduced measures in parliament that would reduce criticism of his regime. His authority over the cabinet ministers, who accounted for over 40 percent of parliament, was established when they were required to sign a letter from the president stating that they were not at liberty to criticize or differ from the government outside immediate government circles. In effect, senior KANU members were no longer able to express criticism of President Moi.

Charged with Human Rights Abuses

In 1987, following the introduction of the 1986 "queue-voting" system and the suppression of the Mwakenya conspiracy during which more than 100 people had been detained, Kenya was cited for human rights abuses. Amnesty International reported on repeated allegations of torture, which was believed to have been used on all political prisoners. Gibson Kamau Kuria, a human rights attorney, began to prepare an unprecedented case against the government. Moi's actions were also opposed by the moderate National Christian Council of Kenya, which opposed the elimination of secret ballots and said, "The party is assuming a totalitarian role. It claims to speak for the people and yet does not allow the people to give their views."

President Moi responded in June 1989 to continuing international criticism of his human rights record by releasing all political prisoners who were being held without charges and by offering an amnesty to dissidents in exile. In light of 1990's developments, though, it seems those actions represented no change in the government's intolerance of political dissent.

As Moi looks ahead to the 1990s and a constitutionally scheduled election in 1993, he must also deal with the problem of declining tourism in the face of escalating violence involving elephant and rhinocerous poaching. Kenya's fabled widlife and its system of national parks have long attracted international tourists, making tourism an important contributor to Kenya's economic well-being. In September 1988, Moi introduced a "shoot-to-kill" policy against the poachers after three Kenyan rangers were murdered.

In April 1989, Moi appointed Richard Leakey the new director of the Kenyan Wildlife Service. Over 100 poachers were shot by game scouts in 1989, and the elephant kill was reduced from 1,500 in 1988 to only 100 in the year following Leakey's appointment. The violence continued, though, when George Adamson, a champion of lions, was killed in his camp at Kora Park in northeast Kenya in August 1989. That July, a Connecticut woman on an Audubon-sponsored photo-safari was killed by poachers-turned-bandits. Most of the poaching and related violence has been attributed to Somali shifta who cross the border from Kenya's northeastern coastal neighbor.

Kenya supported the October 1989 reclassification by CITES (Convention on International Trade in Endangered Species) of the African elephant from a "threatened" species to one "endangered" by trade. The move effectively outlawed the ivory trade among CITES's 103 member nations, with only China and five southern African nations (Malawi, Zambia, Botswana, Zimbabwe, and South Africa) filing reservations to the ban. Earlier that year, President Moi had dramatically set fire to 12 tons of bleached elephant tusks worth an estimated $3.6 million on the international market. Also at risk is Kenya's rhinocerous population, which has been reduced from 20,000 to only 500 over the past 20 years.

Sources

Books

Africa South of the Sahara, 1991, Europa, 1990.

Periodicals

American Spectator, March 1990.
Atlantic, June 1979.
Atlas World Press Review, March 1979.
Audubon, September 1990.
Current History, March 1982; March 1983; May 1987.
Maclean's, August 16, 1982; May 30, 1983; July 31, 1989.
The Nation, September 11, 1982.
New Yorker, September 3, 1990.
Newsweek, July 23, 1990.
Rolling Stone, October 4, 1990.
Time, November 19, 1979; August 16, 1982; October 16, 1989; May 21, 1990.
World Press Review, May 1987.

—David Bianco

Thelonious Monk

1917-1982

Pianist, composer, bandleader

When Thelonious Monk began performing his music in the early 1940s, only a small circle of New York's brightest jazz musicians could appreciate its uniqueness. His melodies were angular, his harmonies full of jarring clusters, and he used both notes and the absence of notes in unexpected ways. He flattened his fingers when he played the piano and used his elbows from time to time to get the sound he wanted. Critics and peers took these as signs of incompetency, treating his music with "puzzled dismissal as deliberately eccentric," *Jazz Journal* noted. "To them, Monk apparently had ideas, but it took fleshier players like pianist Bud Powell to execute them properly." The debate over his talent and skill continued as the years passed, but Monk eventually earned a strong following. By the time of his death in 1982, he was widely acknowledged as a founding father of modern jazz.

The *New York Post* once called Monk "one of jazz's great eccentrics." During concerts and recording sessions he would rise from his bench every so often and lunge into a dance, emphasizing the rhythm he wanted from his bandmembers with his 200-pound frame. With his strange hats, bamboo-framed sunglasses, and goat-

ee, he became an obvious subject for Sunday supplement caricatures. There was also the way he talked: He and his peers were known for popularizing such expressions as "groovy," "you dig, man," and "cool, baby." Most Americans, however, first heard of Monk in the early 1950s when he was arrested for allegedly possessing drugs—for Monk, one of several instances of legal harassment that would create severe obstacles to his work.

Thelonious Sphere Monk was born October 10, 1917, in Rocky Mount, North Carolina. The first music he heard was from a player piano that his family owned. At the age of five or six he began picking out melodies on the piano and taught himself to read music by looking over his sister's shoulder as she took lessons. About a year later the family moved to New York City. Monk's father became ill soon afterward and returned to the South, leaving the boy's mother to raise him and his brother and sister by herself. She actively encouraged her young son's interest in music. Though the family budget was tight, Monk's mother managed to buy a baby grand Steinway; when Monk turned 11 she began paying for weekly lessons. Even at that age it was clear that the instrument was part of his destiny. "If anybody sat down and played the piano," Monk recalled in *Crescendo International,* "I would just stand there and watch 'em all the time."

As a boy Monk received rigorous gospel training, accompanying the Baptist choir in which his mother sang and playing piano and organ during church services. At the same time, he was becoming initiated into the world of jazz; near his home were several jazz clubs as well as the home of the great Harlem stride pianist James P. Johnson, from whom Monk learned a great deal. By age 13 he was playing in a local bar and grill with a trio. A year later he began playing at "rent" parties—thrown to raise money for rent—which meant holding his own among pianists who would each perform marathon displays of virtuosity. Monk gained further distinction at the Apollo Theater's famous weekly amateur contests which he won so often that he was banned from the event. At 16 he left school to travel with an evangelical faith healer and preacher for a year-long tour that indoctrinated him into the subtleties of rhythm and blues accompaniment.

Upon returning to New York, Monk began playing non-union jobs. In 1939 he put his first group together. An important gig came in the early 1940s, when Monk was hired as house pianist at a club called Minton's. It was a time of dramatic innovation in jazz. Swing, the music of older jazzmen, had become inadequate for postwar society. In its place, a faster, more complex style was

developing. The practitioners of this new music, called bebop, created it virtually on the spot, "in jam sessions and discussions that stretched past the far side of midnight," *Keyboard* explained. "According to jazz folklore, this activity centered on Minton's, and as the house pianist there, Monk was at the eye of what would become the bebop hurricane."

Yet while Monk was pivotal in inspiring bebop, his own music had few ties to any particular movement. Monk was an undisputed and independent original, and the proof was in his compositions. "More than anyone else in the Minton's crowd, Monk showed a knack for writing," *Keyboard* remarked. "Years before his piano work would be taken seriously, he would be known for his composing. In fact, most of the classic Monk tunes, such as 'Blue Monk,' 'Epistrophy,' and "Round Midnight,' were written during his gig at Minton's or before 1951."

Charged With Narcotics Possession

As the 1940s progressed and bebop became more and more the rage, Monk's career declined. In 1951 he was arrested with Bud Powell on a questionable charge of narcotics possession. Not only was he confined for 60 days in prison, but the New York State Liquor Authority rescinded his cabaret card, without which he could not play local club dates. For several years he survived only with the help of his good friend and patron the Baroness Nica de Koenigswarter.

By the mid-1950s, though, Monk's fortune took a turn for the better. In 1954 he gave a series of concerts in Paris and cut his first solo album, *Pure Monk* (now out of print). A year later he began recording for the Riverside label. His following grew, and as *Keyboard* reported, his mystique grew as well. "Program notes for the Berkshire Music Barn Jazz Concert in 1955 read, 'Monk is the Greto Garbo of jazz, and his appearance at any piano is regarded as a major event by serious followers of jazz.'" In 1957 Monk opened an engagement at New York's Five Spot, leading a powerful quartet with then jazz newcomer John Coltrane on saxophone. The eight-month gig was pivotal for Monk, who "found himself at the center of a cult," according to *Keyboard.* "Audiences lined up to see his unpredictable performances, his quirky, quietly ecstatic dances during horn solos, his wanderings through the room." Several masterful discs he recorded for Riverside in the late 1950s—*Brilliant Corners, Thelonious Himself,* and *Monk with Coltrane*—increased his notoriety, rendering him "the most acclaimed and controversial jazz improviser of the late 1950s almost overnight." It also didn't hurt that both Coltrane and saxophonist Sonny Rollins were acknowledging him as their guru.

Erratic Behavior

The strange behavior that Monk displayed in public sometimes got him into trouble. A *New York Times* review of the 1989 Monk documentary *Straight, No Chaser* commented on his temperament, revealing that the great pianist was "acutely sensitive and moody and perhaps a manic-depressive. . . . Illness eventually made it impossible for him to perform." In 1958 he was arrested for disturbing the peace and his cabaret license was revoked a second time. Forced to take out-of-town gigs, he was separated from his two main sources of stability—New York City and his wife Nellie—and his eccentricities thus intensified. During one episode in 1959 in Boston, state police picked him up and took him to the Grafton State Hospital, where he was held for a week. Around 1960 his cabaret club card was restored and he returned to playing New York clubs. Now when he played a gig his wife accompanied him.

Toward the end of the 1950s Monk began to receive the prestige he had long deserved. His late-fifties recordings on Riverside fared so well that in 1962 he was offered a contract from Columbia. As a performer he was equally successful, commanding $2,000 for week-long engagements with his band and $1,000 for single performances. In 1964 Monk appeared on the cover of *Time* magazine—an extremely rare honor for a jazz artist.

Withdrew From the Limelight

In the early 1970s, Monk made some solo and trio recordings for Black Lion in London and played a few concerts. But, beginning in the mid-1970s he isolated himself from his friends and colleagues, spending his final years at the home of the Baroness de Koenigswarter in Weehawken, New Jersey. After playing a concert at Carnegie Hall in March 1976, Monk was too weak physically to make further appearances. He died on February 17, 1982, after suffering a massive stroke.

There was "a Monk fever in the jazz world" for at least two years before the pianist's death, observed *Village Voice* contributor Stanley Crouch. But, as record producer Orrin Keepnews observed in *Keyboard,* performing Monk's music is no easy feat. His "material can be basically divided into two categories: difficult and impossible." Monk's eccentric piano technique too raised eyebrows among music critics. Concerning those who criticized his technique, Monk told *Crescendo International,* "I guess these people are surprised when they hear certain things that I've done on records. They must feel awful silly about saying I don't have no technique. Because I know you've heard me make some fast runs. You can dig how stupid the statement is."

Looking back on his career, Monk told *Crescendo International,* "As for the hard times I've had—I've never been jealous of any musician, or anything. Musicians and other people have told lies on me, sure, and it has kept me from jobs for awhile. . . . But it didn't bother me. I kept on making it—recording and doing what I'm doing, and thinking. While they were talking I was thinking music and still trying to play."

Selected discography

(With Sonny Rollins, Frank Foster, Ray Copeland, Julius Watkins, Percy Heath, Curly Russell, Willie Jones, and Art Blakey) *Monk* (recorded 1953-54), Prestige.
The Riverside Trios (recorded 1955-56), Milestone.
The Complete Riverside Recordings: 1955-61, Riverside, 1987.
(With Rollins, Ernie Henry, Oscar Pettiford, and Max Roach) *Brilliant Corners* (recorded 1956), Riverside.
(With Pettiford and Blakey) *The Unique Thelonious Monk* (recorded 1956), Riverside.

He would rise from his bench every so often and lunge into a dance, emphasizing the rhythm he wanted from his bandmembers with his 200-pound frame.

Thelonious Himself (recorded 1957), Riverside, reissued 1987, Fantasy.
Monk with Coltrane (recorded 1957), Jazzland.
European Tour (recorded late 1950s), Denon.
(With Johnny Griffin, Ahmed Abdul Malik, and Roy Haynes) *Misterioso* (recorded 1958), Riverside, reissued 1985.
Alone in San Francisco (recorded 1959), Riverside, reissued 1987, Fantasy.
At Town Hall (recorded 1959), Riverside.
Evidence (recorded 1959 and 1960), Milestone.
In Person (recorded 1959 and 1960), Milestone.
(With Joe Gordon, Charlie Rouse, Harold Land, and others) *At the Blackhawk* (recorded 1960), Riverside, reissued 1988, Fantasy.
Thelonious Monk and the Jazz Giants, Riverside.
Monk in Italy (recorded 1961), Riverside, reissued 1991, Fantasy.
April in Paris/Live, Milestone, 1961.
(With Rouse, Frankie Dunlop, and John Ore) *Monk's Dream* (recorded 1962), reissued 1987, Columbia.

The Composer (recorded 1962-64 and 1968), Columbia, 1988.

Live at the Village Gate (recorded 1963), Xanadu, 1985.

Solo Monk, Columbia, 1965.

(With Blakey, Copeland, Gigi Gryce, Coleman Hawkins, John Coltrane, and Wilbur Ware) *Monk's Music* (recorded mid-1960s), Riverside.

Straight, No Chaser, Columbia, 1966.

The London Collection, three volumes, Black Lion, (Volume 3 recorded 1971; reissued 1990).

The Best of Thelonious Monk: The Blue Note Years, Blue Note, 1991.

Sources

Books

Chilton, John, *Who's Who of Jazz: Storyville to Swing Street,* Chilton, 1972.

Giddons, Gary, *Rhythm-A-Ning: Jazz Tradition and Innovation in the 80s,* 1986.

Hentoff, Nat, *The Jazz Life,* Da Capo, 1975.

Periodicals

Crescendo International, June 1984.

Daily News, February 18, 1982.

Jazz Journal, August 1964.

Jazz Review, November 1958.

Keyboard, July 1982.

New York Post, February 18, 1982; September 30, 1989.

New York Times, September 30, 1989.

Time, February 28, 1964.

Village Voice, March 9, 1982.

—*Kyle Kevorkian*

Garrett Morgan

1877-1963

Inventor

Garrett Morgan was a self-educated and creative individual whose inventions contributed to greater safety and order in our society. He pursued an early interest in things mechanical to develop inventions of surprising technological complexity, considering the fact that he received no formal education beyond the fifth grade. Morgan showed an astute business sense as well, establishing profitable and long-lived companies to manufacture and market his inventions. He was also something of a showman, devising creative and unusual ways to demonstrate his inventions and generate interest in them. Throughout his career, his inventions and activities revealed a deep concern with the safety and welfare of his fellow citizens.

Morgan was born on March 4, 1877, on a farm in the small town of Paris, in a poor and mountainous region of eastern Kentucky. He grew up during the period of Reconstruction following the Civil War, when educational opportunities for young black men were limited. He attended school through the fifth grade, leaving his home at the age of fourteen to seek work and a future across the Ohio River in Cincinnati. He found a job as a handyman for a white landowner but soon became dissatisfied and restless. In 1895, he left Cincinnati for Cleveland, where he settled, married, and spent the rest of his life.

Penniless but hopeful, Morgan arrived in Cleveland and, having taught himself all about sewing machines, found a job as a sewing machine mechanic and adjustor with the firm of Roots and McBride. Over the next few years, Morgan would hold similar positions with other sewing machine companies in Cleveland. He sold his first invention, a belt fastener for sewing machines, in 1901 for $50. In the following years, Morgan's genius for invention and for business would blossom, and he became a successful and independent businessman and inventor.

By 1907, Morgan was able to open a shop that sold and repaired sewing machines. In the first year, he earned enough money to purchase a home and bring his mother to Cleveland. The next year, Morgan married Mary Anne Hassek. By 1909, he owned and operated a tailoring shop that employed 32 people and manufactured dresses, suits, and coats. His involvement in this line of business resulted in an invention that would make enough

At a Glance. . .

Full name, Garrett Augustus Morgan; born March 4, 1877, in Paris, KY; died July 27, 1963, in Cleveland, OH; son of Sydney and Elizabeth Morgan; married Mary Anne Hassek, 1908 (died, 1968); children: John Pierpont, Garrett Augustus, Jr., Cosmo Henry. *Education:* Attended school to the fifth grade.

Left school at age 14 and moved to Cincinnati, where he worked as a handyman; left Cincinnati in 1895 and settled in Cleveland, where he worked as a sewing machine mechanic; sold first invention, a belt fastener for sewing machines, 1901; opened own sewing machine sales and service business, 1907; began tailoring business, 1909; invented gas mask, 1912, formed the National Safety Device Co. to manufacture it, 1914; invented hair straightener and opened G.A. Morgan Hair Refining Cream company to produce it, 1913; invented traffic signal, 1922; owner and publisher of newspaper *Cleveland Call* (later the *Call & Post*) beginning in 1920s; political candidate in Cleveland's City Council race, 1931.

money for Morgan to devote his full energies to new inventions.

Morgan's attention was drawn to a problem at his tailoring shop that involved the sewing of woolen material. The material was frequently scorched by heat generated when the sewing machine's needle moved rapidly up and down. Morgan experimented with chemical solutions that would reduce the friction and eliminate the scorching. As the story goes, when Morgan's wife called him to dinner, he wiped the solution from his hands onto a piece of wiry pony-fur cloth. Upon returning to his workshop, he noticed that the wiry fuzz of the cloth had become straight. The chemical solution had caused the fuzzy hairs to straighten out.

Seeing possibilities in his new discovery, Morgan tried the chemical solution on his neighbor's dog, an Airedale with wiry hair. The solution did such a good job of straightening the dog's hair that the neighbor did not even recognize his own dog. Eventually, Morgan tried the solution on his own hair, a little at a time, then gradually over his entire head. Not noticing any ill effects from his experiment, Morgan began manufacturing and marketing the first human hair straightener under the name G. A. Morgan Hair Refining Cream. In 1913, he set up the G. A. Morgan Refining Company to produce the product. The company has stayed in business, and its profits enabled Morgan to concentrate on other inventions.

Devised First Gas Mask

On August 19, 1912, Morgan filed a patent application for another invention he had been working on, which he called a "breathing device." Also known as the Morgan helmet or safety hood, Morgan would later perfect his "breathing device" into a gas mask that was used extensively in World War I. Morgan himself described his invention as one that was designed "to provide a portable attachment which will enable a fireman to enter a house filled with thick suffocating gases and smoke and to breathe freely for some time therein, and thereby enable him to perform his duties of saving life and valuables without danger to himself from suffocation. The device is also efficient and useful for protection to engineers, chemists, and working men who breathe noxious fumes or dust derived from the materials with which they work." In 1914, Morgan was granted U.S. patent 1,113,675 for his invention.

As illustrated in his patent application, Morgan's device consisted of a hood placed over the user's head, to which a long tube was attached that reached to the ground. In the situations that Morgan envisioned, such as firemen entering a burning building, most of the smoke and fumes would tend to rise, leaving a layer of breathable air along the ground. The tube from the hood had an opening for air, and it was long enough to reach the layer of air beneath dense smoke or gas. The lower end of the tube was lined with an absorbent material, such as sponge, that was moistened with water before use. This would prevent smoke and dust from going up the tube, and it also cooled the air. There was a separate tube containing a valve for exhaled air.

Morgan set up the National Safety Device Company to manufacture and promote the new safety hood. As the company's general manager, Morgan was the only nonwhite officer in the company. He urged his fellow blacks to purchase stock in the company, but most failed to do so. The price of the company's stock rose quickly, from $10 per share in 1914 to more than $250 per share in 1916. Morgan advertised the safety hood extensively, and his talent for creative marketing and showmanship was never more in evidence. He traveled around the country, demonstrating the effectiveness of his invention and trying to drum up interest among industrialists and firefighters.

Excelled as Showman

A particularly spectacular demonstration was described in the October 22, 1914, issue of the *New Orleans Times-Picayune*. As retold in Morgan's profile in *Black Pioneers of Science and Invention,* "A canvas tent, close-flapped and secure, was erected on an open space, and inside the tent a fire was started. The fuel used was made up of tar sulphur, formaldehyde, and manure, and the character of the smoke was the thickest and most evil-smelling imaginable. Charles Salan, former director of public works for Cleveland, conducted the tests.

"Fitting a large canvas affair that had the appearance of a diver's helmet on the head of 'Big Chief' Mason, a full-blooded Indian, Mr. Salan sent Mason under the flaps into the smoke-filled tent. The smoke was thick enough to strangle an elephant, but Mason lingered around the suffocating atmosphere for a full twenty minutes and experienced no inconvenience. He came out after the test 'as good as new,' and a little later gave another exhibition." "Big Chief" Mason was really Garrett Morgan, showman and inventor.

In 1914, the same year his patent was granted, Morgan received the First Grand Prize Gold Medal at the Second International Exposition of Sanitation and Safety in New York City. Several successful demonstrations were topped off by a practical application, when helmets from the exhibit were used by New York firemen to rescue victims from a terrible subway disaster. Shortly afterwards, fire departments in large cities in Ohio, Pennsylvania, and New York began using Morgan's safety hood.

Hailed as National Hero

Although Morgan's breathing device was being used successfully, it received its greatest test on July 24, 1916, when a disastrous explosion rocked the tunnel of crib number five of the Cleveland Water Works. Approximately two dozen men were trapped five miles out and more than 200 feet below Lake Erie. The tunnel quickly filled with smoke, dust, and poisonous gases. The situation required fast action, for the men would soon die of suffocation and gas inhalation. When someone remembered Garrett Morgan and his safety hood, he was quickly summoned to the scene. He arrived with his brother Frank; putting on their safety hoods, they entered the tunnel. The Morgan brothers descended over 200 feet into suffocating darkness, where they gathered up one of the workers and returned to the surface via the tunnel's elevator. They made the trip again and again, bringing back all of the bodies and saving more than twenty lives. It was a true act of heroism that was made possible by Morgan's invention.

Newspapers all over the country carried the story of the heroic deed. Garrett Morgan was given a solid gold, diamond-studded medal by a group of prominent citizens of Cleveland. Its inscription read, "To Garrett A. Morgan, our most honored and bravest citizen." He also received a medal from the International Association of Fire Engineers and was made an honorary member of

> Morgan was given a solid gold, diamond-studded medal by a group of prominent citizens of Cleveland. Its inscription read, "To Garrett A. Morgan, our most honored and bravest citizen."

that association. As a result of the widespread publicity following the Cleveland Water Works explosion, Morgan received many requests from fire departments, police departments, and mining companies to demonstrate his device. Due to racial prejudice, he hired a white person to demonstrate the safety hood in the Deep South; when the racial identity of the inventor became known, orders declined.

Inventor of Traffic Signal

Morgan's concern with the safety and well-being of his fellow citizens led him to invent the first automatic traffic signal. On February 27, 1922, he filed a patent application for a "traffic signal" that would control the stop-and-go of traffic at intersections. His invention came at a time when horse-drawn carriages had to share the road with automobiles, and there were many accidents involving collisions at intersections. Morgan received his U.S. patent (No. 1,475,024) in November 1923, and secured British and Canadian patents as well. He sold the rights for this invention to General Electric for $40,000, a handsome sum in those days. Shortly before his death in 1963, Morgan was cited by the U.S. government for inventing the first traffic signal. His other inventions include a woman's hat fastener, a round belt fastener, and a friction drive clutch.

Morgan's concern with his fellow citizens manifested itself in other ways besides his inventions. Unhappy with the newspaper coverage of events relating to blacks in Cleveland, he started the *Cleveland Call* in the 1920s.

The paper later became the *Call & Post* and was published in Cleveland, Cincinnati, and Columbus, Ohio. It enjoyed a large circulation.

Morgan counted among his friends such notables as John D. Rockefeller and J. Pierpont Morgan, the financier after whom he named his first son. He loved the outdoors and spent time hunting and fishing. He was also a charter member of the Cleveland Association of Colored Men and served as its treasurer from 1914, until the association merged with the National Association for the Advancement of Colored People (NAACP).

Morgan entered politics in 1931, running as an independent candidate for the Cleveland City Council. He promised, "If elected, I will try to lead the people of the third district to equal representation in the affairs of city government." His platform included relief for the unemployed, more efficient administration, improved housing conditions, better lighting, improved sanitation, and improved city-owned hospital accommodations.

Morgan developed a severe case of glaucoma in 1943 that resulted in the loss of 90 percent of his vision. In spite of his near-blindness, he kept busy. At Cleveland's Western Reserve University, he organized a fraternity of black students. One of his last goals in life was to be able to attend the Emancipation Centennial in Chicago, August 1963. However, he died after two years of illness on July 27, 1963.

Sources

Books

Adams, Russell L., *Great Negroes, Past and Present,* third edition, Afro-Am Publishing Co., 1984.

American Black Scientists and Inventors, National Science Teachers Association, 1975.

Georgiady, Nicholas P., et al., *Garrett A. Morgan: American Negro Inventor,* Franklin Publishers, 1969.

A Salute to Historic Black Scientists and Inventors, edited by Richard L. Green, Empak Enterprises, 1985.

Haber, Louis, *Black Pioneers of Science and Invention,* Harcourt, Brace & World, 1970.

Periodicals

Detroit News, February 5, 1991.

Journal of Negro History, Winter/Spring 1985.

—*David Bianco*

Ali Hassan Mwinyi

1925—

President of Tanzania

Tanzania is an East African nation that was formed in 1964 by the union of Tanganyika and Zanzibar, a group of islands off the coast that, under the terms of the union, remains semi-autonomous, electing its own president and legislature. Tanzania's capital, Dar es Salaam, is a port city on the Indian Ocean, and the country shares borders with Kenya to the northeast; Uganda, Rwanda, Burundi, and Zaire to the north and west; and Zambia, Malawi, and Mozambique to the south. Transport routes through Tanzania to its port cities offer central African nations an alternative to transport through South Africa.

Executive powers in Tanzania are vested in a president who is nominated by the sole legal political party, the Revolutionary Party of Tanzania (CCM, Chamo Cha Mapinduzi). The presidential candidate runs unopposed for office and is elected by direct popular vote. Under the most recent constitutional amendments, the presidential term is renewable only once. Since the union of Tanganyika and Zanzibar, Tanzania has had only two presidents. Julius Nyerere, president of Tanganyika since independence in 1961 and then of Tanzania, stepped down in 1985 and was succeeded by Ali Hassan Mwinyi, who

was re-elected for a second term in 1990.

Mwinyi, a devout Moslem, was born in 1925 on the mainland, but his family moved to the island of Zanzibar when he was very young. He entered politics in 1963, leaving his post as principal of the Zanzibar Teacher Training College to become permanent secretary to the minister of education in Zanzibar. In 1970 he was appointed to the Tanzanian cabinet as minister of state in the president's office. He held various government posts in succeeding years, including minister of health and home affairs (1982-83) and minister of natural resources and tourism (1982-83); he also served as ambassador to Egypt for five years.

In April 1984, Mwinyi was elected president of Zanzibar and chairman of the Zanzibar Revolutionary Council. Later that year he was also elected as vice-chairman of the ruling party, CCM. In May 1984, the National Executive Committee (NEC) of CCM proceeded with proposals to change the constitution, reviving the system of two vice-presidents that had lapsed in 1977. Under this system, the president of Tanzania appoints two vice-

At a Glance...

Born on May 8, 1925, in Kivure, Tanganyika; raised in Zanzibar (which joined with Tanganyika in 1964 to form Tanzania). *Education:* Trained to be a teacher. *Religion:* Moslem.

Began professional life as a teacher, became principal at the Zanzibar Teacher Training College. Entered politics in 1963, became permanent secretary to the minister of education in Zanzibar; appointed to the Tanzanian cabinet as minister of state in the president's office,1970; held various government posts in succeeding years, including minister of health and home affairs, 1982-83, and minister of natural resources and tourism, 1982-83; also served as ambassador to Egypt for five years; elected president of Zanzibar and chairman of the Zanzibar Revolutionary Council, 1984; elected vice-chairman of Tanzania's ruling party, CCM, 1984; adopted as the sole presidential candidate by the CCM and elected, 1985; re-elected to a second term in October 1990; became chair of the ruling CCM, 1990.

presidents, one being the president of Zanzibar and the other the prime minister of the Tanzanian government.

When Mwinyi was elected president of Zanzibar, he also became Nyerere's vice-president. The system of two vice-presidents was adopted, in part, to more precisely define Zanzibar's relationship to the mainland within the union. It was hoped that the system would help put an end to secessionist tendencies in Zanzibar, and the constitutional change also consolidated Mwinyi's political position.

The complete integration of Zanzibar into the mainland was one of Nyerere's primary goals. As president of Zanzibar (1984-85), Mwinyi helped maintain Zanzibar's tenuous link to the mainland at a time when Tanzania's pervasive economic problems caused the islands to question the value of the union. He improved relations with the mainland and succeeded in calming fears that the quasi-autonomy of the islands (Zanzibar and Pemba) was being eroded through constitutional changes.

Mwinyi succeeded Zanzibar's President Jumbe, who was forced to resign to take responsibility for the growth of secessionist sentiments in Zanzibar. Mwinyi had been Jumbe's minister of state and was considered a moderate. He sought to reconcile Zanzibar to the union by introducing economic reforms that allowed market for-

ces a larger role than CCM's socialist policies would normally permit. These reforms generally improved the standard of living in the islands. However, tensions between Zanzibar and the mainland would continue even after Mwinyi had become president of Tanzania.

Mwinyi's moderate political stance—together with circumstance—helped to propel him into Tanzania's presidency. After Nyerere had once again reaffirmed his intention to step down, his heir apparent, Prime Minister Edward Sokoine, was killed in April of 1984. Mwinyi was then appointed to fill the vacancy of vice-president of Tanzania and vice-chairman of the ruling CCM. Mwinyi was elected to the latter post in the August 1984 extraordinary Party National Conference, where he received 96 percent of the delegates' votes and defeated six other candidates.

Received Party Endorsement

On August 15, 1985, President Nyerere announced to the special conference of the CCM that Mwinyi would be the sole candidate to succeed him in the October elections. Nyerere introduced him as the party candidate by saying he's "a righteous man, impartial and respectful, [who] has never sought fame or used his position to advance ambition." Commentators regarded Mwinyi as a compromise candidate who was chosen over Salim Ahmed Salim, the prime minister who succeeded Sokoine and who was from Zanzibar, and Rashidi Mfaume Kawawa, the party's secretary-general and a mainlander who was a Nyerere loyalist. Both of these candidates were unacceptable to certain factions within the CCM's executive committee.

Mwinyi and Nyerere together campaigned hard, even though Mwinyi was the sole candidate for president. Nyerere believed it was necessary for the country to rally behind its new president. In the October elections, Mwinyi received 92.2 percent of the votes. His successor as president of Tanzania was Idris Abdul Wakil, who thus also became one of Tanzania's vice-presidents. Interestingly, Wakil only received 61 percent of the votes cast, reflecting his unpopularity with the residents of the island of Pemba.

Since both the new president (Mwinyi) and the prime minister (Salim) were from Zanzibar, the constitution prevented Salim from being prime minister and first vice-president. When he was sworn in as president in November 1985, Mwinyi appointed mainlander Joseph Warioba as prime minister and first vice-president and created the position of deputy prime minister for Salim Salim. The cabinet remained largely unchanged.

Faced Serious Economic Problems

Mwinyi faced serious economic problems when he assumed the presidency. The currency was overpriced, and the country's external debt had reached $3 billion. The most basic goods were unavailable in Tanzania's shops. The socialist policies of Nyerere and the CCM, which included widespread nationalization, were generally recognized as unsuccessful. Mwinyi described Tanzania's economic problems of that time by saying that agricultural production was low and farmers could not produce enough food for the country's citizens. The volume of cash crops (tea, coffee, cotton, sisal) was falling each year, resulting in a shortage of foreign exchange. Tanzania was thus forced to import massive amounts of food from abroad at a time when the country had no money to pay for it.

In addition, Tanzania's economic infrastructure had fallen into disrepair: roads had deteriorated, hospitals had no drugs, schools had no books. The external debt was mounting, so Mwinyi sought to reach an agreement with the International Monetary Fund (IMF), with which Tanzania had been negotiating for six years. One of Mwinyi's first actions upon becoming president was to enter into an agreement with the IMF to abandon socialism and remodel the Tanzanian economy along free-market lines. Although opposed by Nyerere and the CCM, the IMF agreement allowed capital to flow, however slowly, into the country.

As a result of the agreement, donor nations agreed to debt rescheduling, and some nations wrote off Tanzania's debts completely. In 1986, the Paris Club, a loosely knit group of Tanzania's donor nations and institutions, agreed to reschedule Tanzania's accumulated matured debts of about $900 million, suspending payment for five years on 97.5 percent of the loan principal and interest. Principal donors agreed to provide $800 million a year for three years to help cover Tanzania's foreign exchange requirements. In 1987, the 21 donor countries and institutions pledged $955 million for 1987 and $978 million for 1988.

Economic Recovery Plan Unveiled

As part of the 1986 IMF agreement, Mwinyi introduced a three-year Economic Recovery Plan (ERP) that resulted in IMF approval of a standby loan which was replaced in 1987 by a three-year structural adjustment facility. In a December 31, 1986, speech, Mwinyi said the IMF agreement "did not make us change the principals of our policy of socialism and self-reliance." He acknowledged the bad state of affairs that had necessitated negotiating with the IMF.

The ERP was announced at a time when Tanzanians were lining up for the most basic food commodities. The Economic Recovery Plan involved devaluation of Tanzanian currency, raising of agricultural producer prices, and the removal of corruption from some 400 parastatal companies. Mwinyi closed some of the more inefficient state corporations and returned some factories to private ownership. In 1988, Mwinyi described Tanzania's economy as a "mixed economy," pointing to private enterprise as well as public ownership in the different sectors. Tourism, for example, was both private and public. Mwinyi estimated agricultural production at 80-90 percent private, with all cash and food crops being produced by private individuals. Transport was about 60 percent privately run, and Mwinyi noted that he had expanded the role of the private sector in agricultural distribution, which under Nyerere was done only by parastatal organizations.

The ERP was largely designed by Cleopa Msuya, formerly the prime minister and then the finance minister. In 1987, the CCM showed its opposition to the ERP and the IMF agreement by excluding Msuya from its central

> Mwinyi's moderate political stance—together with circumstance—helped to propel him into Tanzania's presidency

committee. To alleviate the effects of the Economic Recovery Plan, under which devaluation made meager wages even more worthless, the minimum wage was increased in 1988, rent assistance was introduced, and income taxes were reduced. Toward the end of 1988, the flow of donor funds into the Tanzanian economy was unblocked, following an IMF agreement, when the government agreed to further devalue the Tanzanian shilling.

The government had been unwilling to further devalue its currency but finally agreed to the IMF's demands. Mwinyi also agreed to reduce public spending and lift import and price controls. He defended the agreement before the CCM as a "lesser evil [between] empty shelves [and] shops full of expensive goods." Commentators noted that Mwinyi had succeeded in bringing basic necessities to the villages, and shops in Dar es Salaam were now filled with local and foreign goods.

Revived Tanzanian Economy

Although Mwinyi's pragmatic and liberalizing policies were credited with reviving the Tanzanian economy, he would deny that he reversed the socialist policies of his predecessor. Mwinyi describes the role of the president and the party in Tanzania by saying, "In our country, the party is supreme and the government is only an instrument which implements the party's policies." Mwinyi continued to assert that socialism is a goal for the Tanzanian economy, but he also acknowledged an active private sector in Tanzania's "mixed economy."

In 1989, Mwinyi launched the country's second five-year plan. Its goal was to raise the real growth in gross domestic product (GDP) by 6 percent per year on the mainland and by 4 percent on Zanzibar. While the budget was likely to have a harsh impact on the population, it was regarded by most donors as disappointing. According to the donors, the plan lacked new measures to encourage investment and restructure the produce-marketing boards.

In March 1990, a new investment code was approved by the ruling CCM and went before parliament in April. As part of the liberalization of the economy, it was designed to "entice private and public investors of local and foreign origin to take a more active role in promoting the development of our national economy." As a result of improved foreign relations, Tanzania received foreign aid from the Nordic countries, the United Kingdom, and the United States. Canada wrote off Tanzania's debt entirely.

Mwinyi has also sought to improve relations with Tanzania's neighbors. In 1986, he signed an agreement with Malawi to allow that nation greater access to the port city of Dar es Salaam. In 1987, he reinforced cordial relations with neighboring Mozambique, Zambia, and nearby Zimbabwe. Mwinyi pledged military support to President Chissano of Mozambique in 1986, to guard the railways and fight against what was perceived as South African-supported destabilizing forces. Toward the end of 1988, though, Tanzanian troops were withdrawn from Mozambique. Relations with neighboring Burundi have been strained, with Tanzania expelling thousands of Burundi nationals allegedly living illegally in Tanzania.

Internal Political Reorganization

Mwinyi gained support for his liberalizing economic policies through a series of cabinet reshuffles, dismissals, and party politicking. Faced with the problem of corruption, he dismissed prominent government administrators. In the middle of his first term, Mwinyi was viewed by some commentators as a transitional president who would be succeeded in 1990 by Joseph Warioba, the prime minister under Nyerere and a dedicated follower of Nyerere and the CCM's socialist policies. In 1987, two cabinet reshuffles resulted in at least three ministers being replaced; they had been regarded as supporters of the traditional party ideology and opposed to Mwinyi's liberalization policies.

At the CCM's third national conference in 1987, Nyerere surprised the 1,800 delegates by announcing he would remain as chairman of CCM, with Mwinyi being renominated as the CCM vice-chairman. In September 1988, Mwinyi strengthened his control over the armed forces by appointing a new chief of general staff, General Ernest Mwita Kiaro, and a new army chief of staff, General Tumainiel Kiwelu. In 1989 Mwinyi created two new ministries and abolished the post of deputy prime minister that had been created for Salim in 1985.

Mwinyi also took over the defense and national service portfolio, sharing responsibilities in this area with Nyerere. In February, the CCM initiated a campaign against corruption in the government, and Mwinyi dismissed seven ministers who had allegedly opposed plans for economic reform and presided over corrupt or irresponsible ministries. This latest reshuffle was seen as a move to secure support for the new investment code, which had reportedly provoked dissent among some socialist ministers.

Mwinyi succeed Nyerere as chair of the CCM in August 1990. In the presidential and general elections set for October 1990, Mwinyi was chosen as the sole candidate for president. Following the elections, Mwinyi appointed a new prime minister, John Malecela, former high commissioner to the United Kingdom. Malecela replaced Joseph Warioba, who had hitherto been considered an eventual successor to Mwinyi.

Sources

Books

Africa South of the Sahara, 1991, Europa, 1990.
Tanzania after Nyerere, edited by Michael Hodd, Pinter Publishers, 1988.
Keesing's Record of World Events, Longman, 1990.

Periodicals

Africa Report, January-February 1988.
Business America, April 10, 1989.

The Economist, October 17, 1987.
New Yorker, March 3, 1986.
Time, November 4, 1985.
U.S. News & World Report, June 27, 1988.

—David Bianco

Youssou N'Dour

1959—

Singer, composer, drummer

Youssou N'Dour is an international star in the field of popular music that has come to be known as "Afro-pop" or "world beat." He is a singer, composer, and drummer whose style has been given the name "mbalax." N'Dour's own particular brand of mbalax has become so popular and widespread that he is often credited with inventing the genre, although Ronnie Graham stated in his authoritative book on contemporary African music that mbalax is a generic Senegalese music characterized by a percussion base and featuring an improvised solo on the sabar drum. Mbalax has also been described as modern Senegalese rock.

Graham described Senegalese pop music of the late 1980s as "a sophisticated blend of the old and the new," with the old being primarily Cuban-influenced melodies and rhythms that dominated Senegalese music prior to the 1970s. The development of local styles was seriously hindered by the French philosophy of exporting their own culture; and local idioms, instruments, and traditions did not begin to appear in urban contemporary music until the 1970s, after Senegal had achieved independence. The tama, a small drum, was introduced in the 1970s and became a popular lead instrument.

N'Dour's own mbalax features a rhythmic dance band consisting of as many as 14 members, including multiple percussionists, guitarists, saxophonists, and backing vocalists. As N'Dour has achieved greater recognition and acceptance among Western audiences in Europe and the United States during the late 1980s, he has been relieved of some of the pressure to incorporate Western rock styles into his own music. Although he is fluent in French, Arabic, and his native Wolof, his English is not very good. Thus, he is at his best when able to present an appealing and authentic brand of African pop, with its own unique rhythms and vocalizations sung in Wolof, one of Senegal's major native languages.

N'Dour was born in 1959 in Dakar, the capital of Senegal, on the west coast of Africa. Historically, Senegal is a part of French or francophone Africa. Musically, external influences within Senegal and other parts of francophone Africa were more restricted than in anglophone or British Africa. N'Dour grew up in a traditional African community within the Medina section of the city. He says of life in the Medina, "Living on the street was like being in a

At a Glance. . .

Born in 1959 in Dakar, Senegal; father was a mechanic; mother was a griot (a community historian and storyteller).

Began singing at ceremonial parties as a child; was performing in front of large audiences by age 14; joined recording/performing group, the Star Band; formed own band, Etoile de Dakar (Star of Dakar), c. 1979, reformed in Paris as Super Etoile de Dakar (Superstar of Dakar), c. 1984. Has toured the United States and Europe and took part in Amnesty International's "Human Rights Now!" world tour, 1988.

family. Everybody knows one another, there's a great feeling of togetherness."

The story of N'Dour's upbringing is that his father was a mechanic who discouraged him from a musical career. His mother, however, was a griot in the community. A griot is a historian and storyteller within the community. N'Dour's mother was a respected elder who kept the oral tradition of the community's history alive through traditional songs and moral teachings.

With his mother's encouragement, N'Dour would sing at kassak, a party to celebrate circumcision. As N'Dour described his work then, "Sometimes on one street there would be four or five kassaks going on at the same time. They would start in the evening and I would go to one and sing two numbers, then on to the next. . . . Sometimes I used to sing at 10 kassaks a night. Gradually, my friends and others encouraged me and gave me confidence, because they liked my singing."

By the age of 14, N'Dour was performing in front of large audiences and had earned the nickname, "Le Petit Prince de Dakar," or "The Little Prince of Dakar." As a teenager he joined the Star Band, the best known Senegalese pop band of the time, recording with them and performing in clubs in Dakar. By the time he was 20, he had left the Star Band to form his own group, Etoile de Dakar (Star of Dakar). They recorded three albums in Dakar and had a hit with their first single, "Xalis (Money)." Then they relocated to Paris and reformed as the Super Etoile de Dakar (Superstar of Dakar).

Toured Europe and the United States

Living in Paris and the European milieu provided N'Dour

with a range of new musical influences to contend with. He says, "When I started to play music, I was playing traditional music. But when I came to Europe to listen to the sounds around me, by 1984 I had a new attitude. I'm a new person now [1990], opening fast. I like to change. I'm African, yes, but I like to play music for everybody. But my identity is African. That will never change."

From his base in Paris, N'Dour and the Super Etoile began to win over Western audiences to the sound of mbalax. The Super Etoile consisted of 14 members, probably the largest aggregation N'Dour would ever perform with. The group used traditional Wolof and African rhythms behind N'Dour's unique tenor. N'Dour sang and continues to sing in Wolof, his vocal style often compared to Islamic chanting reminiscent of mosques and temples.

By the mid-1980s, the group was ready for a major international breakthrough. They had toured the United States, Great Britain, and Holland, in addition to playing at N'Dour's nightclub in Dakar, the Thiosanne. Remembering his audiences in Dakar and his friends from the Medina, N'Dour made it a point to return there. A song he wrote, "Medina," celebrates his old neighborhood and his old friends, who "are still my friends today and are the people I have around me."

N'Dour and Super Etoile released an album in 1985 that became a classic in the Afro-pop field, *Immigres.* It was released in the United States three years later. N'Dour increased his exposure to Western audiences in 1986 by appearing as a drummer on Paul Simon's *Graceland* album. He recorded the *Nelson Mandela* album in Paris that year and toured the United States twice with Super Etoile, once on their own and once opening for Peter Gabriel. N'Dour sang backing vocals on Gabriel's *So* album, and it is Gabriel who is the Western musician most responsible for bringing Youssou N'Dour to America and other Western nations.

N'Dour continued to tour with Peter Gabriel in 1988, reducing the size of his band to six pieces and a dancer. In the summer of that year, N'Dour played New York's first International Festival of the Arts at the Beacon Theatre. The influence of American pop on N'Dour was revealed in his playing half a set's worth of American pop and soul, with Nona Hendryx joining him for a song in English and Wolof. *New York Times* writer Jon Parelis wrote of N'Dour, "What makes Mr. N'Dour an international sensation, along with the dance rhythms of mbalax, is his unforgettable voice, a pure, pealing tenor that melds pop sincerity with the nuances of Islamic singing." Noting that mbalax has always combined international influences with Senegalese traditions, Parelis expressed his concern that American pop was diluting the effect of N'Dour's singing and the band's rhythms. N'Dour would later echo this concern in *Rolling Stone,* when he said, "It's a very difficult balance to keep the roots and bring in a bit of the Western world."

In the Fall of 1988, N'Dour gained even greater international exposure as part of Amnesty International's "Human Rights Now!" world tour. At London's Wembley Stadium, N'Dour joined Bruce Springsteen, Sting, Peter Gabriel, and Tracy Chapman to sing Bob Marley's classic reggae song, "Get Up, Stand Up." It was the start of a 44-day tour of five continents, including such Third World and Eastern bloc nations as Hungary, India, Zimbabwe, Argentina, and Brazil. Only two U.S. dates were included, Los Angeles and Philadelphia.

Diverse Lyrical Content

N'Dour's original songs include political and social commentary. He is also capable of writing and performing songs with a personal lyric content, songs about his old neighborhood and childhood pals, about the youth of his country, and about roaming the countryside with a friend. In 1989, Virgin Records released a new N'Dour album, *The Lion (Gaiende).* It was recorded in Paris, England, and Dakar and was produced by George Acogny and David Sancious, who have combined backgrounds in jazz, pop, and rock. The Super Etoile, by now reduced to an eight-piece band, was joined by some Western musicians, including pop-jazz saxophonist David Sanborn. Peter Gabriel and N'Dour sing a duet on one of the album's tracks, "Shaking The Tree." N'Dour sings in Wolof on the album, but English translations of the lyrics are provided. In a review of the album, *New York Times* reviewer Jon Parelis again expressed his concern that too much Western influence was creeping into N'Dour's music, and he wrote, "Despite an undercurrent of Senegalese drums, the rippling vocal lines and dizzying polyrhythms that made Western listeners notice him are usually truncated."

By the fall of 1989, Super Etoile was back to full strength with 12 pieces for N'Dour's club dates in the United States. The extra percussion and instrumentation helped restore the driving rhythm of N'Dour's music. Reviewing a performance at New York's the Ritz, Jon Parelis described the "two percussionists whose doubletime and tripletime rhythms restored mbalax's sense of swift, sprinting momentum." He noted that the intricate cross-

rhythms combined well with a firm downbeat to provide a mix of Western and Senegalese styles. The show ended with a song about toxic wastes that would be released in 1990 as a single from N'Dour's latest Virgin album, *Set.*

N'Dour's songs on *Set* deal with personal emotions, social problems, and political issues. He says, "Most of the songs I heard in my youth were either love songs or traditional songs recounting the history of the people that I come from—praise songs, historical songs. The lyrics of my own works today I consider to be about the society in which I live, the world in which I live. I want my words to have an educational function."

Selected Discography

Singles

"Toxiques," Virgin, 1990.

Albums

Nelson Mandela, Polydor, 1986.
Immigres, Virgin, 1988.
The Lion (Gaiende), Virgin, 1989.
Set, Virgin, 1990.

Sources

Books

Graham, Ronnie, *The Da Capo Guide to Contemporary African Music,* Da Capo Press, 1988.

Periodicals

Detroit Free Press, October 5, 1990.
Detroit Metro Times, October 3-9, 1990.
Detroit News, October 5, 1990.
Down Beat, May 1987.
New York Times, July 2, 1988; July 2, 1989; November 8, 1989.
Newsweek, September 12, 1988.
People, October 10, 1988.
Rolling Stone, July 13-27, 1989.

—*David Bianco*

Gordon Parks

1912—

Photographer, film director, author

In 1990, at the age of 78, Gordon Parks published his third autobiographical work, *Voices in the Mirror.* The book reveals the personal side of a man whose achievements in photography, literature, film, and ballet have won him more than twenty honorary doctorates and numerous awards. Reviewing the book in the *New York Times Book Review,* Michael Dyson wrote, "Mr. Parks records with unsparing candor the material deprivations, psychic thrashings and moral agonies wrought by his initiation into maturity. It is amazing that he never allowed the ubiquity of racial animosity to obstruct his exploration of the mystery of life or wither his reverence for imagination and experience."

Driven by a self-proclaimed determination to "drive failure from my dreams and to push on," Parks became the first black photographer to work at magazines like *Life* and *Vogue,* and the first black to work for the Office of War Information and the Farm Security Administration. Parks achieved these milestones in the 1940s. Later, in the 1960s, he helped break racial barriers in Hollywood as the first black director for a major studio. He co-produced, directed, wrote the screenplay, and composed the musical score for the film based on his

1963 novel, *The Learning Tree.* The film was later placed on the National Film Register by the Library of Congress.

The youngest of fifteen children, Gordon Parks was born into the devout Methodist family of Sarah Ross Parks and Andrew Jackson Parks in 1912 in Fort Scott, Kansas. It was a town "electrified with racial tension," Parks remembered. The family was dirt-poor, but the children were taught to value honor, education, and equality, as well as the importance of telling the truth. The security that Parks derived from the quiet strength of his father and his mother's love was shattered when she died during his fifteenth year. As he recalled in *Voices in the Mirror,* he spent the night alone with her coffin, an experience he found both "terror-filled and strangely reassuring."

After his mother's death, Parks was sent to live with a sister and her husband in St. Paul, Minnesota. His high school education was cut short when his sister's husband threw him out of the house just before Christmas one year. Suddenly and unexpectedly on his own, Parks was forced to take a variety of temporary jobs that included playing piano in a brothel and mopping floors. As a

At a Glance...

Full name, Gordon Roger Alexander Buchanan Parks; born November 30, 1912, in Fort Scott, KS; son of Andrew Jackson and Sarah (Ross) Parks; married Sally Alvis, 1933 (divorced, 1961); married Elizabeth Campbell, 1962 (divorced, 1973); married Genevieve Young (an editor), August 26, 1973 (divorced, 1979); children: (first marriage) Gordon, Jr. (a filmmaker; deceased), Toni Parks Parson, David; (second marriage) Leslie.

Free-lance fashion photographer in St. Paul, MN, 1937-42; U.S. Farm Security Administration, Washington, D.C., photographer, 1942-43; U.S. Office of War Information, photojournalist war correspondent, 1943; Standard Oil of New Jersey, photographer, 1944-48; *Life* magazine, photojournalist and photoessayist, 1948-68.

Independent photographer and filmmaker, 1954—. Maker of numerous documentary films, including *Diary of a Harlem Family* and *Mean Streets,* and of feature films, including *Shaft,* 1971, *Shaft's Big Score,* 1972, and *The Super Cops,* 1974. *Essence* magazine, founder, 1970, editorial director, 1970-73. Composer and director of ballet *Martin.* Composer of *Piano Concerto,* 1953, *Tree Symphony,* 1967, and piano sonatas and modern works for piano and wind instruments, and film scores, including *The Learning Tree* and *Shaft's Big Score.*

Awards: Recipient of numerous civic and professional awards, including the Julius Rosenwald Fellowship, 1941; Notable Book Award from the American Library Association, 1966, for *A Choice of Weapons;* Emmy Award for documentary, 1968, for *Diary of a Harlem Family;* Spingarn Award, 1972; Christopher Award, 1978, for *Flavio;* National Medal of the Arts, 1988; and Library of Congress National Film Registry Classics film honor, 1989, for *The Learning Tree.*

Addresses: *Home*—860 United Nations Plaza, New York, NY 10017.

busboy at the Hotel Lowry in St. Paul, he played his own songs on the piano there and joined a band that was on tour after the leader heard him play.

Unfortunately, the band broke up when they returned to New York. Stuck in Harlem, living in a rat-infested room and unable to find work, Parks joined the Civilian Conservation Corps (CCC) in 1933. He married Sally Alvis in 1933 and returned to St. Paul in 1934, taking a job there as a dining car waiter and porter on the North Coast Limited. They had three children, Gordon, Jr., Toni, and David.

Began Career in Photography

Parks became interested in photography while working on the railroad. He took his first pictures in Seattle, Washington, in 1937, at the end of his "run" from St. Paul. As Parks recalled for *The Black Photographers Annual,* "I bought my first camera in a pawn shop there. It was a Voigtlander Brilliant and cost $12.50. With such a brand name, I could not resist." He took his first pictures on Seattle's waterfront, even falling off the pier as he photographed sea gulls in flight. Upon his return to the Midwest, he dropped his film off at Eastman Kodak in Minneapolis. "The man at Kodak told me the shots were very good and if I kept it up, they would give me an exhibition. Later, Kodak gave me my first exhibition," Parks recalled.

Against all odds, Parks made a name for himself in St. Paul as a fashion photographer. Heavyweight boxing champion Joe Louis's wife, Marva, saw his photographs on display in a fashionable store and encouraged him to move to Chicago, where she could steer more fashion work his way. Using the darkroom of Chicago's South Side Arts Center, a black community arts center, he supported his family through fashion photography while documenting life in the city's slums. His documentary photographs won him a Julius Rosenwald Fellowship in 1941, paying him $200 a month and offering him his choice of employer. In January 1942, he went to work in Washington, D.C., for Roy Emerson Stryker in the photography section of the Farm Security Administration (FSA), where he joined some of the finest documentary photographers in the country.

Parks took one of his most significant photographs on his first day in the nation's capital. He called it "American Gothic, Washington, D.C.," a portrait of Mrs. Ella Watson, a black woman who had mopped floors for the government all her life, posed with a mop and broom in front of an American flag. Parks was angry when he took the photo, having spent the entire day battling racial prejudice in restaurants and stores. As the first black in the FSA, Parks did all he could to break down racial barriers, and he had the full support of his boss, Roy Stryker. While at the FSA, Parks took documentary photographs of everyday life. He spoke of his camera as if it were a weapon, "I had known poverty firsthand, but there I learned how to fight its evil—along with the evil of racism—with a camera."

After the FSA disbanded in 1943, Parks worked as a war correspondent for the Office of War Information, where he taught himself about "writing to the point." Prohibited from covering the missions of an all-black fighter pilot squadron, Parks left in disgust and moved back to Harlem. In New York, he attempted to land a position with a major fashion magazine. The Hearst Organization, publisher of *Harper's Bazaar,* would not hire a black man. Shocked at Parks's experience, famed photographer Edward Steichen sent him to Alexander Liberman, director of *Vogue* magazine. Liberman put Parks in touch with the senior editor of *Glamour* magazine, and by the end of 1944 Parks's photographs appeared in both publications.

Joined Staff of *Life* Magazine

Parks's former boss, Roy Stryker, offered him a position with Standard Oil of New Jersey in 1944. Parks would stay there until he joined *Life* magazine as a photojournalist in 1948, shooting pictures of the company's executives and doing a notable documentary series for Standard Oil on life in America. Parks's first assignment for *Life* was one of his most significant, a profile of Harlem gang leader Red Jackson. It was an idea Parks himself suggested, and he stayed with the gangs for three months. His most famous photograph of Red Jackson is one in which the gang leader has a .45 pistol in his hand, waiting for a showdown with a rival gang.

Parks would work at *Life* for nearly a quarter of a century, until 1972, completing more than 300 assignments. When asked by *The Black Photographers Annual* to name his most important stories for *Life,* Parks listed the Harlem gang story, his first Paris fashion shoot in 1949, the Ingrid Bergman-Roberto Rosellini love affair on Stromboli, a cross-country U.S. crime series, an American poetry series that interpreted in photographs the works of leading U.S. poets, the Black Muslims and Malcolm X, the Black Panthers, and Martin Luther King's death. By the early 1960s, Parks was writing his own essays to accompany his photographs in *Life.*

Parks provided the readers of *Life* magazine with a unique view of the civil rights movement in the 1960s. As Phil Kunhardt, Jr., assistant managing editor of *Life,* recalled for Deedee Moore, "At first he made his name with fashion, but when he covered racial strife for us, there was no question that he was a black photographer with enormous connections and access to the black community and its leaders." It was Malcolm X's trust of

Parks that allowed him to do a feature on the Black Muslim leader. Malcolm X wrote of Parks in his autobiography, "Success among whites never made Parks lose touch with black reality."

Real life and photography were often closely intertwined in Parks's work. In 1961, he was on assignment in Brazil to document poverty there. He met a young, asthmatic boy named Flavio who was dying in the hills above Rio de Janeiro. Parks's now-famous photoessay on Flavio resulted in donations of thousands of dollars, enabling Parks to bring the boy to a clinic in the United States for treatment. Flavio was cured and lives today outside of Rio; Parks and Flavio have remained friends.

Began Film Career

Parks began his cinematic career by writing and directing a documentary about Flavio in 1962. In 1968, he became the first black to produce and direct a film for a major studio, Warner Bros. Seven Arts. The film, *The*

In the 1960s Parks helped break racial barriers in Hollywood as the first black director for a major studio

---

Learning Tree, was based on Parks's 1963 autobiographical novel and featured lush romanticism. Surprisingly, Parks also directed some highly commercial dramas for Metro-Goldwyn-Mayer (MGM), including *Shaft* (1971), *Shaft's Big Score* (1972), and *The Super Cops* (1974). As described by Donald Bogle in *Blacks in American Films and Television,* "Almost all his films [except *The Super Cops*] reveal his determination to deal with assertive, sexual black heroes, who struggle to maintain their manhood amid mounting social/political tensions. . . . In some respects, his films . . . can generally be read as heady manhood initiation rituals."

The commercial success of the "Shaft" films put MGM studios back on its feet financially after some difficult times, but Parks was not assured of a lasting place in Hollywood. Something of a maverick, Parks found himself in a dispute with Paramount Pictures over the distribution and promotion of his 1976 film, *Leadbelly,* which tells the story of the legendary folk and blues singer Huddie Ledbetter. Paramount's new management denied the film a New York opening, thus lessening its impact, and Parks felt the advertising campaign made the movie appear to be another "blaxploitation" film. Declining to do another Hollywood movie, Parks went on to film several documentaries for television and the Public Broadcasting System, including *Solomon Northrup's Odyssey, The World of Piri Thomas, Diary of a Harlem Family,* and *Mean Streets.*

The Learning Tree, Parks's autobiographical novel and subsequent film, was his first published work of fiction. The story is about a black family in a small Kansas town; it focuses on Newt Winger, the youngest son. As described in the *Dictionary of Literary Biography,* "On one level, it is the story of a particular Negro family who manages to maintain its dignity and self-respect as citizens and decent human beings in a border Southern town. On another, it is a symbolic tale of the black man's struggle against social, economic, and natural forces, sometimes winning, sometimes losing. . . . Because the family is portrayed as a normal American family whose blackness is a natural circumstance and therefore not a source of continual pain and degradation, the book contributes greatly to a positive view of black people."

Parks followed *The Learning Tree* with *A Choice of Weapons.* Published in 1966, it was the first of three autobiographical works he would write. The book details in a fairly straightforward manner the time of his life that was fictionalized in *The Learning Tree,* covering Parks's life from the time of his mother's death to 1944. It was a time that Parks has described as "a sentence in hell."

Parks's second volume of memoirs was published in 1979. *To Smile in Autumn* begins in 1944, when his first fashion photographs were appearing in *Vogue* and *Glamour,* and ends in 1978, when Parks had done just about everything he had set out to do. His creative output during that period was phenomenal. In addition to his work in film and television, Parks published several volumes of his own poetry with accompanying photographs. In 1972, the NAACP awarded him the prestigious Spingarn Medal following the publication in 1971 of *Born Black,* a collection of articles on notable African-Americans. By 1975, Parks was married to his third wife, editor Genevieve Young, and had a major retrospective showing twenty-five years of his photographs in New York. He lived in New York in a large apartment overlooking the East River near the United Nations building.

As *Voices in the Mirror* attests, though, Parks was not about to retire. In 1988, he received the National Medal of Arts from President Reagan, and his autobiographical film, *Moments without Proper Names,* aired on PBS. He completed the musical score and libretto for *Martin,* a ballet about Martin Luther King, Jr., in 1989 and began filming it for PBS, where it was shown on King's birthday in 1990. Grace Blake, the producer of *Martin,* had worked with Parks on some of his Hollywood films. She told writer Deedee Moore, "Gordon's vision of this whole project is so important to all of us. . . . There are not that many good projects being done about black people. . . . [*Martin*] is totally conceived by a black man who is an artist—who wrote the libretto, the music, directed the film, worked on the choreography, narrated, did his own fund raising. Absolutely, we know we are working with a genius."

At age 78, Parks plans to publish another book of photographs, compose sonatas for each of his four children, and finish *Celebrations,* a collection of musical compositions in honor of his mother and father.

Selected writings

Flash Photography, [New York], 1947.
Camera Portraits: The Techniques and Principles of Documentary Portraiture, Franklin Watts, 1948.
The Learning Tree (novel), Harper & Row, 1963.
A Choice of Weapons (autobiography), Harper & Row, 1966.
A Poet and His Camera (poetry and photographs), Viking, 1968.
Gordon Parks: Whispers of Intimate Things (poetry and photographs), Viking, 1971.
Born Black (essays and photographs), Lippincott, 1971.
In Love (poetry and photographs), Lippincott, 1971.
Moments without Proper Names (poetry and photographs), Viking, 1975.
Flavio, Norton, 1978.
To Smile in Autumn: A Memoir, Norton, 1979.
Shannon (novel), Little, Brown, 1981.
Voices in the Mirror (autobiography), Doubleday, 1990.

Sources

Books

The Black Photographers Annual, Volume 4, edited by Joe Crawford, Another View, 1980.
Bogle, Donald, *Blacks in American Films and Television: An Encyclopedia,* Garland, 1988.
Contemporary Authors New Revision Series, Volume 26, Gale, 1989.
Dictionary of Literary Biography, Volume 33, Gale, 1984.
Gordon Parks, Chelsea House, 1990.
Malcolm X and Alex Haley, *The Autobiography of Malcolm X,* Grove, 1965.

Periodicals

American Visions, December 1989.
Detroit Free Press, January 9, 1991.

Modern Maturity, June-July 1989.
New York Times Book Review, December 9, 1990.
Smithsonian, April 1989.

—David Bianco

Rosa Parks

1913—

Civil rights activist

According to the old saying, "some people are born to greatness, and some have greatness thrust upon them." Greatness was certainly thrust upon Rosa Parks, but the modest former seamstress has found herself equal to the challenge. Known today as "the mother of the modern civil rights movement," Parks almost singlehandedly set in motion a veritable revolution in the southern United States, a revolution that would eventually secure equal treatment under the law for all black Americans. "For those who lived through the unsettling 1950s and 1960s and joined the civil rights struggle, the soft-spoken Rosa Parks was more, much more than the woman who refused to give up her bus seat to a White man in Montgomery, Alabama," wrote Richette L. Haywood in *Jet*. "[Hers] was an act that forever changed White America's view of Black people, and forever changed America itself."

From a modern perspective, Parks's actions on December 1, 1955 hardly seem extraordinary: tired after a long day's work, she refused to move from her seat in order to accommodate a white passenger on a city bus in Montgomery. At the time, however, her defiant gesture actually broke a law, one of many bits of Jim Crow legislation

that assured second-class citizenship for blacks. Overnight Rosa Parks became a symbol for hundreds of thousands of frustrated black Americans who suffered outrageous indignities in a racist society. As Lerone Bennett, Jr. wrote in *Ebony,* Parks was consumed not by the prospect of making history, but rather "by the tedium of survival in the Jim Crow South." The tedium had become unbearable, and Rosa Parks acted to change it. Then, she was an outlaw. Today she is a hero.

Parks was born Rosa McCauley in Tuskegee, Alabama. When she was still a young child her parents separated, and she moved with her mother to Montgomery. There she grew up in an extended family that included her maternal grandparents and her younger brother, Sylvester. Montgomery, Alabama, was hardly a hospitable city for blacks in the 1920s and 1930s. As she grew up, Rosa was shunted into second-rate all-black schools, such as the Montgomery Industrial School for Girls, and she faced daily rounds of laws governing her behavior in public places. *Ms.* magazine contributor Eloise Greenfield noted that Rosa always detested having to drink from special water fountains and having to forgo lunch at the whites-

At a Glance...

Born February 4, 1913, in Tuskegee, AL; daughter of James (a carpenter) and Leona (a teacher) McCauley; married Raymond Parks (a barber), c. 1933. *Education:* Attended Montgomery Industrial School for Girls.

Employed in Montgomery, AL, in a series of jobs, 1933-57, including seamstress at Montgomery Fair Department Store. Moved to Detroit, MI, 1957; became administrative assistant to United States Congressman John Conyers. Currently director of the Rosa and Raymond Parks Institute for Self Development, Detroit.

Member: NAACP, Southern Christian Leadership Conference, Distinguished Sons and Daughters of the Civil Rights Movement.

Awards: Has received numerous awards and tributes, including a dozen honorary degrees; honored by several community awards, including Rosa Parks Community Service Award and Rosa Parks Scholarship. A major thoroughfare in Detroit is named after Mrs. Parks.

only restaurants downtown. Still, wrote Greenfield, "with her mother's help, Rosa was able to grow up proud of herself and other black people, even while living with these rules. . . . People should be judged by the respect they have for themselves and others, Mrs. McCauley said. Rosa grew up believing this."

At twenty Rosa married a barber named Raymond Parks. The couple both held jobs and enjoyed a modest degree of prosperity. In her spare time, Mrs. Parks became active in the NAACP and the Montgomery Voters League, a group that helped blacks to pass a special test so they could register to vote. By the time she reached mid-life, Mrs. Parks was no stranger to white intimidation. Like many other Southern blacks, she often boycotted the public facilities marked "Colored," walking up stairs rather than taking elevators, for instance. She had a special distaste for the city's public transportation, as did many of her fellow black citizens.

Jim Crow Laws

The Jim Crow rules for the public bus system in Mont-

gomery almost defy belief today. Black customers had to enter the bus at the front door, pay the fare, exit the front door and climb aboard again at the rear door. Even though the majority of bus passengers were black, the front four rows of seats were always reserved for white customers. Bennett wrote: "It was a common sight in those days to see Black men and women standing in silence and silent fury over the four empty seats reserved for whites." Behind these seats was a middle section that blacks could use only if there was no white demand. However, if so much as one white customer needed a seat in this "no-man's land," *all* the blacks in that section had to move. Bennett concluded: "This was, as you can see, pure madness, and it caused no end of trouble and hard feeling." In fact, Rosa Parks herself was once thrown off a bus for refusing to endure the charade of entry by the back door. In the year preceding Mrs. Parks's fateful ride, three other black women had been arrested for refusing to give their seats to white men. Still the system was firmly entrenched, and Mrs. Parks would often walk to her home to spare herself the humiliation of the bus.

On December 1, 1955, Mrs. Parks had a particularly tiring day. She was employed as a seamstress at the Montgomery Fair department store, and she had spent the day pressing numerous pairs of pants. She has since admitted that her back and shoulders ached terribly that day—she was forty-two at the time—and she deliberately let one full bus pass in order to find a seat on the next one. The seat she eventually found was in the middle section of the bus, because the back was filled. A few stops further down the line, a white man got on and demanded a seat. The driver ordered Parks and three other black customers to move. The other riders did as they were told, but Parks quietly refused to give up her place. The driver threatened to call the police. Parks said: "Go ahead and call them."

Bennett wrote: "There then occurred one of those little vignettes that could have changed the course of history. The [police] officers asked the driver if he wanted to swear out a warrant or if he wanted them to let Rosa Parks go with a warning. The driver said he wanted to swear out a warrant, and this decision and the convergence of a number of historical forces sealed the death warrant of the Jim Crow South."

Parks was driven to the police station, booked, fingerprinted, and jailed. She was also photographed as she was being fingerprinted, a snapshot that has since found its way into history textbooks. Parks was granted one telephone call, and she used it to contact E. D. Nixon, a prominent member of Montgomery's NAACP chapter. Nixon was properly outraged, but he also sensed that in Rosa Parks his community might have the perfect individual to serve as a symbol of Southern injustice. Nixon called a liberal white lawyer, Clifford Durr, who agreed to represent Parks. After consulting with the attorney, her husband, and her mother, Rosa Parks agreed to undertake a court challenge of the segregationist law that had led to her arrest.

Rev. King Organized Bus Boycott

Word of Parks's arrest spread quickly through Montgomery's black community, and several influential black leaders decided the time was ripe to try a boycott of the public transportation system. One of these leaders, the Reverend Martin Luther King, Jr., used the mimeograph machine at his Baptist church to make 7,000 copies of a leaflet advertising the boycott. The message of the leaflet was plain: "Don't ride the bus to work, to town, to school, or any place Monday, December 5. . . . If you work, take a cab, or share a ride, or walk."

The black boycott of Montgomery's city buses was al-

most universal on December 5, 1955. A meeting on the subject that evening drew an overflow crowd numbering in the thousands, and a decision was made to continue the boycott indefinitely. On Tuesday, December 6, Parks was found guilty of failure to comply with a city ordinance and fined $14. She and her attorney appealed the ruling while the boycott wore on. *Ebony* correspondent Roxanne Brown wrote: "For 381 days, Blacks car-pooled and walked to work and church. Their unified effort not only helped put an end to Jim Crow sectioning on the buses, it was also financially devastating for the bus company. It was this monumental event—watched by the world— that triggered the modern-day Black Freedom Movement and made a living legend of Mrs. Parks."

It is not necessarily easy to be a living legend, however. Mrs. Parks and her family received numerous threats and almost constant telephone harassment. The strain actually caused Raymond Parks to suffer a nervous breakdown. In 1957, Rosa and Raymond Parks (and Rosa's mother) moved north to Detroit, Michigan. If Rosa Parks was safer in Detroit, she was never quite allowed to

Parks is fingerprinted in 1956 during the Montgomery Bus Boycott, which was sparked by her refusal to relinquish her seat on a segregated bus.

recede into anonymity. As the years passed she was sought out repeatedly as a dignified spokesperson for the civil rights movement.

A number of universities have awarded her honorary degrees, and she earned a prestigious job on the staff of Detroit congressman John Conyers. In 1988, Roxanne Brown noted: "Thirty-two years after she attracted international attention for sparking the Montgomery Bus Boycott, Mrs. Parks's ardent devotion to human rights still burns brightly, like a well-tended torch that ignites her spirit and calls her to service whenever she is needed."

Still Active in the Struggle

Age has not robbed Rosa Parks of her beauty and grace, nor has it restricted her travels and activities. She still makes some twenty-five to thirty personal appearances per year and is a vocal opponent of apartheid in South Africa. Her crowning achievement, however, is the Rosa and Raymond Parks Institute for Self Development, which she founded in Detroit. The institute offers career training for 12- to 18-year-olds with special attention to education and motivation. "Too many young people are not staying in school and taking advantage of the opportunities they have," Mrs. Parks told *Ebony*. "They're not motivated to learn what is necessary to get the good positions, the good jobs, to go into business for themselves."

In February of 1990 Parks received yet another round of adulation as she was honored at Washington's Kennedy Center on her seventy-seventh birthday. Tribute chairperson C. Delores Tucker praised Parks for her "beautiful qualities" of "dignity and indomitable faith that with God nothing can stop us." In typical fashion, Parks received the tribute with all due modesty—to this day she takes little credit for her role in the history of the civil rights movement. Asked to reveal the secret of her positive attitude, she told *Ebony:* "I find that if I'm thinking too much of my own problems, and the fact that at times things are not just like I want them to be, I don't make any progress at all. But if I look around and see what I can do, and go on with that, then I move on."

Sources

Books

Greenfield, Eloise, *Rosa Parks,* Thomas Y. Crowell, 1973.

Periodicals

Ebony, August 1971; September 1977; February 1988.
Essence, May 1985.
Jet, March 5, 1990.
Ms., August 1974.
Newsweek, November 12, 1979.

—Mark Kram

Anna Perez

1951—

Press secretary to First Lady Barbara Bush

When congressional press aide Anna Perez was selected as press secretary for First Lady Barbara Bush in 1989, she made history by becoming the first African-American to ever hold the position. Mrs. Bush had reportedly been interested in a black or Hispanic for the job and decided upon the highly-qualified Perez, a former congressional press aide who had worked with legislators on Capitol Hill for a number of years. In *Essence* magazine, Bebe Moore Campbell noted that the qualities possessed by Perez which make her ideally suited for the rigors of press secretary work are "her sense of humor, fearlessness and ability to work very hard."

Although Perez was well-qualified for the job, "political savvy is what won her this historic post," commented a contributor to *Jet.* After Perez heard about the position being available, she contacted former employers, in addition to every prominent Republican and Democrat that she knew in Washington, and asked them to write recommendations to the First Lady. She also did extensive research on Mrs. Bush to make sure that she was sufficiently briefed for her initial interview. The fact that she could make history, however, never occurred to

Perez when she applied for the job. As she stated in *Jet:* "I didn't realize it until a dear friend who was with the government many years ago under the Truman administration told me 'you know you're a first.'"

Perez described to Campbell that her main role as press secretary is "to efficiently and unobtrusively help Mrs. Bush help people." She arranges all interviews conducted with the First Lady, and coordinates her busy appointment schedule. Perez has also travelled with the First Lady, and she accompanied the President and Mrs. Bush on their official trip to China in 1989. Although the China trip was a thrill for her, Perez remembers an especially proud moment the first time she met President Bush. It was Martin Luther King, Jr., Day in 1989 and the then President-elect Bush and Mrs. Bush were being interviewed from the vice-presidential residence in Washington. Perez recalled in *Jet,* realizing the significance of being the first black press secretary: "At that time President-elect Bush comes in and he sticks out his hand and says, 'I'm George Bush and you're Anna Perez aren't you? I've been reading about you in the papers.' And it occurred to me what a way to celebrate Martin

At a Glance. . .

Born 1951; native of New York City; married to Ted Sims (chief engineer at Howard University's WHUR-Radio); children: three. *Education:* Attended Hunter College, New York City.

Co-owned a community newspaper with her husband in Tacoma, Wash., late 1970s; press aide to Senator Slade Gorton (Republican of Washington); press secretary to Representative John Miller (Republican of Washington); press secretary to First Lady Barbara Bush, 1989—.

Addresses: *Home*—Takoma Park, MD.

Luther King's birthday . . . dare I hope he would be really proud of his country."

Perez's road to success and achievement was shaped by a painful childhood memory, which she recalled for Campbell: "I was walking home with a very cute, popular girl from school. All of a sudden I looked up and saw the furniture from our house sitting on the pavement two blocks away and realized that my family had been evicted. The blood started draining from my face. . . . Somehow I steered my friend away from my house, and then I went to the library and stayed for hours." Perez's mother, however, managed to pull her family back together, instilling in Anna a valuable attitude to, as she described it, to "always . . . expect the best."

Sources

Essence, August 1989.
Jet, February 6, 1989; May 1, 1989.
Washington Post, January 15, 1989.

—*Michael E. Mueller*

Colin Powell

1937-

Chairman of the Joint Chiefs of Staff

Already highly regarded by political and military leaders in the White House, Congress, and the Pentagon, U.S. Army General Colin Powell achieved national and international prominence in 1990 and 1991 as one of the key leaders of Operations Desert Shield and Desert Storm, the military campaigns to protect Saudi Arabia and liberate Kuwait from Iraqi control. Powell, as the Chairman of the Joint Chiefs of Staff, heads up the Pentagon and serves as the president's top military adviser, placing him among the most powerful policy makers in the world.

During the Persian Gulf War, he was credited with skillfully balancing the political objectives of President George Bush and the *strategy* needs of General Norman Schwarzkopf and other military commanders in the field. Because of his leadership during the war and his experience as an insider in the Washington bureaucracy, Powell has been suggested by analysts as a promising candidate for future political office, either as vice-president or president.

Colin Luther Powell was born in 1937 in Harlem, the son of Jamaican immigrants who had both gone to work In

New York City's garment district. The young Powell grew up in the South Bronx, where he enjoyed a secure childhood, looked after by a closely knit family and a multi-ethnic community. He graduated from Morris High School In 1954 and received his B.A. in geology from the City College of New York in 1958. He was undistinguished as a student, but he excelled in the college's Reserve Officer's Training Corps (ROTC), leading the precision drill team and attaining the top rank offered by the corps, cadet colonel. He was not West Point trained, but his achievements in the ROTC won him a commission as second lieutenant in the U.S. Army.

His first assignment for the U.S. Army was at the Fulda Gap in West Germany, where American and allied troops stood as an obstacle on the Soviet bloc's most likely invasion route of Western Europe. In the 1960s, Powell served two tours of duty in South Vietnam. As an adviser to South Vietnamese troops, he was wounded in 1963 when he fell victim to a Vietcong booby trap. His second tour, from 1968 to 1969, as an Army Infantry officer, also ended when Powell was injured, this time in a helicopter crash from which he rescued two of his

At a Glance. . .

Full name, Colin Luther Powell; born April 5, 1937, in Harlem, NY; son of Luther (a shipping clerk) and Maud Ariel (a seamstress; maiden name, McKoy) Powell; married Alma Vivian Johnson (a speech pathologist), August 25, 1962; children: Michael, Linda, Annemarie. *Education:* City College of the City University of New York, B.S., 1958; George Washington University, M.B.A., 1971; graduate of the National War College, 1976. *Religion:* Episcopalian.

U.S. Army career officer, 1958—; commissioned second lieutenant, 1958, promoted to general, 1989. Served in West Germany, beginning 1958, and in the U.S.; served in Vietnam as a military adviser, 1962-63, and as battalion executive officer and division operations officer, 1968-69, and in South Korea as battalion commander, 1973; commander of the Second Brigade of the 101st Airborne Division, Fort Campbell, KY, 1976-77; assistant commander of the Fourth Infantry Division, Fort Carson, CO, 1981-83; deputy commander of Fort Leavenworth, KS, 1983; commanding general of the Fifth Corps, Frankfurt, West Germany, 1986-87; commander-in-chief of the U.S. Forces Command at Fort McPherson, GA, 1989—; chairman of the Joint Chiefs of Staff, Washington, D.C., 1989—.

Assistant to the deputy director of the Office of Management and Budget, 1972-73; executive assistant to the secretary of energy, 1979; senior military assistant to the deputy secretary of defense, 1979-81; military assistant to the secretary of defense, 1983-86; deputy assistant for the assistant to the President for national security affairs, 1987; assistant to the President for national security affairs, 1987-89.

Awards: Military honors, including the Purple Heart and Bronze Star, both 1963, and the Legion of Merit, 1972.

Addresses: *Home*—Fort Myers, VA. *Office*—Chairman of the Joint Chiefs of Staff, The Pentagon, Room 2E-857, Washington, DC 20318.

fellow soldiers. For his valor in Vietnam, he received two

Purple Hearts, a Bronze Star, a Soldier's Medal, and the Legion of Merit.

Gained Political Experience

Back on the home front, Powell pursued an M.B.A. at George Washington University. After completing his graduate studies in 1971, he was awarded a prestigious White House fellowship, which gave him the opportunity to get his first taste of politics. From 1972 to 1973, he worked for Frank Carlucci, then Deputy Director of the Office of Management and Budget under Caspar Weinberger. It was the beginning of Powell's education in the dynamics of the Washington bureaucracy. Over the next 15 years he returned to the political arena from time to time to continue that education.

From 1979 to 1981, Powell served the Carter administration as an executive assistant to Charles Duncan, Jr., the Secretary of Energy, and as senior military assistant to the Deputy Secretary of Defense. When the Reagan administration came to Washington, Powell worked with Carlucci on the Defense Department's transition team, and then from 1983 to 1986 he joined Weinberger again, this time as military assistant to the Defense Secretary. While there, Powell contributed to the department's involvement in the invasion of Grenada and the bombing raid on Libya.

Between stints in the political arena, Powell continued to advance his military career. In 1973, he travelled to South Korea to take command of a battalion and then a year later he returned to Washington as a staff officer at the Pentagon. He completed his military education at the National War College in 1976 and took command of the Second Brigade of the 101st Airborne Division at Fort Campbell, Kentucky, that same year. In the early 1980s, he completed assignments as the assistant commander of the Fourth Infantry Division at Fort Carson, Colorado, and as the deputy director at Fort Leavenworth, Kansas. He was in West Germany again in 1987, this time as commanding general of the Fifth Corps in Frankfurt, when he was called back to Washington to work again with Frank Carlucci, the new National Security Adviser.

Carlucci had been chosen to head the troubled National Security Council in the aftermath of the Iran-Contra scandal. Powell was not a stranger to the NSC's dealings under Admiral John Poindexter and Oliver North; he had first confronted the issue of arms sales to Iran while working under Weinberger at the Defense Department. Yet, even though he had been aware of the covert activities, he was able to remain above reproach because he had always acted according to law and had not become involved until after presidential approval had been given.

Together Carlucci and Powell reorganized the NSC to reduce the possibility for free lance foreign policy. When in 1987 Carlucci took over as Secretary of Defense for the departing Weinberger, Powell was called upon to take over leadership of the NSC. The move earned widespread approval in Washington because, as Fred Barnes wrote in the *New Republic,* Powell is "a national security adviser strong enough to settle policy disputes but without a personal agenda."

During his tenure at the NSC, Powell did speak out on a number of issues he felt were important to national security, including economic strength, control of technology exchanges, protection of the environment, a stable defense budget, free trade and foreign investment, research and development, and education. He also expressed his opposition to plans for the overthrow of Panamanian dictator Manuel Noriega and to heavy spending on the Strategic Defense Initiative ("Star Wars"). Even so, as he told Barnes, "I'm principally a broker. I have strong views on things, but my job is to make sure the president gets the best information available to make an informed decision."

Named Chairman of Joint Chiefs

In 1989, President Bush rewarded Powell for the knowledge and skills he had acquired in the military and political arenas by naming him to the military's top post, Chairman of the Joint Chiefs of Staff, the youngest man and first black to hold that position. Said the president of Powell: "As we face the challenges of the 90s, it is most important that the Chairman of the Joint Chiefs of Staff be a person of breadth, judgment, experience, and total integrity. Colin Powell has all those qualities and more." In peacetime, the chairman's responsibilities have included overseeing the prioritization of Pentagon spending and keeping the channels of communication open between the military and the White House. They have also included drawing up plans for military action, first in Panama and then in the Middle East.

Because of a 1986 law redefining his role and because George Bush has the utmost trust in Powell, the general has more influence than any Chairman of the Joint Chiefs of Staff since World War II. The Iraqi invasion of Kuwait on August 2, 1990, obliged Powell to exercise that authority. The day after the invasion, Powell advised the president that a number of options were open, including economic and diplomatic sanctions, as well as the use of military force; the Bush administration decided that decisive force was the necessary response. Opera-

tion Desert Shield, requiring the massive movement of troops and supplies to Saudi Arabia, was soon initiated as a show of force and to serve as a deterrent to further Iraqi aggression. After touring the Middle East, the general recommended increasing the number of troops to assure the success of an isolate and destroy strategy if it proved necessary. He told *U.S. News and World Report:* "You go in to win, and you go in to win decisively."

Oversaw War in the Middle East

In the early stages of the operation, Powell again demonstrated his ability to manage people and bureaucracies. As European and Middle Eastern troops joined in a coalition against Iraq, Powell directed the quick integration of communications, operations, and authority into a command network under the direction of General Norman Schwarzkopf. During the planning of the air and land campaigns, he aided the president in making political decisions and kept him informed of military plans, but

> Powell heads up the Pentagon and serves as the president's top military adviser, placing him among the most powerful policy makers in the world

he also convinced the Washington warriors to leave the commanders in Saudi Arabia the space needed to carry out their missions.

He, too, avoided involvement in the minute details of day-to-day operations, exerting his authority only on major issues. He oversaw bombing missions on Baghdad only after the destruction of a suburban Baghdad bunker killed 400 civilians. He rejected Marine requests to launch a true amphibious assault on Kuwait instead of the feint scheduled to aid Schwarzkopf's encirclement of Kuwait by an end run through Iraq. He also convinced President Bush to respond to the February 21 Iraqi peace proposal with an ultimatum: the Iraqis must pull out of Kuwait by noon Washington time, February 23. When the deadline passed, the coalition began its land campaign later that night as scheduled.

With the success of Operation Desert Storm, Powell has been placed in the spotlight of media and public attention. Criticism of him by black leaders who label him a servant of the white Establishment and by peace activists who see him as a trigger-happy hawk has been tempered by praise of him as a positive role model for young blacks and as a committed defender of liberty.

Future Plans

Powell has met with Vice-President Dan Quayle to assure him that the general has no designs on the nation's number two executive post. He has also requested a second tour as Chairman of the Joint Chiefs of Staff. Bruce B. Auster reported in *U.S. News and World Report:* "Powell is able to transfer his unquestioned personal integrity to the institution he leads in part because, while he wields more power than almost any of his Pentagon predecessors, he is not addicted to it."

As a black military leader, Powell has demonstrated his commitment to helping young black men and women succeed in the armed services. He has long contended that the military should not be criticized for putting a disproportionate number of young black men and women in harm's way, but rather praised and imitated for its history of providing opportunities to minorities. Marshall Brown quotes Powell in a profile in *Black Enterprise:* "What we are dealing with now is a changing of hearts, changing of perspectives and of minds. We need to start to erase the cultural filter with respect to minorities."

As a soldier, Powell has demonstrated a firm commitment to protecting his country and securing a world where democratic values can flourish. He said in a March 1990 speech before the Town Hall of California: "I believe that as long as America leads the Free World, there will be no dominating state or region. . . . And the proper safeguards are the same safeguards that have secured the Free World's liberties for over four decades—our strong values, our resilient democracies, our vibrant market economics, our strong alliances, and, yes, our proud and ready armed forces."

Sources

Black Enterprise, October 1989.
Ebony, July 1988.
Los Angeles Times, February 17, 1991.
New Republic, May 30, 1988.
Newsweek, August 21, 1989; March 18, 1990.
New York Times, October 15, 1987; September 16, 1988; December 2, 1988; August 15, 1989.
Time, November 16, 1987; August 21, 1989.
U.S. News and World Report, April 25, 1988; December 24, 1990; February 4,
1991; March 18, 1991.
Washington Post, March 23, 1987; August 7, 1988; August 10, 1989; August 11, 1989.

—Bryan Ryan

Leontyne Price

1927—

Opera singer

When Leontyne Price's angelic voice trailed off that night at New York's Lincoln Center in 1985, signaling the end of her final performance of the title role in Verdi's *Aida*—a role that has become synonymous with her name—the ensuing applause that embraced the great diva's farewell will forever echo, not only through the famed home of the Metropolitan Opera but through Price's heart as well. "That moment, I was a sponge, and I'll have all that moisture the rest of my life," Price told Robert Jacobson of *Opera News*. "I soaked that in. It's the most intense listening I've ever done in my life. For a change, *I* listened. I have *every* vibration of that applause in my entire being until I die. I just will *never* recover from it. I will never receive that much love as long as I live, and I would be terribly selfish to expect that much *ever* again."

Seldom has an artist received applause that was so genuine and so deserved. After all, Price was 57 years old that evening, performing one of the most demanding roles in the repertoire, and yet her voice was as full as the day she first performed *Aida* in 1957 and literally set the standard for its perfection. But then Price's voice, her instrument, was so rare and special to her that she had taken great pains throughout her career to guard it from overuse, and to not destroy it performing roles that she thought she couldn't handle.

If the time was not right, or she didn't think she could handle a certain part, Price was known to reject the invitations of such great conductors as Herbert von Karajan, Rudolf Bing, or James Levine with the wave of a hand. For this, she became known in music circles as arrogant and "difficult," but for the fiercely independent Price it was a matter of survival to be selective. "The voice is so special," she told *Opera News*. "You have to guard it with care, to let nothing disturb it, so you don't lose the bloom, don't let it fade, don't let the petals drop."

Whether she was known as "the girl with the golden voice" or "the Stradivarius of singers," Price was, without question, one of the great operatic talents of all time. The fact that she was the first black singer to gain international stardom in opera, an art-form theretofore confined to the upper-class white society, signified a monumental stride not only for her own generation, but for those that came before and after her.

At a Glance. . .

Born in Laurel, MS, February 10, 1927; daughter of James and Kate (Baker) Price; married William C. Warfield (an opera singer), August 31, 1952 (divorced, 1973). *Education:* Central State College, Wilberforce, Ohio, B.A., 1949; attended the Juilliard School of Music, 1949-52; studied voice with Florence Page Kimball.

Professional opera singer, 1952-85. Made operatic debut in *Four Saints in Three Acts,* 1952; performed in the United States and Europe. Also performed as a soloist and recitalist with symphony orchestras.

Awards: Recipient of numerous awards, including thirteen Grammy Awards; the Presidential Medal of Freedom, 1965; the Kennedy Center Honors for lifetime achievement in the arts, 1980; and was the first recipient of the National Medal of the Arts, 1985.

Addresses: *Office*—c/o Columbia Artists Management, Inc., 165 West 57th Street, New York, NY 10019. *Other*—1133 Broadway, New York, NY 10010.

By the time her career was in full blossom, for example, it was no longer a shock to white audiences to see black singers performing roles traditionally thought of as "white." In opera, the singing and the music are tantamount, and thanks to Price black singers could now be judged solely on their artistic merit. And as the most successful heir of the great African-American vocal tradition, Price's achievements in opera can be seen as a justification for her lesser known, but equally great, predecessors, such as Marian Anderson and Paul Robeson.

Indeed, it was during an Anderson concert in Jackson, Mississippi in 1936 that Mary Violent Leontyne Price, then just nine years-old, first decided that she would dedicate her life to singing. From that day forward, she was driven to recreating the power and beauty which Anderson had brought to the stage. And with her 1985 retirement, Price has just as enthusiastically passed the torch to a new generation of young singers. "You have no idea how wonderful it is to know you had a part in the exposure of some of the great, marvelous talent," she told Jacobson. "I feel like a mother, a mother hen."

Though endowed with a miraculous talent, Price points

to her own mother as the source of her common sense, which in no small way helped her to channel and safeguard that talent for such a long and glorious career. "You need [common sense] as much as you need talent in the career, Robert," Price told Jacobson. "Common sense, which means your own vibes, and going with them. I'm just homespun. I am still homespun. It's sort of down home, very country. I think of myself as a strange mixture of collard greens and caviar."

Musical Studies

Price was born in Laurel, Mississippi, on February 10, 1927. Her father, James Price, worked in a sawmill, and her mother, Kate, brought in extra income as a midwife. Both parents were amateur musicians, and encouraged their daughter to play the piano and sing in the church choir at St. Paul's Methodist Church in Laurel. Price graduated from Oak Park High School in 1944, then left home for the College of Education and Industrial Arts (now Central State College) in Wilberforce, Ohio. There, she studied music education with the idea of becoming a music teacher, but her hopes of becoming an opera singer had not faded. When the prestigious Juilliard School of Music in New York offered her a four-year, full-tuition scholarship, Price leapt at the chance and arrived in the big city in 1949.

With living expenses so high in New York City, Price for a time feared that she would have to follow the path of some of her friends and take a job singing in blues clubs and bars, which would have been a little like Michelangelo working as a housepainter. But Elizabeth Chisholm, a longtime family friend from Laurel, came to Price's rescue with generous patronage, and the young singer was free to study full-time under vocal coach Florence Page Kimball. "It was simply the Midas touch from the instant I walked into Juilliard," Price told *Opera News.* "I learned things about stage presence, presentation of your gifts, how to make up, how to do research, German diction, et cetera." From Kimball, she went on to add, Price learned the steely control which would allow her to perform at top voice over so many performances, "to perform on your interest, not your capital. What she meant was, as in any walk of life, there should be something *more* to give."

Price thrived at Juilliard, and her role as Mistress Ford in a student production of Verdi's *Falstaff* caught the eye of composer Virgil Thomson, who cast her in a revival of his opera *Four Saints in Three Acts,* Price's first professional experience. This in turn led to a two-year stint (1952-54) with a revival of Gershwin's *Porgy and Bess,* which toured the U.S. and Europe. During this time Price married her co-star in that opera, William C. Warfield.

The marriage was a disappointment, however, and the two divorced in 1973 after years of separation.

Began Professional Career

In 1954 Price made her concert debut at New York's Town Hall, where she exhibited great skill with modern compositions; a magnetic performer, she enjoyed the concert format and continued to tour regularly throughout her career, much to the chagrin of opera purists. Fast becoming a darling of the New York critics, Price soon saw her career take off. In 1955 she appeared in Puccini's *Tosca* on NBC television, thus becoming the first black singer to perform opera on television. And she was so well-received that she was invited back to appear on NBC telecasts of Mozart's *Magic Flute* (1956), Poulenc's *Dialogues of the Carmelites* (1957), and Mozart's *Don Giovanni* (1960).

One of the most fruitful associations of Price's career began in 1957, when she was invited by conductor Kurt

Herbert Adler (he had seen her NBC *Tosca*) to make her American operatic debut as Madame Lidoine in *Dialogues of the Carmelites* with the San Francisco Opera. In later years, San Francisco seemed to be the place where Price returned to challenge herself with new roles, thus expanding her repertoire.

In fact, Price first performed *Aida* there—under quite unusual circumstances. "The first *Aida* I did, period, anywhere, was on that stage, by accident," Price said in *Opera News*. "I've always threatened to give two wonderful medals to two wonderful colleagues who happened to have two wonderful appendectomies and gave me two wonderful opportunities to sing *Aida*. They are Antonietta Stella in San Francisco in 1957 and Anita Cerquetti at Covent Garden in 1958. The year I did *Dialogues*, Stella had an emergency appendectomy. Adler walked into the room and asked if I knew *Aida*. I told him yes, and I was on. I went through the score with Maestro Molinari-Pradelli, and I knew every single, solitary note and nuance. I had it ready to travel. After

Price (right) meets her idol, Marian Anderson, the first black to perform at the Metropolitan Opera.

that *Aida* was definitely part of my repertoire. That was being in the right place at the right time.''

Achieved International Acclaim

In the following years, Price expanded her repertoire significantly on American soil, with such distinguished companies as the Chicago Lyric Opera and the American Opera Theater as well as the San Francisco Opera. She credits the great Herbert von Karajan with introducing her to European audiences. Price's debut on that continent came at Vienna's Staatsoper in 1958 as Pamina in *Zauberflote*, not in *Aida* as has been commonly written. Her second European performance was in *Aida* at the same theater, and she quickly forged a reputation in Europe with a string of appearances on such venerable stages as London's Covent Garden, Verona's Arena, the Salzburg Festival, and Milan's historic La Scala, where her *Aida* won the hearts of Verdi's own countrymen.

Her international prominence now secure, Price returned home to make her debut at the mecca of American opera, New York's Metropolitan Opera, and thus began a long, often controversial, but always glorious association with that revered institution. Her Leonora in *Il Trovatore* on January 27, 1961, brought a standing ovation of 42 minutes, the longest ever given at the Met. Over the next several years Price was a staple in Metropolitan productions. When the company moved its home to the impressive new Metropolitan Opera House at Lincoln Center, director Rudolf Bing extended Price the ultimate honor of opening the house in the world premier of Samuel Barber's *Antony and Cleopatra.*

Although the opera itself was not well received, Price was magnificent, having dedicated herself to the role with total commitment. "*Antony and Cleopatra* was *the* event of the century, operatically speaking," Price told *Opera News*. "I was there! I lived the life of a hermit for a year and a half, so as not to have a common cold. From the moment I was asked to do this, I simply did everything I possibly could to have it be right. I accepted that responsibility with the greatest happiness. This was the greatest challenge of my life.''

Clearly on top of the opera world, Price appeared in 118 Metropolitan productions between 1961 and 1969, when she drastically cut back her appearances not only in New York but elsewhere. It was here that she began to strike some opera insiders as ungrateful, vindictive, and arrogant, but Price insists that she was merely protecting herself from overexposure. "If I don't want to do something, I don't do it—nothing against anyone or the institution," she told Jacobson. "If you say yes to something that may not go, *you* are discarded—not the people who asked you to do it. They have something else to do. You are part of a unit, and they need your expertise to make the unit better. . . . The thing that's been misunderstood is that I don't give a lot of rhetoric before I say no. I just say no. It saves everybody time, and maybe because I don't give a reason, it's taken in a negative way.''

In the 1970s Price drastically cut the number of opera appearances, preferring to focus instead on her first love—recitals—in which she enjoyed the challenge of creating several characters on stage in succession. Her career credits include countless recordings, many of them on the RCA label, which enjoyed an exclusive 20-year contract with the diva. She has won 13 Grammy Awards, the Presidential Medal of Freedom (the nation's highest civilian award) in 1965, the Kennedy Center Honors for lifetime achievement in the arts in 1980, and the First National Medal of Arts. She has appeared on the cover of *Time* magazine, and she performed at the White House in 1978. Price has lived alone for years in a townhouse in New York's Greenwich Village.

Sources

Books

Baker, Theodore, *Baker's Biographical Dictionary of Musicians,* Schirmer, 1984.

Hitchcock, H. Wiley, *The New Grove Dictionary of American Music,* MacMillan, 1986.

Souther, Eileen, *The Biographical Dictionary of Afro-American and African Musicians,* Greenwood Press, 1982.

Periodicals

Opera News, July 1985; August 1985.

—David Collins

Queen Latifah

1970(?)—

Rap singer

Queen Latifah, whom Lisa Kennedy of *Mother Jones* called one of the hottest artists on the burgeoning Tommy Boy label, has worked hard for her success, but not by stepping on fellow rappers on her way to the top. Latifah is known for her refusal to participate in the well-publicized feuds among various factions of rap performers. "I might rebut if somebody challenged me, but I'd make it funny, not nasty," she said in *Rolling Stone.* Attesting to her feelings of solidarity with other rappers, she has stated that she would rather present a united artistic front than suggest a clique fractured by in-fighting and clashing ambitions.

Applauded for her social politics as well as her gift for rhyme, Latifah—from an Arabic word meaning "delicate" or "sensitive"—seems to pursue a well-rounded image, with social commentary in its place, but entertainment firmly in the foreground. "I'd rather throw in a line or two about drugs," she has said, "just to make you think. I can have fun and still show I'm on the ball." Her music, according to *Interview,* borrows freely "from hip-hop, House, jazz, and reggae," all saturated by Latifah's sense of self and a pride seemingly untouched by vanity.

While some vocal artists are never quizzed about the message of their music, rappers are often asked to philosophize about fellow musicians and ideas in rap; Latifah holds her own, but will not be made into a spokesperson. Her strength is often misinterpreted as a feminist message. *Rolling Stone* contributor Alan Light testified that "Latifah bristles at the suggestion that she is part of a 'women's movement' sweeping rap. 'Me, M.C. Lyte, Roxanne Shante, we got record deals because we're good,' she said. 'We deserve them, not because we happen to be women.'"

Like many young women, Latifah dislikes the label "feminist," believing it carries strident overtones. "I'm not a feminist. . . . I'm just a proud black woman. I don't need to be labeled," she said in *Interview.* According to Dominique DiPrima in *Mother Jones,* "'Ladies First,' [Latifah's] duet with British rapper Monie Love, touches female pride without preaching. Her whole style is a feminist statement—she is the Queen, never the victim." Not surprisingly, several of the cuts on Queen Latifah's LP *All Hail the Queen* begin with tongue-in-cheek references to her "royal" status, such as "All hail the queen," and "Dance for me."

At a Glance. . .

Born Dana Owens c. 1970; raised in East Orange, NJ.

Began performing in high school as human beat box in rap group *Ladies Fresh;* solo recording artist, 1989—; recorded re-mix of the single "Fame" with David Bowie, 1990.

Addresses: *Record company*—Tommy Boy Records, 1747 First Ave., New York, NY 10128

Related to the debate over feminism in women's rap is the dominance of men in rap—and all music—production. In her *Mother Jones* article about women in rap, DiPrima described the business and its relationship to gender: "The rap music business, like most other businesses, is controlled by men, making it risky to really speak out. In addition to the business end, many female groups rely on the artistic support of men to write, produce, and advise them." By way of example, Latifah co-mixed only two of the 15 tracks on her album.

DiPrima also pointed out that "popular male rappers make guest appearances on women's records, feature women on theirs, and plug them on stage and on vinyl." This is true of *All Hail the Queen,* which features Daddy-O of Stetsasonic, KRS-One, and members of De La Soul. Latifah, however, seems to find her current level of artistic control sufficient; she firmly calls *All Hail the Queen* "hers" and discusses the album's concept as her own. Suggesting that a live setting transcends gender roles, the Queen told Kennedy: "This is a business where you sell off your talent, and to me the proof is usually at the show. There's no double standard with your fans."

Queen Latifah, usually clad in what *Entertainment Weekly* described as "African-print pajama suits, skull caps, and big wooden bracelets and earrings," *is* critical of the sexist images of women presented by some male rappers. In a rare moment of universal criticism she stated: "Those women are pretty shallow. They look like skeezers, and that's the problem. A lot of those females don't have respect for themselves. Guys are exploiting them." Dimitri Ehrlich of *Interview* congratulated Latifah on her positive image: "I think it's great that the women you chose for your dancers have the kind of image that young people can look up to." She sees materialism as one cause of the acceptance of male-dependent women, contending that

"females don't respect themselves; they only think materialistically. They want money, but they don't think, I'm gonna get this money on my own. They think, I'm gonna get money from this guy."

Latifah's larger commitment to unity in rap is apparent in her defense of male rappers; she told *Entertainment Weekly* that the most memorable entertainment-world moment in 1990 was "when the [censorship] controversy over 2 Live Crew pushed their album to double platinum status and when they were cleared of charges." Although her own lyrics are not considered sexually provocative—as were 2 Live Crew's—Latifah believes fervently in an artist's unfettered freedom to express him or herself. In this way she is among the mainstream of her colleagues; where her opinion varies is in her defense of male rappers against charges of hating women.

She told *Interview:* "I wouldn't even say it's sexist. It's sexist in the sense that they're talking about a female, but that's usually exaggerated for the humor. Others speak the truth. They are not talking about women like me and you; they're rapping about women who wear dresses halfway up the behind—women who use their bodies, not their minds. I'd say the guys are wrong, because instead of educating women, they're exploiting them. But I can't say they're wrong for what they're saying. I've been on the road and seen girls who don't know a guy sleep with him in twenty minutes 'cause he's in a group. That's the kind of girl they're talking about. . . ."

DiPrima summed up the importance of Queen Latifah's success: "Women like Latifah provide role models—models of women in control, speaking their minds and getting their own, without being an accessory to some guy. These role models aren't just important to young girls but to young men as well who are getting accustomed to the independent women as a peer. Everywhere I go I hear guys listening to Latifah or Lyte, not as FEMALE RAPPERS but simply as def lyricists."

Selected discography

All Hail the Queen, Tommy Boy, 1989.

Sources

Entertainment Weekly, December 28, 1990.
Interview, May 1990.
Mother Jones September/October 1990.
Nation, April 16, 1990.
Rolling Stone, February 22, 1990.

—*Christine Ferran*

Ola Rotimi

1938—

Playwright, director

The dramatic works of Ola Rotimi are known throughout Africa and have made him one of the most significant playwrights on that continent. His dramatic works have been performed in Europe and Africa and are the focus of study in Europe and in American universities with African studies programs. He has also published short stories and critical articles on African theater. An accomplished play director, Rotimi has taken many works directly to the people with the University of Ife Theatre, a repertory company that performs works in the Yoruba language, Nigerian pidgin, and English.

The youngest of three children, Olawale, known as Ola, was born on April 13, 1938. His father, Samuel Enitan Rotimi was a steam-launch engineer from the Yoruba ethnic group of Western Nigeria, and his mother, Dorcas Oruene, was an Ijo from Nembe in Eastern Nigeria. The young boy grew up learning four of the three hundred full-blooded languages spoken in Nigeria, as well as English, the administrative language of the country.

The Rotimis were interested in the arts: Ola's mother excelled in traditional dance and managed her own dance group from 1945 to 1949. His father often wrote and recited, and he organized the community theater in Port Harcourt where Ola grew up. Ola's uncle, Chief Robert Dede, was the lead performer in a traditional dance troupe called a masquerade. Dede and his dancers, dressed in elaborate costumes, danced, sang, and acted in what was one of the most spectacular of such troupes in Rivers State. The young boy first appeared on stage at age four in a play directed and produced by his father.

Rotimi attended the Methodist Boys High School in the capitol city of Lagos from 1952 to 1956, during which time he earned the nicknames "Shakespeare incarnate" and "the Poet" for his writing. Some of his works were broadcast on Nigerian radio and published in institutional magazines. On a scholarship from the Nigerian government, Rotimi studied theater at Boston University, and from 1963 to 1966 he earned a Master of Fine Arts degree in playwriting and dramatic literature at Yale University on a Rockefeller Foundation Fellowship. His socio-political comedy *Our Husband Has Gone Mad Again* was chosen Yale's student play of the year in 1966.

Since then Rotimi has become a household name among

At a Glance...

Full name, Emmanuel Gladstone Olawale Rotimi; born April 13, 1938; son of Samuel Enitan (a steam-launch engineer) and Dorcas Oruene (a dancer) Rotimi; married, wife's name, Hazel Mae Gaudreau; children: Enitan, Oruene (daughter), Biodun, Kole. *Education:* Holds undergraduate degree from Boston University; Yale University, M.F.A., 1966.

Playwright, director. Head of Department of Creative Arts at the University of Port Harcourt, Nigeria; has also served as visiting professor, playwright, and director in Germany and Italy, as well as at DePauw University and Wabash University.

Awards: Awarded two Fullbright Scholarships.

Addresses: *Office*—Dept. of Creative Arts, Faculty of the Humanities, University of Port Harcourt, PMB 5323, Rivers State, Nigeria.

the educated of Nigeria. The driving force of his artistic endeavor is to achieve what he calls total theater. Rotimi extends the boundaries of traditional Western theater by embracing dance, mime, music, and song, as well as the ritual aspects of traditional African life. Because he believes that theater should be a medium of the people, Rotimi elicits audience participation, targeting as his audience the literate minority who speak English—those who determine the social course of the nation.

"When I studied in America, there is no doubt that my scholarship gained immense depth. My self-confidence in writing and teaching grew tremendously," Rotimi told Mike Lillich of the *DePauw University Alumnus.* "But I was inundated with Americanisms. I had to link up with my people. So my immediate audience has been the Nigerian people within my own cultural context. Any other kind of writing for me would be artificial. Once my people accept me, the world will look at me. It has taken me a long time to get out and test the world market." Rotimi continued by saying that he "tampers with the English language in order to temper its Englishness, to experiment with the English language to create an elegant simplicity." Trademarks of Rotimi's works are his use of mostly monosyllabic and disyllabic words and his incorporation of traditional languages, song, and dance.

Rotimi's literary popularity also derives from the histori-

cal reaches of his plays. "I'm concerned with history first of all because of the pedagogic motivation," Rotimi stated in an interview with Kunle Ajibade of the *African Concord.* "Most of us Africans are ignorant of our history. When I was in secondary school, we learnt tangentially African History and usually from a myopic, jaundiced perspective of Western scholars. . . . The play tries to teach history through drama. My second mission is, of course, to see whether we could emulate some heroic figures in history." With these goals in mind, Rotimi tries to answer this question: Who runs the political landscape of Africa?

In *Our Husband Has Gone Mad Again,* Rotimi depicted the cocoa farmer and businessman Lejoka-Brown as a self-seeking, opportunistic leader who could make better contributions to Nigeria outside the political arena. In *Ovoranwen Nogbaisi,* the title character simply luxuriates in the grandeur of his office. Although he is a custodian of culture who inspires people, he does not actively participate in their struggles. Similarly, in *If . . .* the young firebrand Hamidu is nowhere to be found when a real commitment is required. *Kurunmi* from the play of the same name is a jingoistic narrow-minded leader, and in *The Gods Are Not to Blame* Odelwale, a man of the people, comes to grief because of his ethnicism, according to Rotimi, the bane of modern Africa.

In contrast to these negative portrayals, in *Hopes of the Living Dead,* Rotimi depicts a different kind of leader in Harcourt Whyte. "Now we have a selfless, result oriented, committed leadership complimented by a followership that believes in the good of the generality of its members through the application of itself to the cause that is beneficial," the author told Ajibade. "*Hopes of the Living Dead* illustrates what I consider as a very good leadership and an approximation of an ideal followership."

Selected writings

The Gods Are Not to Blame, Oxford University Press, 1971; reprint Ibadan, Nigeria: University Press, 1985.
Ovoranwen Nogbaisi: An Historical Tragedy, Ethiope Publishing Corporation, 1974.
Our Husband Has Gone Mad Again, Oxford University Press Nigeria, 1977.
If . . . , Heinemann Educational Books, 1983.
Everyone His/Her Own Problems, 1986.
Hopes of the Living Dead, Spectrum Books, 1988.
Kurunmi, University Press Limited, 1989.

Sources

African Concord, April 1, 1991.
DePauw University Alumnus, Winter 1990.
LACE Occasional Publications, Vol. 1, No. 3 (June 23,

1984), Theatre Department, University of Gbadan, Nigeria.
Weekend Concord, April 20, 1991.

—*Jeanne M. Lesinski*

Carl T. Rowan

1925—

Journalist

Familiar to Americans as a nationally-syndicated columnist and a panelist on the television program *Inside Washington,* Carl T. Rowan has been called by the *Washington Post* "the most visible black journalist in the country." In his long and distinguished career in journalism, and as the author of six books, Rowan has documented some of the biggest political and social stories of the last fifty years, including the Cold War, the American Civil Rights Movement, the Vietnam War, and the economic policies of the Reagan administration. He has also held government posts in the Kennedy and Johnson presidential administrations, serving as director of the United States Information Agency and U.S. Ambassador to Finland. Rowan's 1991 bestselling autobiography, *Breaking Barriers: A Memoir,* recounts his ground-breaking career as one of the nation's few black journalists, from his early days in poverty, to his becoming one of the first black officers in the U.S. Navy, one of the first black reporters on a U.S. national daily newspaper, his tenure as the highest-ranking black official in the federal government, and his often outspoken career as a nationally-syndicated columnist.

Rowan grew up in poverty in McMinnville, Tennessee, in the midst of the segregated "Jim Crow" South, where his father struggled to support his family on a meager salary stacking lumber, and his mother occasionally took in laundry. Like many black youths, Rowan did various menial jobs for the white community, and while the economic and social situation in McMinnville offered little hope for the future, Rowan found an outlet in education. Particularly important to him were teachers who stressed the values of education and persistence as the way to confront the obstacles facing him as a black youth. One high school teacher in particular, "Miss Bessie," to whom Rowan dedicated a 1980 column, smuggled him books out of the all-white library in McMinnville. Rowan recounted the important message imparted to him by Miss Bessie in *Breaking Barriers:* "If you don't read, you can't write, and if you can't write, you can stop dreaming."

Rowan excelled as a student at McMinnville's all-black Bernard High School, where he graduated as valedictorian of his class. After graduation, Rowan headed for Nashville with only 77 cents to his name but hopes of attending college. He moved in with his grandparents and worked as an attendant at the hospital where his

At a Glance...

Full name, Carl Thomas Rowan; born August 11, 1925, in Ravenscroft, TN; son of Thomas David and Johnnie (Bradford) Rowan; married Vivien Louise Murphy, August 2, 1950; children: Barbara, Carl Thomas, Jr., Geoffrey. *Education:* Attended Tennessee State University, 1942-43, and Washburn University, 1943-44; Oberlin College, A.B. (mathematics), 1947; University of Minnesota, M.A. (journalism), 1948.

Minneapolis Tribune, copy editor, 1948-50, staff reporter, 1950-61; U.S. Department of State, deputy assistant secretary for public affairs, 1961-63; U.S. Ambassador to Finland, 1963-64; director of United States Information Agency, 1964-65; *Chicago Daily News,* columnist for Field Newspaper Syndicate, 1965—. National affairs commentator, *The Rowan Report* (national radio program); political commentator for radio and television stations of Post-Newsweek Broadcasting Co.; panelist, *Agronsky & Co.* and *Inside Washington* (syndicated television shows); frequent panelist, *Meet the Press,* NBC-TV. Former member of U.S. delegation to United Nations. Lecturer. *Military service:* U.S. Navy, communications officer.

Awards: Sidney Hillman Award, 1952, for best newspaper reporting; "Best Book" citations, American Library Association, 1953, for *South of Freedom,* and 1956, for *The Pitiful and the Proud;* Anti-Defamation League of B'nai B'rith communications award, 1964; named "Washington Journalist of the Year," Capital Press Club, 1978; American Black Achievement Award, *Ebony,* 1978; George Foster Peabody Award, 1978, for *Race War in Rhodesia;* Alfred I. DuPont-Columbia University Silver Baton, 1987, for television documentary *Thurgood Marshall: The Man.*

Addresses: *Home*—Washington, DC. *Office*—1101 7th St. N.W., Washington, DC 20036.

grandfather was employed, earning $30 a month for his college expenses. He enrolled at all-black Tennessee State University in 1942, and the following year was recommended by a professor for an opportunity to take an examination for a U.S. Navy commission. Rowan passed the examination, and was later assigned to

Washburn University in Topeka, Kansas, as one of the first fifteen blacks in Navy history to be admitted to the V-12 officer-training program. Rowan later attended Oberlin College in Ohio as part of the program, and then the Naval Reserve Midshipmen School in Fort Schuyler, the Bronx. He was eventually commissioned an officer and was assigned to sea duty, where he excelled as deputy commander of the communications division.

Rowan's naval duties ended in 1946 and he briefly returned to McMinnville, but his time in the Navy had pointed him towards new goals in his life. "When you are plucked out of a totally Jim Crow environment at age seventeen and thrown into a totally white environment where more is at stake than your personal life, you mature rapidly," he wrote in *Breaking Barriers.*

Rowan returned to Oberlin to complete his college degree, with hopes of eventually becoming a journalist. He found Oberlin's "egalitarianism" a positive experience, and learned much from students who, unlike himself, "came from homes where political, economic, and social issues were discussed daily." Rowan majored in mathematics, and obtained work as a free-lance writer for the Negro newspaper chain, the *Baltimore Afro-American.* When he was accepted into graduate school in journalism at the University of Minnesota, Rowan worked as a northern correspondent for the *Afro-American,* and also wrote for the Twin Cities' two black papers, the *Minneapolis Spokesman* and the *St. Paul Recorder.*

Began Journalism Career

Rowan got a big break after graduate school when he was hired at the copy desk of the all-white *Minneapolis Tribune.* Two years later, he became that paper's first black reporter, and one of the few in the entire United States. Rowan was working as a general-assignment reporter when he remembered the advice of a white Texan he had met in the Navy who told him that if he became a writer, he should "tell all the little things it means to be a Negro in the South, or anyplace where being a Negro makes a difference." Rowan proposed to the *Tribune* management that he take a trip through the deep South and report on the effects of Jim Crow discrimination laws on Negroes. The *Tribune* enthusiastically agreed to Rowan's proposal, and he embarked upon a 6,000-mile journey through thirteen states, writing a series of eighteen articles in 1951 entitled, "How Far From Slavery?"

Rowan's articles caused a sensation among *Tribune* readers and brought him wide critical recognition, in addition to earning him the Sidney Hillman Award for the best newspaper reporting of 1952. *Time* magazine praised the articles as "a perceptive, well-written series on segregation and prejudice in the South as only a Negro could know them." Rowan noted in *Breaking Barriers,* his objective was "to tell the American people some truths they do not know, explain some things that they clearly do not understand, and ... fulfill every journalistic obligation that burdens any reporter of any race." The articles also became the basis for Rowan's first book, *South of Freedom,* published in 1952.

Hodding Carter, white editor of a liberal Mississippi newspaper (and father of State Department spokesperson Hodding Carter, Jr.), wrote in the *New York Times* that *South of Freedom* was "a vivid reminder that changes which a white Southerner thinks are swift seem snail-like and indecisive to a southerner who is not white and who suffers from color barriers" and called the book "a noteworthy contribution to the sad folklore of American interracial relations." Reviewer Harold Fleming in the *New Republic* noted that Rowan's "return to the South was a profound personal experience, and he communicates that experience to the reader with unusual skill."

Rowan returned to the South for a second series of articles entitled "Jim Crow's Last Stand," which reviewed the various court cases comprising the historic 1954 *Brown* vs. *Board of Education of Topeka Supreme Court* decision, outlawing racial segregation in public schools. Rowan gained further recognition with "Jim Crow's Last Stand," and in 1954 received the prestigious Sigma Delta Chi Journalism Award for the best general reporting of 1953, in addition to being named by the U.S. Junior Chamber of Commerce as one of America's ten most outstanding men of 1953.

In 1954, Rowan was invited by the U.S. State Department to travel to India and lecture on the role of a free press in a free society. Rowan wrote a series of articles for the *Tribune* on India, which earned him his second consecutive Sigma Delta Chi Award, this time for best foreign correspondence. Rowan's trip was extended to include Southeast Asia, and he wrote another series of articles on the tense political climate in the region, in addition to covering the 1955 Bandung Conference, a gathering of twenty-three underdeveloped nations. For these articles, Rowan won an unprecedented third straight Sigma Delta Chi Award, while his 1956 book, *The Pitiful and the Proud,* which recounted his Asian journeys, was named one of the best books of the year by the American Library Association.

Covered Montgomery Bus Boycott

Rowan returned to the United States and continued as a reporter for the *Tribune.* In the late 1950s, he covered

the burgeoning Civil Rights Movement in the South, including the historic Montgomery (Alabama) bus boycott in 1955, resulting from Rosa Parks's refusal to relinquish her bus seat to a white passenger. As the only black reporter covering the story for a national newspaper, Rowan struck a special friendship with the boycott's leaders, including Martin Luther King, Jr. When news of an unlikely compromise settlement of the boycott came to Rowan's attention across the Associate Press wire, he notified King, who made quick steps to discredit the story which was about to appear in a Montgomery newspaper, thus ensuring the continuance of the boycott. Rowan wrote an acclaimed series of articles for the *Tribune,* "Dixie Divided," which explored efforts in the South to resist the Supreme Court's desegregation orders.

In addition to his reporting, Rowan was a member of the Committee of 100, a group of citizens who raised money across the United States for the NAACP Legal Defense Fund. As one of the country's few black reporters, Rowan was increasingly called upon to comment upon the impact of the Civil Rights Movement, and his articles

> Carl T. Rowan has been called by the *Washington Post* "the most visible black journalist in the country"

appeared throughout the country in a number of magazines and newspapers. His 1957 book, *Go South to Sorrow,* which generated both controversy and acclaim was, as he describes in *Breaking Barriers,* a "lashing out at President Eisenhower, Hodding Carter, and other gradualists who, in my view, were compromising away the freedom of America's black people."

In 1956, Rowan was called away from the South to cover the United Nations, as the world witnessed two events of major international importance: the Suez Canal crisis in which England, France, and Israel attempted to seize the canal from Egypt, and the Hungarian uprising against the Soviet Union, both in late 1956. Rowan was especially outraged at the brutal Soviet reprisal against the Hungarians, and reflected in *Breaking Barriers* on its relation to the U.S. Civil Rights Movement: "In the mentalities of our White House, our Congress, our media, there were no 'troublemakers on both sides' in Hungary. The villains were the brutal Soviet rapers of innocent Hungarians who had dared to reach out for freedom. But in America the air was filled with cries, even by Eisenhower and Stevenson, for a 'moderate' approach to ending segregation and a national rejection of 'the extremists on both sides.'"

Joined Kennedy Administration

In 1960, Rowan had the opportunity to interview presidential candidates Richard M. Nixon and John F. Kennedy for the *Tribune*. After Kennedy was elected, the new President contacted Rowan and asked him to become his Deputy Assistant Secretary of State for Public Affairs, responsible for press relations of the State Department. Rowan was involved in the sensitive area of news coverage of increasing U.S. military involvement in Vietnam, and was also trusted to the negotiating team that secured the exchange of pilot Francis Gary Powers, who was shot down over the Soviet Union in his U2 spy plane. He also accompanied Vice-President Lyndon Johnson on a tour through Southeast Asia, India, and Europe. In 1963, Kennedy named Rowan U.S. Ambassador to Finland, making him the youngest ambassador in diplomatic service, and only the fifth black to ever serve as an envoy.

When Johnson became President following Kennedy's assassination, he named Rowan head of the United States Information Agency (USIA), a position which made him the highest-ranking black in the federal government and the first to ever attend National Security Council meetings. As head of USIA with a staff of 13,000, Rowan was responsible for overseeing a vast government communications network, which included the international Voice of America radio system and the daily communiques to U.S. embassy personnel around the world. Rowan was assigned the task of developing a massive psychological warfare program to assist the Vietnam War effort, and was criticized for drawing away from the other USIA activities. In 1965, Rowan resigned from USIA, and took a lucrative offer to write a national column for the Field Newspaper Syndicate, in addition to three weekly radio commentaries for the Westinghouse Broadcasting Company.

Return to Journalism

As a columnist and commentator on the national scene, Rowan developed a reputation as an independent and often controversial voice on national political and social issues. He publicly urged Martin Luther King, Jr., to remove himself from his increasing anti-war stance, in that it was damaging the thrust of the Civil Rights Movement. He called for the resignation of powerful FBI director, J. Edgar Hoover, holding that Hoover's lengthy tenure was leading to serious abuses of power, including unethical and illegal investigations of citizens. When

Ronald Reagan became president, Rowan became a passionate critic of the President's policies, noting that the gains made in the Civil Rights Movement for disadvantaged groups were seriously being undermined by cuts in vital social and economic programs.

While Rowan has been throughout the years a frequent spokesman for civil and economic rights for blacks and other disadvantaged groups, he has also been critical of those blacks he feels should more aggressively address the serious issues that affect them. Neil A. Grauer, in his book *Wits & Sages,* calls Rowan "a vigorous exponent of self-improvement . . . and has little patience for those who won't work at it."

In 1988, Rowan made national headlines when he shot and wounded an intruder in his Washington, DC, home. A frequent advocate of national gun control laws, Rowan was charged with possession of an unregistered firearm, charges which were later dropped in court. Rowan accused former Washington, DC, Mayor Marion Barry—a frequent target of criticism in Rowan's column—of extortion by offering to not pursue the charges against Rowan if the columnist would tone down attacks on the mayor's administration. Rowan came under criticism again for speaking out against Barry, yet responded with a statement: "I have learned over four decades as a journalist that 'City Hall' becomes more and more corrupt as more and more citizens lose the guts to fight."

Breaking Barriers, a *New York Times* bestseller, was praised by Roy Larson in the *New York Times Book Review* as an "anecdotally rich memoir" which appeals to the "interests of a whole spectrum of readers." UPI White House correspondent Helen Thomas, on the book's dust jacket, calls Rowan "one of the most respected and admired journalists on the Washington scene" who "has held the liberal banner high for the disadvantaged and the afflicted." Throughout his career, Rowan has held the rare position of, as Larson noted, "a prophet with honor on both sides of a biracial society divided against itself."

Selected writings

South of Freedom, Knopf, 1952.
The Pitiful and the Proud, Random House, 1956.
Go South to Sorrow, Random House, 1957.
Wait Till Next Year: The Life Story of Jackie Robinson, Random House, 1960.
Just between Us Blacks, Random House, 1974.
Race War in Rhodesia, PTV Publications, 1978.
Breaking Barriers: A Memoir, Little, Brown, 1991.

Contributor of articles to numerous periodicals. Contributing editor to *Reader's Digest.* Host of documentaries, including *Searching for Justice: Three American Stories* and *Thurgood Marshall: The Man,* both 1987.

Sources

Books

Contemporary Issues Criticism, Volume 1, Gale, 1982.
Grauer, Neil A., *Wits & Sages,* Johns Hopkins University Press, 1984.
Rowan, Carl T., *Breaking Barriers: A Memoir,* Little, Brown, 1991.

Periodicals

Christian Science Monitor, August 4, 1952.
New York Times, August 3, 1952.
New York Times Book Review, January 20, 1991.
Time, June 27, 1988.
Washington Post, October 28, 1978.

—*Michael E. Mueller*

Barry Sanders

1968—

Professional football player

Although he describes himself as an "average person," Barry Sanders has amassed a string of accomplishments in his football career that suggest someone extraordinary. In his three years at Oklahoma State University, Sanders broke or tied 24 NCAA records on his way to winning college football's top honor, the Heisman Trophy. He followed by signing a $6.1 million professional football contract, one of the largest ever offered to a first-year player. His rookie year in the National Football League was also impressive: coming ten yards short of the season individual rushing title, selected as a starter for the Pro Bowl, and being named the league's "Rookie of the Year." After watching two of Sanders's performances in his first season, ex-Chicago Bear Walter Payton, the NFL's all-time leading rusher, said of the speedy 5' 8", 200-pound running back: "I don't know if I was *ever that* good."

The talented Sanders has been admired by teammates, coaches, and opponents throughout his football career. "Trying to tackle him has got to be like hitting a rock that's moving real fast," commented OSU quarterback and Sanders's former teammate Mike Grundy in *Sporting News*. "The only way to tackle Barry is to try to get him by both ankles, like a calf roper." Defensive players, in turn, remark on the challenge of facing Sanders. "I remember bracing myself to hit him," recalled Chicago Bears defensive end Trace Armstrong in *Sports Illustrated*. "He just stopped and turned, and he was gone. He's like a little sports car. He can stop on a dime and go zero to 60 in seconds."

Green Bay Packers linebacker Brian Noble similarly remarked: "He runs so low to the ground and is so strong and elusive; it makes him very difficult to get a piece of him. You never get *the* shot at him. Usually, when you get to him, he's not there anymore." Pat Jones, Sanders's college coach, had this to say in *Sporting News:* "If someone was to ask me who the most explosive back I've coached is, that would be Barry, as far as a guy who can take your breath away and is liable to score on every down. . . . I don't know that I've ever seen anyone like him with my own eyes."

Not everyone always expected so much of Sanders. When he graduated from North High School in Wichita, Kansas, and despite being a high school All-State and honorable All-American player, Sanders was overlooked

At a Glance. . .

Born in 1968; son of William (a carpenter and roofer) and Shirley Sanders. *Education:* Attended Oklahoma State University, 1985-88.

Professional football player with the Detroit Lions of the National Football League, 1989—.

Awards: Heisman Trophy, Maxwell Award, and "Player of the Year," *Sporting News,* all 1988; "Rookie of the Year," National Football League and Marlboro/*Sporting News,* both 1989; selected to Pro Bowl, 1989; named to Associated Press All-Pro Team, 1990.

Addresses: *Office*—Detroit Lions Football Team, Pontiac Silverdome, 1200 Featherstone Rd., Box 4200, Pontiac, MI 48057.

by many Division 1-A schools because of his small size. As a result, he received only two scholarships, to Wichita State and Oklahoma State. By his sophomore year at OSU, however, Sanders had made quite a statement, leading the nation in both kick-off returns and punt returns. The following year, Sanders set thirteen NCAA rushing records, including gaining the most yards in one season (2,628) and the most touchdowns in one season (39). As a result, Sanders overwhelmingly won the 1988 Heisman Trophy, becoming only the eighth junior to receive the award, and winning in the tenth-largest point margin ever.

Sanders decided to forego his senior year at college and make himself eligible for the NFL draft, a move prompted by the NCAA putting the OSU Cowboys on probation after the 1988 season and Sanders's desire to relieve financial burdens on his family. His $6.1 million five-year contract with the Detroit Lions—which carried with it a $2.1 million bonus—was one of the largest ever in the NFL for a rookie. And as the statistics in his first year

indicate, Sanders was worth the money. Although he didn't start the first two games of the season and missed parts of two others, Sanders managed to set the Lions's season rushing record and came just 10 yards short of the NFL's individual season rushing record—which he accomplished with 90 fewer carries than the winner, Christian Okoye.

Off the playing field, Sanders is modest about his accomplishments and prefers not to discuss them. He was quoted by Tom Kowalski in *Sporting News* about being "uncomfortable being valued because of how well I play football" and that he sees a liability in realizing he is an exceptional player. "If that's the case, I can prove it on the field. I don't have to talk about [it]. That's where athletes have problems off the field. People treat them differently and you start thinking you're better than everybody else. You're not."

In the 1989 final season game for the Lions, Sanders had the opportunity to enter the game and obtain the 10 yards he needed for the league season rushing record. Sanders insisted, however, that Coach Wayne Fontes continue playing back-up running back, Tony Paige. When Sanders was later asked if he had any regrets about not winning the rushing title, he told Austin Murphy in *Sports Illustrated:* "I satisfied my ego last season." A deeply religious person, he also prefers to keep that side to himself. Said Fontes in *Sports Illustrated:* "He doesn't wear his beliefs on his sleeve. . . . Barry's not the type of guy who scores a TD and kneels down in front of everyone in the world. He's not for show, he's for real."

Sources

Jet, January 9, 1989; February 13, 1989; May 29, 1989.
New York Times, November 23, 1988; December 4, 1988; January 1, 1989; March 31, 1989; April 5, 1989; September 12, 1989; September 15, 1989.
Sporting News, October 24, 1988; April 24, 1989; November 20, 1989; January 15, 1990.
Sports Illustrated, April 10, 1989; September 10, 1990.

—Michael E. Mueller

Kurt Schmoke

1949—

Mayor of Baltimore

Kurt L. Schmoke made history in 1987 by being the first black man elected mayor of Baltimore, Maryland. The Ivy League-educated Schmoke now finds himself at the head of America's eleventh largest city, and his administration is attempting to address Baltimore's problems from a whole new perspective. Schmoke's impressive academic credentials and his studious, professional demeanor have proven surprisingly popular in blue-collar Baltimore. As Timothy Noah puts it in the *Washington Post,* Schmoke has won a wide following by presenting himself "as a candidate worthy of both black pride and white approval."

Schmoke's rise to the Baltimore mayor's office was both swift and unique. His relative youth and inexperience notwithstanding, he beat an older and highly popular candidate (also black) who had the backing of the city's former mayor and a circle of powerful friends. Schmoke won the race by appealing to young and liberal voters—and by addressing the many problems still facing Baltimore despite the city's well-publicized cosmetic improvements. Schmoke's agenda is not nearly as flamboyant as that of his predecessor, William Donald Schaefer, but it is certainly more pragmatic. The new mayor of

Baltimore wants to improve the city's school system, fight illiteracy and teenage pregnancy, and prepare Baltimore's citizens for a job market that requires high-tech skills. "There comes a time when people feel it's time for a change," Schmoke told the *Washington Post* in 1987. "To a great extent, people [are] looking for a fresh start."

Kurt Schmoke was *not* born into poverty or illiteracy. His parents were both college graduates with good jobs, and he was their only child. Growing up in Baltimore, Schmoke was encouraged to excel in school not only by his parents but also by Marion Bascom, the pastor of the Douglas Memorial Community Church. Everyone assumed Schmoke would attend college too, preferably his father's alma mater, Morehouse University in Atlanta. In the *Washington Post,* Bascom remembered the young Kurt Schmoke as "a quiet, unassuming boy, but always a boy whom you felt had great depth of mind and spirit."

Schmoke is the first to admit that he profited from the controversial Supreme Court decision that mandated integration of all public schools. Because he became a student shortly after the landmark *Brown* vs. *Board of*

At a Glance. . .

Full name, Kurt Lidell Schmoke; born December 1, 1949, in Baltimore, MD; son of Murray (a chemist) and Irene Schmoke; married Patricia Locks (an ophthalmologist); children: Katherine, Gregory. *Education:* Yale University, B.A., 1971; studied at Oxford University under Rhodes Scholarship; Harvard University, J.D., 1978.

Associate of Piper & Marbury, Baltimore, MD, 1978-79; member of White House Domestic Policy Staff, 1977-78, and employed in the Department of Transportation, Washington, DC, 1979-81. State's attorney for the city of Baltimore, 1982-87; mayor of Baltimore, 1987—.

Addresses: *Office*—Mayor of the City of Baltimore, 250 City Hall, 100 N. Holliday St., Baltimore, MD 21220.

Education ruling, he was given the opportunity to attend predominantly white schools, where he earned good grades while participating in a variety of sports. Schmoke attended Baltimore's City College (a public high school), serving as both school president and starting quarterback in his senior year. Even before he turned eighteen he was a minor celebrity in Baltimore for leading City College to a state championship in football.

Schmoke's poise and maturity as a teenager caught the attention of Robert Hammerman, a white Baltimore city judge who devoted his spare time to running a club for boys. Hammerman invited Schmoke to join the club, known as the Lancers, and the two quickly became close friends. It was Hammerman who suggested that Schmoke aim high in his choice of a college, and it was also Hammerman who told Schmoke about the Rhodes Scholarship for study at Oxford University in England. Schmoke had already decided upon a career in politics and law, so Hammerman introduced him to a number of influential Baltimore lawyers and legislators. Some observers feel it may have been Hammerman who suggested Schmoke aim for the mayor's office, but others claim that Schmoke had wanted to be mayor of Baltimore from the time he was a small boy.

Attended Yale

At any rate, failure was almost unknown to Kurt Schmoke

as a youth. After graduating from City College he enrolled in Yale University, continuing to distinguish himself as an athlete and a student leader. Schmoke found himself in college in the late 1960s, when anti-war sentiment turned many campuses into near battlegrounds. In the spring of 1970 tensions erupted at Yale during the New Haven murder trial of Black Panther activist Bobby Seale. As Seale's trial progressed downtown, a group of Yale students massed outside the campus administration building, quickly becoming an angry mob. Inside the building, as faculty members predicted the university's imminent destruction, Yale president Kingman Brewster agreed to hear one representative from the students outside. Kurt Schmoke was chosen to be that representative.

If the assembled Yale faculty expected an avalanche of abuse that day, it was only because they did not know Kurt Schmoke. Not yet 20, Schmoke calmly took the podium and merely said: "The students on this campus are confused, they're frightened. They don't know what to think. You are older than we are, and more experienced. We want guidance from you, moral leadership. On behalf of my fellow students, I beg you to give it to us." Schmoke was awarded a standing ovation as he left the hall, and order was restored on the Yale campus.

The Rhodes scholarship is one of academia's most prestigious awards. Rhodes scholars win the opportunity to study for two years at Oxford University; competition is rife for the few available positions. After graduating from Yale, Schmoke was chosen for the Rhodes scholarship by a committee from his home state of Maryland. He spent two years in England and travelled through Europe and Africa when he was out of class. Upon his return to America he enrolled in Harvard Law School, earning his law degree in 1978. Elsewhere Schmoke might have been an unknown, but many eyes in Baltimore were already on him, and expectations for his success in local politics were growing day by day.

Entered Government Service

Schmoke passed the Maryland bar and joined Piper & Marbury, one of Baltimore's most influential law firms. He did not work there long, however—he was recruited by the Carter Administration in Washington, D.C. to work in the Department of Transportation under Stuart Eizenstat. Noah wrote: "It was the kind of job hordes of bright Ivy Leaguers would give their eye teeth for, but Schmoke was restless." Even though he met regularly with President Carter's cabinet members and even Carter himself, even though he had a high-paid and high-visibility position, Schmoke had other aspirations for himself. He wanted to be mayor of Baltimore. He returned to his hometown and threw himself into the political arena.

While in law school Schmoke had married Patricia Locks, a Baltimore native who was studying ophthalmology. Schmoke's father-in-law had been a member of the Maryland General Assembly and was full of advice for the young would-be candidate. Schmoke rejected most of the advice, centered as it was on the traditional step-by-step system that had long been part of Baltimore politics. Noah noted: "Times had changed, and the city's once-powerful [neighborhood] clubhouses were no longer the gateways to political power. Instead, Schmoke would work as a prosecutor for the U.S. attorney, involve himself in assorted civic activities, and begin scouting political opportunities. The opening came in 1982, in the race for Baltimore district attorney, a position known somewhat confusingly as 'state's attorney.'"

Won Elective Office

In order to win as state's attorney, Schmoke had to defeat a white incumbent whose law-and-order rhetoric was very popular among the citizenry. Schmoke did not attack his opponent for racial insensitivity, as many of his predecessors had, but instead presented himself as an able young professional who would be more aggressive on drug prosecutions. He won by a landslide, carrying almost all of the black vote and a good many white votes besides. Schmoke served as state's attorney for four years—heading an office of 133 lawyers—and he sought the death penalty in several cases where narcotics policemen were shot by drug dealers. His years as a district attorney gave Schmoke an insider's awareness of the scope of the illegal narcotics industry, and that awareness has shaped his attitude toward illegal drugs to this day.

It is unlikely that Schmoke—or anyone else—could have beaten William Donald Schaefer in a race for mayor of Baltimore. In the fifteen years that Schaefer ran Baltimore (1972-87), the city experienced a transformation. Whole regions around the harbor that once housed rotting warehouses and abandoned homes bloomed into tourist attractions and upscale neighborhoods. Many Baltimoreans felt that Schaefer was solely responsible for the city's renaissance, and when the popular mayor moved on to become governor of Maryland, it was widely assumed that his hand-picked successor, Clarence "Du" Burns, would fill his shoes.

Schaefer was flamboyant and perennially optimistic. From the outset of his campaign Schmoke presented an entirely different picture. He was quiet, deliberate, and anything but optimistic about Baltimore's future. The

civic improvements, he pointed out, were laudable but completely inadequate for solving the many problems still besetting the city. Schmoke called for immediate attention to the soaring teen pregnancy rate and the numbers of high school dropouts. Claiming that Baltimore had become "prettier but poorer," Schmoke struck a chord among those who had not benefitted from the city's so-called recovery. At the age of thirty-eight he was elected mayor in a very close race.

Controversial Views

Mayor Schmoke became controversial almost immediately. Only four months after he was elected he stunned the audience at the National Conference of Mayors by suggesting that at least some drug use should be made legal. Schmoke told the *Washington Post:* "I started to think, maybe we ought to consider this drug problem a

> Many political observers feel that Schmoke is one of the most promising representatives of a new generation of black politicians, men and women who will ascend to positions of national power in the twenty-first century

public health problem rather than a criminal justice problem." Schmoke may have been thinking of the police officers gunned down in drug busts, the dangers of AIDS-infected needles being passed among drug users, and the daunting scale of the illegal drug industry, but his remarks brought an avalanche of criticism down upon him. It was suggested that he was "too soft" on the drug issue and that his suggestions would only intensify an already epidemic social problem. Noah concluded, however, that Schmoke did at least take a strong stand on the issue. "Right or wrong," the reporter noted, "it's hard not to give Schmoke points for political bravery."

Today Schmoke still faces a host of problems in his native Baltimore. He is trying to improve city services even as his tax base grows narrower, and his constant encouragement seems to have had little effect on the city's soaring school dropout and illiteracy rate. "Even with the best of intentions and a long-term strategy for change, success can be maddeningly elusive," Noah wrote. "Tough urban problems do not easily yield to even the most innovative solutions, and Schmoke is already drawing criticism for not showing enough results, especially in the schools."

His critics notwithstanding, Schmoke is seen in Baltimore—among black and white voters alike—as a strong leader with his city's best interests at heart. Many political observers feel that he is one of the most promising representatives of a new generation of black politicians, men and women who will ascend to positions of national power in the twenty-first century. Still in his first term as mayor, Schmoke maintains that he has no further ambitions beyond running—and improving—Baltimore. He has not ruled out higher office, however, and his background and current performance make him a likely candidate for the Senate, at least. Like many in his generation, Schmoke wants to be judged for his record and not for his accomplishments as a black man. Reflecting on his own hopes for the future, he told the *Washington Post:* "We are moving slowly but surely to a time when people are judged by their character and not their color."

Sources

Washington Post, August 25, 1985; September 16, 1987; December 8, 1987; December 20, 1988; May 27, 1990.

—*Mark Kram*

Art Shell

1946—

Professional football coach, player

When Art Shell was named head coach of the Los Angeles Raiders in 1989, he became the first black head coach in modern National Football League history. A former star offensive lineman for the Oakland Raiders, and part of two Super Bowl championship teams, Shell replaced Mike Shanahan, a second-year coach who was previously with the Denver Broncos. By appointing Shell, Raiders management hoped to rejuvenate the franchise, which, after moving to Los Angeles from Oakland in 1982, had lost the mark of the dominant Raiders teams of the late 1970s and early 1980s. "I wanted a Raider," general manager Al Davis was quoted as saying in the *New York Times* after naming Shell early in the 1989 season. "When we went back in Oakland for an exhibition game two months ago, the one thing lacking was a link to the past in our coaching leadership."

Shell's history with the Raiders runs deep. In fifteen seasons as an offensive lineman, he was considered one of the N.F.L.'s finest. At 6'5" and 300 pounds, Shell could, as Jill Lieber noted in *Sports Illustrated,* "intimidate opponents with his size alone." He was selected to the Pro Bowl a total of eight times, the most of any Raider

ever, and played in a total of 207 games, the third highest number of any Raider. One of his career highlights came when Oakland defeated Minnesota in the 1977 Super Bowl, and Shell's defensive opponent had neither a tackle or sack the entire game. Former Raiders fullback Mark van Eeghen recalled to Lieber: "Art had extremely high standards. He prided himself in keeping his guy off [quarterback] Ken Stabler; a sack hurt Art more than it did Kenny." In 1989, Shell was honored for his career achievements by being elected to the Professional Football Hall of Fame.

In addition to his stellar playing career, Shell possessed a knowledge of Raiders football that distinguished him as prime coaching material. Former Raiders head coach John Madden remarked in the *New York Times:* "When I watched Art Shell play, I always felt he would make a good coach and a good head coach. . . . He's a very bright, studious person, who not only played the game physically but knew everything about what he did, what everybody else did and why. He took that approach to the game, he was very, very knowledgeable." Madden added: "Some players never think about anything but their own jobs, but Art always thought about everybody else's job. When I was coaching the Raiders, he used to come up to me and say, 'I was thinking last night, what if we did this.' That's the way a coach thinks, but not many players think like that."

Following games, Shell would enjoy listening to other players respond to the media, especially fellow lineman Gene Upshaw. "I'd listen to Gene answer the questions. He always said the right things and he was so good, so quotable," Shell told Thomas George in the *New York Times.* "I paid close attention. I learned a lot that way about football, about life, by just listening." After Shell retired from playing football in 1983, he was named the Raiders offensive line coach, and continued to learn from others. He commented to Lieber on the various Raiders coaches he worked under: "John Madden taught me about the game of people. I learned that you have to

understand each individual, when to push his buttons and when not to. From Tom Flores [the Raiders coach from 1979 to 1987] I learned patience. He was a quiet, stoic leader. Mike Shanahan was one of the most organized people I ever met."

Loyal and patient as a coach, Shell makes it a priority to maintain a closeness with his players. "Even in the bad games, his communion with the players is obvious," commented Jeannie Park and Lorenzo Benet in *People.* "Unlike more mercurial coaches, Shell doesn't scream or throw tantrums. When things go wrong, he gently pulls the offender aside, wraps a beefy arm around his shoulder and speaks his mind quietly." A family approach has always been important to Shell, as he already demonstrated when he was a young man. The eldest of five children whose mother died when he was fifteen, Shell played a major role raising his siblings. Shell's sister, Eartha Smalls, told Park and Benet: "He ran the house as my dad would. . . . He told us life must go on and we had to pull together."

Since becoming head coach, the Raiders under Shell have started their climb back to the top of professional football. In his second year as coach, the team advanced all the way to the American Football Conference championship game, before losing to Buffalo. Shell seemed to be living up to his game plan, as he was quoted in *New York Times* as saying that the Raiders were "going to try and regain the power, toughness and explosiveness we had in the past." Shell has a good chance of being, as general manager Davis hopes, "the guy . . . to restore the identity of this franchise."

Sources

New York Times, January 25, 1989; October 4, 1989; October 5, 1989; October 8, 1989.
People, December 4, 1989.
Sports Illustrated, October 23, 1989.

—*Michael E. Mueller*

Russell Simmons

1957(?)—

Record company executive, producer, music promoter

The explosive entry of rap music onto the national music scene in the late 1980s is greatly due to the efforts and vision of rap record producer and artist manager Russell Simmons. Co-owner and founder of the rap label Def Jam Records and head of Rush Artist Management, which produces such top-selling rap acts as Run-DMC, Public Enemy, L. L. Cool J, and Oran "Juice" Jones, Simmons took "rap music, an often misunderstood expression of inner-city youth, and . . . established it as one of the most influential forms of Black music," wrote Nelson George in *Essence*. Often deemed by the media as the "impresario" and "mogul" of rap, Simmons began as a fledgling promoter of a new breed of street music, and today is at the helm of a multimillion-dollar entertainment company—complete with its own film and television division—which is the largest black-owned music business in the United States.

Some have described Simmons as the "Berry Gordy of his time," referring to the man who brought the cross-over black Motown sound to pop America in the 1960s, yet Simmons's approach is fundamentally different. According to Maura Sheehy in *Manhattan, Inc.,* "Like Gordy, Simmons is building a large, diverse organization into a black entertainment company, only Simmons's motivating impulse is to make his characters as 'black' as possible."

Simmons is insistent on presenting rap images that are true to the tough urban streets from which rap arose; as a result, his groups don such recognizable street garb as black leather clothes, high-top sneakers, hats, and gold chains. He explained his objectives to Stephen Holden in the *New York Times:* "In black America, your neighbor is much more likely to be someone like L. L. Cool J or Oran 'Juice' Jones than Bill Cosby. . . . A lot of the black stars being developed by record companies have images that are so untouchable that kids just don't relate to them. Our acts are people with strong, colorful images that urban kids already know, because they live next door to them."

Simmons grew up in a middle-class neighborhood in the New York City borough of Queens, and as a youth was himself involved with a street gang. It was while he was enrolled in the mid-1970s at the Harlem branch of City College of New York studying sociology that he became aware of rap music and its appeal to young inner-city blacks. He saw rappers as they would converge in parks and on street corners, and then take turns singing rap songs to gathering crowds.

Sheehy depicted the exchange between rappers and their audience in those beginning days of rap: "Rappers, called MCs (emcees) then, told stories and boasted—about street life, tenements, violence, and drugs; about their male prowess, their talents; about 'sucker MCs'; and about women. Their raps romanticized the danger-ous, exciting characters of the street, sanctified its lessons into wisdom, made poverty and powerlessness into

At a Glance. . .

Born c., 1957; raised in Hollis, Queens, New York City; father's name, Daniel Simmons (a public school attendance supervisor). *Education:* Attended City College of New York.

Co-founder and owner of Def Jam Records and Rush Productions, beginning 1985; owner of Rush Artist Management. Production associate of rap films *Krush Groove,* 1985, and *Tougher Than Leather,* 1988. Director of music videos.

Addresses: *Home*—New York, NY. *Office*—Def Jam Records, 298 Elizabeth St., New York, NY.

strength by making rappers superhuman, indomitable. The audience followed, finding their power in dancing and dressing styles of the moment; in mimicking the swaggering, tougher-than-leather attitude; and by worshiping their street 'poets.'"

Simmons saw in rap enthusiasts a vast audience that the recording industry had not tapped into. He left his college studies and began tirelessly promoting local rap artists, producing recordings on shoestring budgets and conducting "rap nights" at dance clubs in Queens and Harlem. In 1984, he teamed up with a fellow aspiring rap producer named Rick Rubin to form Def Jam Records, and caught the attention of CBS Records who agreed to distribute the label. Within three years, Def Jam albums such as the Beastie Boys' *Licensed to Ill,* L. L. Cool J.'s *Bigger and Deffer,* and Run-DMC's *Raising Hell* dominated the black music charts.

Throughout, Simmons has been the manager of all Def Jam acts and has emphasized authenticity with each particular group. "Our artists are people you can relate to," he told Fayette Hickox in *Interview.* "Michael Jackson is great for what he is—but you don't know anybody like that. The closest Run-DMC comes to a costume is a black leather outfit. . . . It's important to look like your audience. If it's real, don't change it."

Some critics find the image of rappers disturbing. "It is the look of many rap artists—hard, belligerent, unassimilated,

one they share with their core audience—that puts many folks on edge," noted George. The group Public Enemy, which carries the logo of a black teen in the scope of a police gun, is representative, as Simmons told George, of how many black teenagers feel like "targets that are looked down upon." Simmons added: "Rush Management identifies with them. That's why we don't have one group that doesn't look like its audience."

The lyrics and antics of some male rap artists have also infuriated women's groups, who find misogynistic messages in the songs and stage acts, while public officials have brought charges of lewdness against some rappers in concert. Simmons distances himself from censoring the content of his rap groups' songs, telling George that "rap is an expression of the attitudes of the performers and their audience." He does, however, ultimately uphold rappers as positive role models for many black youths.

As an example, Simmons commented to Holden that the members of Run-DMC, which include Simmons's younger brother Joseph, "are more than musicians. . . . They're from a particular community, and have succeeded on their own terms without any compromise. . . . If you take a look at the pop cultural landscape or the black political landscape now, there aren't a lot of heroes. If you're a 15-year-old black male in high school and look around, you wonder what you can do with your life. How do you better yourself? Run-DMC has opened up a whole new avenue of ambition. You can grow up to be like Run-DMC. It's possible."

Sources

Books

George, Nelson, *The Death of Rhythm and Blues,* Pantheon, 1988.

Periodicals

Essence, March 1988.
Interview, September 1987.
Jet, May 28, 1990.
Manhattan, Inc., February 1990.
New York Times, February 20, 1991.

—*Michael E. Mueller*

Sinbad

1957(?)—

Comedian, actor

Known for his "clean comedy," stand-up comic Sinbad pulls off a rare feat of delivering stage monologues that are funny and outrageous without being profane. The son of a Baptist minister and married father of two children, Sinbad strongly feels that stories of life itself are the stuff of humor, and that profanity is not necessary to make people laugh. As he told Aldore Collier in *Jet:* "Life unedited is funny."

does. Only a husband or boyfriend could make a woman act the way she acts." Sinbad frequently draws upon stories of his own family in his act, in particular tales of his own marriage (he describes his wife as "understanding"). He commented in *Ebony* that such "comedy really works because it's about being on a stage and talking about everything that is wrong with all of us. And we realize, 'Man, I'm not the only one who's messed up like this.'"

Early in his career Sinbad found that getting rid of profanity in his act was a way of trusting his own comic instincts. "I'll never forget it," he related to Collier. "I was on stage and I was dying. I didn't really know how to do comedy and I was trying to write stuff rather than just be what I am. And I remember I cursed on stage. And it was the worst feeling I ever had. People were laughing, but I said I would quit comedy before I had to do that. . . . I went home and learned how to be myself. I learned that your life is funny."

The follies of male-female relationships are often the focus of Sinbad's monologues. "Relationships are just plain funny," he was quoted as saying by Collier. "Only a wife or girlfriend could make a man act the way he

Being funny has always part of Sinbad's life. The native of Benton Harbor, Michigan, was always "the goofy kid," as he told a contributor to *People*. At 6' 5", Sinbad originally aspired to be a basketball player, and thought that someday he might mix comedy and sports by being one of the Harlem Globetrotters. While he attended the University of Denver on a basketball scholarship, a knee injury forced him to give up the sport, and he left in 1978. Sinbad later joined the U.S. Air Force, and began working at stand-up comedy after he won a talent contest. "Inspired," as the contributor to *People* relates, "[Sinbad] set out to get himself discharged by walking off duty in his underwear. 'Just kick me out,' he begged. 'Let's work as a team.'"

At a Glance...

Full name, David Atkins; born c. 1957; native of Benton Harbor, Mich.; father's name, Donald (a Baptist minister); married, 1985; wife's name, Meredith; children: Paige, Royce. *Education:* Studied at University of Denver.

Began performing comedy in the early 1980s; served in the U.S. Air Force until 1983; played Walter Oakes on NBC-TV series, *A Different World,* c. 1986—; host of *Showtime at the Apollo,* beginning in 1989.

After he left the Air Force in 1983, Sinbad became a success on the comedy nightclub circuit in Los Angeles, and eventually was a seven-time winner on the television talent show, *Star Search.* He also performed as an opener for music groups the Pointer Sisters and Kool and the Gang, and was a regular on the short-lived *The Redd Foxx Show.* Eventually, he did warm-ups for studio audiences on *The Cosby Show,* during which time his idol, Bill Cosby, helped land him a role on the hit NBC-TV series, *A Different World.*

Sinbad's role on *A Different World*—which humorously depicts the lives of students and faculty at an all-black college—was the irreverent dormitory director and gym teacher Walter Oakes. A reviewer in *Variety,* who comments that the show's strength is its "likable and energetic cast," added that "dorm antics are infectiously led by the single-named Sinbad, who is delightful as the big guy struggling to keep order in a nonstop party house." In 1990, Sinbad's character on the show was broadened to become a counselor. According to co-executive producer Susan Fales, as quoted in *Jet,* the move to make Sinbad's character more serious was to increasingly "address social problems, like sex education, teen pregnancy, and drugs" and to have the popular Sinbad become "the voice of what's happening in the Black community."

Sources

Ebony, April 1990.
Jet, February 12, 1990; August 13, 1990.
People, September 29, 1986.
Variety, October 4-10, 1989.

—*Michael E. Mueller*

Henry Ossawa Tanner

1859-1937

Painter, photographer

At the beginning of the twentieth century, Henry Ossawa Tanner was highly regarded in Europe and America as the foremost African-American painter of the day. In 1991, nearly a century later, a major retrospective containing more than 100 paintings, drawings, photo graphs, and memorabilia was sponsored by the Philadelphia Museum of Art. Shown in four major American museums, the exhibit served to refocus attention on this expatriate American artist who spent most of his adult life in France.

Born in Pittsburgh on June 21, 1859, Henry Ossawa Tanner was the first child of Benjamin Tucker Tanner and Sarah Miller Tanner. His middle name, Ossawa, stems from Osawatomie, Kansas, where the abolitionist John Brown murdered five slavery sympathizers in 1856. Although born in Pittsburgh, he grew up in Philadelphia, where his parents moved in 1866 when his father was assigned to the Bethel Church there. The Tanner family would grow to include seven children.

Tanner's parents were cultured and educated, and they owned property. His father was born into a family that had been free for several generations. Benjamin Tucker

Tanner attended Avery College and Western Theological Seminary, both located in Pennsylvania. He was a minister and later a prominent bishop in the African Methodist Episcopal Church. Tanner's mother, Sarah Miller Tanner, was the granddaughter of a white plantation owner. She was born in Winchester, Virginia; and although born into slavery, Sarah was sent north on the Underground Railroad by her parents and raised in freedom. Sadly, she never saw her parents again. Henry Tanner would paint portraits of both his parents in 1897. His mother's portrait was done in a style similar to that used by the American artist James Whistler for his mother's portrait.

Only a handful of African-American artists preceded Tanner, including Joshua Johnston (active 1796-c.1824), a Maryland portrait painter; Robert Duncanson (1817-1872), a Cincinnati landscape painter; Edward Bannister (1828-1901) of Providence, Rhode Island; and Edmonia Lewis (1845-c.1890), a noted sculptor. While Tanner devoted most of his paintings to biblical subjects, he also created some notable black genre paintings, such as *The Banjo Lesson* (1893) and *The Thankful Poor* (1894). Interestingly, and disappointingly for some critics, Tanner devoted his energies to black genre paintings for only a couple of years before abandoning the genre in 1895. During this brief period he was able to produce paintings that one commentator praised as "dignified images of his race in everyday settings."

By the 1890s, images of blacks painted by white artists like Winslow Homer, Thomas Eakins, and Thomas Hovenden were not uncommon. Tanner, however, accepted the new challenge of correcting their misconceptions and stereotypes, something previous African-American artists had not done. Tanner had personal contact in Philadelphia with Eakins, his teacher at the Pennsylvania Academy of Fine Arts, and Hovenden, who worked in Philadelphia. Eakins was a realistic painter who "approached his art with scientific precision." He depicted African Americans as individuals, not as caricatures. Eakins, who was an exceptional role model for Tanner, showed that African Americans could be represented with dignity.

Hovenden also influenced Tanner, giving him, as one commentator wrote, "a comprehension of and sympathy with the broader and deeper things of life and art." Hovenden was born in Ireland and came to the United States at the age of 23. His house was used for abolitionist meetings and as a station on the Underground Railroad. He developed a deep personal concern for the black cause and produced paintings of black subjects far superior to any other American artist of the time.

Hovenden's *The Last Moments of John Brown* is typical of the paintings that influenced Tanner.

Tanner's Black Genre Period

Hovenden's *I'se So Happy,* which depicts an older black banjo player, is likely to have inspired Tanner's *The Banjo Lesson.* Tanner painted *The Banjo Lesson* in Philadelphia while he was recovering from a bout with typhoid fever that he had contracted in France. It was during this convalescence that Tanner decided to address African-American themes in his paintings. He wrote in his third-person autobiography, "The Story of an Artist's Life," which appeared in 1909 in *The World at Work,* "Since his [i.e., Tanner's] return from Europe he has painted many Negro subjects. He feels drawn to such subjects on account of the newness of the field and because of a desire to represent the serious and pathetic side of life among them, and it is his thought that other things being equal, he who has most sympathy with the subject will obtain the best results."

The Banjo Lesson, as well as several other of Tanner's paintings, was also influenced by a French tradition established by Jean-Francois Millet, whose studies of everyday peasant life included several with teaching themes, such as *The Knitting Lesson* (1854), *The Reading Lesson* (1860), and *The Sewing Lesson* (1874). Art history professor Maurice Frank Woods praised *The Banjo Lesson* in *American Visions* by writing, "Tanner skillfully and sympathetically captured a tender exchange between the wisdom of age and the innocence of youth in the form of an elderly man instructing a boy on how to play the banjo." The painting was purchased in 1894 by the Hampton Institute after being shown at Earle's Gallery in Philadelphia.

Tanner's affinity for lesson paintings, which typically show an older person passing along a tradition of skill or knowledge to a younger individual, also revealed itself in such works as *The Young Sabot Maker,* which was exhibited at the Salon in Paris in 1895. While not strictly speaking a lesson, the painting shows a youth making wooden shoes while an older man, probably his father and teacher, looks on with pride in the background. The later biblical paintings for which his wife and son posed, *Christ and His Mother Studying the Scriptures* (1910) and *Christ Learning to Read* (1910-1914), also embody this theme.

Tanner painted *The Thankful Poor* in 1894 before abandoning his black genre paintings. It is based on a similar painting called *Le repas en famille,* painted in 1891 by Elizabeth Nourse, a Cincinnati-born painter who also studied in France at the Academie Julien. Tanner had a chance to view the painting when it was exhibited at the World's Columbian Exposition in 1893. According to Professor Woods, "The message is the same in both paintings. Despite their humble surroundings and meager meals, these two groups of people have found spiritual sustenance in their lives of struggle. Both pictures quietly reassure the viewer that the souls of the downtrodden are perhaps the purest and their faith in God the strongest." Lost for many years, *The Thankful Poor* was discovered in 1970 by the headmaster at the Pennsylvania School for the Deaf. It was exhibited for eleven years at the Philadelphia Museum of Art and then sold in 1981 to actor Bill Cosby and his wife, Camille, for $250,000.

Henry Ossawa Tanner decided he wanted to be a painter around the age of 12, when he saw a landscape painter at work in Philadelphia's Fairmount Park. "It set me on fire," he wrote. His mother loaned him 15 cents to buy paints and brushes. "From this time forward, I was all aglow with enthusiasm, working spare times between school hours." Tanner started out to be a marine painter, painting various seascapes, harbor scenes, and ships in storms before being accepted at the Pennsylvania Academy of Fine Arts in Philadelphia in 1880. Tanner was also interested in painting animals and made paintings and clay models of the animals at the Philadelphia Zoo. Around 1880, he painted *"Pomp" at the Zoo,* showing well-dressed townspeople viewing a caged animal. He also painted horses, dogs, lions, deer, and other animals.

At the Pennsylvania Academy of Fine Arts, Tanner was taught by the well-known realist, Thomas Eakins, who was professor of drawing and painting. A "charismatic and headstrong" teacher, Eakins instructed Tanner how to render the human form, manipulate light and shadow to express a mood, and probe the depths of his subject. In 1902, Eakins would pay tribute to his former pupil by painting his portrait. By that time, Tanner had become the more acclaimed artist of the two.

Tanner tried to raise money for a trip to Europe by selling paintings and photographs in Philadelphia and doing magazine illustrations, but he realized few sales and received little financial support from his family. In 1888, he went to Atlanta, then known as a major center for black education. He opened a photography studio, hoping the well-educated black community would support him. However, he soon closed the shop and took a teaching position at Clark University. He spent the summer of 1889 photographing and painting mountainous landscapes in North Carolina's Highlands.

Traveled to Europe

In 1890, Tanner raised money for his European voyage through an exhibit of his works in Cincinnati that was organized by Bishop Joseph Hartzell of the Methodist Episcopal Church. When no one appeared to buy the paintings, Hartzell purchased the entire exhibit as a sign of support. In 1902, Tanner would paint a large portrait of Bishop Hartzell in tribute to his earliest patron. On January 4, 1891, Tanner sailed from New York for Europe. He arrived in Paris via Liverpool and London and enrolled in the Academie Julien. He spent his first summers in the countryside, painting the landscape and its people. After a summer at Port-Aven, he painted his first entry into the Salon. Although not accepted, *The Bagpipe Lesson* (1892-93) is a well-executed painting of Breton peasants. Although peasants were a traditional French subject, bagpipes were not; and Tanner also introduced an uncharacteristic element of humor into this painting.

Tanner became ill during his second year in France, contracting typhoid fever. He returned to Philadelphia

> Henry Ossawa Tanner was highly regarded in Europe and America as the foremost African-American painter of the day

for two years to recuperate and convalesce. It was during this period that he began to address black themes in his paintings. In the summer of 1893, he delivered a paper on "The American Negro in Art" before the World's Congress on Africa, held in Chicago in conjunction with the World's Columbian Exposition. Although the text has been lost, Tanner preserved his views on black genre paintings in his autobiographical sketch published in *The World at Work* (1909). When Tanner returned to Paris in 1894 after finishing *The Thankful Poor,* he worked hard to get his work accepted by the prestigious Salon of Paris. He would never return to the theme of African-American genre paintings.

Biblical Themes Period

After producing *The Young Sabot Maker* for the Salon exhibition of 1895, Tanner turned to biblical themes in his work. *Daniel in the Lion's Den* received an honorable mention from the Salon in 1896; and Tanner triumphed at the 1897 Salon exhibition when *The Raising of Lazarus* was awarded a medal there. The painting was later purchased by the French government for the Luxembourg Gallery, where the works of living artists were displayed. Tanner thus joined the exclusive company of John Singer Sargent and James A. McNeil Whistler, the only other American artists whose works had also been purchased by the French government. Today, *The Raising of Lazarus* is on exhibit at the Musee d'Orsay.

According to James K. Kettlewell, curator of the Hyde Collection, "Religious themes were for Tanner, like Rembrandt, very personal modes of expression." Perhaps his interest in religious paintings stemmed from his upbringing in the church (his father was a prominent bishop in the African Methodist Episcopal Church) and his own spiritual beliefs. Tanner clearly was a religious man who believed in the biblical stories he depicted. He may have believed the biblical myths he painted could illustrate the struggles and hopes of his fellow black Americans. Some commentators, including the artist's own son, have referred to the "poetic mysticism" of Tanner's biblical paintings.

In 1897 and 1898, Tanner traveled to Palestine, Egypt, and the Holy Land. He entered another major biblical work, *The Annunciation* (1898) in the 1898 Salon. Painted after his trip to Palestine, the painting introduced textiles, ceramics, and white-washed, stone-floored architecture that Tanner would use in his later interior scenes of biblical subjects. *The Annunciation* became the first of Tanner's works to be purchased for an American museum; it was acquired in 1899 by the W.P. Wilstach Collection for display in the Pennsylvania Museum (now Philadelphia Museum of Art).

Marriage and Family Life

Tanner met his wife, Jessie Macauley Olssen (1873-1925) in the summer of 1898 at Barbizon and later in Paris. Of Swedish descent, she was raised in San Francisco, where her father was an electrician in the shipbuilding industry. She was a gifted musician and moved to France to study voice. She married Henry in London on December 14, 1899, and settled in Paris. Jessie had posed for *The Annunciation* (1898) and would serve as a model for many of Henry's paintings, including *The Three Marys* (1910). Their only child, Jessie Ossawa Tanner, was born September 25, 1903, in New York city during a stay in the United States.

In 1899, Tanner painted *Flight into Egypt,* the first of more than 15 versions he would paint on this theme. Other paintings reflecting his trips to the Holy Land

include *A View in Palestine* (1898-99) and *Nicodemus Visiting Jesus* (1899), which was signed by Tanner in Jerusalem. Following a two-year stay in the United States (1902-1904), during which his son Jesse Ossawa Tanner was born, Tanner returned to France and continued to paint biblical scenes. A favorite theme appeared in *The Good Shepherd* (1902-1903), a metaphor illustrating the relationship between God and man. In 1906, *The Two Disciples at the Tomb* was purchased by the Art Institute of Chicago. That same year, the French government purchased Tanner's *The Disciples at Emmaus.*

Tanner's early interest in marine painting manifested itself in some of his mature biblical work, including *The Disciples See Christ Walking on the Water* (c.1907) and *Christ and His Disciples on the Sea of Galilee* (c.1910). The 1991 retrospective also featured the first public showing of Tanner's *Fishermen at Sea* (c.1913-14). This boldly composed and freely painted work was discovered underneath another painting when the first canvas was removed for conservation. It shows a dramatic view from above of a fishing boat tossed about in a fairly rough sea.

Visited North Africa and Palestine

Tanner traveled to Algeria and Morocco in 1908 and the years prior to World War I. His trips there and to Palestine helped him capture the historical essence of his biblical subjects. While in Morocco and Algeria he painted in the Orientalist tradition, popular with French artists since Napoleon's conquest of North Africa. Tanner and other artists were attracted by the exotic nature of Islamic countries in the Mediterranean region. Tanner painted street scenes in Tangier and the Casbah.

Tanner's painting activities were interrupted in 1914 by the start of World War I. He was profoundly depressed by the war and did very few paintings until the war was over. Tanner served with the American Red Cross in France from the time the United States entered the war in 1917 until 1919. While serving, he proposed a therapy program in which convalescing patients would grow vegetables on vacant land around hospitals and base depots. The program was very successful.

After the war's end in November of 1918, Tanner returned to painting. He received permission to make sketches in the restricted war zone of Neufchateau, where he was stationed. His permit limited him to painting Red Cross activities, and his work was reviewed by censors. At the end of the war, Tanner presented three large works to the American Red Cross, including *American Red Cross Canteen, Toul, France, WWI* (1918).

Following World War I, Tanner continued to paint biblical scenes. He began to receive more honors as well. In 1923, the French government honored him by electing him a Chevalier of the Legion of Honor. When he was elected a full academician to the National Academy of Design in 1927, he presented the painting, *Miraculous Haul of Fishes* (c.1913) as his reception piece.

When Tanner's wife died of pleurisy in 1925, Tanner was griefstricken and unable to paint for a while. He became reclusive, and his paintings became more mystical. *The Burning of Sodom and Gomorrah* (1932) is a good example of his later style of thickly painted mysterious landscapes. He spent his last years caring for his son, Jesse, who had suffered a nervous breakdown after graduating from Cambridge University and the Royal School of Mines in London. Tanner helped his son achieve a complete recovery, and Jesse eventually married and started his own business.

During the Harlem Renaissance of the 1920s and 1930s, when black writers and artists sought a new aesthetic, Tanner was criticized for not painting more black subjects. By the 1930s, though, Tanner was a respected elder whose work may have seemed "old-fashioned" to the younger generation. Tanner continued to pursue his inner vision, and he completed his final painting, *Return from the Crucifixion,* in 1936. When he died in his sleep in Paris on May 25, 1937, there was still wet paint on his canvases.

The first major American exhibition of Tanner's work took place in 1969. Co-sponsored by the Frederick Douglass Institute and the National Collection of Fine Arts, the exhibit contained 90 oils, watercolors, drawings, and etchings. After opening in Washington, D.C., at the National Collection of Fine Arts, it traveled to seven American museums, thus becoming the first one-man show by a black artist to tour the country's major museums.

Sources

Books

The Art of Henry Ossawa Tanner, Hyde Collection, 1972.
Henry Ossawa Tanner, Philadelphia Museum of Art, 1991.
Mathews, Marcia M., *Henry Ossawa Tanner,* University of Chicago Press, 1969.

Periodicals

American Heritage, February-March 1991.
American Visions, February 1991.
Connoisseur, January 1991.
Detroit Free Press, May 9, 1991.
Ebony, March 1991.
New York Times, February 17, 1991.
The World's Work, June 1909.
The World's Work, July 1909.

—David Bianco

Alice Walker

1944-

Author

Recognized as one of the leading voices among black American women writers, Alice Walker has produced an acclaimed and varied body of work, including poetry, novels, short stories, essays, and criticism. Her writings portray the struggle of black people throughout history, and are praised for their insightful and riveting portraits of black life, in particular the experiences of black women in a sexist and racist society. Her most famous work, the award-winning and best-selling novel *The Color Purple,* chronicles the life of a poor and abused southern black woman who eventually triumphs over oppression through affirming female relationships. Walker has described herself as a "womanist"—her term for a black feminist—which she defines in the introduction to her book of essays, *In Search of Our Mothers' Gardens: Womanist Prose,* as one who "appreciates and prefers women's culture, women's emotional flexibility . . . women's strength" and is "committed to [the] survival and wholeness of entire people, male *and* female."

A theme throughout Walker's work is the preservation of black culture, and her female characters forge important links to maintain continuity in both personal relationships and communities. According to Barbara T. Christian in *Dictionary of Literary Biography,* Walker is concerned with "heritage," which to Walker "is not so much the grand sweep of history or artifacts created as it is the relations of people to each other, young to old, parent to child, man to woman." Walker admires the struggle of black women throughout history to maintain an essential spirituality and creativity in their lives, and their achievements serve as an inspiration to others. In *Our Mother's Gardens,* Walker wrote: "We must fearlessly pull out of ourselves and look at and identify with our lives the living creativity some of our great-grandmothers were not allowed to know. I stress *some* of them because it is well known that the majority of our great-grandmothers knew, even without 'knowing' it, the reality of their spirituality, even if they didn't recognize it beyond what happened in the singing at church—and they never had any intention of giving it up."

Walker's women characters display strength, endurance, and resourcefulness in confronting—and overcoming—oppression in their lives, yet Walker is frank in depicting the often devastating circumstances of the "twin afflic-

the burdens that everyone else—*everyone else*—refused to carry," Walker stated in *Our Mothers' Gardens.* Mary Helen Washington in *Sturdy Black Bridges: Visions of Black Women in Literature* noted that "the true empathy Alice Walker has for the oppressed woman comes through in all her writings. . . . Raising an ax, crying out in childbirth or abortion, surrendering to a man who is oblivious to her real name—these are the kinds of images which most often appear in Ms. Walker's own writing." Washington adds that the strength of such images is that Walker gives insight into "the intimate reaches of the inner lives of her characters; the landscape of her stories is the spiritual realm where the soul yearns for what it does not have."

Early Influences

Walker's beginnings as a writer are in the small rural town of Eatonton, Georgia, where she was the youngest of eight children of impoverished sharecroppers. Both of her parents were storytellers, and Walker was especially influenced by her mother, whom she described in *Our Mothers' Gardens* as "a walking history of our community." A childhood accident at the age of eight left Walker blind and scarred in one eye, which, partially corrected when she was fourteen, left a profound influence on her. "I believe . . . that it was from this period—from my solitary, lonely position, the position of an outcast—that I began really to see people and things, really to notice relationships and to learn to be patient enough to care about how they turned out. . . . I retreated into solitude, and read stories and began to write poems." Walker has commented that as a southern black growing up in a poor rural community, she possessed the benefit of "double vision." She explained in *Our Mothers' Gardens:* "Not only is the [black southern writer] in a position to see his own world, and its close community . . . but he is capable of knowing, with remarkably silent accuracy, the people who make up the larger world that surrounds and suppresses his own."

Walker was an excellent student, and received a scholarship to Spelman College in Atlanta, and later to Sarah Lawrence College in the Bronx, New York. While in college, she became politically aware in the Civil Rights Movement and participated in many demonstrations. Her first book of poems, *Once,* was written while she was a senior at Sarah Lawrence and was accepted for publication the same year. Walker wrote many of the poems in the span of a week in the winter of 1965, when she wrestled with suicide after deciding to have an abortion. The poems recount the despair and isolation of her situation, in addition to her experiences in the Civil Rights Movement and of a trip she had made to Africa. Though

tions" of racism and sexism. "Black women are called, in the folklore that so aptly identifies one's status in society, 'the *mule* of the world,' because we have been handed

not widely reviewed, *Once* marked Walker's debut as a distinctive and talented writer. Carolyn M. Rodgers in *Negro Digest* noted Walker's "precise wordings, the subtle, unexpected twists . . . [and] shifting of emotions." Christian remarks that already in *Once,* Walker displayed what would become a feature of both her future poetry and fiction, an "unwavering honesty in evoking the forbidden, either in political stances or in love."

Walker returned to the South after college and worked as a voter register in Georgia and an instructor in black history in Mississippi. She was inspired by Martin Luther King Jr.'s message, as she recounted in *Our Mothers' Gardens,* that being a southern black meant "I . . . had claim to the land of my birth." Walker continued to write poetry and fiction, and began to further explore the South she came from. She described in *Our Mothers' Gardens* of being particularly influenced by the Russian writers, who spoke to her of a "soul . . . directly rooted in the soil that nourished it." She was also influenced by black writer Zora Neale Hurston, who wrote lively folk accounts of the thriving small, southern black community she grew up in. Walker stated in *Our Mothers' Gardens* how she particularly admired the "racial health" of Hurston's work: "A sense of black people as complete, complex, *undiminished* human beings, a sense that is lacking in so much black writing and literature."

Objections to Her Portrayal of Black Males

With the help of a 1967 McDowell fellowship, Walker completed her first novel, *The Third Life of Grange Copeland,* published in 1970. The novel depicts cycles of male violence in three generations of an impoverished southern black family (the Copelands), and displays Walker's interest in social conditions that affect family relationships, in addition to her recurring theme of the suffering of black women at the hands of men. The novel revolves around a father (Grange) who abandons his abused wife and young son (Brownfield) for a more prosperous life in the North, and returns years later to find his son similarly abusing his own family. Christian writes that the men in the novel are "thwarted by the society in their drive for control of their lives—the American definition of manhood—[and] vent their frustrations by inflicting violence on their wives." Critics praised the realism of the novel, including *CLA Journal* contributor Peter Erickson, who noted that Walker demonstrated "with a vivid matter-of-factness the family's entrapment in a vicious cycle of poverty." However, Walker was also faulted for her portrayal of black men as violent, an aspect which is frequently criticized in her work. Walker responded to such criticism in an interview with Claudia Tate in *Black Women Writers at Work:* "I know many Brownfields, and it's a shame that I know so many. I will not ignore people like Brownfield. I want you to know I know they exist. I want to tell you about them, and there is no way you are going to avoid them."

Walker's short story collections, *In Love and Trouble* (1973) and *You Can't Keep a Good Woman Down* (1981) expand upon the problems of sexism and racism facing black women. *In Love and Trouble* features thirteen black women protagonists—many of them from the South—who, as Christian notes, "against their own conscious wills in the face of pain, abuse, even death, challenge the conventions of sex, race, and age that attempt to restrict them." In *Our Mothers' Gardens,* Walker stated that her intent in the stories was to present a variety of women—"mad, raging, loving, resentful, hateful, strong, ugly, weak, pitiful, and magnificent"—as they "try to live with the loyalty to black men that characterizes all of their lives." Barbara Smith in *Ms.* praised the collection, stating it "would be an extraordinary literary work if its only virtue were the fact that the author sets out consciously to explore with honesty the

> Walker was inspired by Martin Luther King Jr.'s message that being a southern black meant "I . . . had a claim to the land of my birth."

textures and terror of black women's lives." Smith added: "The fact that Walker's perceptions, style, and artistry are also consistently high makes her work a treasure."

Subject Matter Evolved

The stories in *You Can't Keep a Good Woman Down* represented an evolution in subject matter, as Walker delved more directly into mainstream feminist issues such as abortion, pornography, and rape. Although a number of critics remarked that the polemic nature of the stories detracted from their narrative effect, Walker again demonstrated, according to Christian, "the extent to which black women are free to pursue their own selfhood in a society permeated by sexism and racism."

Walker explored similar terrain in her acclaimed 1976 novel, *Meridian,* in which she recounts the personal evolution of a young black woman against the backdrop of the politics of the Civil Rights Movement. Structurally complex, the novel raises questions of motherhood for the politically-aware female, and the implications for the individual of being committed to revolution. Writing in the *New York Times Book Review,* Marge Piercy praised *Meridian* as "a fine, taut novel that accomplishes a remarkable amount" and noted that Walker "writes with a sharp critical sense as she deals with the issues of tactics and strategy in the civil rights movement, with the nature of commitment, the possibility of interracial love and communication, the vital and lethal strands in American and black experience, with violence and nonviolence." The novel received much critical recognition and was praised for its deft handling of complex subject matter. Years after its publication, Robert Towers commented in the *New York Review of Books* that *Meridian* "remains the most impressive fictional treatment of the 'Movement' that I have yet read."

In her 1982 novel, *The Color Purple,* Walker brought together many of the characters and themes of her previous works in a book which Peter S. Prescott in *Newsweek* proclaimed "an American novel of permanent importance." *The Color Purple* is a series of letters written by a southern black woman (Celie), reflecting a history of oppression and abuse suffered at the hands of the men. The book was resoundingly praised for its masterful recreation of black folk speech, in which, as Towers noted, Walker converts Celie's "subliterate dialect into a medium of remarkable expressiveness, color, and poignancy." Towers added: "I find it impossible to imagine Celie apart from her language; through it, not only a memorable and infinitely touching character but a whole submerged world is vividly called into being."

The Color Purple Became a Pulitzer Prize-winner

The novel charts Celie's resistance to the oppression surrounding her, and the liberation of her existence through positive and supportive relations with other women. Christian notes that "perhaps even more than Walker's other works, [*The Color Purple*] especially affirms that the most abused of the abused can transform herself. It completes the cycle Walker announced a decade ago: the survival and liberation of black women through the strength and wisdom of others." The novel won both the Pulitzer Prize and the American Book Award, and was made into a popular motion picture which received several Academy Award nominations.

Her 1989 novel, *The Temple of My Familiar,* described by Walker as "a romance of the last 500,000 years," represents a departure of sorts for the author, and critical opinion was mixed upon its publication. J. M. Coetzee in the *New York Times Book Review* described it as "a mixture of mythic fantasy, revisionary history, exemplary biography and sermon" which is "short on narrative tension, long on inspirational message." In the novel, Walker features six characters, three men and three women, who relate their views on life through recounting memories of ancestors and spirits from past cultures. While a number of reviewers faulted the ideological weight of the novel, others commented that the book remained faithful to the concerns of Walker's works. Luci Tapahonso noted in the *Los Angeles Times Book Review* that the novel focuses on familiar Walker themes, such as "compassion for the oppressed, the grief of the oppressors, acceptance of the unchangeable and hope for everyone and every thing."

While Walker's works speak strongly of the experiences of black women, critics have commented that the messages of her books transcend both race and gender. According to Gloria Steinem in *Ms.,* Walker "comes at universality through the path of an American black woman's experience. . . . She speaks the female experience more powerfully for being able to pursue it across boundaries of race and class." Jeanne Fox-Alston in the *Chicago Tribune Book World* called Walker "a provocative writer who writes about blacks in particular, but all humanity in general." In her 1988 prose collection, *Living by the Word: Selected Writings, 1973-1977,* Walker discusses, through essays and journal entries, topics such as nuclear weapons and racism in other countries. Noel Perrin in the *New York Times Book Review* wrote that although Walker's "original interests centered on black women, and especially on the ways they were abused or underrated . . . now those interests encompass all creation." Derrick Bell commented in the *Los Angeles Times Book Review* that Walker "uses carefully crafted images that provide a universality to unique events." *Living by the Word* presents "vintage Alice Walker: passionate, political, personal, and poetic."

Selected writings

Poetry

Once: Poems, Harcourt, 1968.
Revolutionary Petunias and Other Poems, Harcourt, 1973.
Goodnight, Willie Lee, I'll See You in the Morning, Dial, 1979.
Horses Make a Landscape Look More Beautiful, Harcourt, 1984.

Fiction

The Third Life of Grange Copeland (novel), Harcourt, 1970.
In Love and Trouble: Stories of Black Women, Harcourt, 1973.

Meridian (novel), Harcourt, 1976.
You Can't Keep a Good Woman Down (stories), Harcourt, 1981.
The Color Purple (novel), Harcourt, 1982.
To Hell with Dying (juvenile story), Harcourt, 1988.
The Temple of My Familiar (novel), Harcourt, 1989.

Other

Langston Hughes: American Biography (for children), Crowell, 1973.
(Editor) *I Love Myself When I'm Laughing . . . and Then Again When I Am Looking Mean and Impressive: A Zora Neale Hurston Reader,* Feminist Press, 1979.
In Search of Our Mothers' Gardens: Womanist Prose (essays), Harcourt, 1983.
Living by the Word: Selected Writings, 1973-1987 (essays and journal entries), Harcourt, 1988.

Media adaptations

The Color Purple was made into a film and released by Warner Bros. in 1985.

Contributor to numerous books, anthologies, and periodicals; contributing editor to periodicals, including *Freedomways* and *Ms.*

Sources

Books

Bell, Roseann P., Bettye J. Parker, and Beverly Guy-Sheftall, editors, *Sturdy Black Bridges: Visions of Black Women in Literature,* Anchor Press, 1979.
Bestsellers 89, Issue 4, Gale, 1989.
Contemporary Authors New Revision Series, Volume 27 (entry contains interview), Gale, 1989.
Contemporary Literary Criticism, Gale, Volume 5, 1976; Volume 6, 1976; Volume 9, 1978; Volume 19, 1981; Volume 27, 1984; Volume 46, 1988.
Dictionary of Literary Biography, Gale, Volume 6: *American Novelists since World War II,* 2nd series, 1980; Volume 33: *Afro-American Fiction Writers after 1955,* 1984.
Evans, Mari, editor, *Black Women Writers (1950-1980): A Critical Evaluation,* Anchor Press/Doubleday, 1984.

Periodicals

Chicago Tribune Book World, August 1, 1982; September 15, 1985.
CLA Journal, September 1979.
Los Angeles Times Book Review, May 29, 1988; May 21, 1989.
Ms., February 1974; June 1982.
Negro Digest, September/October 1968.
Newsweek, June 21, 1982.
New York Review of Books, August 12, 1982.
New York Times Book Review, May 26, 1976; June 5, 1988; April 30, 1989.

—Michael E. Mueller

Herschel Walker

1962—

Professional football player

Outstanding running back Herschel Walker has been a stellar performer in both collegiate and professional football. As a junior at the University of Georgia, the 6'1'', 223-pound Walker won the Heisman Trophy, college football's highest honor, en route to a collegiate career in which he set ten NCAA records. His subsequent career as a professional player in both the United States Football League (USFL) and National Football League (NFL), has shown him to be one of the sport's premiere rushers and receivers. Walker, who has played for the Minnesota Vikings since 1989, is "arguably the most devastating running back in today's world," according to a contributor to *The Football Abstract.* "Whether running or catching, Herschel is a threat to score every time he touches a football."

Walker's prowess was evident already in high school, where he excelled in both football and track, leading Johnson County (Georgia) High School to state championships in both sports. At the Georgia state track championships, Walker won the shot put, the 100-yard dash, and the 200-yard dash; and while in his senior season on the football team, he rushed for 3,167 yards, averaging 211 yards per game. Walker received two major national

honors for his high school athletic achievements. In 1979 he represented Georgia at the Hertz Number 1 Awards, which annually honor the best high school track-and-field athletes from each of the 50 states, and the following year Walker was named *Parade* magazine's national high school running back of the year.

When Walker set out for college in 1980, he was offered over 100 athletic scholarships. He finally chose to attend the University of Georgia, nearest his hometown of Wrightsville. Walker quickly brought himself and the Georgia football program into the national spotlight. In his first year, he set the NCAA freshman running record with a total of 1,616 yards, leading the Georgia Bulldogs to an undefeated season and the school's first-ever national football championship. In the Sugar Bowl, which Georgia won over Notre Dame, Walker played with a dislocated shoulder, yet managed to gain 150 yards and two touchdowns on his way to being named the bowl game's most valuable player. He was also third in the balloting for the Heisman Trophy, in which a freshman had never before finished in the top ten.

The following year Walker finished second in the Heisman

At a Glance. . .

Full name, Herschel Junior Walker; born March 3, 1962, in Augusta, GA; son of Willis and Christine (Taylor) Walker; married Cynthia De Angelis, March 31, 1983. *Education:* Attended University of Georgia, 1980-83.

Played professional football with the New Jersey Generals (United States Football League), 1983-86, with the Dallas Cowboys (National Football League), 1986-89, and with the Minnesota Vikings (National Football League), 1989—. Owner, Diversified Builders Inc., Athens, GA. Appears on video, *Hershel Walker's Fitness Challenge for Kids,* HPG Home Video, 1989.

Awards: Hertz Number 1 Award, 1979; named national high school back of the year by *Parade,* 1980; three-time All American football player at University of Georgia; Heisman Trophy as outstanding college football player in the United States, 1982; named most valuable player in the United States Football League, 1985.

balloting, while Georgia ended the season ranked number two in the nation. He finally won the Heisman his junior year—in a landslide—and was the nation's second leading ground rusher. He decided to forego his senior year of eligibility at Georgia and play professional football, capping off a collegiate career in which he set ten NCAA records, including the most yards gained by a rusher (5,259). In addition to his football accomplishments at Georgia, Walker was also a stand-out on the track team, and at one point was ranked in the top five nationally in the 60-yard dash.

In 1983 Walker signed a record $1.5 million annual contract with the New Jersey Generals of the USFL. His salary, under team owner Donald Trump, made him one of the highest-paid players in all of professional football. Walker continued to dominate the playing field in his first two years of professional football. With the Generals, he set the record for the highest single-season rushing record in professional football, running for 2,411 yards in 1985, and the same year was named the USFL's most valuable player.

The USFL folded in 1986, and Walker was signed by the Dallas Cowboys of the NFL for a reported five-year, $5 million contract. His performance with the Cowboys was one of the few bright spots in a series of otherwise disappointing seasons for the team. In 1986, while the Cowboys finished the regular season with 7 wins and 9 losses, Walker topped the team in receiving and finished a close second to fellow Cowboy Tony Dorsett in the rushing category. In 1987, which the Cowboys finished with 7 wins and 8 losses, Walker led the entire NFL in combined rushing and receiving, amassing a total of 1,606 yards.

Early into the 1989 season Walker was traded to the Minnesota Vikings, after the struggling Cowboys changed coaches and converted to a more pass-oriented offense which gave Walker less of an opportunity to play. Walker received a reported $1.2 million in the form of "exit money" in the deal, while he gained for the Cowboys a total of five players and rights to a number of draft choices. The Vikings, ready to utilize Walker's running talents, provided a good atmosphere for Walker. Carl Banks of the New York Giants commented in the *New York Times* on the change in Walker after he joined the Vikings: "He's a much-inspired runner now. Aside from his abilities, he has an offensive line that gives him a crack to get into the secondary. . . . With Dallas this year, just playing against him, you saw he was giving 100 percent, but things were not going as smoothly as in the past. You've got to have other guys doing things to have success as a runner. I think he has that element now."

Sources

Books

Carroll, Bob, Pete Palmer, and John Thorn, *The Football Abstract,* Warner Books, 1989.
Neft, David S., and Richard M. Cohen, *The Sports Encyclopedia: Pro Football,* 6th edition, St. Martin's, 1988.

Periodicals

Ebony, November 1987.
New York Times, October 13, 1989; October 29, 1989.
Sports Illustrated, October 23, 1989.

—*Michael E. Mueller*

Sippie Wallace

1898-1986

Blues singer, songwriter, pianist, organist

Sippie Wallace, "The Texas Nightingale," was one of the major blues artists of the 1920s, whose renown as a performer carried well into the 1980s. Wallace was respected as both a blues singer and songwriter. Jon Pareles in the *New York Times* described such original songs as "Mighty Tight Woman" and "Women Be Wise"—which found new audiences with younger music listeners in the 1970s—as "earthy and self-assertive blues songs." She is best remembered, however, as one of the foremost interpreters of the blues. Paul Oliver in *Jazz on Record* called Wallace "one of the major singers in the Classic blues idiom. . . . Possessing a mellow and tuneful voice, [she] had the qualities of shading and inflection in her singing that marked the classic blues artist."

One of Wallace's specialties was the "shout," a precursor to the modern blues, in which the singer often repeats two lines of a song, and improvises a third. Wallace, who frequently sang without a microphone, was influenced by blues great Ma Rainey, yet developed a style all her own. A contributor to *The New Grove Dictionary of Jazz* wrote: "In her earliest work she attempted to project a vocal weightiness similar to that of Ma Rainey. Later she sang in a manner better suited to the lighter, prettier qualities of her voice, which may be heard to advantage on [the album] *I'm a Mighty Tight Woman*. . . . Wallace composed most of her own songs, which are notable for the shapeliness and dignity of their melodies."

Wallace learned music in her father's Baptist church in Houston, Texas, where she played the organ and sang gospel music. (She was nicknamed "Sippie" because, as Pareles quoted her, "my teeth were so far apart and I had to sip everything.") Around 1910, she moved with her family to New Orleans, where Sippie's brother George W., Jr., a professional musician and composer, lived. The family later returned to Houston, and while she was in her late teens she began performing with traveling tent shows. Wallace learned blues and ragtime music in the shows, in addition to performing in chorus lines and acting in comedy skits. These experiences influenced her contributions as a blues artist. As LeRoi Jones commented in *Blues People: Negro Music in White America*, Wallace was of a line of distinguished performers who "brought a professionalism and theatrical polish to blues that it had never had before."

At a Glance...

Original name, Beulah Thomas; born November 1, 1898, in Houston, TX; died November 1, 1986, in Detroit, MI; daughter of George W., Sr. (a Baptist deacon) and Fanny Thomas; married Frank Seals, c. 1914 (marriage ended c. 1917); married Matt Wallace, c. 1917 (died, c. 1936). *Education:* Attended high school in Houston.

Performed with traveling tent shows, c. 1916-1920s; moved to Chicago, IL, 1923; recorded with Okeh Records, Chicago, 1923-27; moved to Detroit, MI, 1929; Leland Baptist Church, Detroit, organist and singer, 1929-1970s; National Convention of Gospel Choirs and Choruses, Chicago, director, beginning mid-1930s; played at folk and blues festivals in the United States and Europe, 1966-1980s.

In the 1920s, Wallace gained a national reputation as a recording artist, working with Okeh Records in Chicago. She recorded a number of solo albums, and also worked with other jazz greats, including Louis Armstrong and Sidney Bechet. She continued theatrical touring in the 1920s, and frequently worked with another brother, Hersal, himself a respected jazz pianist. In 1929 Wallace settled in Detroit, where she would live for the rest of her life. In the 1930s she became active again in gospel music, and played the organ and sang for the Leland Baptist Church. Wallace only occasionally recorded in the 1940s through early 1960s.

Wallace revived her blues career in the mid-1960s at the urging of fellow blues singer Victoria Spivey. In the autumn of 1966 Wallace traveled to Europe with the American Folk Blues Festival, and throughout the rest of the 1960s frequently performed at various blues and jazz festivals in the United States. "Visiting Europe in 1966,... Wallace astonished by the breadth of her singing and a delivery recalling Bessie Smith," noted Oliver. The same year, her album *Sippie Wallace Sings the Blues* likewise demonstrated she still had her touch. A contributor to *The New Grove Dictionary of Jazz* remarked: "The importance of the present disc . . . is that she can still sing these blues. . . . Her wide range of material and masterful reinterpretations are clearly shown in the efforts 'I'm a Mighty Tight Woman,' 'Shorty George Blues,' and 'Special Delivery Blues.'"

Singer and guitarist Bonnie Raitt broadened interest in Wallace's music by featuring two of the blueswoman's songs on Raitt's 1971 debut album. Wallace toured and recorded with Raitt in the 1970s and 1980s, while continuing to perform on her own. In 1980 Wallace was featured at New York City's Avery Fisher Hall in a salute to prominent blueswomen. *New York Times Magazine* contributor Ariel Swartley said that Wallace, the show's oldest participant at 81, offered "her own, still-fresh remedies for heart ache." Swartley commented on Wallace's popularity with a new generation of music lovers. "It's one of the program's bittersweet ironies that, of all the performers, it's probably the aging Sippie Wallace who's best known to audiences under 30. . . . And yet it shouldn't be surprising that a young audience appreciated her—the blues, after all, is the root of both jazz and rock and roll."

Selected discography

(With C. Williams) *Caldonia Blues,* Okeh, 1924.
Special Delivery Blues, Okeh, 1926.
The Flood Blues, Okeh, 1927.
I'm a Mighty Tight Woman, Victor, 1929.
Bedroom Blues, Mercury, 1945.
(With L. B. Montgomery and R. Sykes) *Sippie Wallace Sings the Blues,* Storyville, 1966.
Sippie, Atlantic, 1982.

Sources

Books

Harris, Sheldon, *Blues Who's Who,* Arlington House, 1979.
Jones, LeRoi, *Blues People: Negro Music in White America,* Morrow, 1963.
Kernfeld, Barry, editor, *The New Grove Dictionary of Jazz,* Macmillan, 1988.
McCarthy, Albert, Alun Morgan, Paul Oliver, and Max Harrison, *Jazz on Record: A Critical Guide to the First 50 Years, 1917-1967,* Hanover Books, 1968.

Periodicals

New York Times, November 4, 1986.
New York Times Magazine, June 29, 1980.

—*Michael E. Mueller*

Denzel Washington

1954—

Actor

Denzel Washington describes himself as "that minority among minorities—a working black actor." Indeed, in an era that offers few opportunities for black men—especially in feature films—Washington has forged a solid career with a string of highly-regarded performances. *Chicago Tribune* correspondent Hilary de Vries wrote: "From his smoldering Private Peterson in *A Soldier's Story* to the coolly understated Steve Biko in *Cry Freedom* to the defiant Civil War infantryman Trip in *Glory,* Washington creates morally complex characters shaded by wit, intelligence and barely concealed anger." The critic added that Washington "is riding a series of cinematic successes that are not only buoying his own career but also helping shape the role of black Americans in Hollywood."

An actor blessed with good looks and a wide range of talent, Washington has chosen his roles with care. *Washington Post* contributor Donna Britt noted: "It's ironic that this man whose race almost certainly has diminished his opportunities as an actor has used his career to explore his blackness." Washington admits that he has felt stifled by the "role model" and "torch bearer" tags by which critics identify him, but at the same time he is a dedicated artist seeking to make an impression. "All I can do is play the part," he told the *Washington Post*. "I can't do [a] part for 40 million black people, or orange or green. On the other hand I'm not going to do anything to embarrass my people."

Denzel Washington was born late in 1954, the son of a Pentecostal minister and a gospel singer. He grew up right on the edge of the Bronx, in the middle class neighborhood of Mt. Vernon, New York. "My father was down on the movies, and his idea of something worthwhile would be *The King of Kings, The Ten Commandments* and *101 Dalmatians,"* the actor told the *Chicago Tribune*. "And I knew no actors. It's a wonder I ever went into acting." Washington was a good student as a youth, and he drew his friends from the melting pot of races that formed the Bronx. He described his childhood as "a good background for somebody in my business. My friends were West Indians, blacks, Irish, Italians, so I learned a lot of different cultures."

When Washington was 14, his parents divorced. The subject is still sensitive for him, although he remains on cordial terms with both his mother and his father. "I

At a Glance. . .

Born December, 1954, in Mt. Vernon, NY; son of a pentecostal minister and a beautician; married Pauletta Pearson (an actress), c. 1983; children: John David, Katia. *Education:* Fordham University, B.A., ca. 1981.

Actor in motion pictures, stage plays, and television dramas, 1981—. Selected television appearances include *Flesh and Blood, St. Elsewhere* (as Dr. Phillip Chandler), c. 1982-87; *Licence To Kill,* and *Wilma.* Selected stage appearances include *A Soldier's Play, Richard III, Othello, The Emperor Jones, Ceremonies in Dark Old Men,* and *When the Chickens Come Home To Roost.* Selected film appearances include *Carbon Copy, A Soldier's Story, Cry Freedom, Power, The Mighty Quinn, For Queen and Country, Glory, Mo' Better Blues,* and *Heart Condition.*

Awards: Obie Award for best performance in an Off-Broadway play, for *A Soldier's Play.* Academy Award nomination for best supporting actor, 1989, for *Cry Freedom;* Academy Award for best supporting actor, 1990, for *Glory.*

ism, and took an acting workshop "but underwent no great revelation." During the summer recess, however, he served as a counselor at a YMCA-sponsored camp. "I had grown up in the organization and had worked as a leader," he told the *Chicago Tribune.* "I organized a talent show, and someone told me, 'You seem real natural on the stage; did you ever think of becoming an actor?' Bing! That's all it took." When he returned to Fordham in the fall, he auditioned for the university's production of Eugene O'Neill's *The Emperor Jones,* and won the part over a number of theater majors. He went on to star in several more dramas at Fordham, including Shakespeare's *Othello.*

Robinson Stone, a retired actor, was Washington's drama instructor at Fordham. Remembering his gifted student, Stone told the *Chicago Tribune:* "Oh, God, he was thrilling even then. Denzel was from the Bronx campus—not even a theater major—and he got the lead in the school production of *Othello.* He was easily the best Othello I had ever seen, and I had seen Paul Robeson play it. I remember Jose Ferrer came to look at it. He and I agreed that Denzel had a brilliant career ahead of him. He played Othello with so much majesty and beauty but also rage and hate that I dragged agents to come and see it."

Cast in Television's *St. Elsewhere* Series

The agents too were impressed. Even before Washington graduated from Fordham he was offered a small role in a television drama, *Wilma,* based on the life of runner Wilma Rudolph. After he earned his degree, Washington embarked on a hectic round of professional activities, including theater work, television, and films. Early in his career he appeared opposite George Segal in *Carbon Copy,* a comic movie, and he also took a role in the television mini-series *Flesh and Blood.* These parts introduced Washington to the Hollywood production companies, and he was cast as doctor Phillip Chandler in the television drama *St. Elsewhere.* Although he was not nearly as demanding about his *St. Elsewhere* character as he has since become, Washington was nevertheless able to infuse the role with non-stereotyped humanity. *Washington Post* writer Megan Rosenfeld concluded that the actor's five-year association with *St. Elsewhere* gained him "the kind of popular recognition that is both the boon and the curse of serious actors. Chandler is an intelligent and ambitious young man, portrayed not as a black paragon, but as a human being with all the flaws and problems of anyone else."

It was a stage role that assured Washington's success, however. Early in the 1980s he was cast in the pivotal role of Private Peterson in the drama *A Soldier's Play.*

guess it made me angry," he told the *Washington Post.* "I went through a phase where I got into a lot of fights. Working it out, you know." A guidance counselor at his high school suggested that Washington apply to a private boarding school ("very rich and very white") in upstate New York. He did, and to his astonishment was accepted with a full scholarship. After graduating from that academy, he attended Fordham University in the Bronx, where he declared a pre-med major. In retrospect, Washington attributes his strong showing as a youngster to his mother's influence. "She was very, very tough, a tough disciplinarian," he told the *Washington Post.* "Even when I was 15 or 16, I had to be home by the time the street lights went on. She saw to it I was exposed to a lot of things. She couldn't afford it, but she was very intelligent. She is basically responsible for my success."

Decided on Acting Career

A longstanding membership in the YMCA also contributed to Washington's career choice. In college he drifted through several majors, including biology and journal-

The part won Washington an Obie Award for his Off-Broadway performance, and he was invited to work as Peterson in the film version of the play. Washington took a break from *St. Elsewhere* to undertake the film role, and he was quite pleased when *A Soldier's Story* earned the respect of film critics worldwide. In *A Soldier's Story,* Washington turned in a memorable performance as the young private goaded to murder by an abusive drill sergeant. After viewing *A Soldier's Story, Chicago Tribune* correspondent Bob Thomas called Washington "one of the most versatile of the new acting generation."

The Hollywood establishment recognized that Denzel Washington possessed a near phenomenal potential. He was at once handsome, articulate, and dignified, and he appeared to be at ease in both comic and dramatic situations. Inevitably (and unfortunately), his race still restricted the number and size of roles he was offered. Even after he appeared in the Oscar-nominated role of activist Steve Biko in *Cry Freedom,* he was still not considered a high-visibility star. As late as 1989 the actor told the *Washington Post* that he often found himself "waiting for an opportunity to come [my] way but realizing there's no group of people like [me] who are successful, who can give you the faith to say, 'Well, if I wait, it will come.' So you end up taking [roles] . . . that are not necessarily the best, that aren't optimum."

Insisted That the Script for *Glory* be Revised

One of the roles Washington did not consider "optimum" was that of the runaway slave Trip in the film *Glory.* The original script for *Glory* concentrated on the Civil War general, Robert Gould Shaw, who led the first black regiment into battle and died with them in an unsuccessful assault. At Washington's suggestion, the screenplay for *Glory* was significantly revised in order to explore the concerns of the black foot soldiers. Satisfied with the revisions, Washington accepted the part of Trip. He studied histories of the Civil War and of slavery in the South, learning enough to assure that both he and his character would be in a fit of controlled rage. "When we were making *Glory,*" he told the *Chicago Tribune,* "people kept asking me, 'Why are you so angry?' I haven't been through anything like [slavery and soldiering], but I've read about it. I've studied the history, and that's enough to make you angry. How can I be 35 and never been taught about black soldiers being a part of the Civil War. That's something to ask: How can that happen?"

Washington's performance in *Glory* earned him an Academy Award for best supporting actor in 1990. It was his second nomination, but more importantly, it was only the fifth Oscar ever won by a black actor. Since he won the prestigious award, Washington has finally been able to secure leading-man roles, both in dramas such as *For Queen and Country* and Spike Lee's *Mo' Better Blues* and in comedies such as *Heart Condition.* The actor is also planning to star in a major film about the slain activist Malcolm X. *Detroit Free Press* movie critic Kathy Huffhines observed that Washington has "the knife's-edge intensity that makes quick, deep impressions. Usually, actors begin with comic, romantic or action roles, then move toward seriousness. Washington is taking that trip in reverse, keeping serious roles while trying to move toward romance, action and comedy."

The question remains: is Hollywood ready for a romantic leading man who happens to be black? Like Sidney Poitier—to whom he is often compared—Washington may find that producers shy away from offering him certain romantic roles. His work in love stories to date is sparse, consisting mainly of *Mo' Better Blues,* but as a dynamic and riveting actor he should win more such work. If he does, he may indeed become a ground-

> "Denzel is magnetic, he's a great actor, and women love him. Women love them some Denzel."
>
> —*Spike Lee*

breaking star who could pave the way for black opportunity in Hollywood. "Denzel is magnetic, he's a great actor, and women love him," Spike Lee told the *Detroit Free Press.* "Women love them some Denzel."

Washington is not particularly forthcoming about his private life, but his family is very important to him. In his rare moments of leisure he stays home, avoiding the celebrated Hollywood party circuit. In the *Washington Post,* the actor called his wife and two children "the base that keeps me solid." He added: "Acting is just a way of making a living. Family is life. When you experience a child, you know that's life." The actor is careful to keep a humble perspective on the praise he has received, and he completely refuses to consider himself "sexy" despite persistent claims in the press. Acting, he said, is a way for him to explore the spiritual self, irrespective of race or creed. "I enjoy acting," he told the *Washington Post.* "This is when I feel most natural. This is really my world. I was obviously destined to get into this, and I guess I have the equipment to do it."

Sources

Boston Globe, February 1, 1990.
Chicago Tribune, March 15, 1986; December 30, 1987;
   August 5, 1990.
Detroit Free Press, July 29, 1990.
Washington Post, September 18, 1985; August 25, 1989.

—*Mark Kram*

Bill White

1933(?)-

Baseball executive

Bill White, the president of baseball's National League, is the highest-ranking black executive in all of professional sports. History was made on April 1, 1989 when White assumed his duties in the offices of the National League. He will earn some $250,000 per year in a demanding administrative position that requires resolution, judgment, and a thorough grounding in the game of baseball. As Rich Ashburn put it in the *Philadelphia Daily News,* "The National League should be in pretty good hands. . . . Bill White is intelligent, articulate, firm and fair. And he's determined."

Although blacks are well represented on teams in virtually every American sport, they are rare indeed in managerial and executive positions. White does not see his appointment as a means to correct that imbalance. Both he and the baseball team owners who chose him agree that his experience, his maturity, and his love of the game make him ideally suited for the job. Peter O'Malley, chairman of the search committee and owner of the Los Angeles Dodgers, remarked to the *New York Times:* "Bill White was selected because he was the best man for the job. He was the only man who was offered the job and, fortunately, he was the only man who accepted. Race was not a factor."

For his own part, White had this to say about his new position. "I've been in the game since 1952," he told the *Boston Globe.* "It wasn't integrated. When I came into baseball, spring training wasn't integrated. The country wasn't integrated. I think we've both come along. I'm here now, and there have been quite a few improvements in hiring at certain levels. I feel that will continue, and the people here feel the same way. . . . I've told people the most important thing that has happened in baseball history was Jackie Robinson getting a chance to play. It gave a lot of people before who had no hope a lot of hope. I'm glad for the opportunity, and I will do the best that I can. If I didn't think I could do this job, I'd be foolish to take it."

White earned a reputation as an outspoken player almost from the moment he signed with his first major league team. Perhaps because he came to professional baseball after several years in college, he was quicker to address injustices than others, and more forceful in demanding that changes be made. As *New York Times* correspondent Claire Smith wrote: "Bill White has long

At a Glance. . .

Full name, William DeKova White; born in Lakewood, FL, c. 1933; divorced; five children. *Education:* Attended Hiram College.

Professional baseball player, 1956-69; joined the New York Giants, 1956, moved to the St. Louis Cardinals, 1959, traded to the Philadelphia Phillies, 1965, and returned to the Cardinals for final season, 1969. Play-by-play broadcaster, 1970-89; began in St. Louis and Philadelphia, moved to New York Yankees televised games, 1971. President of the National League, 1989—.

Awards: Named to National League All-Star team six times; awarded Gold Glove for first base seven times.

prided himself on being a person who cannot be easily fitted into any mold. In the early 1960's, when it was safer for one's career as well as health to acquiesce quietly to the nation's Jim Crow laws, White was among a vocal minority of black players who spoke out vociferously against inadequacies at Florida spring-training sites and in minor league cities throughout the South." White originally agreed to play baseball with the New York Giants merely as a means to earn college tuition (he was enrolled in pre-med courses). He made the Giants' roster in 1956, however, and moved with the team to San Francisco, embarking on a fine 13-year career.

White hit twenty-two home runs as a rookie with the Giants. In 1959 he was traded to the St. Louis Cardinals, where he batted .286 and played first base. The beginning of the 1965 season found White with the Philadelphia Phillies, where he played until the end of 1968. For his last season he returned to the Cardinals, performing well despite severe injuries to his Achilles tendon. His career statistics are far above the average for a sport that uses players like fodder: in 1,673 games he had 5,972 at bats, with 1,706 hits, 202 home runs, and 870 runs batted in. Six times he was named to the National League All-Star team, and seven times he brought home the Gold Glove for first base.

After retiring from baseball, White found work as a radio and television announcer in St. Louis and then in Philadelphia. Howard Cosell happened to catch White doing play-by-play for a college basketball game and recommended him to the New York Yankees. In 1971 White entered the broadcast booth with Phil Rizzuto and began

an 18-year tenure as the Yankees' play-by-play man for televised games. White carried his strong opinions on affirmative action with him into the booth, but he resisted using his power to become a spokesman for special interest groups. Instead he concentrated on baseball and became immensely popular with the hard-to-please Yankee fans.

White never made any bones about it: he loved being an announcer for the Yankees. The job paid a princely salary of $300,000 per year for about 60 days' work each summer, allowing him to purchase a stately home in Bucks County, Pennsylvania, for his family of five children. In 1989, White told the *Philadelphia Daily News:* "The Yankees took a trip to the West Coast last summer. I worked a game in Seattle and then I flew to Alaska and fished for five days. I flew back to Oakland for a game and then fished another four days in northern California. That's the kind of thing I'm going to miss."

His years of experience with baseball notwithstanding, White was surprised when he was approached about taking the presidency of the National League. White told the *New York Times:* "My first comment was, 'Are you serious?' But in meeting with people, I found out they were dead serious. Once I knew that, we proceeded from there." White was the unanimous choice of the National League team owners to succeed A. Bartlett Giamatti, who was named Baseball Commissioner. As president of the league, White must arbitrate disputes between players and umpires and supervise contracts for the league's professional players. He must determine the rules under which the teams will play—including the controversial Designated Hitter regulation. Most importantly, he will preside over a major expansion of major league teams, expected to bring baseball into a number of new American cities. As Larry Whiteside put it in the *Boston Globe:* "[White's] been on the baseball scene for more than 30 years, but what [he] is sure to face is a plethora of duties, responsibilities and issues he never came across as a player or broadcaster. He's been outside the closed door; now he'll be inside."

No doubt the issue of race will continue to dog White, despite his evident qualifications for the position. White's appointment came at a moment in the history of sports—especially baseball—when insiders were openly lamenting the lack of black leadership. White became baseball's first black leader, and that issue is just another that he must address. White told the *Boston Globe:* "My goal is to be the best president I can be. I hope that in the opinion of the committee, I met those qualifications. I know my hiring will be symbolic and important to some people. To me, it's getting on with my life and doing something that I enjoy."

Some two years into his four-year contract now, White

has surprised some people with his style of management. For the most part he has shunned the media and has indeed conducted his business behind that "closed door" where management decisions are made. The consensus on White among the owners who hired him is quite positive, however—such executives as Phillies owner Bill Giles and Mets co-owner Fred Wilpon laud White for his integrity, his honesty, and his independent agenda. White himself told the *New York Times:* "[Those owners] could get a black man they could control or they could get a black man who's been around this game as long, if not longer than they have. I think that's what they got. What they didn't get was a puppet. And they know my reputation, so it's to their credit that they did not just bring in someone who would just fill the position in name only." White added: "I'm not close to anyone in baseball, period. I'm independent, you could say. By choice."

Sources

Boston Globe, February 4, 1989; February 13, 1989.
Philadelphia Daily News, February 16, 1989.
Philadelphia Inquirer, February 4, 1989.
New York Times, February 4, 1989; February 5, 1989; September 17, 1990.
Washington Post, February 4, 1989.

—Mark Kram

Malcolm X

1925-1965

Human rights activist

"When I talk about my father," said Attallah Shabazz to *Rolling Stone*. "I do my best to make Malcolm human. I don't want these kids to keep him on the pedestal, I don't want them to feel his goals are unattainable. I'll remind them that at their age he was doing time." The powerful messages of Malcolm X, his dramatic life, and his tragic assassination conspire to make him an unreachable hero. Events in the 1960s provided four hero-martyrs of this kind for Americans: John F. Kennedy, Robert F. Kennedy, Rev. Martin Luther King, Jr., and Malcolm X. These idealistic men believed in the possibilities for social change, the necessity of that change, and the truth of his vision of change.

Of the four, Malcolm came from the humblest roots, was the most radical, most outspoken, and angriest—"All Negroes are angry, and I am the angriest of all," he often would say. The powerful speaker gathered huge crowds around him when he was associated with Elijah Muhammad's Lost-Found Nation of Islam movement, and afterwards with Malcolm X's own organization. Many Americans, white and black, were afraid of the violent side of Malcolm X's rhetoric—unlike Rev. Martin Luther King, Jr.'s, doctrine of non-violent resistance, Malcolm X believed in self-defense.

But Malcolm X cannot be summed up in a few convenient phrases, because during his life he went through distinct changes in his philosophies and convictions. He had three names: Malcolm Little, Malcolm X, and El-Hajj Malik El-Shabazz. Each name has its own history and illuminates a different facet of the man who remains one of the most compelling Americans of the 20th century.

Malcolm X's father was a Baptist minister and a member of the United Negro Improvement Association. Founded by Marcus Garvey, the group believed that there could be no peace for blacks in America, and that each black person should return to their African nation to lead a natural and serene life. In a parallel belief, Nation of Islam supporters in Malcolm X's time held that a section of the United States secede and become a nation onto itself for disenfranchised blacks. It seems possible that Malcolm X was predisposed to the separatist ideas of the Nation of Islam partly because of this early exposure to Marcus Garvey.

Malcolm X described in his autobiography (written with Alex Haley) the harassment of his father, including terrifying visits from the Ku Klux Klan; one of Malcolm X's first memories is of his home in Omaha burning down. The family moved to Lansing, Michigan, in 1929 and there Malcolm X's memories were of his father's rousing sermons and the beatings the minister gave his wife and children. Malcolm X believed his father to be a victim of brainwashing by white people, who infected blacks with self-hatred—therefore he would pass down a form of the abuse he received as a black man.

The minister was killed in 1931, his body almost severed in two by a streetcar and the side of his head smashed. In the autobiography, Malcolm X elaborated, saying that there were many rumors in Lansing that his father had been killed by the Klan or its ilk because of his preachings, and that he had been laid on the streetcar tracks to make his death appear accidental. After his father was killed, the state welfare representatives began to frequent the house, and it seemed to Malcolm X that they were harassing his mother. Terribly stricken by her husband's death and buckling under the demands of raising many children, Louise Little became psychologically unstable and was institutionalized until 1963.

Trouble With the Law

After his mother was committed, Malcolm X began what was to be one of the most publicized phases of his life. His brothers and sisters were separated, and while living with several foster families, Malcolm began to learn to steal. In his autobiography, he used his own young adulthood to illustrate larger ideas about the racist climate in the United States. In high school, Malcolm began to fight what would be a lifelong battle of personal ambition versus general racist preconception. An English teacher discouraged Malcolm X's desire to become a lawyer, telling him to be "realistic," and that he should think about working with his hands.

Lansing did not hold many opportunities of *any* kind for a young black man then, so without a particular plan, Malcolm X went to live with his half-sister, Ella, in Boston. Ella encouraged him to look around the city and get a feel for it before trying to land a job. Malcolm X looked, and almost immediately found trouble. He fell in with a group of gamblers and thieves, and began shining shoes at the Roseland State Ballroom. There he learned the trades that would eventually take him to jail—dealing in bootleg liquor and illegal drugs. Malcolm X characterized his life then as one completely lacking in self-respect. Although his methods grew more sophisticated over time, it was only a matter of four years or so before he was imprisoned in 1946, sentenced to ten years on burglary charges.

Many journalists would emphasize Malcolm X's "shady" past when describing the older man, his clean-cut lifestyle, and the aims of the Nation of Islam. In some cases, these references were an attempt to damage Malcolm X's credibility, but economically disadvantaged people have found his early years to be a point of commonality, and Malcolm X himself was proud of how far he had come. He spared no detail of his youth in his autobiography, and used his Nation of Islam (sometimes called Black Islam) ideas to interpret them. Dancing, drinking, and even his hair style were represented by Malcolm X to be marks of shame and self-hatred.

Relaxed hair in particular was an anathema to Malcolm X for the rest of his life; he described his first "conk" in the autobiography this way: "This was my first really big step toward self-degradation: when I endured all of that pain [of the hair-straightening chemicals], literally burning my flesh to have it look like a white man's hair. I had joined that multitude of Negro men and women in America who are brainwashed into believing that the black people are 'inferior'—and white people 'superior'—that they will even violate and mutilate their God-created bodies to try to look 'pretty' by white standards. . . . It makes you wonder if the Negro has completely lost his sense of identity, lost touch with himself."

Discovered Islam

It was while Malcolm X was in prison that he was introduced to the ideas of Elijah Muhammad and the

Nation of Islam. Fundamentally, the group believes in the racial superiority of blacks, a belief supported by a complex genesis fable, which includes an envious, evil white scientist who put a curse on blacks. The faith became a focus for Malcolm X's fury about his treatment (and his family's) at the hands of whites, about the lack of opportunity he had as a young black man, and the psychological damage of systematic anti-black racism—that is, the damage of self-hatred.

Malcolm X read "everything he could get his hands on" in the prison library. He interpreted history books with the newly-learned tenets of Elijah Muhammad, and told of his realizations in a *Playboy* interview with Alex Haley. "I found out that the history-whitening process either had left out great things that black men had done, or the great black men had gotten whitened." He improved his penmanship by copying out a dictionary, and participated in debates in jail, preaching independently to the prisoners about the Nation of Islam's theories about "the white devil." The group also emphasizes scrupulous personal habits, including cleanliness and perfect groom-ing, and forbids smoking, drinking, and the eating of pork, as well as other traditional Muslim dietary restrictions.

Began Ministry

When Malcolm X left prison in 1952, he went to work for Elijah Muhammad, and within a year was named assist-ant minister to Muslim Temple Number One in Detroit, Michigan. It was then that he took the surname "X" and dropped his "slave name" of Little—the X stands for the African tribe of his origin that he could never know. The Nation of Islam's leadership was so impressed by his tireless efforts and his fiery speeches that they sent him to start a new temple in Boston, which he did, then repeat-ed his success in Philadelphia by 1954.

Malcolm X's faith was inextricably linked to his worship of Elijah Muhammad. Everything Malcolm X accom-plished (he said) was accomplished through Elijah Mu-hammad. In his autobiography, he recalled a speech

Malcolm X (right) meets with Dr. Martin Luther King, Jr.

which described his devotion: "I have sat at our Messenger's feet, hearing the truth from his own mouth, I have pledged on my knees to Allah to tell the white man about his crimes and the black man the true teachings of our Honorable Elijah Muhammad. I don't care if it costs my life." His devotion would be sorely tested, then destroyed within nine years.

Differences With Rev. King

During those nine years, Malcolm X was made a national minister—he became the voice of the Nation of Islam. He was a speechwriter, an inspired speaker, a pundit often quoted in the news, and he became a philosopher. Malcolm used the teachings of the Nation of Islam to inform blacks about the cultures that had been stripped from them and the self-hatred that whites had inspired, then he would point the way toward a better life. While Rev. Martin Luther King, Jr., was teaching blacks to fight racism with love, Malcolm X was telling blacks to understand their exploitation, to fight back when attacked, and to seize self-determination "by any means necessary." Malcolm spoke publicly of his lack of respect for King, who would, through a white man's religion, tell blacks to not fight back.

In his later years, though, Malcolm X thought that he and King perhaps did have the same goals and that a truce was possible. While Malcolm X was in the process of questioning the Nation of Islam's ideals, his beliefs were in a creative flux. He began to visualize a new Islamic group which "would embrace all faiths of black men, and it would carry into practice what the Nation of Islam had only preached." His new visions laid the groundwork for a break from the Black Muslims.

In 1963 a conflict between Malcolm X and Elijah Muhammad made headlines. When President John F. Kennedy was assassinated, Malcolm said that it was a case of "chickens coming home to roost." *Rolling Stone* reported that many people believed Malcolm X had declared the president deserving of his fate, when he really "meant the country's climate of hate had killed the president." Muhammad suspended Malcolm X for ninety days "so that Muslims everywhere can be disassociated from the blunder," according to the autobiography.

Became Disillusioned With Nation of Islam

Muhammad had been the judge and jury for the Nation of Islam, and had sentenced many other Black Muslims to terms of silence, or excommunication, for adultery or other infractions of their religious code. Malcolm X discovered that Muhammad himself was guilty of adultery, and was appalled by his idol's hypocrisy. It widened the gulf between them. Other ministers were vying for the kind of power and attention that Malcolm X had, and some speculate that these men filled Elijah Muhammad's ears with ungenerous speculations about Malcolm X's ambitions. "I hadn't hustled in the streets for years for nothing. I knew when I was being set up," Malcolm X said of that difficult time. He believed that he would be indefinitely silenced and that a Nation of Islam member would be convinced to assassinate him. Before that would come to pass, Malcolm X underwent another period of transformation, during which he would take on his third name, El-Hajj Malik El-Shabazz.

A "hajj" is a pilgrimage to the holy land of Mecca, Saudi Arabia, the birthplace of the Prophet Muhammad; "Malik" was similar to Malcolm, and "Shabazz," a family name. On March 8, 1964, Malcolm X had announced that he was leaving the Nation of Islam to form his own groups, Muslim Mosque, Inc., and the Organization of Afro-American Unity. In an effort to express his dedication to Islam, and thereby establish a more educated religious underpinning for his new organization, Malcolm X declared he would make a hajj. His travels were enlarged to include a tour of Middle Eastern and African countries, including Egypt, Lebanon, Nigeria, and Ghana.

These expeditions would expand Malcolm X in ways that would have seemed incredible to him earlier. He encountered fellow Muslims who were caucasian and embraced him as a brother, he was accepted into the traditional Islamic religion, and he was lauded as a fighter for the rights of American blacks. "Packed in the plane [to Jedda] were white, black, brown, red, and yellow people, blue eyes and blond hair, and my kinky red hair—all together, brothers! All honoring the same God Allah, all in turn giving equal honor to the other." As a result of his experiences, Malcolm X gained a burgeoning understanding of a global unity and sympathy that stood behind America's blacks—less isolated and more reinforced, he revised his formerly separatist notions.

Returned to U.S.

Still full of resolve, Malcolm X returned to the States with a new message. He felt that American blacks should go to the United Nations and demand their rights, not beg for them. When faced with a bevy of reporters upon his return, he told them, "The true Islam has shown me that a blanket indictment of all white people is as wrong as when whites make blanket indictments against blacks." His new international awareness was evident in statements such as: "The white man's racism toward the black man here in America has got him in such trouble all over the world, with other nonwhite peoples."

This new message, full of renewed vigor and an enlarged vision, plus the fact that the media was still listening to Malcolm X, was not well-received by the Nation of Islam. Malcolm X was aware that he was being followed by Black Muslims, and regularly received death threats. His home was firebombed on February 14, 1965—his wife and four daughters were unharmed, but the house was destroyed, and the family had not been insured against fire. It was believed that the attack came from the Nation of Islam. A week later, Malcolm X, his wife (pregnant with twin girls), and four daughters went to the Audubon Ballroom in Harlem, New York, where he would speak for the last time. A few minutes into his message, three men stood and fired sixteen shots into Malcolm X, who died before medical help could arrive. The three were arrested immediately, and were later identified as members of the Nation of Islam.

Malcolm X gave African-Americans something no one else ever had—a sense that the race has a right to feel anger and express the power of it, to challenge white domination, and to actively demand change. Politically sophisticated, Malcolm X told everyone who would listen about the tenacious and pervasive restraints that centuries of racism had imposed on American blacks. His intelligence and humility was such that he was not afraid to revise his ideas, and he held up the example of his transformations for all to see and learn from.

Although Malcolm X's own organizations were unsteady at the time of his death, the posthumous publication of his autobiography insures that his new and old philosophies will never be forgotten. In 1990, twenty-five years after his assassination, Malcolm X and his ideas were still a huge component in the ongoing debate about race relations. Plays and movies focus on him, new biographies are written, and several colleges and societies survive him. "Malcolm's maxims on self-respect, self-reliance and economic empowerment seem acutely prescient," said *Newsweek* in 1990. The words of Malcolm X and the example of his life still urge Americans to fight racism in all of its forms.

Selected writings

(With Alex Haley) *The Autobiography of Malcolm X,* intro-duction by M.S. Handler, epilogue by Ossie Daivs, Ballantine Books, 1964.

Malcolm Speaks: Selected Speeches and Statements, edited with prefatory notes by George Breitman, Merit Publishers, 1965.

The Speeches of Malcolm X at Harvard, edited and with an introductory essay by Archie Epps, Owen, 1969.

Malcolm X Talks to Young People, Young Socialist Alliance, 1969.

Malcolm X and the Negro Revolution: The Speeches of Malcolm X, edited and with an introductory essay by Archie Epps, Owen, 1969.

Two Speeches by Malcolm X, Merit Publishers, 1969.

By Any Means Necessary: Speeches, Interviews, and a Letter by Malcolm X, edited by George Breitman, Pathfinder Press, 1970.

The End of White World Supremacy: Four Speeches, edited and with an introduction by Benjamin Goodman, Merlin House, 1971.

Work represented in anthologies, including *100 and More Ouotes by Garvey, Lumumba, and Malcolm X,* compiled by Shawna Maglangbayan, Third World Press, 1975.

Sources

Books

(With Alex Haley) *The Autobiography of Malcolm X,* intro-duction by M.S. Handler, epilogue by Ossie Daivs, Ballantine Books, 1964.

McGraw-Hill Encyclopedia of World Biography, McGraw-Hill Book Company, 1973.

Political Profiles: The Johnson Years, edited by Nelson Lichtenstein, Facts on File, 1976.

Political Profiles: The Kennedy Years, edited by Lichtenstein, Facts on File, 1976.

Periodicals

Newsweek, February 26, 1990.
Playboy, January 1989.
Rolling Stone, November 30, 1989.

—Christine Ferran

Coleman Young

1918-

Mayor of Detroit

The feisty and colorful Coleman Alexander Young is now serving an unprecedented fifth term as mayor of the city of Detroit. Not one to shy from unpleasant tasks, Young presides over an urban area beset with problems, from rampant crime to high unemployment to ever-dwindling population. He is an outspoken and opinionated man whose strongly-worded views have earned him both passionate supporters and bitter enemies, both in his city and nationwide.

Opinions aside, however, few would argue with a *Detroit Free Press* editorial in which Young was characterized as "a successful mayor and a consummate politician who has put what's good for Detroit—or, more exactly, what Coleman Young thinks is good for Detroit—above all else."

During 1990 both Detroit and its mayor were targets of highly critical feature stories in the *New York Times* and on national television. Much has been written about Detroit's sagging economy and brutal crime statistics, its "white flight" to the suburbs and its general air of despair. Young does not see his city in that light. Under his administration, the city has managed to balance its budget despite a dramatic cutback in federal and state

aid. A number of its neighborhoods have undergone renovation, and at least one new automobile manufacturing plant has opened within the city limits. As Frank Washington put it in *Newsweek,* "any other incumbent mayor could ride comfortably into re-election on [Young's] record."

Young defended his agenda in the *Detroit Free Press:* "Today, the big debate is whether the country's heading into another damned depression—the truth of the matter is, Detroit never came out of depression. Since I've been mayor, our unemployment level has been twice the national average. That is why we need to take radical steps to preserve this city—but this city is worth preserving. It has all the natural assets that it needs to make it: its geographical location, the strength of character of its people. . . . You pool all these people who have a heritage of struggle and you have a powerful force. This city will not be overcome."

Coleman Young is certainly a Detroiter with a "heritage of struggle." He was born in Tuscaloosa, Alabama and spent most of his early years in Huntsville, where his family was sometimes terrorized by the Ku Klux Klan.

Like many black Americans, Young's father eventually moved the family north, to Detroit, in search of a more congenial environment and better economic opportunity. Young's family settled in the Black Bottom section of Detroit in the late 1920s, and his father opened a small dry cleaning business. In an interview with the *Cleveland Plain Dealer,* Young remembered that his old neighborhood "was a cohesive community, a mixture of working-[and] middle-class people. In many ways it was more secure and comfortable than today's communities."

Young is almost silent on his private life, his early years included. An aide, Joyce Garrett, told the *Detroit Free Press* that the mayor had a difficult childhood that accounts for his solitary character today. "The mayor never grew up in what we would call a normal, middle-class family situation," Garrett said; "that has made quite a difference in that he doesn't care about home, really." Despite excellent grades in public school, Young was denied financial aid to the University of Michigan due to his race. Unable to attend college, he was forced to go to work to help support his four brothers and sisters. In the late 1930s he enrolled in an apprentice electrician program at the Ford Motor Company. He finished first in the program but was passed over for the only available electrician job in favor of a white candidate.

Lobbied for Equal Treatment

In the early 1940s Young took a job on the Ford Assembly line and became an underground union organizer and civil rights activist. Within his first few months on the job he became the target for racial slurs by "company goons," leading eventually to a fistfight that caused him to be fired. He continued his union activities when he earned a position with the post office, and by the time he was drafted to the Second World War he was well known in Detroit for demanding equal employment and fair treatment for blacks in the automobile industry. During the war Young served with the Tuskegee Airmen, an elite black flying unit. He became a second lieutenant and flew missions as a bombardier-navigator. Near the end of the war he was one of several black officers who were arrested and jailed for demanding service at a segregated officers' club. The incident generated a great deal of publicity, and the Army eventually integrated the club.

Young returned to Detroit after the war and drifted from job to job for nearly a decade. His principal interest during the 1950s was union organizing, and he also campaigned for the Progressive Party. During that decade he also founded the National Negro Labor Council, an organization devoted to civil rights in the workplace. Young's projects on behalf of black workers brought him to the attention of the House Un-American Activities Committee, who investigated him for possible Communist ties. Called to testify in Washington, D.C., Young refused to answer questions about his Negro Labor Council, and he disbanded the organization rather than turn its membership list over to the United States Attorney General. The adverse publicity made it quite difficult for Young to find and keep a job in Detroit, but it did not quell his spirit or dampen his enthusiasm for the cause of civil rights.

Toward the end of the 1950s Young began to have some success as an insurance salesman, and he became active in the Democratic party. In 1960 he was elected a delegate to the Michigan Constitutional Convention. Gradually Young gained popularity in Detroit, and in 1964 he won a seat in the state senate. He quickly proved to be a strong legislator in Lansing, fighting for open housing legislation and for busing to integrate public schools. His liberal views and pro-labor stance won him many supporters in the Democratic party, and he received a wide base of support in Detroit from the black clergy and the unions.

Won First Mayoral Election

Young declared his candidacy for mayor in 1973 and

mounted a vigorous campaign for the office. He finished second in a nonpartisan primary election and faced stiff competition from John F. Nichols, a white police commissioner. While Nichols ran on a standard "law-and-order" platform, Young maintained that blacks were being treated with undue brutality by the city's policemen. He promised that his administration would maintain order without repressive tactics, bringing better racial relations to a region under strain. The election was decided by a mere 17,000 votes. Young won, taking 92 percent of the black vote. Nichols carried more than 91 percent of the white vote.

"We are going to turn this city around," Young promised in his inaugural address. The new mayor called for a coalition of business and labor to preserve the industries remaining in Detroit and attract new ones. He also set about reforming the police department, adding more black officers and promoting those already in the ranks. He saw to it that all police officers—indeed, all of Detroit's civil servants—were required to live within the city limits, and he opened neighborhood "mini-stations" in high crime areas. William Beckham, formerly Young's deputy mayor, told the *Detroit Free Press* that the early years of the Young administration were marked by a sense of struggle against a common enemy. "When Coleman took office, he was fighting [to reform] the Police Department, fighting federal cutbacks and the recession—real big enemies," Beckham said. "This is still a strong administration because of its foundations. But it has lots of pitfalls based on its longevity."

Young has won every election since 1973 by a wide margin. He is the only mayor in the history of Detroit to serve five consecutive terms—indeed, some reporters note that he is "mayor for life." A close ally and political adviser to president Jimmy Carter, Young turned down a cabinet position in Washington, D.C. in order to remain in Detroit. Needless to say, the salty mayor has been a vocal critic of the Reagan and Bush administrations, with their massive cutbacks in federal aid to urban areas. Nor has the federal government remained sanguine about Coleman Young. His administration has been investigated on more than six different charges, including improprieties in the awarding of city contracts and illegal personal use of city funds by the police department. Young himself has never been personally implicated in the scandals, however, and his popularity has been undiminished—some might even say enhanced—by the publicity.

Helped City Rejuvenate

Mayor Young can point to a number of improvements in Detroit since he took office. Expansion of riverfront attractions has brought convention and tourist traffic to the city, and favorable tax abatements have attracted new businesses, including two major automobile plants. Young would like to see more diversification in the region's employment profile, noting that the automobile industry is prone to cyclical layoffs. Even his most vocal critics admit that Young is a tireless worker for his city who has the area's best interests at heart. As Patricia Edmonds put it in the *Detroit Free Press,* "There is little Young likes more than talking deals for his city."

A number of daunting problems remain for Detroit, chief among them its dwindling population. Middle-class flight to the suburbs continues, robbing the city's coffers of essential tax revenue. Some critics argue that Young has contributed to this phenomenon by promoting the idea that suburban dwellers are hostile or indifferent to the city's woes. Indeed, in recent years Young has endured a barrage of disapproval in the press for his management style—which is described as autocratic—his blunt language, and his concentration on cosmetic improvements while the city's core decays. Young makes no apologies

> Even his most vocal critics admit that Young is a tireless worker for his city who has the area's best interests at heart.

for his methods or his style. "I'm not seeking to stay in office by being a Teflon goddam mayor, taking positions to enhance my popularity," he told *Newsweek.*

Young told the *Detroit Free Press* that he considered retirement in 1985 but hasn't since. He feels that he has a great deal of unfinished business to attend to in Detroit, and that he can indeed turn the city around. He characterized his years at the top as "very positive," adding: "What I set out to do has been done and is taking place." On the other hand, he said, "It's been in crisis constantly. And sure it wears me out. But when you get into a fight with a damned bear, you don't get tired until the bear gets tired. If you do, it's your a—. You can't afford to quit, can you?"

Sources

Cleveland Plain Dealer, March 17, 1974.
Detroit Free Press, April 5, 1987; April 7, 1987; January 3, 1988.
Ebony, February 1974.

Newsweek, July 31, 1989.
Time, February 24, 1983.
U.S. News and World Report, September 25, 1989.

—Mark Kram

Nationality Index

Occupation Index

Subject Index

Name Index